THE EVOLVING PROJECT OF
CORMAC McCARTHY

THE EVOLVING PROJECT OF
CORMAC McCARTHY

Edited by Jonathan Elmore and Rick Elmore

LOUISIANA STATE UNIVERSITY PRESS
BATON ROUGE

Published by Louisiana State University Press
lsupress.org

Copyright © 2024 by Louisiana State University Press
All rights reserved. Except in the case of brief quotations used in articles or reviews, no part of this publication may be reproduced or transmitted in any format or by any means without written permission of Louisiana State University Press.

Designer: Kaelin Chappell Broaddus
Typeface: Dolly Pro, text; Acumin Pro, display

Cover photographer courtesy Unsplash/Tahir Osman.

Cataloging-in-Publication Data are available at the Library of Congress.

ISBN 978-0-8071-8280-2 (cloth) | ISBN 978-0-8071-8342-7 (paper) | ISBN 978-0-8071-8341-0 (pdf) | ISBN 978-0-8071-8340-3 (epub)

Contents

Acknowledgments vii

Introduction: McCarthy's Positive Project 1
JONATHAN ELMORE AND RICK ELMORE

His Disastrous Wrath:
Monstrosity in *Child of God* 20
AHMED HONEINI

Woods That No One Owned:
Rereading *Child of God* through *The Road* 45
JORDAN J. DOMINY

Sorrow at the Moving World:
Nihilistic Despair and American Exceptionalism
in the Border Trilogy and *The Road* 65
RACHEL B. GRIFFIS

"Whales and Men" and Its Echoes
in the Border Trilogy 88
KATEŘINA KOVÁŘOVÁ

Cormac McCarthy's Idea of Race 109
JOHN VANDERHEIDE

The Black and White Jacksons:
Nonarbitrary Racial Conflict and the Resonance of the
Racial Sign in Faulkner and McCarthy 132
PETER LURIE

Unsettling Testimony:
Settler Law and Native Persistence in *Blood Meridian* 155
ALEX HARMON

The Frailty of Everything Revealed at Last:
Cormac McCarthy and Radical Atheism 184
DAVID DEACON

The Darker Picture and the Ghost of Culture:
The Sunset Limited 206
TREVOR JACKSON

Chaos, Law, and the Materiality of
McCarthy's Language 230
VERNON W. CISNEY

McCarthy's Foundational Critique of
Individualism and the Western Mythos in
the Epilogue of *Cities of the Plain* 249
JONATHAN ELMORE AND RICK ELMORE

Contributors 267
Index 271

Acknowledgments

Volumes such as these are in every way a reflection of the quality of the work of their contributors, and this volume is no exception. We would like to thank Vernon W. Cisney, David Deacon, Jordan Dominy, Rachel B. Griffis, Alex Harmon, Ahmed Honeini, Trevor Jackson, Kateřina Kovářová, Peter Lurie, and John Vanderheide for trusting us with their work and for the incredible quality of their contributions. We are very grateful to James Long and his entire team at LSU Press. Their support and efforts in bringing this volume to print have been amazing. The Cormac McCarthy Society is composed of the most generous, intelligent, enthusiastic, and kind collection of colleagues imaginable. While there are too many people deserving of mention from the society, we are especially grateful to Stacey Peebles, Steven Frye, Lydia Cooper, Dianne Luce, Scott Yarbrough, Russell Hillier, and Nell Sullivan for their friendship and support in all our work on Cormac McCarthy.

None of us work or think alone, and this volume would not have been possible without an entire community of folks supporting us. Rick would like to thank Jon for suggesting a few years ago that we write a piece together on the work of Cormac McCarthy, that first project the seed of what has become an incredible intellectual collaboration. There is no one I'd rather write with. I am grateful as always for brian bean, James Manos, and Joe Weiss, whose friendship, love, and intellect are part of everything I do. My colleagues Kevin Schilbrack and Davis Hankins I thank for their friendship and support. Maddy and Misty Elmore for their love, support, care, and humor. You remind me everyday of what is best in this life, and how incredibly lucky I am. Let's be so for real. Jon would like to thank his colleagues at Savannah State University for their friendship, encouragement, and intellectual curiosity, especially Lisa Yount, Nick Silberg, Jordan Dominy, Jenni Halpin, and Isadora Hefner. No one thinks alone and living and working in this community is a profound privilege. I remain, as ever, beyond grateful for the love and encouragement of my family. My son, Damian, who left home for college during this project, consistently reminds me that this work is fun and extraordinary; he keeps me young. And my wife, Paige, who makes everything I do possible, fun, and always a little unpredictable.

THE EVOLVING PROJECT OF
CORMAC McCARTHY

Introduction

McCarthy's Positive Project

JONATHAN ELMORE AND RICK ELMORE

Following the March 2022 announcement of the forthcoming publication of *The Passenger* and *Stella Maris*, *Literary Hub* published a short interview that McCarthy had given two industrious high school students in March of 2014.[1] The students, Lily Wilhelm and Carly Oseran, were completing an Advanced Placement literature project on *All the Pretty Horses*, and, fortuitously, Wilhelm's boyfriend happened to live next to one of McCarthy's neighbors. The two students drafted a set of questions and emailed them to the neighbor not knowing whether the notoriously reclusive author would reply.[2] Yet reply he did. Asked how he develops the ideas for his stories and why he chooses to narrate in the third person, McCarthy tells the teens that, for him, "writing is very subconscious and the last thing I want to do is think about it. [...] I write what comes to mind" (Carpenter). Similarly, speaking of his intended audience, McCarthy remarks, "I'm not writing for a particular audience. The reader in mind is me. If someone else would write these books I could go play golf" (Carpenter). While brief and informal, these comments shed light on the nature of McCarthy's project. For him, writing novels is less a creative act of world making and more a subconscious drive, the idea that if others would write these books he would not have to suggesting both a necessity to write and that this act of writing speaks to something outside of himself, something to which others have access. This notion that his writing is motivated by something in the world and potentially felt by many, is further developed when McCarthy comments, "everything in life influences style and therefore it is difficult if not impossible to pinpoint a specific influence" (Carpenter). For McCarthy, the distinctive style of his prose is not a reflection of personal taste or literary convention, but the unsortable sum of his life experiences, these experiences giving to his novels their distinctive rhythm, sound, and form. Yet this notion of style as a reflection of life, when combined with the idea that others could "write these books," presents McCarthy's project not as a reflection of his own life so much as an exploration of life in general. Moreover, while the pessimist tone of McCarthy's work is well-documented, he here resists the idea of his work as primarily elegiac.

Speaking of *All the Pretty Horses*, McCarthy comments, "the loss of a bygone era is certainly a theme of the book but not necessarily a purpose of it" (Carpenter). Despite the importance of loss and death to McCarthy's oeuvre, this comment emphasizes the prescriptive promise of his work, McCarthy interested not simply in diagnosing the ills of the world but in offering some vision of how humans ought to live in light of them. For example, asked about his own commonalities with the character of John Grady Cole, McCarthy muses, "I think he is an admirable kid, and maybe I wish I'd been more like him when I was his age" (Carpenter). John Grady Cole, like perhaps Billy Parham or the son from *The Road*, represents something like an "admirable" life, McCarthy committed to the notion that there are better and worse ways to live in a world defined by violence, corruption, and death. Hence, while brief and informal, this interview presents McCarthy's project as concerned primarily with the exploration of life and reality, and with how one ought to live in the face of this reality. It is these two questions, moreover, that have, by and large, organized the scholarly engagement with McCarthy's work from its inception, his bleak vision of the world central to this engagement.

As is well known, the initial studies of McCarthy's fiction, by scholars such as Vereen Bell, read his depictions of the world as fundamentally pessimistic and nihilistic.[3] For these scholars, McCarthy's novels show us a world defined by arbitrary suffering and violence, a world devoid of any essential meaning or values. As Bell famously puts it, in McCarthy's work, "existence seems both to precede and preclude essence, and it paradoxically derives its importance from this fact alone" (31). Faced with the unknowable absurdity of existence, McCarthy renders life a desperate and decidedly sorted affair, the characters of many of his early novels in a perpetual state of existential ambiguity, seeking whatever shards of meaning and purpose they can scrounge from the circus of violence and corruption all around them. From the murderous evil of Kenneth Rattner and the incest-fueled guilt of Culla Holme to the necrophilic perversity of Lester Ballard and the doomed aimlessness of the denizens of McAnally Flats, McCarthy's early work paints a profoundly dark and pessimistic picture of existence and humanity's place in it. Yet, while existential absurdity and depraved violence are defining features of McCarthy's work, some initial scholarship pushed back against this vision of McCarthy as mere prophet of nihilism.

Contra this notion of McCarthy's work as purely pessimistic, early scholars like Edwin Arnold and Dianne Luce find in his fiction—with its plethora of religious themes and illusions—the possibility of, and hope for, something beyond the bleakness and violence of the existing world. As Arnold puts it emphatically, "there is always a possibility of grace and redemption even in the darkest of [McCarthy's] tales" (46). Despite the cosmic and malign forces arrayed against them, McCarthy's characters are, nonetheless, compelled to address the problems in their lives, "the narratives" of his novels "driven by distinct," and profoundly human, "thematic concerns [that] move at least *in the direction* of some form of resolution" (44).[4] There is, Arnold shows, a sense of moral ethos to McCarthy's texts, "each novel" providing readers with "a moral gauge by which [...] to judge the failure or limited success of McCarthy's characters" (44). Yet, while Arnold, among other scholars, influentially interprets this possibility of "resolution" in distinctly Christian theological terms, Luce takes a more mystical and philosophical approach.

Speaking, for example, of *Suttree*, Luce writes, "McCarthy synthesizes Platonic, gnostic, Christian, and existentialist images and concepts to inform Suttree's anguished alienation from the world and his final transcendence through freeing himself both from the guilt and life-denial inculcated by the Roman Catholic Church and from his gnostic obsessions with the mortal captivity in matter, arriving at his affirmations of an uncomplicated love for the natural world, of a true ministry in communion with his brothers and sisters in the streets, and of his own voice as an emerging artist and Messenger" (203). For Luce, McCarthy's work brings together various philosophical and theological themes in order to reveal, if only obliquely, fundamental truths about the nature of reality and human existence. For her and many other scholars, the darkness, alienation, suffering, and violence of McCarthy's novels is revelatory as well as descriptive. For example, speaking of the role of evil in McCarthy's early novels, Kenneth Lincoln contends that McCarthy's texts "force readers to 'witness atrocity without moralizing,'" this lack of any simple opposition between good and evil forcing readers to confront their own entanglement with evil (22). Similarly, Lydia Cooper charts what she calls McCarthy's "southern grotesque," his "obscene and sometimes comic exaggeration [...] of physical deformity or sexual deviance," "a visual catalyst for the apprehension of uncomfortable, perhaps even terrifying, realities" (*Companion Piece* 42). For these scholars, McCarthy's fascination with the world's structural and institutional denials of life and community aims not only at describing these denials but offering at least the possibility of moving beyond them. Hence, along with the theological or redemptive readings of McCarthy's work, a range of scholars find in his novels an ethical impulse, even if the character of this impulse remains, for many of them, far more oblique than a religious hope for grace and redemption. In fact, the character of McCarthy's morality has been a topic of much debate.[5]

While McCarthy is often lauded for the complex scope of his philosophical, theological, literary, and historical thematics and allusions, this complexity has also tended to complicate the desire to find a moral message in his work. For example, scholars such as Ty Hawkins and David Holloway caution against ascribing too much positivity to McCarthy's philosophical and literary project. For Hawkins, while McCarthy's early novels represent nothing short of a fundamental interruption of "progressivisms" and the "creating [of] spaces wherein he can imagine alternatives to modernization," these alternatives are, ultimately, impossible to articulate, since McCarthy's critique leaves them "no metaphysical leg on which to stand" (438). Having "relentlessly remind[ed] us of how progressive worldviews are assimilatory vehicles that close out alternatives," McCarthy is, Hawkins contends, constitutively unable "to represent a form of community that would transcend the individual," since to do so, would hazard presenting "an assimilatory vision" of his own (438–39). Similarly, David Holloway argues against the possibility of drawing any concrete moral prescription from McCarthy's works, insofar as humans are trapped within systems of language and representation. As Holloway puts it, "the tool of the storyteller, language itself, is a flawed mechanism, the words used to articulate his story's meaning referring always to other meanings and other contexts beyond those which are intended" (189–90). Taking as his example, McCarthy's oft-cited notion of "the world as tale," Holloway contends that humans are, on McCarthy's account, trapped within the prison house of language, constitutively unable to access any meaning outside their own systems of representation. As he puts it, "McCarthy's narrative always points beyond itself into a web of signification whose textual spread—whose expropriation of concrete meaning—is potentially without limit" (189).[6] For both Hawkins and Holloway, the paradoxical and aporiatic structure of McCarthy's philosophical and literary worldview fundamentally troubles the possibility of gleaning from his work a concrete and prescriptive moral or political project, the "moral" point of McCarthy's work to reveal this impossibility itself. And yet, while the philosophical and metaphysical complexities of McCarthy's thought continue to generate rich and conflicting scholarly analysis, many readers find in McCarthy's work an explicit social and political critique.[7]

Despite its philosophical, theological, and metaphysical depth and opacity, scholars have long noted McCarthy's essential and relatively straightforward critique of modernization and progress, the industrial, profit-driven ethos of capitalism consistently depicted in his novels as profoundly damaging to both human life and the natural world. From the Marxist-inflected eco-pastoralism of John Wesley and Ather Ownby to the postapocalyptic, *laissez faire* cannibalism of *The Road*, scholars find, across McCarthy's corpus, a condemnation of the evils of unfettered self-interest and industrialization. Moreover, in works such as *No Country for Old Men*, *Child of God*, and *The Road*, among others, McCarthy develops a robust and thoroughgoing critique of capitalist market logic and neoliberalism. Alongside this critique of modern industrialization, there has been considerable scholarly attention given to the pastoral and ecocritical elements of McCarthy's work, particularly in his Appalachian novels, where the extractive poisoning of the natural world and destruction of rural communities figure prominently.[8] In addition, McCarthy's Western novels contain what many scholars see as an explicit critique of American exceptionalism and manifest destiny, McCarthy painting a vivid picture of the violent colonial history of the U.S./Mexico border both past and present. Hence, despite its metaphysical complications, there is a widespread consensus that McCarthy forwards a forceful and consistent critique of contemporary American society, and its violent economic and ideological commitments. Yet, while the notion of McCarthy as social critic has gained widespread acceptance, there remains considerable debate over the character of McCarthy's "politics," some scholars seeing in McCarthy's social critique, and particularly the masculinist timbre of his work, a profoundly traditional, even reactionary "politics."

While critics have long commented on the nostalgic and elegiac elements of McCarthy's fiction, manifest, for example, in the pastoralism of his Appalachian novels and the frontier setting of his Western fictions, the most explicit evidence for McCarthy's traditionalism comes around his depiction of women and the feminine. As Nell Sullivan puts it bluntly, "a merely cursory reading of Cormac McCarthy's novels reveals an unmistakable ambivalence about women, even an outright misogyny" (230). From "the objectification of women as dead bodies in *Child of God*" and the "one dimensional stereotyp[ing]" of them as "witch, virgin, or whore in *Suttree*" to the relative absence of women in the Border Trilogy (and much of the rest of McCarthy's fiction), Sullivan see McCarthy's work as explicitly patriarchal. In addition, his move from the genre of southern gothic to the Western corroborates, Sullivan argues, the sexism of his work, the Western a genre long recognized by critics as "a reaction against feminism and female authority" (230). Following the spirit of Sullivan's argument, scholars such as Jennifer A. Reimer connect this critique of sexism to McCarthy's treatment of race and coloniality as well. For Reimer, "Cole's relationships with Alejandra and Magdalena," in the Border Trilogy, "reify stereotypes about the availability and hypersexualization of Mexican women on the US-Mexico border in service of constructing a dominant, if ambivalent, white masculinity" (423). Reimer is not alone in admonishing McCarthy's fiction for being bad on questions of race, gender, and coloniality, yet she extends this critique to the field of McCarthy scholarship itself; as she puts it, "even a cursory glance at the major edited anthologies of Cormac McCarthy scholarship prove how marginal analyses of race, gender, and their intersections remain" (423). Hence, while stridently insisting on the conservative character of McCarthy's politics, scholars such as Reimer and Sullivan highlight the need for a more serious analysis of the role of gender and race in McCarthy's novels. And yet, while there is certainly more work to be done in this regard, some recent analyses have, interestingly, tended to complicate rather than confirm the picture of McCarthy as simply bad on questions of race, gender, coloniality, and imperialism.

While conscious of the cis, white, and masculine tendencies of McCarthy's novels and protagonists, a growing body of scholarship has complicated the picture of McCarthy's politics as a reactionary pining for the perceived loss of white, cismale dominance. For example, Dianne Luce, Stacey Pebbles, and Erin K. Johns see in McCarthy's novels a much more sophisticated engagement with patriarchy, McCarthy troubling rather than affirming traditional systems of male mastery and control. Anne Fisher-Wirth goes even further, arguing that "McCarthy is" nothing less than "a brilliant symbolist of 'the feminine,'" his representations of women and use of feminine imagery capturing something essential about the constitutive vulnerability of subjectivity itself (127). Similarly, Josef Benson and Sara Spurgeon see in McCarthy a critical depiction of the sexist and racist nature of America's jingoistic fantasies of subduing and conquering the western frontier and its people. As Benson puts it, "McCarthy paints an entirely different story than the national fantasy, one that suggests that the winning of the West relied on a philosophy of violence and racism that disavowed any moral law, human law, or governmental law" (22). Likewise for Spurgeon, the "the legacy of an American history cut through with racism, slavery, invasion, conquest, the exploitation of poor and working-class people, and the attempted genocide of Native Americans in the United States and Mexico" is a central "theme that runs through McCarthy's oeuvre" (16). Hence, while varied in their assessments of the prescriptions to be drawn from McCarthy's accounts, these more "progressive" readings tend to emphasize the descriptive, historical, and geographically embedded character of McCarthy's fiction, his graphic depictions of sexism, racism, imperialism, and violence aimed not at affirming these realities but at recognizing their historical, ideological, and cultural power.[9] Moreover, while this emphasis on the descriptive register of McCarthy's fiction need not entail a progressive politics—McCarthy telling us what is, not what ought to be—there has been a growing consensus that this unrelenting assessment of the ills and horrors of modern life offers an alternative, even revolutionary vision, of a world beyond these horrors.

Given McCarthy's stern depiction of the historical, economic, ideological, and social violences of modern society, alongside his critical assessment of the life and community denying forces of capitalism, extraactivism, imperialism, patriarchy, nationalism, and white supremacy, scholars have increasingly seen in McCarthy's fiction not just the promise of an ethical message *via negativa*, but an explicit and concrete ethical imperative. For example, Raymond Malewitz, Christopher Lawrence, Jordan Dominy, and Rachel Griffis see McCarthy as not simply critiquing capitalist consumerism but offering an alternative vision of social and economic relations. Speaking of *No Country for Old Men*, Griffis writes that "McCarthy's interaction with both the Tom Sawyer and Huck Finn traditions suggests that the refusal to participate in degrading, consumerist transactions without abandoning human community is the ethical imperative for a society sustained by the ideological assumptions of optimism and individualism" (4). Similarly, an array of scholars find in the son from *The Road* an alternative model of social life, "McCarthy develop[ing]" in the son, "an ethos towards community and the alleviation of suffering, one that the novel suggests might be the only hope for humans at the end of the world" (Elmore and Elmore 134). While profoundly pessimistic about the possibility of contemporary life, this scholarship highlights how McCarthy's pessimism concerning life was never aimed at life *itself*, but at the particular figurations of life found in modern, industrial, consumerist societies, the organization of modern life by the horrifically violent forces of individualism, self-interest, nationalism, racism, and patriarchy all but guaranteeing life's inability to flourish or even survive.

From the promise of a new "alien" life to come at the end of *The Orchard Keeper* to the son finding a family at the conclusion of *The Road*, McCarthy's work has always been interested in the nature and possibility of a life that might truly live, a life, as he portends in *The Orchard Keeper*, so different from its modern form that we existing humans are neither its "scion" nor "avatar," our "names" falling from its lips as "myth, legend, dust" (246). Like the father of *The Road*, McCarthy's work has always been traveling alongside the promise of a new life, one it knows it cannot fully understand but to which it is, nonetheless, utterly beholden. Seen in this way, the metaphysical and philosophical complexity of McCarthy's work appears not at odds with his social critique but as the recognition of just how deep the life-denying forces of modern society go. For McCarthy, these forces are not just social and historical but metaphysical and ontological, the very structures of Western metaphysics itself—with its commitment to Cartesian dualism and the Enlightenment subject—consumed, as he puts it in the opening section of *Suttree*, by "*a longing that nothing save dark's total restitution could appease*" (5). In McCarthy's fiction, "the western world" is figured as a death cult all the way down, from its metaphysics to its social relations, the quest for a life that might truly live requiring a total transformation not only of society's cultural and ethical relations but its metaphysical and philosophical commitments as well (5). Hence, it is the recognition of the thoroughgoing depth and complexity of the critique of contemporary society from the metaphysical to the social found in McCarthy's fiction and its vision of a life beyond this society that, for us, indicates the need for a programmatic reassessment of McCarthy's project attuned to the interrelatedness of his metaphysical and social thinking as a whole.

In many ways, the field of McCarthy scholarship has always been driven by a desire to give a full or complete account of McCarthy's project, to unearth the subterranean framework that organizes his complex array of influences, references, ideas, and provocations. From Vereen Bell's 1988 classic *The Achievement of Cormac McCarthy* to Steven Frye's 2020 companion *Cormac McCarthy in Context*, one can trace, across nearly five decades, the evolving character of this desire, critics and readers demonstrating how every element of McCarthy's texts form part of a carefully planned whole from the smallest subtleties of word choice, syntax, and (sparse) punctuation to the grandest complexity of its philosophical and theological musings. As Luce and Arnold comment in their landmark 2001 collection, *A Cormac McCarthy Companion: The Border Trilogy*, this desire for "full-length explorations" of McCarthy's work must be built out of "in-depth studies of McCarthy's writings, both southern and western," the task of understanding the character of McCarthy's project requiring not just careful readings, but a willingness to work through the seeming tensions between the various claims, allusions, motifs, and thematics of his work. Given McCarthy's work is guided most fundamentally by the question of to what degree life is still livable, his work a kind of empirical exploration of the profoundly life-denying forces of contemporary society, it follows that the task of giving a "full-length exploration" of his work is more than a mere academic exercise, the tensions and paradoxes of his novels a reflection of the tensions and paradoxes of the world these novels attempt to understand. In this sense, to fail to work through the interrelated complications of McCarthy's work, the way in which the theological, scientific, metaphysical, ethical, political, and social elements are, on his own account, necessarily interconnected, is to risk misunderstanding both the character and depths of his critique of modern society and his positive project. Hence, to speak of a programmatic reassessment of McCarthy's work is to call for scholarship that not only explores the various elements of McCarthy's thought, developing accounts of issues such as race, morality, gender, history, metaphysics, law, economics, ecology, and science in his novels, but to do so with an eye to the interrelated totality of these themes. If for McCarthy, the life-denying forces of contemporary society are metaphysical and moral as much as social and political, then to attempt to articulate a notion of life beyond these forces requires that we think on all of these levels at once, the exploration of this interrelatedness the primary challenge, we would argue, of thinking McCarthy's positive project. This is the challenge around which this collection is constellated, the essays exploring issues of race, morality, history, metaphysics, law, economics, and ecology in McCarthy's work with an eye to how these themes intersect in McCarthy's overarching, positive project. Taken together, these studies reinforce a view of McCarthy's work as profoundly critical of contemporary society, and as insistent on the possibility of life and community beyond their existing manifestations.

In this volume, in "His Disastrous Wrath: Monstrosity in *Child of God*," Ahmed Honeini revisits the theme of moral culpability in McCarthy's fiction around one of his most iconic and disturbing protagonists: Lester Ballard. Against the dominant reading of Ballard's homicidal necrophilia as a product of his ostracization and mistreatment by the community of Sevierville, Honeini reads Ballard's fall into monstrousness as primarily Ballard's own doing, his willful "stripping [of] his victims' [...] right to life and ownership over their bodies," the "assertion of his own individuality and agency." For Honeini, the existing literature pays too little attention to the way in which McCarthy paints Ballard as the architect of his own monstrosity, Ballard's descent into evil not a result of his social treatment or programming but the product of his own twisted actions and desires. Hence, Honeini stakes out a clear and original claim for the moral prescriptiveness of McCarthy's work, evil not simply a product of dysfunctional and malign social forces, for McCarthy, but a determinable and condemnable trait of certain individuals.

Developing the moral lesson of *Child of God* from a markedly different perspective, Jordan Dominy's "'Woods That No One Owned': Rereading *Child of God* through *The Road*" takes a long view of the lessons of McCarthy's figurations of evil and societal collapse. Following the failures and abuses of the community of Sevierville and its reduction of human relations to a logic of transaction and self-preservation, Dominy sees in Ballard's community a forecasting of the total loss of society found in The Road. Building on McCarthy's long-recognized critique of the self-destructive logic of neoliberalism, Dominy charts a direct continuity between the absence of community in *Child of God* and the total social collapse of *The Road*, the reduction of human life to self-interested market exchange all but ensuring the impossibility of community found in *The Road*. For Dominy, McCarthy was, from his earliest work, thinking the utter destitution of modern life under the forces of capitalist production, Ballard's homicidal necrophilia and the cannibalism of *The Road* just the most extreme expressions of this ethos of self-interested indifference to the needs and lives of others.

Similarly, Rachel Griffis's "Sorrow at the Moving World: Nihilistic Despair and American Exceptionalism in Cormac McCarthy's Border Trilogy and *The Road*" develops the unlivable destitution of modern life via McCarthy's critique of the myth of American exceptionalism. For Griffis, the Border Trilogy demonstrates how easily the belief in exceptionalism flips over into nihilism and despair, the failure of the ideological promise of assured success leaving its adherent "decenter[ed] and disorient[ed]," incapable of making sense of themselves or the world. Unable to abandon the belief in their own success, and faced with the world's indifference to their individual and national desires, McCarthy's protagonists are caught in the grips of exceptionalism even as it leads them into nihilism and despair. In fact, it is not, for Griffis, until *The Road*, that McCarthy offers us, in the figure of the son, a character who transcends this nihilistic logic of exceptionalism, the boy's insistence on a communal ethic of self-sacrifice offering "an antidote to the moral poverty of contemporary American life." Hence, we see in Griffis's account the ways in which McCarthy's foundational critique of the life-denying forces of modern society bends always, even in its very insistence on nihilism and despair, towards an alternative vision of the world.

Developing an important element of this alterative vision, Kateřina Kovářová's "'Whales and Men' and Its Echoes in the Border Trilogy," offers an analysis of McCarthy's unfinished screenplay alongside his treatment of animality and nature in *The Crossing*. Highlighting the parallels between whales and wolves in McCarthy's work, Kovářová shows how McCarthy's rendering of these two iconic species offers insight into his thinking on "environmental ethics, [the] material reality of nature, and [the] spiritual relationship between humankind and nature." Attentive to the ways in which humans misunderstand the intelligence and sociality of these creatures, McCarthy's texts depict the natural world as having its own drives, motivations, forces, and desires, ones that are often at odds with the dominant, Western conception of nature as a resource to be consumed, mastered, and controlled. Thus, to attend to the specificity and alterity of the nonhuman in McCarthy's texts is, for Kovářová, to recognize just how little humans understand nature and their place in it, this recognition a first step "in challenging the anthropocentric perspective" and developing "more humble and respectable views of the world."

Returning to the character of McCarthy's social critique, John Vanderheide's "Cormac McCarthy's Idea of Race" argues that McCarthy's fiction develops, from his earliest novels, a critical conception of race and racial difference. Following the work of Afropessimists such as Frank Wilderson III, Vanderheide traces the complex figuration of race across McCarthy's oeuvre, showing how McCarthy's careful attention to racial difference marks these differences as "social and metaphysical" problems to be solved. For McCarthy, race is a social rather than biological construct, a material, semiotic, and metaphysical category "foundational" to America's "social or political ontology." Yet while, presenting white supremacy and racial difference as foundational to the American project historically, socially, and metaphysically, Vanderheide shows how McCarthy's later fiction attempts a "solution" to the problem of racial difference via the figure of the "common man" in *The Stonemason* and Quijada's figure of "the poor man" in *The Crossing*. For Vanderheide, McCarthy offers up these "generic" figures of the human as indexes to a different kind of social or political ontology than "Anglo-Saxon white supremacist capitalist patriarchy," McCarthy searching for some commonality or solidarity that might transcend racial difference. Yet while only partially successful, on Vanderheide's account, the fact that McCarthy maintains a critical understanding of white supremacy as foundational to the American project points to how McCarthy's fiction offers potential resources to help us think questions of racism and racial difference in America, these resources developed in the following two essays.

Peter Lurie's "The Black and White Jacksons: Nonarbitrary Racial Conflict and the Resonance of the Racial Sign in Faulkner and McCarthy" contests the common reading of McCarthy's work as "apolitical." Through a meticulous reading of the tone, imagery, historical embeddedness, and aurality of the beheading of the White Jackson in *Blood Meridian*—alongside its resonance with Faulkner's *Light in August*—Lurie shows how this scene serves as a tonal anchor for the racial politics of McCarthy's text. For Lurie, the resonance of this scene, expressed in the "rebounding sound" of the use of racial epithets in McCarthy's and Faulkner's fiction, calls attention to the continuing force of the history of racial animus. Specifically, Lurie sees in McCarthy's work the development of what he calls an *"acoustical democracy that extends from Faulkner to McCarthy,"* the permeating force of racial animus resonating in the sonic structures of McCarthy's text, drawing our attention to the ways in which white supremacy saturates the American project from first to last. Hence, like Vanderheide, Lurie illustrates the way in which McCarthy positions race, racism, and racial difference as structural and persistent features of contemporary American life, this conception of race not only at odds with any notion of McCarthy's work as apolitical but also crucial for an understanding of the nature of McCarthy's political project.

Continuing an exploration of McCarthy's racial politics, Alex Harmon's "Unsettling Testimony: Settler Law and Native Persistence in *Blood Meridian*" takes up the question of McCarthy's depiction of Native characters in *this novel*. Against the common view of McCarthy's depiction of Native peoples as uncritical, even xenophobic, Harmon contends that a careful, historically embedded reading of these figures positions them as *"bear[ing] witness* to the mythologizing of the West and the ways in which that mythologization was achieved." Framing McCarthy's depiction of the Glanton Gang in the context of federal foreign policy and federal Indian law of the time, Harmon shows the way in which McCarthy's novel traces the transformation of the West into an historical place of law and order, the racialized violence of the Glanton Gang not opposed to the supposed racial equality of law, but an element in the construction of the racial apartheid of the American West. Hence, for Harmon, the racial politics of *Blood Meridian* are best read as a kind of bearing witness of the American project "against itself," McCarthy's "novel refus[ing] either to obscure or to apotheosize the violence of the colonial project," the ubiquity of this violence showing the way in which the American project is, for McCarthy, racialized violence all the way down.

Taking up, from a different perspective, the question of America's foundational mythos, David Deacon's "The Frailty of Everything Revealed at Last: Cormac McCarthy and Radical Atheism" returns to the longstanding question of the theological in McCarthy's fiction, exploring what he sees as McCarthy's commitment to a radical atheism. Rejecting the "false dichotomy" between "theological revelation and nihilism" in McCarthy's work, Deacon traces the secular "veneration of life" in McCarthy's text, showing how, against more theological readings, McCarthy develops a notion of life defined not by theology or nihilism but by an appreciation of the transience and radical contingency of life. Reading *The Road* and *The Sunset Limited* in the context of post 9/11 America, Deacon explores the way in which McCarthy deploys a theological conception of life not to expose this conception as merely false—life shown to be absurd or meaningless, rather than sacred and meaningful—but to illustrate the way in which the very longing for a life defined theologically appears ultimately life-denying. Just as the calls to defend the American way of life post 9/11 led to policies, like the Patriot Act, that profoundly restricted the very freedom they claimed to protect, so too, for Deacon, McCarthy's work illustrates the way in which the longing for a life understood as sacred, in the sense of pure and unscathed, works to undermine the actual survival of the life. Hence, for Deacon, to follow McCarthy's "radical atheism" is not to claim that McCarthy is an atheist (although he might be), but to recognize the ways in which McCarthy's work is motivated, politically and philosophically, by a critique of the life-denying forces of contemporary American society, and by the insistence on developing another, less theological and more affirming, conception of life.

Further developing the complexity of McCarthy's conception of life, Trevor Jackson's "The Darker Picture and the Ghost of Culture: *The Sunset Limited*" traces an important shift in McCarthy's thinking of life from the theological to the social and scientific. Where much of the scholarship is organized by the question of who wins the debate between White's atheistic pessimism or Black's religious conviction, Jackson focuses on how Black's faith survives even in the face of his seeming inability to convince and thereby save White from suicide. Following the importance of language to this survival, Jackson argues that it is the constructive power of language to provide a life and meaning sustaining narrative in the face of White's pessimistic, even nihilistic, disenchanting of the world that is the ultimate lesson of this encounter. For McCarthy, science is, like theology or ethics, a name for this kind of life-sustaining narrative, the contingency of existence requiring humans to give meaning to their lives, not as a defense against life's ultimate meaninglessness, but as a creative act of world building that defines the very character of human life itself. Hence, for Jackson, McCarthy's scientific rendering of life retains rather than dismisses the mythical and utopian potential of life to be radically different than it is, this potential highlighting the truth moment in Black's faith in the meaningfulness of life, as well as the importance of the exploration of language to McCarthy's philosophical worldview.

Developing further the philosophical implications of McCarthy's account of language and the unconscious, Vernon Cisney's "Chaos, Law, and the Materiality of McCarthy's Language" explores the way in which language, although a crucial theme of McCarthy's work, proves for him "woefully inadequate" as a vehicle to maintain the social, material, or metaphysical order of reality. Language can, Cisney notes, "just as easily sanction slavery as [...] emancipation, murder as healing [...] genocide as justice." For Cisney, the limits of language explored throughout McCarthy's work lead him to develop a notion of the unconscious as the true moral and philosophical teacher of human life. "In place of the dispassionate morality of duty for duty's sake, or the enlightened self-interest of *homo economicus*," McCarthy offers up "love, the groundless" and unconscious "upsurge of care, affirmation, and hope," as the ultimate pedagogue of human life, one that both exposes the narrowness of rational self-interest and connects us to the fundamental metaphysical structures of reality, structures defined, for McCarthy, by "absolute risk" and contingency. For Cisney, it is McCarthy's insistence on love and the unconscious as receptivity to reality's absolute risk that reveals not only the limits of language in McCarthy's work but the basic moral imperative of his thought as well.

Developing the character of McCarthy's account of reality, we conclude the volume with our collaboratively composed essay, "McCarthy's Foundational Critique of Individualism and the Western Mythos in the Epilogue of *Cities of the Plain*." Reiterating many of the philosophical claims of *The Crossing* concerning, for example, the ontological dynamism and ever-changing nature of reality, McCarthy's conclusion to the Border Trilogy insists on the ontological unity of reality as a means to critique the dualism at the heart of Western metaphysics. For McCarthy, existence is an ever-unfolding, dynamic process, one which eschews, by definition, any limit, whether between representation and reality, signifier and signified, or self and other. Hence, to recognize the nature of existence is to challenge all limits or boundaries whether between self and other, dream and reality. Hence, McCarthy's account of ontology constitutes "a thoroughgoing critique of the most essential metaphysical convictions of the Western genre, the mythos of the rugged individual with all it entails in terms of morality, ethics, and politics at odds with the very ontological nature of reality itself," the instability of the limit between self and other exposing the instability of Western individualism *tout court*.

NOTES

1. https://lithub.com/rare-thoughts-on-writing-from-cormac-mccarthy-in-this-unlikely-interview

2. This reputation as reclusive has been somewhat modified with the recent publication of a number of interviews that McCarthy gave between 1968 and 1980. As editors Dianne C. Luce and Zachary Turpin write in their abstract to these interviews, "Together, they suggest that McCarthy was often willing to be interviewed when it would please his friends and neighbors" (108).

3. Early reviews and initial studies of McCarthy's first novels tended to agree with Bell that McCarthy was a pessimistic and even nihilistic writer. See, for example, Robert Coles's "The Stranger," Thomas Daniel Young's *Tennessee Writers*, and John Ditsky's "Further into Darkness: The Novels of Cormac McCarthy." This sense of McCarthy as a pessimistic writer has persisted. See, for example, Gerhard Hoffman's "Strangeness, Gaps, and the Mystery of Life: Cormac McCarthy's Southern Novels."

4. Although one of the most influential proponents of a theological reading of McCarthy, Arnold was not the first scholar to see and explore the theological resonances of McCarthy's texts. See for example, Robert Coles's "The Empty Road" and William Schafer's "The Hard Wages of Original Sin." In addition, the theological character of McCarthy's work remains an important locus of scholarly interest. See for example, Manuel Broncano's *Religion in Cormac McCarthy's Fiction* and Matthew Potts's *Cormac McCarthy and the Signs of the Sacrament*.

5. See, for example, Alexandra Blair's "'The Wanted Stared Back': Biopolitics, Genre, and Sympathy in Cormac McCarthy's *Child of God*," Gary Adelman's "The Quest to Find Hope in a Savage World: The Novels of Cormac McCarthy," Nicholas Monk's *True and Living Prophet of Destruction: Cormac McCarthy and Modernity*, Hannah Stark's "'All These Things He Saw and Did Not See': Witnessing the End of the World in Cormac McCarthy's *The Road*," and Phillip Snyder's "Hospitality in Cormac McCarthy's *The Road*."

6. Holloway is not the only scholar to find resonances between McCarthy's work and a poststructuralist or deconstructive view of language and representation. See for example, Linda Woodson's "'The Lighted Display Case': A Nietzschean Reading of Cormac McCarthy's *Border Trilogy*" and "Deceiving the Will to Truth: Semiotic Foundations of *All the Pretty Horses*."

7. See Patrick O'Connor's "Literature and Death: McCarthy, Blanchot, and Suttree's Mortal Belonging."

8. For example, see Georg Guillemin's *The Pastoral Vision of Cormac McCarthy*, David Huebert's "Eating and Mourning the Corpse of the World: Ecological Cannibalism and Elegiac Protomourning in Cormac McCarthy's *The Road*," Christopher Lawrence's "'Because we carry the fire': An Eco-Marxist Reading of Cannibalism in Cormac McCarthy's *The Road*."

9. For scholars such as David Cremean, much of this debate circles around a biocritical tendency of reviewers and scholars to read certain characters, for example, Sheriff Ed Tom Bell in *No Country for Old Men*, as voicing McCarthy's own political and social views, views taken to be those of a "southern conservative" (21).

WORKS CITED

Adelman, Gary. "The Quest to Find Hope in a Savage World: The Novels of Cormac McCarthy." In *Sorrow's Rigging: The Novels of Cormac McCarthy, Don DeLillo, and Robert Stone*. McGill-Queen's University Press, 2012.

Arnold, Edwin. "Naming, Knowing, and Nothingness: McCarthy's Moral Parables." In *Perspectives on Cormac McCarthy*. Edited by Edwin Arnold and Dianne Luce. University of Mississippi Press, 1993: 45–70.

Arnold, Edwin, and Dianne C. Luce. "Introduction." In *A Cormac McCarthy Companion: The Border Trilogy*. Edited by Edwin T. Arnold and Dianne C. Luce. University of Mississippi Press, 2001: vii–xi.

Bell, Vereen. *The Achievement of Cormac McCarthy*. Louisiana State University Press, 1988.

———. "The Ambiguous Nihilism of Cormac McCarthy." *Southern Literary Journal*. Volume 15, number 2, 1983: 31–41.

Benson, Josef. *Hypermasculinities in the Contemporary Novel: Cormac McCarthy, Toni Morrison, and James Baldwin*. Rowman and Littlefield, 2014.

Blair, Alexandra. "'The Wanted Stared Back': Biopolitics, Genre, and Sympathy in Cormac McCarthy's *Child of God*." *Southern Literary Journal*, Volume 47, number 2, Spring 2015: 89–106.

Broncano, Manuel. *Religion in Cormac McCarthy's Fiction: Apocryphal Borderlands*. Routledge, 2013.

Carpenter, Murray. "Rare Thoughts on Writing from Cormac McCarthy in This Unlikely Interview." *Literary Hub*. March 15, 2022.

Coles, Robert. "The Empty Road." *New Yorker*, 22 March 1969.

———. "The Stranger." *New Yorker*, 26 August 1974.

Cooper, Lydia R. "McCarthy, Tennessee, and the Southern Gothic." In *The Cambridge Companion to Cormac McCarthy*. Edited by Steven Frye. Cambridge University Press, 2013: 41–53.

———. *No More Heroes: Narrative Perspective and Morality in Cormac McCarthy*. Louisiana State University Press, 2011.

Cremean, David. "For Whom the Bell Tolls: Conservatism and Change in Cormac McCarthy's Sheriff from *No Country for Old Men*." *Cormac McCarthy Journal*, Volume 5, number 1, 2005: 21–29.

Ditsky, John. "Further into Darkness: The Novels of Cormac McCarthy." *Hollins Critic*. Volume 18, number 2, 1981: 1–11.

Elmore, Rick, and Jonathan Elmore. "'You can stay here with your Papa and die or you can go with me': The Ethical Imperative of *The Road*." *Cormac McCarthy Journal*. Volume 16, number 2, 2018: 133–48.

Frye, Steven. *Cormac McCarthy in Context*. Cambridge University Press, 2020.

Fisher-Wirth, Ann. "Abjection and 'the Feminine' in *Outer Dark*." In *Cormac McCarthy New Directions*. Edited by James D. Lilly. University of New Mexico Press, 2002, 125–40.

Griffis, Rachel B. "'Track the money': The Moral Consequences of Tom Sawyer in *No Country for Old Men*." *Cormac McCarthy Journal*. Volume 19, number 1, 2021: 2–20.

Guillemin, Georg. *The Pastoral Vision of Cormac McCarthy*. Texas A&M University Press, 2004.

Hawkins, Ty. "The Eruption of Sordid: Cormac McCarthy's Resistance to Modern Ideology." *Critique*, Volume 55, number 4, 2014: 437–51.

Hoffman, Gerhard. "Strangeness, Gaps, and the Mystery of Life: Cormac McCarthy's Southern Novels." *American Studies*, Volume 42, number 2, 1997: 217–38.

Holloway, David. "'A false book is no book at all': The Ideology of Representation in *Blood Meridian* and the Border Trilogy." In *Myth, Legend, Dust: Critical Responses to Cormac McCarthy*. Edited by Rick Wallach. Manchester University Press, 2000: 185–200.

Huebert, David. "Eating and Mourning the Corpse of the World: Ecological Cannibalism and Elegiac Protomourning in Cormac McCarthy's The Road." *Cormac McCarthy Journal*, Volume 15, number 1, 2017: 66–87.

Lawrence, Christopher. "'Because we carry the fire': An Eco-Marxist Reading of Cannibalism in Cormac McCarthy's *The Road*." *International Journal of Humanities and Social Sciences*. Volume 1, number 13, 2011: 162–67.

Lincoln, Kenneth. *Cormac McCarthy: American Canticles*. New York: Palgrave, 2009.

Luce, Dianne C. *Reading the World: Cormac McCarthy's Tennessee Period*. University of South Carolina Press, 2009.

Luce, Dianne C., and Zachary Turpin. "Cormac McCarthy's Interviews in Tennessee and Kentucky, 1968–1980." *Cormac McCarthy Journal*, Volume 20, number 2, 2022: 108–35.

Malewitz, Raymond. "'Anything can be an Instrument'; Misuse Value and Rugged Consumerism in Cormac McCarthy's *No Country for Old Men*." *Contemporary Literature*. Volume 50, number 4, 2009: 721–41.

McCarthy, Cormac. *The Orchard Keeper*. New York, Vintage, 1965.

———. *Suttree*. Vintage, 1979.

Monk, Nicholas. *True and Living Prophet of Destruction: Cormac McCarthy and Modernity*. University of New Mexico Press, 2016.

O'Connor, Patrick. *Cormac McCarthy, Philosophy and the Physics of the Damned*. Edinburgh University Press, 2023.

Potts, Matthew L. *Cormac McCarthy and the Signs of the Sacrament: Literature, Theology, and the Moral of Stories*. Bloomsbury Academic, 2017.

Reimer, Jennifer A. "All the Pretty Mexican Girls: Whiteness and Racial Desire in Cormac McCarthy's *All the Pretty Horses*. *Western American Literature*, Volume 48, number 2, 2014: 422–42.

Schafer, William. "The Hard Wages of Original Sin." *Appalachian Journal*, Volume 4, number 2, 1977: 105–19.

Snyder, Phillip A. "Hospitality in Cormac McCarthy's *The Road*." *Cormac McCarthy Journal*. Volume 6, number 1, 2008: 69–86.

Spurgeon, Sara. "Introduction." *Cormac McCarthy: All the Pretty Horses, No Country for Old Men, The Road*. Edited by Sara Spurgeon. Continuum, 2011: 14–40.

Stark, Hannah. "'All These Things He Saw and Did Not See': Witnessing the End of the World in Cormac McCarthy's *The Road*." *Critical Survey*. Volume 25, number 2, 2013: 71–84.

Sullivan, Nell. "Boys Will Be Boys and Girls Will Be Gone: The Circuit of Male Desire in Cormac McCarthy's Border Trilogy." In *A Cormac McCarthy Companion: The Border Trilogy*. Edited by Edwin T. Arnold and Dianne C. Luce. University of Mississippi Press, 2001: 228–255.

Woodson, Linda. "Deceiving the Will to Truth: The Semiotic Foundation of All the Pretty Horses." *Sacred Violence: Cormac McCarthy's Western Novels*. Edited by Wade H. Hall and Rick Wallach. Texas Western Press, 2022: 51-56.

———. "'The Lighted Display Case': A Nietzschean Reading of Cormac McCarthy's Border Fiction." *Southern Quarterly*. Volume 38, number 4, 2000: 48-60.

Young, Thomas Daniel. *Tennessee Writers*. Tennessee Three Star Books, 1981.

His Disastrous Wrath

Monstrosity in *Child of God*

AHMED HONEINI

Throughout the scholarly history of *Child of God*, critics have frequently asserted that Lester Ballard is made a monster by his community. This standpoint is exemplified by Jay Ellis, who argues that "the implicit argument of [the novel] is that Lester Ballard is *made* a necrophilic murderer by the circumstances and forces of the society that refuses, repeatedly, to claim him in the absence of his family" (80). Opposing this claim, this essay focuses on Lester's free will, agency, and conscious decision to commit murder and necrophilia, actions which constitute his own self-fashioned monstrosity. My reading of Lester's monstrosity is informed by Stephen T. Asma's contention that "*monster* is a flexible, multiuse concept" that is frequently applied "to *inhuman* creatures of every stripe, even if they come from our own species. The concept of the monster has evolved to become a moral term in addition to a biological and theological term. [...] The term *monster* is often applied to human beings who have, by their own horrific actions, abdicated their humanity." Since "our humanity is indeed a fragile mantle, one that can be corrupted by forces internal and external to us," Asma concludes, "everyone has the potential to become monstrous" (7–8). The "internal forces" that Asma gestures toward drive Lester's transition to monstrosity: by committing violence, murder, and necrophilia, Lester deliberately fashions himself into a monstrous entity, becoming an embodiment of evil. His actions disregard the lives and individual agencies of the members of the wider community of Sevier County. Indeed, his transition from human to monster becomes the ultimate assertion of his own individuality and agency, which is possible only at the expense of completely stripping his victims of their right to life and ownership over their bodies to fulfill his base desires. In other words, Lester Ballard is not made a monster so much as he makes himself one.

This reading of *Child of God* challenges previous readings of the novel which have also attempted to read Lester as a monster, most notably one by Ashley Craig Lancaster. Lancaster argues that Lester is "a man who exists not just as a stigmatized Other but as a monstrous version of humanity": "By presenting Lester's descent into madness as a gradual process of social disenfranchisement, McCarthy rejects the argument that social outsiders are born deviants; in fact, he implicates society as a main contributor to this social deviance from which it yearns to separate itself" (132). Lancaster does not take into account Lester's own agency and his total rejection of any normative connection to the people of Sevier County from the beginning of his life to its end. As such, my reading of the novel is precisely that Lester "has terrorized their community his entire life, even as a young child, and as an adult, Lester intrigues them and frightens them by carrying a gun wherever he goes and by his ability to shoot the gun so accurately. These people piece together a version that makes him seem like a creature of disorder, rebellion, and displacement," a characterization of Lester that Lancaster rejects, but which is central to my own account and understanding of McCarthy's authorial intentions throughout the novel (140).

"A Malign Star Kept Him"

Critical assessments of *Child of God* typically begin with the assumption that the townspeople of Sevier County have purposefully excluded and alienated Lester Ballard. That assumption is rooted in, I would argue, a misunderstanding of the novel's opening chapter, during which Lester's "aged clapboard house" is auctioned off and he is, as a result, left untethered to any conventional sense of family and community (3). On this point, Ellis asserts that, "whatever the mental insufficiencies and psychological deformities of Lester Ballard, the plot is launched by this act of unhousing; every subsequent action of Lester Ballard—including necrophilia—follows from this initial scene" (70). On the surface, Lester does, indeed, appear to be excluded and alienated from the community. The townspeople converge "like a caravan of carnival folk" upon Lester's property, singing and forming "a ghost chorus among old ruins" (3 and 5). McCarthy purposefully contrasts their gathering to Lester who, in the opening moments of the novel, stands alone, isolated "at the barn door" (4). This deliberate juxtaposition has been interpreted by critics such as Christopher Coughlin as demonstrating that Lester, from the outset of *Child of God*, has no proper place among the community, to the extent that even his house, "aged" and decrepit though it is, has been forcibly taken from him. Coughlin maintains that Lester "is not a symbol of the 'other,' the social outsider, he *is* the 'other.' He has been heavily scrutinized by the townspeople and rejected as a problem. Therefore, he is fated to be a transgressive and strange nuisance" (133). Thus, readings such as Ellis's and Coughlin's cast Lester as an essentially sympathetic victim of social alienation.[1] As a result, such readings imply that his subsequent campaign of violence against Sevier County can be understood though not necessarily condoned.

Yet, such readings also minimize the palpable threat and menace that Lester himself openly displays toward the townspeople during the auction and, indeed, the overwhelming hostility that characterizes his encounters with them throughout his life. McCarthy places particular emphasis on the fact that, as the auction begins, Lester emerges upon the scene "holding a rifle," sending a disturbed, fearful "murmur [. . .] through the crowd" (6–7). There is no sense that Lester's fury at the townspeople converging upon his property can be attributed to their having excluded him. Instead, I read Lester's confrontation of these people as McCarthy's explicit attempt to establish that he desires no such place among them. He actively attempts to force them away from his home, saying "I want you to get your goddamn ass off my property. [. . .] I don't give a fuck who's present" (7). Far from harboring a rage-fueled resentment for their refusal to accept him, Lester performs actions that deliberately disrupt any notion that he wishes to become an integrated member of the community. As Brian Evenson notes, throughout his life and, indeed, from the outset of the novel, Lester "lives absolutely on the fringe, [and] his dependence on society [is] reduced to a minimum" (44). In my view, readings of *Child of God* that argue to the contrary fundamentally misunderstand the tense dynamic between Lester and the community that

McCarthy works to establish from the beginning of the novel, and which he also underscores through Lester's clear capacity for violence. Armed with his rifle and demanding these "sons of bitches off of my goddamned property" (7), Lester proves that he is a willful communal outcast who voluntarily lives at a distinct remove from the collective whole of Sevier County. As Matthew Guinn writes, Lester "exists on the margins of society with a pervasive hostility towards those at the center" and "drifts along the fringe of his culture," thereby becoming "a displaced agrarian figure" (101). Given his recourse to violence in the opening passage, Lester's relations with the townspeople are clearly grounded in malevolence.

Having threatened the townsfolk and subsequently lost his familial home, Lester retreats to the Appalachian backwoods to live in a dilapidated "outhouse" (14). Again, the common critical perspective on this moment is that Lester, now dispossessed of his home, has been debased, humiliated, and rendered "half crazy" by the town's inhumane actions (15). Katie Owens-Murphy, for instance, argues that because the community "must resort to labels like 'crazy' to explain the behavior of nonconformists" like Lester, that label "reveals the community's nervous intolerance to challenges to the social order" (168). Likewise, Ferma Lekesizalın claims that the "dehumanizing aspects of Lester's conditions, including the social hostility displayed toward him, lend an inevitability to the evolution of his destructive and deviant behavior" (374). In other words, the severity of Lester's subsequent actions, along with his need to revenge himself against the townspeople, has frequently been figured within McCarthy scholarship as being a consequence of Lester's societal debasement, including his having to live among and defecate like the animals he encounters "in the clumps of jimson and nightshade" and sleeping alone in the outhouse, "with his mouth open like a dead man" (14–16). Yet, in the context of my overarching argument regarding his self-determined monstrosity, Lester's retreat to the backwoods can also be read as his purposefully fashioning a new form of existence for himself. This new existence emerges in the absence of any normative connection to society, which has explicitly rejected him (in the view of common critical orthodoxy) and which he himself has also openly rejected through the violence and antipathy he exhibits toward them. Lester, in Evenson's terms, "exists outside of (and in spite of) fixed routes, off both moral and intellectual paths, his existence amounting to a constant movement" (42).[2] Lester is driven by his acute, unwavering reliance upon violence, such as when McCarthy describes how "he got up and got the rifle from where it stood by the fireplace" in the outhouse "and laid it on the floor by his mattress" (16). His capacity for violence and the hatred which he has always harbored for the community gives his life purpose, and subsequently metastasizes and corrupts his entire being from now to the end of his life. Instruments of violence such as his rifle, John Cant observes, "is all that he can care for and is the agent of destruction—his victims and his own" (100). Retreating to the woods, Lester begins to fashion himself into a monster, and yet it is precisely that monstrosity which ironically brings about his own downfall by the novel's end.

McCarthy further amplifies Lester's willful hostility and self-determined social otherness through the various anecdotes about his reputation for violence and intimidation, which are strategically placed early within the novel.[3] One such anecdote details his assault of a young boy, Finney, during his childhood:

> [Finney] lost a softball down off the road that rolled down into this field about . . . it was way off down in a bunch of briers and stuff and he told this boy, this Finney boy, told him to go and get it. [. . .] Finney boy said he wasn't about to do it and Lester told him one more time, said: You don't get down in there and get me that ball I'm goin to bust you in the mouth. [. . .] He seen the boy wasn't goin to do what he ast him. He just stood there a minute and then he punched him in the face. Blood flew out of the Finney boy's nose[.] (17–18)

This anecdote emphasizes that Lester's outburst during the auction is not an isolated, aberrant episode, nor do his actions in that instant merely constitute his wish to defend himself against the townspeople encroaching upon his land. Instead, McCarthy purposefully weaves together various accounts of Lester's violent history to show that he has long been antagonistic toward the townsfolk and has repeatedly attempted to force his violent will upon them. Lester's social interactions are frequently undergirded by a tendency to threaten and coerce those around him into obeying his commands under penalty of violence. McCarthy urges his readers to question what precisely Finney did to be assaulted, much like he compels them to ask why Lester felt justified in charging at the townspeople with his rifle during the auction. Regardless of whether Sevier County itself has a long history of violence and moral degradation (which, as I will soon acknowledge, is certainly the case), to place the responsibility of Lester's violence upon the community for 'trespassing' upon his property or upon Finney for accidentally losing the ball implies that these moments merited Lester's violent, confrontational behavior. Such a reading is inherently questionable, because it places the onus upon the townsfolk and upon Finney specifically as having engineered their own victimization. To do so also overlooks Lester's purposeful, consistently aggressive behavior as an individual simply because of the town's murky moral architecture. Such an oversight fails to consider that Lester has been gradually fashioning himself into a violent person since childhood. As Steven Frye notes, Lester's "cruelties are foreshadowed by his bullying behavior as a young boy, and malevolence seems a feature of his essential character" (40). He has been deliberately attempting to cultivate a lurid reputation for himself within the town's collective consciousness, and his adolescent behavior is proleptic of his future turn toward monstrosity in adulthood.

Years following his assault of Finney, Lester encounters an unnamed "lady sleeping under the trees in a white gown" on the Frog Mountain turnaround (41). Lester's encounter with the lady has frequently been misinterpreted by critics who strongly proclaim Lester innocent of any wrongdoing and, indeed, condemn the lady for her subsequent, false accusation of rape that she charges him with (49). For example, Vereen M. Bell describes the lady as "a drunken whore" who beats Lester and has him "put in jail" (53). Similarly, Lekesizalın declares that during "this particular incident, Lester acts out not because of perverted or voyeuristic impulses, but because he is misunderstood and shown hostility" by the lady, who does not comprehend that Lester is apparently "concerned for her safety" (373). While no act of rape actually occurs in this passage, McCarthy implicitly urges his readers to suspect Lester's intentions with the lady as he watches her sleep. Specifically, McCarthy mentions that Lester "could see her heavy breasts sprawled under the thin stuff of her nightdress" and "the dark thatch of hair under her belly" (41). Such details imply that Lester's gaze here is inherently sexualized and predatory; he focuses upon the sleeping lady's body in a carnal, covetous fashion. That the lady is asleep during this moment leaves her vulnerable to Lester, a vulnerability that McCarthy emphasizes when Lester "knelt down and touched her" (41). As Nell Sullivan highlights, "Lester prefers inanimate, 'sleeping' women—women whose movements he alone controls" (74). The details I have highlighted within this passage reflect a definite maliciousness on Lester's part, which the lady herself is aware of when she awakes and defends herself against him with a rock (42). Although no rape is committed here, the fact that Lester strikes "her so hard" across the face that he "spun her back round facing him" and that he then rips her gown off, "leaving her stark naked on the ground" are, in my view, coded examples of the sexualized menace he does in fact pose to her (42–43). Stripping away her clothes, Lester takes a trophy of his—admittedly unsuccessful—tryst with her in order to humiliate her. Although Lester fails to rape the lady here, the threat his actions pose to her, when seen in the wider context of his subsequent campaign of murder and necrophilia, is proleptic of the numerous acts of sexualized violence he later commits against the women of Sevier County.

Alongside these actions of violence, McCarthy also introduces early within the narrative various attempts by the community to explain and rationalize Lester's aberrant behavior. A representative example of just such a rationalization is their invocation of Lester's traumatic childhood, which is mentioned after his confrontation with the townsfolk during the auction:

> They say he was never right after his daddy killed hisself. They was just the one boy. The mother had run off, I don't know where to nor who with. Me and Cecil Edwards was the ones cut him down. He come in the store and told it like you'd tell it was rainin out. We went up there and walked in the barn and I seen his feet hangin. We just cut him down, let him fall to the floor. Just like cuttin down meat. He stood there and watched, never said nothin. He was about nine or ten years old at the time. (21)

This communal voice does not suggest that Lester's actions are at all the responsibility of the wider citizenry of Sevier County. Instead, from the community's perspective, the overarching cause for Lester's crimes is rooted in external factors, namely the death of his father and the absence of his mother. Such factors are positioned as being of greater significance to comprehending Lester than any wrongdoing the townspeople themselves may be accused of. There is a tacit refusal by the community to accept any liability for Lester; as Travis Franks writes, by purposefully invoking Lester's childhood as a leading cause of his violence later in life, "the community members frame a way of talking about Lester that allows them to avert talking about themselves and their complicity in his wretchedness" (88). Yet, even this attempt at rationalizing Lester's monstrosity does not consider the internal factors at play within him that made him "crazy" (22) and that caused him, in Asma's terms, to "abdicate [his] humanity" through his own "horrific actions" (7). Such an oversight on the community's part, and on the part of critics such as Ellis who insist that Lester's crimes are rooted in the "social structure of the home [being] broken" from the outset of the novel (73), betrays a foolhardy eagerness to find an overarching cause for what made Lester a monster, rather than—and more usefully, I would argue—looking closely at Lester's own behavior. Focusing on these factors within Lester's childhood is futile because to do so completely ignores any question of his own free will and agency that contributed to his murderousness.

The temptation by the community to focus on Lester's traumatic childhood is, Franks writes, also "a means of controlling the narrative in order to insulate the community by not admitting that they possess knowledge" of his crimes: "Doing so would force them into a potentially ruinous discourse about the community's complex history of violence" (87). Indeed, throughout the novel, McCarthy makes clear that Lester's actions are not unique to the community. Instead, his monstrosity is seen as part of a wider pattern of behavior that is exhibited throughout human history, and which is rampant throughout Sevier County. Indeed, at one point, a member of the community declares: "I'll tell you one thing about Lester though. You can trace em back to Adam if you want and goddamn if he didn't outstrip em all" (81). Sevier County itself is explicitly figured as a place with a long history of violence, tribalism, and moral degradation, as seen through the dumpkeeper's rape of his own daughter (28), "them other two sons of bitches" that the lady under the tree subsequently demands be jailed for rape (51), and the "fugitive" from Pine Bluff whom Lester encounters while in jail and who boasts that he "cut a motherfucker's head off with a pocket knife" (53). Situating Lester's crimes within this wider context of social corruption and depravity, McCarthy suggests that monstrosity can be located anywhere. Lester, then, is not a limit-case of the world's evils, nor even of the community's evils—he is only an (admittedly potent and by far the most extreme) example among many. In *Child of God*, McCarthy shows his readers how one such monster is created by his own self-determined, inexhaustible capacity for violence and murder.

"A Crazed Gymnast Laboring over a Cold Corpse"

As highlighted at the beginning of this essay, a common critical perspective of Lester's relationship with Sevier County places responsibility for his monstrosity within the community itself. However, considering that many of Lester's subsequent victims are women who are not only brutally murdered but whose bodies are sexually violated after their deaths, the remainder of this essay challenges any critical position that suggests that one can sympathize with or, indeed, tacitly understand Lester's engagement in murder and necrophilia because of his fundamental need to belong to a family. Such a reading has most forcefully been advanced by Ellis, who insists that "McCarthy challenges us to recognize that the natural longings of any lonely person are present" within Lester's crimes: "the desire for home, companionship, romance" (87). Such readings substantially minimize Lester's own culpability for his crimes; instead, as Georg Guillemin observes, the novel overtly works to establish Lester as "a sentient human being, ethically derailed and socially estranged to be sure, but not unaccountable for his actions" (42). Like Guillemin, I do not believe that Lester can be seen as "unaccountable for his actions," nor can one argue that he has no will or agency in his treatment of his victims. Instead, the remainder of this section emphasizes the willful, deliberate cruelty that underpins Lester's crimes. I argue that, by murdering and sexually violating several women after death, Lester disregards the individual agencies of his victims in order to assert his own power and dominance over them. By doing so, he heightens his own need to embody maleficence and monstrosity.

Lester discovers his first victim of necrophilia, a "young and pretty girl," at random: she and her lover are dead within their car, which is "idling" off Frog Mountain Road (88 and 85). While Lester does not murder these people, McCarthy nonetheless outlines an ethical dilemma that Lester finds himself in: after discovering the couple's "half naked bodies," Lester "kept on walking. Then he stopped. A pair of eyes staring with lidless fixity. He turned and came back" (86). Lester's initial hesitancy notwithstanding, the fact that he returns to the scene suggests that his curiosity here is driven by precisely those deviant, violent impulses that he has repeatedly been shown to be attracted to, and which were exemplified during his earlier encounter with the lady sleeping under the tree. As John Cant claims, Lester is "driven by the irresistible appetite of sexuality," and although "his economical, social and personal circumstances combine to deny Lester any human outlet for his sexuality," these circumstances are "not sufficient to suppress it altogether" (91). The same sexualized gaze that Lester focuses upon the lady under the tree is replicated once he notices that the girl's "blouse [is] open and her brassiere [is] pushed up" (87). Lester's desire for the dead "pretty girl" is then manifested physically and corporeally when "finally he reached across the dead man's back and touched the breast. It was soft and cool. He stroked the full brown nipple with the ball of his thumb. He was still holding the rifle. [. . .] He reached and stroked her other breast. He did this for a while and then he pushed her eyes shut with his thumb" (87). Lester's physical, sexual contact with the corpse is fundamentally an act of violation, especially since he is fully cognizant that she cannot resist his advances. In fact, to Lester, she is merely a material possession devoid of any personal history. Her significance to Lester arises only because, through his violation of her body, he is finally able to utter "into that waxen ear everything he'd ever thought of saying to a woman" (88). My reading of this moment is diametrically opposed to Lancaster's claim that "Lester never treats this woman with any disrespect": "Although all of these passionate and loving acts with the dead woman seem demented, they actually reveal a sensitive side of Lester" (143). Instead, my reading mirrors Harriet Poppy Stilley's characterization of Lester's "merciless misogyny," which, for Stilley, is "a means to a practical, sexual end, adopting the theme of necrophilia so as to stress the reality of woman as sexual property" (98). Lester actualizes his own monstrosity in this moment because, by exploiting this corpse for his own pleasure, he places his own needs and carnal appetites above any conventional sense of respect or solemnity for the dead. He relinquishes himself to those grotesque "inner forces" which Asma, rightly, claims can lead human beings to commit monstrous acts. Lester's myopic, single-minded pursuit of his long-frustrated sexual desires causes him to become a "crazed gymnast laboring over a cold corpse," a deliberate rhetorical gesture on McCarthy's part that imposes a moment of stark reality upon the outlandish, mad act occurring within the car (88).

Lester's subsequent, repeated engagement in necrophilia with this corpse calls into question the sentimentality and sympathy for Lester's supposed plight that critics such as Ellis or Lancaster advocate. Indeed, McCarthy emphasizes the degree to which Lester finds no value or importance in this woman's right to a proper burial when he describes Lester's insistence upon making her "rise again" with the use of "some old lengths of plowline" that he places around her waist (95). Lester aims to extend the means through which the corpse functions as a corporeal vessel through which to satiate his monstrous lusts. Unlike Lancaster, who characterizes her corpse as "the lover whom he has always wished to have," I view Lester's interactions with the girl as being fundamentally impersonal in nature (143). She has no name within the novel and no identity or will of her own; instead, she resembles the "crude wood manikin headless and mounted" that Lester spots in a store window while in town (97). Lester instills within her a grotesque, perverse simulacrum of life, placing her corpse into a "red dress," a "pretty red" slip, and black lingerie adorned "with pink bows" (98–99). That Lester repeatedly violates her body while he insists that she "been wantin it" can only be read as a posthumous experience of rape (103). Lester's actions do not, in any way, constitute his becoming "the middle-class husband with the perfect stay-at-home wife that loves him unconditionally and certainly will never leave him," in Michael Madsen's terms (23). Instead, as Stilley writes, McCarthy frames Lester's actions as his own authorial "indictment of the reality of women as sexual chattel, emphasizing the extent to which man uses objects, and insensate beings called objects, to feel his own power and presence and to know himself at once as man and as subject" (103). Repeatedly exploiting this body for his own sexual gratification, Lester makes this corpse a helpless victim of his unbridled menace. She has no means of resisting his grossly manipulative abuse of her body after death.

Having taken possession of and, subsequently, losing the "young and very pretty" girl when the outhouse accidentally burns down, leaving only a "blackened chimney with a pile of smoldering boards at its feet," Lester ventures to find another victim (105). He targets another young local girl, the daughter of his acquaintance, Ralph (118). Lester considers this girl as simply another sexualized, carnal possession that he preys upon and, ultimately, captures. He is concerned only with the continual, unabated fulfilment of his sexual needs, which have been momentarily frustrated because of the unintended cremation of the first corpse during the outhouse fire, that has left "not so much as a bone" in its "ruins" (107). Although the second girl does not acquiesce to Lester's crude advances and refuses to "show [him] them nice titties," Lester is not deterred from his pursuit of her, because he can now easily strip away her own agency and control over her own body from her through the act of murder (118). After leaving the house, "he picked up the rifle where he'd left it leaning against a crabapple tree and he went along the side of the house and stepped up into a low wall of cinder block and went along it past the clothesline and the coal pile to where he could see in the window there. He could see the back of her head above the sofa. [. . .] Ballard fired." (118) Lester's initial engagement in necrophilia was a formative, life-altering moment, one which revealed to him the extent of the power he possesses and harnesses over his victims. No possible threat or demonstration of resistance disturbs him here; his sole endeavor is to possess this body. Indeed, a total affectlessness inflects his actions as he sets about murdering the girl, placing "another shell into the chamber and [raising] the rifle then she fell" (119). Here, Lester seems to be completing a series of scripted, mechanical gestures with the goal of obtaining his coveted prize, a new "dead girl" who is "slick with blood" (119). As per Asma's aforementioned definition of monstrosity, Lester's murderous actions here, in combination with his unabated engagement in necrophilia until the end of his life, demonstrates the extent to which he has conclusively "abdicated [his] humanity" because of his "own horrific actions" (7). Lester totally disregards humanity and community; these traits, which were present even during his childhood through his victimization of the Finney boy, reach an uncontrollable fever pitch at this point in his life.

As the murder of Ralph's daughter suggests, Lester's actions, by now, constitute his purposeful, deliberate attack upon the township's most vulnerable and helpless members. Lester subsequently targets a couple in a "pickup truck" (150). After shooting the 'boy' "through the neck," he places "the muzzle of the rifle at the base of" the 'girl's' "skull and fire[s]" (150–51). Where his assault and murder of the girl specifically is concerned, Lester strips her of agency and power over her own body, leaving her defenseless as she places "her hands in the air as if she didn't know where to put them"

(150). Immediately after she is shot, McCarthy notes "she dropped as if the bones in her body had been liquefied": "Ballard tried to catch her but she slumped into the mud" (151). As such, she is yet another dead body that Lester will defile and demean in pursuit of his deviant lusts and his fundamental need to intimidate, menace, and control his victims.[4] In view of the necrophilic intentions he has in mind, Lester, at this stage, treats his victims as always already dead: as Yi Yang notes, his "hunting of women suggests a willed blindness and a willful descent into the slavery of objects" (545). Now a "crazed mountain troll" who "call[s] out a high voiced gibberish" (152), Lester's monstrous fall suggests that, despite whatever power or satisfaction he may gain from murder and necrophilia, his actions place him at the absolute edge of any identifiable connection to humanity. Thus, in Dianne C. Luce's terms, Lester's actions emblematize McCarthy's own challenge to "the limits of our own optimistic definitions of humanity" (2009, 134). Indeed, he has become, in James R. Giles's words, "a ghoulish figure so consumed by madness as to be scarcely recognized as human" (35–36). Lester's monstrosity results, then, from his willingness to desecrate, destroy, and pervert the lives and bodies of his weak, defenseless victims with no qualms or compunction.

"His Wrath Seemed to Buoy Him Up"

Once the outhouse has burned down and he has lost the first "young and very pretty" corpse, Lester retreats to a "cave" situated deep within Frog Mountain, which he must enter through a "crawlway" that leaves him "slick with red mud down the front of him" (107). He also finds refuge within his own, inner metaphorical "cave" where he can continue to abuse and plot against the townsfolk. Although by normative standards Lester's retreat into this cave exacerbates his sustained withdrawal from any recognizable form of humanity, his actions can also be seen as part of a wider pattern of aberrant behavior that, as I have acknowledged, has been rooted within him since childhood. His position within the cave recalls Richard Kearney's assertion that monstrosity is typically located within "those phantasmal boundaries where maps run out"; in fact, according to Kearney, monstrous beings like Lester are "figures of Otherness" that "occupy the frontier zone where reason falters and fantasies flourish" (3). Indeed, by withdrawing into "the bowels of the mountain" (135), Lester's monstrous "fantasies" are allowed to fully "flourish" and take on a grotesque aesthetic form, as seen on the "ledges or pallets of stone where dead people"—Lester's subsequent victims—are displayed "like saints" (135). Displaying these corpses in this manner allows Lester to fulfill his wish to make "things more orderly in the woods and in men's souls"; he is able to position his victims within an insane "orderly" form that only he can comprehend. Enmeshed within his own hidden idyll, the corporeal products of his depraved lusts are literally on display. Monsters, as Kearney reminds us, are "by definition unrecognizable": "they defy our accredited norms of identification" and are, instead, considered "unnatural, transgressive, obscene, contradictory, heterogeneous, mad" (4). By this point in *Child of God*, Lester has offended murderously against the natural order of humanity, and his depravity has now escalated beyond all rationality and comprehension. He has entered the "clefts of bedlam" surrounding him and is ensconced within "his disastrous wrath," having rejected "the name of sanity" and, by extension, whatever humanity remains within him (145–50). Now, in Gary M. Ciuba's terms, Lester "lives by the very violence he has engendered" (82).

Lester's turn toward monstrosity is not free of consequence, however. Although he chooses "wrath" as the guiding principle of his life, such a decision has dire, "disastrous" consequences upon his body and psyche. McCarthy makes clear that Lester has become a ruin of a man, in constant "agony" and reduced to "gibbering a sound not quite like crying" (159). While his turn toward murder and necrophilia initially enabled him to cultivate a new form of existence entirely outside of social dictates, McCarthy makes clear that the consequences of Lester's campaign of threatening, terrorizing, and, ultimately, murdering the townsfolk results in a life underscored by misery and desperation. In other words, the fundamental irony of Lester's self-determined monstrosity is that it is not the community who has destroyed his life. Rather, *Lester himself* has engendered his own destruction and has reduced himself to a subhuman, "gibbering" creature. The abject suffering he now experiences is the inevitable consequence of his murderous, vindictive rejection of society, community, and humanity.

The final phase of Lester's "disastrous wrath" is figured in his carefully planned yet ultimately unsuccessful assault on John Greer, a native of Grainger County who, more importantly, now lives on Lester's former familial property (11). Lester's attack on Greer is consistent with the palpable hatred that he has always displayed toward Sevier County; he, in other words, wants to revenge himself against Greer for having dared to encroach upon his property. Lester, initially, displays a purposeful and deliberate menace toward Greer by standing at an unseen distance and watching as Greer sits "before Ballard's very stove with his stockfeet up": "Ballard laid the rifle foresight on his chest. He swung it upward to a spot just above the ear. His finger filled the cold curve of the trigger. Bang, he said" (109). The fact that Lester does not shoot Greer here suggests that he, in fact, finds a perverse joy in watching over his apparently oblivious and defenseless prey. The prospect of a direct, violent confrontation is, implicitly, much more satisfying to Lester than discreetly and impersonally dispatching his enemy, his "house's new tenant," from a covert distance (109). As Frye acknowledges, by this point in the novel, Lester is "the personification and the dark embodiment of the very chaos he apparently laments. But he is also a master of method, a survivor who for a time makes his way alone, and he plots his exploits precisely if not always successfully" (45). During Lester's actual assault on Greer, he emerges bedecked in a "frightwig and skirts" upon the property: advancing on Greer, he "raise[s] the rifle and cock[s] the hammer silently, holding back the trigger and easing it into the notch as hunters do" (172). Aiming to reclaim his property, Lester displays no hesitancy toward the violence he is about to commit and, indeed, acts beyond even a rational sense of justice for having been robbed of what Ellis describes as the "social structure of the home" (73). Instead, he is fully immersed in this process of frightening and destroying Greer, having exchanged his humanity in favor of the "frightwig" he has "fashioned whole from a dried human scalp" (172–73).[5] Any possibility of redemption is now closed to him because of his violent antipathy toward humanity and the macabre abuse of his victims' bodies. Yet, whatever catharsis or victory Lester may have achieved by attacking Greer is immediately destroyed when Greer manages to defend himself against and shoot Lester, sending his attacker's "arm flying out in a peculiar limber gesture, a faint pink cloud of blood and shredded clothing and the rifle clattering soundless on the porchboards amid the uproar" (173). Now Lester is incapacitated and injured: his missing arm symbolizes his irrevocable disconnection from humanity—he is simply a "thing" that has been shot (173).[6] Ironically, Lester's failed attack upon Greer implies that, much like the physical and psychic agony he experiences prior to this moment, "his disastrous wrath" has been rendered ineffectual because of his injury—his all-encompassing, monstrous disdain for the townspeople has backfired against him.

"What Did You Want with Them Dead Ladies?"

During his confrontation with Lester, Greer is forced to commit violence in order to save his own life and—unbeknownst to him—effectively terminate Lester's campaign of terror against Sevier County. Through Greer's actions, McCarthy makes clear that, while Lester attempts to repeatedly disturb and menace the townsfolk, they are capable of resisting and, indeed, combatting the threat he poses. In fact, Greer's actions are anticipated in the opening moments of the novel, during Lester's altercation with the townspeople during the auction. In that moment, one of the townsmen, Buster, strikes him, leaving him "bleeding at the ears" with an "awful pumpknot on his head" (9). Buster's reaction to Lester's threats has been read, by critics such as Ellis, as emblematizing the community's insistence upon encroaching upon and forcibly stripping Lester of his rights an individual. That insistence, in Ellis's terms, causes Lester's "descent into psychopathic violence" (74). However, seen in the wider context of the novel and especially his immediate turn toward murder and necrophilia and, later, his attack upon Greer's property, the injury Lester sustains from Buster is a moment of narrative prolepsis wherein McCarthy makes clear that the town, when confronted by Lester's violence, refuses to be intimidated by or acquiesce to him. Sevier County as a whole, and Buster and Greer as its representatives, also have recourse to violently resist Lester—violence is as engrained into their own collective consciousness as it is in Lester's behavior as an individual subject. They endeavor to preserve peace and civility and uphold a sense of order that Lester's actions disturb, because, from their perspective, the severity of his behavior leaves them with no alternative.

After Lester has been shot, he is not left to die on Greer's property like an animal or an inhuman "thing" (173)—he is not, in other words, treated with the complete inhumanity and cruelty that his victims suffered at his hands. Instead, he is kept alive, his wounds are treated at the hospital, and he is clothed, fed, and medicated (174–76). Despite the severity of his crimes, he is treated with basic human decency from, ironically, the very society he has emphatically and murderously rejected. As John Lang notes, the townspeople, like the reader, are "never permitted to evade the knowledge of Lester's fundamental humanity, however violent or grotesque" (88). A posse of men, erroneously described as "hunters" and "tormentors" from Lester's perspective (168–73), subsequently demand to find Lester's victims, "so they can be give[n] a decent burial"; they assure him that "we'll put you back in that hospital and let you take your chances with the law" once the bodies have been recovered (182). These "hunters" are not driven by a tribal pursuit of mob justice; instead, their actions emerge from a common respect for the dead that is also consistent with the basic decency shown to Lester after he is shot. Their search for these defiled corpses, then, is not undergirded by a perverse bloodlust but, rather, by an insistence upon upholding a moral, ethical standard—the proper burial of the dead—that Lester has disregarded and disrespected to an extreme extent. As Hillary Gamblin notes, Lester, by "placing the living among the dead in ways that society would label 'wrong' illustrates that in creating his own space [he] abandons the world that the local community lives in, and doing so severs his accordance with social norms" (31–32).

Through the posse's actions, McCarthy purposefully challenges any ambivalence his readers may have toward extrajudicial justice, especially since they are acting to restore the solemnity that death demands and that Lester's perverse treatment of these "dead ladies"—namely "fuckin em"—has perverted (182). Early in the novel, McCarthy makes clear that Lester has been frequently arrested for a variety of crimes and misdemeanors, including for "failure to comply with a court order, public disturbance, assault and battery, public drunk[enness], [and] rape" (56), and that he is known to Fate Turner, the "high sheriff of Sevier County" (56). Yet, despite the sheriff's open hostility toward Lester and his tacit awareness of Lester's capacity for "meanness" and murder (56), Fate is unsuccessful in ridding Sevier County of Lester and, ultimately, cannot prevent Lester's crimes. Any attempt made by local law enforcement, as embodied by Sheriff Fate, to protect social order from Lester's menace is explicitly shown to be futile, especially because of Lester's own fundamental contempt for the law in general and for Fate in particular. By juxtaposing Fate's ineffectualness to the posse's endeavors, McCarthy implies that Lester's monstrosity not only causes his own and his victims' debasement, but also leads those around him into choosing a violent means of responding to and correcting his crimes. In other words, they capitulate to the undercurrent of "violent backwardness" that Franks identifies is engrained into life within the community (89).

However, Lester remains sustained by "his disastrous wrath" even after the injuries he has sustained at this point. His disdain and contempt for Sevier County is uncompromised, and he shows no remorse or contrition for his crimes—after learning that Greer has survived the attack, for example, Lester declares: "I wish the son of a bitch was dead" (176). Indeed, the prospect of relinquishing his victims' corpses to the posse for burial is anathema to him; he considers these bodies as being his property. To allow them "a decent burial" would be to capitulate to the demands of his "tormentors" and operate within a conventional social and ethical code that he has long rejected. Even at his most vulnerable, therefore, Lester remains monstrous, deceitful, and dangerous—although he offers to take the posse to the location of the corpses, he manipulates their trust and comically escapes their grasp: "Goddamn if that little bastard ain't played us for a bunch of fools. [. . .] We've rescued the little fucker from jail and turned him loose where he can murder folks again" (186). Lester consistently refuses to be tethered to the community's moral standards. Instead, he exploits the fraction of human decency they treated him with and chooses to remain unapologetically menacing.

Why, then, does Lester return to "the county hospital" three days after escaping the posse and retreating to his cave? *Why* does he declare to the "nightduty nurse" that "I'm supposed to be here"? (192). Critics have debated the logic behind this baffling and enigmatic narrative turn. Giles, for instance, argues that this moment "evokes a recognition in Lester of the sheer madness of his crimes" (40). Cant, meanwhile, asserts that Lester's "choice is a kind of suicide, because [he] belongs to the ancient mountain and not to modern society." Thus, this "enigmatic conversion leads ultimately to his evisceration" (15). In my view, Lester's return to the hospital functions as his own tacit acknowledgment that the freedom of movement and power over his victims that his embrace of monstrosity once afforded him has been irrevocably compromised and, thus, is no longer feasible. He will be hunted by the entire community now for having dared to escape, and the means through which he previously sustained his wrath against them—including his rifle and his physical strength—are now irretrievably lost. He has been reduced, instead, to a "weedshaped onearmed human swaddled up in outsized overalls and covered all over with red mud" (192). Any return or reconnection to a normative framework of humanity is now impossible for Lester, because he has been undone by the sheer extent of his own capacity for monstrosity, and the consequences of his "wrath" are now as apparent as the "red mud" that visibly cakes his body. Thus, he surrenders himself to the "wrath" of the townsfolk, tacitly accepting whatever punishment he will be subjected to.

"Monsters Worse to Come"

Lester's life ends on the ironic note that he "was never indicted for any crime" (193) by reason of insanity—as Ciuba speculates, because "the courts recognize Ballard as insane, he is spared not only the vengeance of the mob but also any formal indictment" (193). Lester's crimes, therefore, are seen by the state to completely transgress and disturb any sense of rationality or explanation. From the state's perspective, his crimes were those of a madman who was not acting willfully or even consciously. Instead, like the "demented gentleman" who he is placed "in a cage next door to" in the Knoxville state hospital (193), Lester is considered by the state as being beyond even conventional judicial punishment because of the "enormity of his crimes" (193). In other words, the decision not to indict him is undergirded, once again, by a deference toward basic human decency and, indeed, sympathy and empathy for a man who treated his victims with none of these qualities. The fact that Lester ultimately dies of "pneumonia," a painless death in comparison to the suffering his victims experienced, suggests that, ultimately, he escapes justice and persecution.

A predominant impulse within scholarly readings of Lester's autopsy, during which he is "laid out on a slab and flayed, eviscerated, [and] dissected" by "four young medical students who [are] bent over him like those haruspices of old," has been to position Lester as an ironic victim of the state's complete inhumanity (194). According to this interpretation, Lester, after death, is now subject to precisely the same cruelty that he subjected his victims to. Russell M. Hillier, for instance, maintains that Lester's "final indignity is to undergo a process of physical as well as social and moral disintegration" (109). Similarly, Cant asserts that "McCarthy manages to make this dehumanized treatment of Lester's mortal remains seem as horrific as has been Lester's treatment of his own victims" (97). Yet, I would argue, instead, that this atomization of Lester's body, during which his "muscles [are] stripped from his bones" and his "heart [is] taken out," implies that these medical examiners are desperate to locate a tangible, scientific reason for Lester's monstrosity. Regardless of whatever inhumanity they may be accused of, the students are compelled, in my view, to rationalize the barbarity of Lester's actions, an explanation that they fail to pinpoint. In that sense, the students' actions ironically replicate the attempts by the community to find an underlying cause for Lester's fate within the trauma of his childhood (22–23). The prejudices of the community and the stark, scientific objectivity of the students are ironically juxtaposed here, because they are each driven by a desperate need to understand why humanity itself is vulnerable to "monsters worse to come" (194). My reading here is aligned with Guinn's assessment that, during the autopsy, "the very idea of civilized progress is subjected to a powerful irony," because the medical students "are unlikely to lay bare the precise source or character of a degeneracy that McCarthy sees as ingrained" (102). Even after stripping Lester to his core, no substantive explanation for his innate depravity is determined: his body provides no answers.

In 2007, McCarthy asserted that "we know how to make serial killers": "You just take a Type A kid who's fairly bright and just beat the crap out of him day after day. That's how it's done" (Kushner, n.p.). On one level, McCarthy's statement here may be helpful in explaining the position that critics—and Ellis chief among them—have often taken as being central to explaining Lester's acts: the corrosive, destructive influence of his community. In light of this volume's wish to achieve "a programmatic reassessment of the character of McCarthy's project," however, this essay has not only rejected the idea that Lester is a helpless victim of communal pressure and "social forces beyond [his] control" (Elmore 141), but has also questioned McCarthy's assertion that serial murderers are themselves victims of oppressive societal abuse who, by implication, bear no culpability for their own crimes. Instead, my work throughout this essay has attempted to make clear Lester's own fundamental responsibility for his monstrous crimes, which have been determined by his own agency.

The temptation to simply and unquestioningly accept Lester Ballard as an unfairly maligned "child of God" who is the victim of years of societal exclusion is a critical mainstay that scholars have frequently relied upon to conveniently justify and rationalize his actions. In stark contrast to that overarching trend within critical readings of *Child of God*, I have asserted that one must also accept Lester as being fundamentally accountable for engineering his own monstrosity. The novel itself makes abundantly clear that Lester lost his family during his childhood and that Sevier County is a morally repugnant area with an undeniable history of violence and depravity. Thus, Lester's upbringing and his existence within such a society undoubtedly did impact his adulthood to a degree. Yet, within *Child of God*, McCarthy also urges his readers to question whether wider society must bear sole responsibility for the actions of an individual. As far as my position within this essay is concerned, I conclude that the moral repugnance of Sevier County did not, in itself, strip Lester of his own culpability for the crimes he willfully committed. The historical strain of violence within the community notwithstanding, Lester's fate was not predetermined by or imbricated within society's violent past. Instead, as the events of the novel make clear, his actions, along with the consequences of "his disastrous wrath," were his own.

NOTES

The impetus behind this study of *Child of God* was a desire for a full-length comparison between Lester's crimes and those of Ed Gein's. Although my focus subsequently shifted beyond my original intentions, I wish to honor here the memory of Gein's victims, Mary Hogan and Bernice Worden.

1. McCarthy scholars such as Alexandra Blair (2015) and John Lang (1995) have also advocated for a sympathetic, empathetic reading of Lester's actions. On the other hand, Jonathan and Rick Elmore (2019) provide a noteworthy reconsideration of these readings, to which this essay is indebted.

2. In that respect, my argument here is indebted to Stephen Greenblatt's concept of "self-fashioning" in sixteenth-century England (1980), principally the idea that self-fashioning allows one "the power to impose a shape upon oneself" and, indeed, to achieve "a profound mobility in social and economic terms" (1–7). Seen in the context of Greenblatt's argument, Lester's embrace of his own inner monstrosity gives his life form and substance, fueled by wrath.

3. Further examples of Lester's maliciousness and predation include when he observes a couple making love in a car parked on the Frog Mountain turnaround, "his heart hammering against the earth" as he masturbates and ejaculates on the car's fender (19–20). His victims are also not exclusively human, as seen when he attacks a pack of dogs who come "howling" into the outhouse; he sets upon one of them with "great drumlike thumps that echoed in the near empty room among the desperate oaths and wailings" of his assault (23–24). These instances emphatically suggest that Lester is a figure so disconnected from normative society that he is always predisposed toward violence and predation, which thus foreshadows his inevitable turn toward murder.

4. My reading of Lester's victims here is antithetical to Sullivan's characterization of McCarthy's authorial method. Sullivan argues that the novel is undergirded by a "narrative misogyny that excludes live women from the text" and which "also allows the projection of guilt onto the victims themselves, a sort of blaming of the victim" (75). As my reading here makes clear, however, McCarthy explicitly advocates readerly sympathy for Lester's victims and, indeed, urges an empathetic revulsion toward the grotesque sexual abuse they posthumously suffer. In that regard, my reading of Lester's victims is informed by Jane Caputi's pioneering observation that "sexual murder is a product of the dominant [patriarchal] culture. It is the ultimate expression of sexuality that defines sex as a form of domination [and] power; it is, like rape, a form of terror that constructs and maintains male supremacy" (2).

5. The image of Lester in the "frightwig and skirts" and, earlier, "the underclothes of his female victims [...] [and] their outerwear as well," resembling a "gothic doll in illfit clothes, its carmine mouth floating detached and bright" (140), calls to mind specific, real-life examples of serial murderers such as the "Plainfield Butcher" Ed Gein. Gein, throughout the 1950s, deliberately robbed graves and, later, committed murder, fashioning the corpses of his victims into stockings, soup bowls, vests, masks, drums, chairs, and jewelry (Vronsky, 113–14). Dianne C. Luce (2009) identifies Gein's crimes as a direct influence on the novel (144–46). Unfortunately, Gein's sordid legacy has also contributed to what Ryan Lee Cartwright describes as "the fabrication of the transgendered 'psycho' killer myth": "Informed by the *Diagnostic and Statistical Manual (DSM)*'s twisted taxonomy of sexual deviation, observers from 1957 through the early years of the twenty-first century have described Gein as though wearing parts of corpses was a perfectly logical extension of a man wearing a dress. It is not. Because it seems this must be said, I will say it directly: wearing skin flayed from an embalmed corpse is not 'carrying transvestism a step further,' nor does transsexualism involve stealing corpses in order to procure a 'woman's skin.' These are absurd insinuations that cause real harm to trans women" (98). Following Cartwright's lead, I reject any impulse to read Lester as a trans coded character, a reading that scholars such as Sullivan gesture toward by stating that Lester's crimes escalate to the point where "he must also *be* the women" he murders and, by doing so, he "incarnates his victims' femininity" (76). Such a reading implies that being transgender is a form of psychosis and would, as such, perpetuate the harmful characterization of trans people that Cartwright outlines.

6. The injury that Lester sustains to his arm during his confrontation with Greer and, indeed, his aforementioned retreat to his cave recall the downfall of Grendel in *Beowulf*, a literal monster who, after suffering "a tremendous wound" to his arm during combat with the poem's titular warrior, retreats, "fatally hurt, / To his desolate lair" (ll.815–19). Dianne C. Luce (2023), in fact, asserts that Lester "suffers the monster Grendel's fate, but the later century into which [he] is born means that he is not fated to bleed out from his terrible wound, the sole benign intervention of fate or chance in his life" (216). While I would not go so far as to suggest that McCarthy is rewriting Grendel's confrontation with Beowulf here, nor that Greer is cast as an ironic, unintended hero, the resonances between this moment in *Child of God* and Grendel's confrontation with Beowulf are clear enough to acknowledge. Indeed, scholars such as Rick Wallach, Peter Josyph, and Michael Lynn Crews have also identified *Beowulf* as a key point of reference for McCarthy as he was composing *Suttree* and *Blood Meridian*.

WORKS CITED

Asma, Stephen T. *On Monsters: An Unnatural History of Our Worst Fears*. Oxford University Press, 2009.

Bell, Vereen M. *The Achievement of Cormac McCarthy*. Louisiana State University Press, 1988.

Blair, Alexandra. "'The Wanted Stare Back": Biopolitics, Genre, and Sympathy in Cormac McCarthy's *Child of God*." *Southern Literary Journal*, Volume 47, number 2, 2015: 89–106.

Cant, John. *Cormac McCarthy and the Myth of American Exceptionalism*. Routledge, 2008.

Caputi, Jane. "The New Founding Fathers: The Lore and Lure of the Serial Killer in Contemporary Culture." *Journal of American Culture*, Volume 13, number 3, 1990: 1–12.

Cartwright, Ryan Lee. *Peculiar Places: A Queer Crip History of White Rural Nonconformity*. University of Chicago Press, 2020.

Ciuba, Gary M. "McCarthy's *Enfant Terrible*: Mimetic Desire and Sacred Violence in *Child of God*." In *Sacred Violence: A Reader's Companion to Cormac McCarthy*. Edited by Wade Hall and Rick Wallach. Texas Western Press, 2002: 77–85.

Coughlin, Christopher. "Gothic Commodification of the Body and the Modern Literary Serial Killer in *Child of God* and *American Psycho*." In *Monsters and Monstrosity from the Fin de Siècle to the Millennium*. Edited by Sharla Hutchinson and Rebecca A. Brown. McFarland & Company, Inc., 2015: 129–43.

Crews, Michael Lynn. *Books Are Made Out of Books: A Guide to Cormac McCarthy*. University of Texas Press, 2017.

Ellis, Jay. *No Place for Home: Spatial Constraint and Character Flight in the Novels of Cormac McCarthy*. Routledge: 2006.

Elmore, Jonathan, and Rick Elmore. "'You reckon there are just some places the good lord didn't intend folks to live in?': The Absence of Community in McCarthy's *Child of God*." *Cormac McCarthy Journal*, Volume 17, number 2, 2019: 134–47.

Evenson, Brian. "McCarthy's Wanderers: Nomadology, Violence, and Open Country." In

Sacred Violence: A Reader's Companion to Cormac McCarthy. Edited by Wade Hall and Rick Wallach. Texas Western Press, 2002: 41–48.

Franks, Travis. "'Talkin about Lester': Community, Culpability, and Narrative Suppression in *Child of God*." *Mississippi Quarterly*, Volume 67, number 1, 2014: 75–98.

Frye, Steven. *Understanding Cormac McCarthy*. University of South Carolina Press, 2011.

Gamblin, Hillary. "Discovering the Romantic in a Necrophiliac: The Question of Misogyny in *Child of God*." *Cormac McCarthy Journal*, Volume 9, number 1, 2011: 28–37.

Giles, James R. *The Spaces of Violence*. University of Alabama Press, 2006.

Greenblatt, Stephen. *Self-Fashioning: From More to Shakespeare*. University of Chicago Press, 1980.

Guillemin, Georg. *The Pastoral Vision of Cormac McCarthy*. Texas A&M University Press, 2004.

Guinn, Matthew. *After Southern Modernism: Fiction of the Contemporary South*. University Press of Mississippi, 2000.

Heaney, Seamus. *Beowulf: A Verse Translation*. W. W. Norton & Company, 2002.

Hillier, Russell M. "'Monsters Worse to Come": A Reconsideration of the Influence of Mary Shelley's *Frankenstein* upon Cormac McCarthy's *Child of God*." *The Explicator*, Volume 79, number 3, 2021: 104–10.

Josyph, Peter. "Blood Music: Reading *Blood Meridian*." *Sacred Violence: A Reader's Companion to Cormac McCarthy*. Edited by Wade Hall and Rick Wallach. Texas Western Press, 2002: 51–75.

Kearney, Richard. *Strangers, Gods, and Monsters: Interpreting Otherness*. Routledge, 2002.

Kushner, David. "Cormac McCarthy's Apocalypse." *Rolling Stone*, Thursday, December 27, 2007.

Lancaster, Ashley Craig. "From Frankenstein's Monster to Lester Ballard: The Evolving Gothic Monster." *Midwest Quarterly*, Volume 49, number 2, 2008: 132–48.

Lang, John. "Lester Ballard: McCarthy's Challenge to the Reader's Compassion." *Sacred Violence: A Reader's Companion to Cormac McCarthy*. Edited by Wade Hall and Rick Wallach. Texas Western Press, 1995: 87–93.

Lekesizalın, Ferma. "Possessing Cold Bodies: Necrophilia and the Conflicts of Private Property in Cormac McCarthy's *Child of God*." *Critique*, Volume 61, number 3, 2020: 370–80.

Luce, Dianne C. *Embracing Vocation: Cormac McCarthy's Writing Life, 1959–1974*. University of South Carolina Press, 2023.

———. *Reading the World: Cormac McCarthy's Tennessee Period*. University of South Carolina Press, 2009.

Madsen, Michael. "The Uncanny Necrophile in Cormac McCarthy's *Child of God*: or, How I Learned to Understand Lester Ballard and Start Worrying." *Cormac McCarthy Journal*, Volume 9, number 1, 2011: 17–27.

McCarthy, Cormac. *Child of God*. Vintage, 1993.

———. *No Country for Old Men*. Picador, 2007.

Owens-Murphy, Katie. "The Frontier Ethic behind Cormac McCarthy's Southern Fiction." *Arizona Quarterly*, Volume 67, number 2, 2011: 155–78.

Stilley, Harriet Poppy. "'White pussy is nothin but trouble': Hypermasculine Hysteria and the Displacement of the Feminine Body in Cormac McCarthy's *Child of God*." *Cormac McCarthy Journal*, Volume 14, number 1, 2016: 96–116.

Sullivan, Nell. "The Evolution of the Dead Girlfriend Motif in *Outer Dark* and *Child of God*." In *Myth, Legend, Dust: Critical Responses to Cormac McCarthy*. Edited by Rick Wallach. Manchester University Press, 2000: 68–77.

Vronsky, Peter. *American Serial Killers: The Epidemic Years 1950–2000*. New York: Berkley, 2021.

Wallach, Rick. "From *Beowulf* to *Blood Meridian:* Cormac McCarthy's Demystification of the Martial Code." *Southern Quarterly*, Volume 36, number 4, 1998: 113–20.

Watson, Jay. "William Faulkner." *Cormac McCarthy in Context*. Edited by Steven Frye. Cambridge University Press, 2019: 47–58.

Yang, Yi. "Segregation and Exclusion: A Politics of Fear in Cormac McCarthy's *Child of God*." *Critique*, Volume 58, number 5, 2017: 538–47.

Woods That No One Owned

Rereading *Child of God* through *The Road*

JORDAN J. DOMINY

Cormac McCarthy's 1973 novel *Child of God*, which explores Lester Ballard's devolution from impoverished and property-deprived citizen to necrophiliac serial killer, can be a difficult text to read. It vividly narrates scenes of murder, sexual assault, rural squalor, and catastrophe. The narration provides no explicit purpose or moral for the reader's exposure to such brutality. The earliest critics of McCarthy's work, such as Vereen M. Bell, have attributed this to a nihilistic streak in McCarthy's earliest work, reading *Child of God* as a story about the nadirs of human activity.[1] However, more recent critical attention paid to *Child of God* focuses largely on the community from which Ballard emerges. Several scholars, such as Edwin Arnold, Dianne Luce, and Alexandra Blair, claim that Ballard's transformation in the novel is the result of his abuse by members of the community, negligent policing, and the failure of social and government institutions. Even more recently, Jonathan and Rick Elmore further contend that such failures extend to the entire community of Sevier County, and that Ballard's actions are an extreme reaction to the endemic loss of community due to prejudice, neoliberalism, and patriarchy.[2] Such forces are also present in McCarthy's 2006 novel, *The Road*, in which extreme self-interest in the face of global catastrophe leads roving gangs to indulge in keeping human livestock for cannibalism. Similarities between *Child of God* and *The Road* do not end here: both share the setting of the southeastern United States, specifically Appalachia, and depictions of gruesome violence. The East Tennessee mountains in *Child of God* and the countryside the father and son see along the road in *The Road* have both been spent via speculation, industrial processes, and their long-term consequences. There are also striking similarities in particular word choices and lyrical passages McCarthy uses to describe the landscape traversed by Ballard in *Child of God* and the father and son in *The Road*.

Given these resonances, *Child of God* requires a reassessment through the lens of *The Road*. The former prefigures the latter in setting, themes, and critique of neoliberal society. *Child of God* presents readers a region of waste that might have been a paradise if left untouched by quarrying, farming, and other human enterprises. But the failure of the community as well, in its abject poverty, violent past, and distrust of one another has also been created by the people of Sevier County. Edwin T. Arnold argues that Lester Ballard "is created by those around him, a necessary figure of the community, the scapegoat that embodies their weird alienation and stoked violence but also their terrible sadness, their potential nothingness" (57). Jonathan and Rick Elmore reiterate this in their assessment of *Child of God*, explaining that "Lester appears an extreme reaction to what is, in actuality, a widespread loss of community brought about by the systematic violence of deindustrialization, individualism, and patriarchy" (135). My reassessment of *Child of God* reads the abuses to and by Ballard's community as an early manifestation of the cataclysm that comes to fruition in *The Road*. This later novel has been approached in many ways, ranging from moral parable to religious allegory to critique of capitalism.[3] However, the strongest resonances lie in how both *Child of God* and *The Road* depict the reduction of human interaction to transactional logic. Ballard's exertion of his violent will over his victims, which critics tend to describe as understandable if not excusable, reflects his action upon and emphasis on transactional relationships with others and an ill-defined moral imperative of self-preservation. That ill-defined imperative mirrors the vague "fire" the father in *The Road* tells his son that they carry. Both Ballard and the father of *The Road* come to emphasize self-preservation against a violent landscape and even more violent community. Looking at these two novels in tandem reveals an evolution of the narrative forecasting from a fatalistic collapse of humanity under the weight of its own neoliberal activities to a slightly more hopeful conjecture that humans, even without society, can persevere under such a collapse. This tandem consideration also shows the extent to which the notion that capitalism is the force that will lead society to ruin has been present in McCarthy's work throughout his career.

The parallels between *Child of God* and *The Road* begin with the opening events of the earlier novel: "They came like a caravan of carnival folk up through the swales of broomstraw and across the hill in the morning sun, the truck rocking and pitching in the ruts and the musicians on chairs in the truckbed teetering and tuning their instruments, the fat man with guitar grinning and gesturing to other in a car behind and bending to give a note to the fiddler who turned a fiddlepeg and listened with a wrinkled face" (3). In this opening scene in which readers meet Ballard, he faces a crowd of fellow denizens of Sevier County come to enjoy the spectacle of his home and farm being auctioned off to pay defaulted tax debts to the county. Likely very few of the individuals in attendance can afford to bid on Ballard's farm; nevertheless, a carnival pops up for the occasion. Ballard must hear the auctioneer's cries about the "real future in this property" (5) when his own future with it has been foreclosed. "There's no sounder investment than property," the auctioneer goes on, "You all know that a dollar won't buy what it used to buy. A dollar might not be worth but fifty cents a year from now, [. . .] But real estate is going up, up, up" (6). Before Ballard can interrupt the auctioneer, he also relates to his audience the story of an uncle who bought the "Prater place" a few years back and sold it for a considerable profit and suggests the same could be done with Ballard's farm. The assemblage of locals there at the farm waiting to make a boon from Ballard's misfortune—or at least enjoy the spectacle of the societal conventions that have abused him—bears resemblance to the caravans of "bloodcults" (16) that the father and son encounter numerous times in *The Road*. Both groups are bound by a respecting of property, both real estate and chattel, and are thriving on the material substance lost as consequences of disrespecting notions of private property. Ballard may care about losing his house and farm, but he does not respect the notion that he must pay taxes to the county for the privilege of owning land that he inherited. Likewise, the bloodcults of *The Road* can understand nothing more than ownership of things and persons wholly as the system of survival in their postapocalyptic world. Just as the people of Sevier County find entertainment in the spectacle of the auction and the vivid interlude of Buster subduing Ballard with the axe to end his confrontation with the auctioneer, the bloodcults of *The Road* seize the property and bodies of their victims, their violence leaving a "tableau of the slain and the devoured" (91).

The confiscation and sale of his property is but one of many ways in which the social structures and community of Sevier County fail Ballard. While one narrator reports that Ballard's clocking by Buster prevented some locals from bidding on the farm, the locals do not prevent an outside interest, a John Greer from Grainger County, from purchasing it. A different narrator relates how Ballard's father hanged himself, which they learned from the young Lester who simply "come in the store and told it like you'd tell it was rainin out" (21). Even though Lester is "nine or ten," the men who cut his father down from the barn rafter focus more on their own discomfort from the corpse's bulging eyes and tongue rather than how this might have traumatized the young Lester Ballard and what they might do to comfort him. With his mother "run off," the narrator says, "They say he [Ballard] was never right after his daddy killed hisself" (21). Another narrator tells of a time when a child Ballard punched a younger boy in the face for refusing to retrieve a ball that Ballard had lost in a thicket of briars. "I never liked Lester Ballard from that day. I never liked him much before that. He never done nothin to me" (18). These instances all reflect a lack of compassion for Ballard that begins when he is young, a lack of compassion that none of the narrators can explain. Even though Ballard punching the younger boy is a reason not to like him, the narrator reports not liking him before, and for no particular reason. These narrators and the people at the auction have no affection for Ballard, nor does he for them. Their no love lost is a manifestation of the inability of Ballard and the people of Sevier County to understand that their relationships can be anything other than transactional—that one is owed agency or property via an unstated social contract or exchange of understanding or value.

This conflict between Ballard and his neighbors is the source of his turn toward serial murder and necrophilia. Critics have frequently termed Ballard's behavior as it includes more and more acts of violence and transgressions that breach sexual taboos as a descent into madness. Indeed, by the end of *Child of God*, Ballard is clearly not well. However, I would like to put some pressure on its characterization as a descent by considering Ballard's behavior in light of the events and condition of society in *The Road*. Echoing my previous arguments about cannibalism progressing from a metaphor for consumer capitalism to a literal consumptive practice, rather than devolving into some kind of deranged, subhuman activity, Ballard instead takes his own community's selfish, consumptive practices and literalizes them decades before the calamity of *The Road*.[4] This perspective complements Harriet Poppy Stilley's, who helpfully reads *Child of God* as "condemning the social ills of nationalistic ideals by positioning the serial killer as both reflective and symptomatic of an American culture of materialism. Ballard's violent manifestations of excess literalize the conjoining of mass production with mass consumption" (98). The culmination of his choices to confiscate for his own desires and survival, in the same way that the county confiscated his farm, is Ballard's rejection by community. Nowhere along the way do the social institutions or community act to slow the intensification of Ballard's materially transactional relationships with the people of Sevier County. When Ballard wanders into a service at Six-Mile Church, it is not the preaching that catches his attention, but the bulletins at the back of the church: "This week's offering. Last week's offering. Six dollars and seventy-four cents. The numbers in attendance" (31–32). The congregation does not ask Ballard to quiet his cold-induced sniffing during the remainder of the service because "nobody expected he would stop if God himself looked back askance so no one looked" (32). What the narrator does not specify here is just as important as what is detailed: if no one in the congregation thought to ask Ballard to keep his coughing down, likely no one approached him afterward to inquire on his well-being or offer any Christian charity. What must stand out to Ballard about church service is its interest in quantifiable relationships. How much does the church collect from week to week and from how many congregants? The exchange is not a spiritual, but an economic one from Ballard's perspective on the back pew. The congregation does not allow or expect him to participate in these economic exchanges, nor does it extend charity to Ballard. He comes to expect and accept no spiritual or emotional relationships and interactions among the community as he grows further alienated from them.

    Ballard developed a sense of transactional interactions with people from an early age. He expects to deal with people in concrete, consistent terms, even if only at his convenience. One narrator states that a young Ballard bought his prize possession, a rifle, by working "for old man Whaley settin fenceposts at eight cents a post to buy it. Told me he quit midmornin right in the middle of the field the day he got enough money. I don't remember what he give for it but I think it come to over seven hundred posts" (57). The anecdote demonstrates that Ballard is motivated by material goals. He works for that goal then abandons the labor when it is met. That is the extent to which Ballard understands twentieth-century economic relation of wages for labor: a means to an end. Ballard feels alienated from the world without participating in its economy of relations and earning some material, practical gain from his labor. In the instance of the gun, his prized possession, it develops into one of his most effective instruments for creating transactions, especially violent ones, to assert his will as he isolates himself further from the community that rejects him. These material, transactional relations between the community and an individual seeking to survive and impose their will upon a fragmented society foreshadows the dystopian social of *The Road*. Accumulation is not of money or wages, but of material items—or bodies—of utility that augment survival and the capability to act and impose on others whose survival threatens their own.

Child of God shows that Ballard becomes an accumulator of things and bodies because the local community refuses him the ability to interact transactionally with them in any other way. Ballard emphasizes survival and the fulfillment of base hungers as his primary reasons for existence in the face of his abjuration. His experience with arbitrary rules of carnival prize games demonstrates a parallel between how the barkers and fair goers alienate him similarly as citizens of Sevier County who have access to the capital and resources of the area cut him out. At a fishing game in which players catch "celluloid goldfish" with small nets to win a prize that corresponds with the number on the fish's bottom, Ballard takes a moment to pull up several fish, studying the numbers underneath and the corresponding prizes. A woman discombobulated by another contestant splashing water on her gestures at Ballard and tells the operator, "That man yonder is cheatin" (62). The operator allows Ballard one losing play and dismisses him. He moves on to a target shooting game. Just as before, Ballard assesses the game, replying "I'm studyin it. [...] What do ye get?" to the barker asking if he is ready to play (63). Upon learning that he must shoot out the red dot on the target to win the biggest prizes, he ponies up the thirty cents for the game, taking five shots and picking his prize. However, the barker shows Ballard his card, which has "a single hole in the middle of it. Along one edge of the hole was the faintest piece of red lint." It did not win the big prize because "all of the red must be removed" (64). Ballard curses in reply, paying to play again and this time obliterating the red on the target. After three wins, the pitchman cuts him off to Ballard's protest. "You never said nothin about how many times you could win" (64). The pitchman replies not directly to Ballard but by revising his siren song to prospective gamers: "Three big grand prizes per person is the house limit" (64). Despite capitalism's self-professed emphasis on merit and hard work, Ballard's talent gets ostracized rather than rewarded.

These exchanges show Ballard seeking to understand and participate in transactional relations: complete a task, receive a thing; pay money, purchase a good or service. In his experiences at the carnival, the system is hostile to his desire to understand to the fullest of his capabilities how it works. He is expelled from the fishing game for attempting to understand the prize scheme. And when Ballard applies his expertise to a shooting game, the ruling that he left a sliver of red lint on the target negates the uncanny precision of his grouping of shots, presumably all five bullets passing through the same hole of the target. Like other local relations—the church, capitalism—consistency is not rewarded; the emphasis shifts to suit the person in power. Constituents who do not respect the idiosyncrasies of capitalism, such as "cheatin" by attempting to understand a prize scheme or being talented enough to meet ludicrous qualifications, are abused by or refused participation in the system. Ballard's turn toward serial murder and necrophilia is not a descent into madness and evil, but an attempt to reconcile his community's rejection of his entry into community relations on his own terms by exploiting his own talents, desires, and preferences for interacting with the material world.

Indeed, Ballard's rejection and vilification by the community render both incapable of seeing any value in working together or building a collective. Neither can Ballard appreciate others' skills in the way he expects his skills, such as his marksmanship, to be respected. An important example of this is his interaction with the blacksmith, to whom Ballard takes an old axe head that he presumably found to be sharpened. He figured he could have such work done cheaply. Ballard is surprised (and annoyed), however, to learn from the smith that the axe head requires more serious maintenance. He balks at the cost of the repair compared to the cost of purchasing a new one, but the smith insists, "I'd better to have thisn and it right than two new ones" (71) and begins an involved restoration of the axe head. He carefully heats it in the furnace and repairs it, explaining in careful detail to Ballard what colors of hot steel to look for to know how much to heat it, then tempers, polishes, and prepares the axe head to accept a new handle. After going to such lengths, the smith asks, "Reckon you could do it now from watchin?" Ballard replies, "Do what?" (74). Ballard's response shows that he was not paying attention to the smith's actions; the narrator mentions Ballard only once during the process of working the axe to indicate that he "glanced about the shop," that is, looked everywhere but the smith's demonstration (73). The time that Ballard spends in the smith's forge is merely time spent to acquire a service. His lack of attention demonstrates a lack of care for the skills of others, reciprocal of prior interactions in which others disrespected his skills or did not value them adequately. Whatever reason the smith's demonstration provides for why "I'd better to have thisn" is lost on Ballard, but having this one that the smith repaired indicates a community's respect for a skilled craftsman. It also indicates an acknowledgment that the consumer is supporting a local skilled laborer rather than a hardware selling brand new axes stamped out by unskilled laborers in a factory exploiting its workers. However, these concerns appear not even to cross Ballard's mind: he is a materially conscious consumer, as are many of the residents of Sevier County as indicated in their interactions with Ballard. Alexandra Blair goes further by interpreting this vignette as a critique of rugged individualism as a redeemable value of the people of Appalachia, a common trope in fiction about the region. "With Lester Ballard as the novel's frontiersman, the pioneer values quickly become exhausted, the butt of a joke rather than a beautiful ideal" (95). As the butt of a joke, Ballard shows how rugged individualism has failed his Appalachian community more than strengthened it. That rugged individualism persists in *The Road* as well. The father expects no one to show him and his son charity, and he places inordinate emphasis on his resourcefulness. But in what is an afterthought to the father, his son acknowledges that they're actually benefiting from the work and preparation of others, such as when they find the pristine fallout shelter underneath the backyard of an abandoned city. In that instance, the son asks, "Do you think we should thank the people?" (*The Road* 145). This puzzles the father at first, but he quickly understands the question; nevertheless, when his son asks him to do it, he instead has his son do the thanking. This becomes the critical difference between Ballard and the father and the son. The former two do not understand or value community, whereas the son does.

Returning to Ballard, his disregard for the immaterial value of a person's skills extends to utter disregard for the intrinsic value of others' lives, their agency, and their bodily autonomy. Just as his cruelty and indifference to others began long before his first acts of murder and necrophilia in *Child of God*, so do Ballard's misogyny and objectification of women. His first interactions with women that readers get to see both portray Ballard as a voyeur: he masturbates while looking on at a young couple having sex in a car on Frog Mountain (19–20) and he has dialogue—internal and external—with Reubel, the dumpkeeper's daughter, noting that "he'd never seen [Reubel's daughter] in a pair of shoes but she had a different color pair of drawers for every day of the week" and entertains an offer for her to flash her breasts to him for a quarter (28–29). Ballard repeatedly treats and talks to and about women as pleasure objects, calling the woman who accused him of cheating at the fair a "busynosed old whore" (63). One of Ballard's most significant interactions with a woman happens one cold morning on Frog Mountain, when he finds a woman asleep wearing a white nightgown. After watching her for a moment and ascertaining that she is alive, Ballard "knelt and touched her" (41) without her consent before she wakes. The woman fights back against Ballard, who responds by stripping her gown from her, leaving her naked in the cold morning. Their interactions conclude after the high sheriff brings Ballard in assuming that he is one of the two men that the woman reports to have attacked and abandoned her the previous night. Mistaken identity or not, the woman remembers the interaction with Ballard and asks to press rape and assault charges against him. Ballard vehemently protests, calling his accuser "nothin but a goddamned old whore" before she severely beats him, even with the sheriff and his deputy attempting to intervene (52). The narrator never makes it clear what becomes of the two men that the victim originally sought to press charges against, but Ballard spends nine days in the county jail before he's finally released. At first reading, this seems to be more bad luck that has befallen Lester Ballard, and indeed it seems poor policing practice to simply bring in Ballard because of his reputation. Nevertheless, this fits a consistent, cyclical pattern in which Ballard interacts with society and is rejected, then he retaliates against that rejection by taking the actions (and the things and bodies) that he wants, for which he is then further ostracized by society. Both the sheriff and the local government are indifferent to Ballard's victim's accusations. Moreover, they are at ease with releasing him from jail. This shows that Ballard's misogyny is not unique to him.

In fact, I would go so far as to argue that the murderous Ballard is a monster of Sevier County's own making. Sevier County releases Ballard after the episode discussed above, and the sheriff indicates that he believes Ballard will continue to cause trouble. He asks him, "What sort of meanness have you got laid out for next?" (56). Ballard answers, "I ain't got any laid out," to which the sheriff retorts, "I figure you ought to give us a clue. Make it more fair. Let's see: failure to comply with a court order, public disturbance, assault and battery, public drunk, rape. I guess murder is next on the list ain't it? Or what things is it you've done that we ain't found out yet" (56). The sheriff knows Ballard is more than capable of "meanness," and even predicts that he will become a murderer before Ballard kills his first victim. The sheriff's nonchalance in this exchange, the congregation's indifference to Ballard's attendance, the carnival barker's changing of the rules to disadvantage Ballard: all of these do nothing to prevent Ballard's disenfranchisement and turning toward engaging the community in the only ways that he has left, via transactional exchanges that feed his base desires.

Importantly though, Ballard does not feed those desires on impulse. He turns toward necrophilia as a careful act of consideration, making the most of the circumstances presented to him. This is as obvious in his "studyin" of the carnival game as it is in his first act of necrophilia, which is calculated and methodical. Ballard slowly and cautiously approaches a still-running car he finds one cold morning, finding the bodies of a man and woman in states of undress. After waiting for a moment, he shuts off the engine and "knelt in the seat and leaned over the back and studied the other two" (87). Ballard's actions and thoughts during this sequence are not impulsive, as might be characterized by a character descending into the depths of madness and evil; rather, he is methodical and calculating as he decides to have sex with the dead woman in the back seat of the car. He listens and watches out for anyone who may see him before he climbs into the back seat with her, becoming "[a] crazed gymnast laboring over a cold corpse. He poured into that waxen ear everything he'd ever thought of saying to a woman. Who could say she did not hear him?" (88–89). "Gymnast" and "laboring" connote careful choreography, precise movement, and adherence to a set of conventions. These do stand in contrast to "crazed," and he indeed has been crazed in his attempt to understand social mores under which Sevier County could deprive him of his land and jail him without conviction for over a week. Ballard whispers his desires into his deceased victim's ear, along with his understanding that material accumulation is what matters. In defiance of how he has been treated, he believes that there is no wrong in studying the world in calculating terms, taking what no one else is using, and unlike at the auction, the carnival, or the courthouse, no one is present to challenge that view of the world.

Even as Ballard brings this first corpse back to his dwelling (a run-down house owned by a man named Waldrop) for later use, he is not impulsive or reckless in the decision making. He walks away from and returns to the car four times, first to retrieve his forgotten squirrels, second to search for money and valuables, a third time to leave the radio on as he found it, and the last time to take the dead woman's body with him back to his cabin. Ballard seems to be calculatingly taking with him all the spoils that he can before the rules are changed on him again, which will likely be when the police appear in search of a disappeared man and woman. In this regard, his first dead lover is no different from the large tiger and two bears that he wins from the shooting gallery at the carnival. Similar to his first night home with his carnival winnings, which "watch[ed] from the wall, their plastic eyes shining in the firelight and their red flannel tongues out" (67), Ballard uses the dead woman as a furnishing within his squatter's home. Michael Madsen considers this sequence and Ballard's later accumulation of bodies as evidence of a critique of consumerism: "Much as we will furnish our homes with furniture and other belongings, Lester populates his home with dead people. His attachment to them is as strong as twentieth-century white middle-class attachment and attraction to household items" (25). Even in his isolation, Ballard recreates the spectacles of a consumerist society. He "inspect[ed] her body carefully, as if he would see how she were made," as a careful consumer would want to be sure he receives a quality product; "He went outside and looked in through the window at her lying naked before the fire," thereby creating his own storefront window displays (91–92). After a long trip to town to buy clothing for the dead woman, Ballard again repeats this ritual, posing the woman in various stages of undress to peer at her form outside through the window (102–3), thereby using her to create his first "tableau of the slain" (91). In procuring the products that he needed to fulfill his fantasies with the dead woman, Ballard crosses from commodity fetishization to what could be described as a different fetish, necrophilia. Indeed, to Ballard, the woman is only a prize.

However, with seizing his prize of opportunity, Ballard begins his final sundering from Sevier County society. It is that very evening that Ballard loses the house that he is squatting in, along with this first corpse, in a spectacular fire he has caused attempting to stay warm on a freezing night. After saving what he can of his belongings, including the shooting gallery prizes, Ballard finds a cave and makes it his grotto, a manifestation of his retraction from the living denizens of the community. When he is arrested by the sheriff on suspicion of causing the fire at the Waldrop place, an unnamed man behind a desk, presumably the justice of the peace, questions him about his previous run-ins with the sheriff and his connection to the fire. The man concludes their conversation by telling Ballard, "You are either going to have to find some other way to live or some other place in the world to do it" (123). This is his final banishment from the civic society of Sevier County, and Ballard follows this with an abjuration of his own. In Mr. Fox's store he makes his final purchase for cash after being denied credit. In one last effort to participate in the exchange of goods on terms with the community, he crosses over to Blount County to attempt to sell three watches, presumably ones that he has taken from his victims. Rather than getting his desired price—five dollars for each—he sells the lot for eight dollars to one of the men in the story huddled around the woodstove. He immediately begins selling the watches to the other men at a small profit margin, but a profit nonetheless (131–32). Again, Ballard sees the logic for the transaction change before his eyes; just a moment before he had seen these men "watching him to see what price used watches would bring" suddenly being able to command more favorable pricing from each other. The haggling reinforces to Ballard his limited access to the local economy.

As Ballard accelerates his separation from civilization, he begins prioritizing his survival and the satiety of his desires. Since he can no longer buy provisions on credit, he begins raiding his former homestead for food and obsessively watching its new owner, Greer's, pattern of behavior. Rather than stumbling upon necrophiliac sexual partners, he begins securing them through murder. *Child of God* depicts two of these murders, and the first reveals that Ballard continues to act with calculation. In what seems to be his first murder, or at least the first that the novel narrates, Ballard visits Reubel's house. After failing at negotiating with one of Reubel's daughters, who is at home alone babysitting one of the dumpkeeper's mute grandchildren, Ballard shoots her through the window with his rifle. He starts a fire that will consume the house and the child he leaves there before carrying her lifeless body and his rifle out of the house (115–120). The choice to burn the house down to cover his crime demonstrates that Ballard learned from his previous misfortune of burning down Waldrop's house and leaving no trace of his first corpse. Ballard likely understands that burning the house will easily have investigators conclude that the daughter died in the fire rather than being harvested by him for his growing necropolis deep in the caves.

Near the novel's end, though, Ballard's subsistence wrought out of the East Tennessee society and wilderness begins to crumble. He makes a mistake in one of his attacks, allowing a victim he presumed dead to drive off (151–52). In the aftermath, Ballard observes parties searching for the missing getting close to his regular haunts; at night "Ballard passed beneath them, scuttling with his ragged chattel down stone tunnels within the mountain" (154). The use of "chattel" here indicates that Ballard understands his victims as his property. His rapacious murdering is a transaction, an acquisition. With the authorities closing in, Ballard must relocate his property, and he finds himself doing so in the middle of a catastrophic flood. During the relocation, he loses some of his belongings down a swollen creek, and both his mattress and rifle get waterlogged. This ordeal is the one in which readers first see Ballard showing signs of suffering and anguish. After being rejected by society, the environment into which Ballard retreats rejects him as well.

But the environment also rejects the community that Ballard abandons. The chapter subsequent to Ballard's relocations depicts the sheriff, Fate Turner, boating with Deputy Cotton through town on a skiff surveying a flood of historic proportions. The pair make stops to converse with citizens about local history, meanness, and the White Caps, an extralegal organization of rural farmers akin to the Ku Klux Klan that would enforce their version of law and order through murder. Lester Ballard's ancestors were members. After a Mr. Wade recounts the history of how a brave deputy finally put an end to the White Caps in Sevier County, Cotton asks Mr. Wade,

"You think people was meaner then than they are now?" In response, Mr. Wade "look[s] out at the flooded town. No, he said, I don't. I think people are the same from the day God first made one" (168). This exchange serves as commentary on the characters and events of the novel and is further significant when reading *Child of God* backward through *The Road*. If people have not changed since the first one made in the setting of *Child of God*, they likely are no different in the setting of *The Road*. And when one narrator earlier in *Child of God*, a man of Sevier County, attempts to single Ballard out by saying of the Ballards generally and Lester specifically, "You can trace em back to Adam if you want and goddamn if he didn't outstrip em all" (81), he reinforces Mr. Wade's point, lumping all of humans together from Adam.

We can glean from Mr. Wade's commentary that if people have not changed, the communities that they create likely have not either. This is one of the more significant reasons that reconsidering *Child of God* through the lens of *The Road* is a worthwhile undertaking. Whether it be the stories that the earliest humans told themselves to justify ostracizing and waging war against other, the White Caps paramilitary securing of their interests, the Sevier County excluding Lester from its social and economic community, or the roaming bloodcults of *The Road* devouring all they see in the name of survival, in all phases of historical development people build transactional relations that have their most important meaning in material relations. Lester Ballard literalizes his county's consumption of his property through the consumption of his neighbors via the fulfillment of his necrophilia. While Ballard avoids death at the hands of the state, his body is consumed by the state in the training of doctors at the state medical school, who dissected his body. "Ballard was scraped from the table into a plastic bag and taken with other of his kind to a cemetery outside the city and there interred" (194). Both the local and state community's dealings with Ballard have been unceremonious, and in the end, Ballard becomes just like his victims, an object of study and fulfillment. Much later in the timeline, the characters of *The Road* also unceremoniously deal with each other, such as when the father and his son find the entrails of a man field dressed by his own associates (*The Road* 71) or when the father strips a man who robbed them of "every goddamned stitch" of clothing he had, leaving him to die in the barren landscape (256–57).

Turning more pointedly to more specific textual parallels between *Child of God* and *The Road*, the most chilling is the one between Ballard's roaming of the mountainside and valley for victims of his lust and the bloodcults of *The Road* traversing the road in search of bodies to consume. The most harrowing example of this are the phalanx of redscarves rhythmically marching down the road, behind them their "wagons drawn by slaves in harness and piled with goods of war and after that the women, perhaps a dozen in number, some of them pregnant, and lastly a supplementary consort of catamites illclothed against the cold and fitted in dogcollars and yoked each to each" (*The Road* 92). Ballard's individual acts of murder and keeping human chattel, his movement along the mountainside with his possessions on his back, is an accumulation and consumption of property prefiguring that portrayed in *The Road*. Moreover, *Child of God* describes the cave where Ballard keeps the bodies of his victims: "Here in the bowels of the mountain Ballard turned his light on ledges or pallets of stone where dead people lay like saints" (*Child of God* 135). Ballard moves them from this cave to another during the flood, and at the novel's conclusion a sink hole opens in a field underneath a team of mules. The sinkhole provides access to that final "chamber in which the bodies of a number of people were arranged on stone ledges in attitudes of repose" (195). The father and son in *The Road* also stumble into a cave of horrors, the padlocked basement of a plantation house containing human livestock, one of whom had "his legs gone to the hip and the stumps of them blackened and burnt" (110). With pleas for help behind them, the father and son barely escape becoming chattel themselves. In both *Child of God* and *The Road* human bodies, dead and alive, are held as property by those who seeking to survive in the face of a collapsing or collapsed society. Ballard, dispossessed of his homestead, standing in the community, and access to markets, finds survival and fulfillment in the consumption of his victims sexually or erotically. In *The Road* the cannibals further that literalization began in *Child of God* via the eating of human bodies for nourishment.

The similarity of the descriptions of settings and the word choices between *Child of God* and *The Road* further reinforce how the former prefigures themes that McCarthy goes on to explore and fulfill in the latter. These become apparent looking backward, especially from the descriptions in *The Road* of a landscape scarred by a human-caused apocalypse. The father and son are traveling a road that has "charred and limbless trunks of trees stretching away on every side. Ash moving over the road and the sagging hands of blind wire strung from the blackened lightpoles whining thinly in the wind. A burned house in a clearing and beyond that a reach of meadowlands stark and gray and a raw red mudbank where a roadworks lay abandoned" (8). They cross rivers in which "skeins of ash and slurry moved slowly in the current" (51). Descriptions of the disused landscape abound in *The Road*, and they echo some of the descriptions of the same mountains in *Child of God*. Early in the novel, Ballard leaves Reubel's and descends into a quarry. "The great rock walls with their cannelured faces and featherdrill holes composed about him an enormous amphitheatre. The ruins of an old truck lay rusting in the honeysuckle. He crossed the corrugated stone floor among chips and spalls of stone. The truck looked like it had been machine-gunned. At the far end of the quarry was a rubble tip and Ballard stopped to search for artifacts, tilting old stoves and water heaters, inspecting bicycle parts and corroded buckets" (38–39). In both instances, readers see environments utterly spent from human activity. The quarrying of rock, presumably limestone, from the biome of the Appalachians to be used in the construction of a built environment is a consumption that leaves behind not just the "chips and spalls of stone" but an opportune place for inhabitants of the mountain to dump large items not easily discarded through public works, or to avoid any fees associated with the municipal dump. The scenery of *The Road* is spent on a grander scale, the culmination of a world and its climate abused by human forces.

Moreover, Ballard's scavenging of the quarry is the closest similarity between the father of *The Road* and Ballard. Both are calculating consumers, choosing carefully what objects are useful for their ends. However, Ballard has perhaps more in common with the cannibalistic brigands in *The Road* than the father, except for the fact that the father has also abandoned any hope of being part of a community again. He distrusts all other persons and would rather refuse to share food and supplies with travelers that he and his son meet on their journey south. Rick and Jonathan Elmore, however, argue that his son quite clearly is a substantive foil to the father's and consequently Ballard's ways of dealing with others. "In the figure of the son, McCarthy develops an ethos towards community and the alleviation of suffering, one that the novel suggests might be the only hope for humans at the end of the world" (2018, 134). The son's insistence that there must be some community not based in material transaction and consumption that they can survive as a part of is what saves the boy in the end. This notion that community relations can be anything other than transaction is absent from *Child of God*. Most of the denizens of Sevier County only consider themselves and their livelihood, and thereby harry the destruction of society and its world.

In closing, there is a passage in *Child of God* describing the woods that Ballard haunts whose meaning is enhanced when reread using the closing passage of *The Road* as a lens. At the end of *The Road*, the narrator recounts that "once there were brook trout in the streams in the mountains" whose backs bore "maps of a world in its becoming"; "in the deep glens where they lived all things were older than man and they hummed of mystery" (286–87). I have previously argued that this closing passage of *The Road* imagines a world in which "items in the world were held in common" and no one person or group of people claimed ownership of land and its resources, and that the possibility of recovering this common use is difficult if not impossible ("Cannibalism, Consumerism, and Profanation," 155). As Ballard crosses from Sevier County into Blount County after Mr. Fox refuses him credit, the narrator describes the woods he traverses in a strikingly similar manner: "Old woods and deep. At one time in the world there were woods that no one owned and these were like them. He passed a windfelled tulip poplar on the mountainside that held aloft in grip of its roots two stones the size of fieldwagons, great tablets on which was writ only a tale of vanished seas with ancient shells in cameo and fishes etched in lime" (127–28). In both passages, McCarthy imagines wilderness that tells its own story untouched by human designs. In *Child of God*, the stones in the tree roots tell a story that is ancient history and of a landscape that transformed from the depths of briny seas to the tops of ancient mountains without human influence. These woods are like those that were a wilderness truly untouched and not owned by humans. As Ballard walks through this primitive woodland, he is retreating from a society that failed him and is failing itself, and there is a finality in that. The fossils the narrator describes are a record of a past of no ownership to which Ballard cannot, nor wishes, to return to considering his violent accumulation; at the end of *Child of God*, Ballard is dead and forgotten. This is a subtle contrast from the final outlook of *The Road*, in which the son survives in a world that has possibilities of the brook trout, whose maps are those "of a world in its becoming." Rather than tales of what the world has been, the narrator of *The Road* ends with possibilities of what the world could become. The world at the end of *The Road*, though brutish and cruel and very difficult to change, promises more hope than the world that Ballard consumes and is consumed by. At the conclusion of *Child of God*, there is only Ballard's shared internment with other spent cadavers and the all-but-forgotten crypt of his victims, and consequently no hope that people are any different "from the day God first made one," as Mr. Wade concludes (168). The more optimistic, even if limited in realization, ending of *The Road* demonstrates an evolution of the worldview of McCarthy's fiction. Many readers of *The Road* note its obvious critiques of late capitalism and neoliberal society; however, my reading of a much earlier novel through *The Road* shows how this critique has been both present and central to McCarthy's project.[5] Revisiting *Child of God* through engagement with his much later work provides a significant opportunity to recognize how McCarthy's writing has always identified capitalism's problems and to note his evolving proposed solutions for its destruction of communities. In the case of *Child of God* and *The Road*, such reassessment of his work reveals a shift from an outlook devoid of any purpose other than consumption and competition to one with a sliver of hope for cooperation. Indeed, such a reassessment casts at least the shadow of a doubt on the notion that humans in contemporary times are not any different from our earliest progenitors.

NOTES

1. See Bell's *The Achievement of Cormac McCarthy*.
2. See Arnold's "Naming, Knowing and Nothing: McCarthy's Moral Parables," Luce's *Reading the World: McCarthy's Tennessee Period*, Blair's "'The Wanted Stared Back': Biopolitics, Genre, and Sympathy in Cormac McCarthy's *Child of God*," and the Elmores' "'You reckon there are just some places the good lord didn't intend folks to live in?': The Absence of Community in McCarthy's *Child of God*."
3. See Lydia Cooper's "Cormac McCarthy's *The Road* as Apocalyptic Grail Narrative," Erik J. Wielenberg's "God, Morality, and Meaning in Cormac McCarthy's *The Road*," and Brian Donnelly's "'Coke It Is!: Placing Coca-Cola in McCarthy's *The Road*."
4. My reading here leads me to assume that the Sevier County of *Child of God* exists some decades prior but in a similar temporal setting as *The Road*, but I would go further to argue that part of the man and the boy's journey in *The Road* in fact takes them in areas

of what would have been considered the mountains of East Tennessee if local governments had not collapsed. See Dominy, "Cannibalism, Consumerism, and Profanation: Cormac McCarthy's *The Road* and the End of Capitalism."

5. While there have been many works on critiques of capitalism in McCarthy's fiction and film (see Lydia Cooper's "Diamonds, Drugs, and the Digital Age: Global Capitalism in Cormac McCarthy's *The Counselor*"; Casey Jergenson's "'In what Direction Did Lost Men Veer?': Late Capitalism and Utopia in *The Road*"; Carl F. Miller's "The Cultural Logic of Post-Capitalism: Cormac McCarthy's *The Road* and Popular Dystopia"; and Dan Sinykin's "Evening in America: *Blood Meridian* and the Origins and Ends of Imperial Capitalism"), very few have recognized it as an enduring theme since his Tennessee period. One exception is Christine Chollier in "'I aint come back rich, that's for sure,' or the Questioning of Market Economies in Cormac McCarthy's Novels," in *Myth, Legend, Dust: Critical Responses to Cormac McCarthy*.

WORKS CITED

Arnold, Edwin T. "Naming, Knowing and Nothing: McCarthy's Moral Parables." In *Perspectives on Cormac McCarthy*. Edited by Edwin T. Arnold and Dianne C. Luce. University of Mississippi Press, 1999: 45–69.

Bell, Vereen M. *The Achievement of Cormac McCarthy*. Louisiana State University Press, 1988.

Blair, Alexandra. "'The Wanted Stared Back': Biopolitics, Genre, and Sympathy in Cormac McCarthy's *Child of God*." *Southern Literary Journal*, Volume 42, number 2, 2015: 89–106.

Chollier, Christine. "'I aint come back rich, that's for sure,' or the Questioning of Market Economies in Cormac McCarthy's Novels." In *Myth, Legend, Dust: Critical Responses to Cormac McCarthy*. Edited by Rick Wallach. Manchester University Press, 2000: 171–76.

Cooper, Lydia. "Cormac McCarthy's *The Road* as Apocalyptic Grail Narrative." *Studies in the Novel*, Volume 43, number 2, 2011: 218–36.

———. "Diamonds, Drugs, and the Digital Age: Global Capitalism in Cormac McCarthy's *The Counselor*." *Critique: Studies in Contemporary Fiction*, Volume 5, number 4, 2018: 445–58.

Dominy, Jordan J. "Cannibalism, Consumerism, and Profanation: Cormac McCarthy's *The Road* and the End of Capitalism." *Cormac McCarthy Journal*, Volume 13, number 1, 2015: 142–57.

Donnelly, Brian. "'Coke It Is!: Placing Coca-Cola in McCarthy's *The Road*." *Explicator*, Volume 68, number 1, 2010: 70–73.

Elmore, Jonathan, and Rick Elmore. "'You Can Stay Here with Your Papa and Die or You Can Go with Me': The Ethical Imperative of *The Road*." *Cormac McCarthy Journal*, Volume 16, number 2, 2018: 133–48.

———. "'You reckon there are just some places the good lord didn't intend folks to live in?': The Absences of Community in McCarthy's *Child of God*." *Cormac McCarthy Journal*, Volume 17, number 2, 2019: 134–47.

Jergenson, Casey. "'In What Direction Did Lost Men Veer?': Late Capitalism and Utopia in *The Road*." *Cormac McCarthy Journal*, Volume 14, number 1, 2016: 117–32.

Luce, Dianne C. *Reading the World: Cormac McCarthy's Tennessee Period*. University of South Carolina Press, 2009.

Madsen, Michael. "The Uncanny Necrophile in Cormac McCarthy's *Child of God:* or, How I Learned to Understand Lester Ballard and Start Worrying." *Cormac McCarthy Journal*, Volume 9, number 1, 2011: 17–27.

McCarthy, Cormac. *Child of God*. 1973. Vintage, 1991.

———. *The Road*. Vintage, 2006.

Miller, Carl F. "The Cultural Logic of Post-Capitalism: Cormac McCarthy's *The Road* and Popular Dystopia." In *Blast, Corrupt, Dismantle, Erase: Contemporary North American Dystopian Literature*. Edited by Brett Josef Grubisic et al. Wilfrid Laurier University Press, 2014: 45–60.

Sinykin, Dan. "Evening in America: *Blood Meridian* and the Origins and Ends of Imperial Capitalism." *American Literary History*, Volume 28, number 2, 2016: 362–80.

Stilley, Harriet Poppy. "'White pussy is nothin but trouble': Hypermasculine Hysteria and the Displacement of the Feminine Body in Cormac McCarthy's *Child of God*." *Cormac McCarthy Journal*, Volume 14, number 1, 2016: 97–116.

Wielenberg, Erik J. "God, Morality, and Meaning in Cormac McCarthy's *The Road*." *Cormac McCarthy Journal*, Volume 8, number 1, 2010: 1–16.

Sorrow at the Moving World

Nihilistic Despair and American Exceptionalism in the Border Trilogy and *The Road*

RACHEL B. GRIFFIS

 Several of Cormac McCarthy's characters, especially across the Border Trilogy and *The Road*, have experiences wherein they are startled and pained by the coldness of a world impervious to their suffering. For example, at the end of *All the Pretty Horses*, John Grady Cole "held out his hands [...] as if to slow the world that was rushing away and seemed to care nothing for the old or the young or rich or poor or dark or pale or he or she. Nothing for their struggles, nothing for their names. Nothing for the living or the dead" (301). In *The Crossing*, after the atomic bomb test, "the right and godmade sun did rise, once again, for all and without distinction" (426). And in *The Road*, "the pilgrims sank down and fell over and died and the bleak and shrouded earth went trundling past the sun and returned" both "trackless" and "unremarked" (181). The characters in these books express many violent emotions at the realization that the world continues to spin and circle the sun after atrocities occur, and, rather than move on from this unwelcome realization, they each, to varying degrees, mourn what John Cant calls "the myth of American Exceptionalism" ("Myth of American" 15). Cant suggests, "most are destroyed by it; one or two escape, but not unscathed" (15).

Characters who mourn the myth of American exceptionalism in McCarthy's work are consequently often tempted by a quality of despair that resembles nihilism as an alternative to the elevation of the self. By placing despair before characters deeply startled by the world's coldness, McCarthy suggests that dismantling American exceptionalism has a decentering and disorienting effect on its adherents. If these characters cannot make the world stand still, despair appears with the temptation to embrace meaninglessness. McCarthy's multiple depictions of his characters' temptation to replace exceptionalism with despair not only excoriates an ideology that leaves its believers with nothing but also demonstrates its power in a culture wherein both individuals and the nation are considered exceptional and destined to succeed in their endeavors. Through recurring images of the spinning world and the sun in the Border Trilogy, McCarthy narrates the struggles of characters who cannot extricate themselves from the grip of American exceptionalism. Then, with the publication of *The Road*, McCarthy offers a prominent character who mourns the myth of American exceptionalism, accepts nihilism's critique of the ideology, and yet rejects nihilism's claim to meaninglessness. Indeed, the man in *The Road* submits to the moral authority of his son, who espouses a communal ethic that eschews exceptionalism and finds meaning in the willing sacrifice of one person for another. The interplay between exceptionalism and despair as characters consider their place in, and relation to, the world heightens the effect of the boy's communal ethic in *The Road*, forwarding this perspective as an antidote to the moral poverty of contemporary American life.

Scholars of McCarthy have long observed the author's interaction with narratives and ideologies associated with American exceptionalism, particularly in his Western *Blood Meridian* and the novels that comprise the Border Trilogy. Robert L. Jarrett, for example, argues that McCarthy uses the Western to challenge the illusion that men are autonomous, suggesting that John Grady Cole and Billy Parham are "a pastiche, a postmodern form of parody, of the sentimental and popular figure of the Last Cowboy" (99).[1] In their engagement of McCarthy's use of the Western genre, other critics have focused on the link between exceptionalism and imperialism in the Border Trilogy.[2] A body of criticism also exists on the Border Trilogy that examines McCarthy's presentation of cowboy heroes as nostalgia for the past and a way of life that is lost.[3] In these discussions, many scholars focus on the characters' loss of idealism—which tends to spring from the ideology of exceptionalism. Stacey Peebles, for example, has studied the ways in which the Western environment serves to dismantle the characters' heroic ideals, and Gail Moore Morrison writes that what instigates John Grady's "fall from innocence to experience" is his own failure to uphold the Western heroic code (Peebles 131; Morrison 179). Petra Mundik describes *All the Pretty Horses* as a story that "traces John Grady Cole's painful initiation into an awareness of evil, suffering, and death" ("A Bloody" 101). Also concerned with John Grady's heroism and idealism, Dianne C. Luce argues that by the end of *All the Pretty Horses*, he learns "that romantic dreams of the past or the future have little enough to do with real human experience" ("When You Wake" 66). Although the existing scholarship on the Border Trilogy connects McCarthy's characters' loss of idealism to the ideology of exceptionalism, these studies do not fully investigate the characters' temptation to despair as a moral and philosophical critique of exceptionalism rather than as an inevitable stage in the maturation process.[4]

John Grady Cole's Exceptional Errand

In her broad definition of American exceptionalism, originating with Puritan culture, Deborah L. Madsen asserts, "America and Americans are special, exceptional, because they are charged with saving the world from itself and," they "must sustain a high level of spiritual, political and moral commitment to this exceptional destiny—America must be as a 'city upon a hill' exposed to the eyes of the world" (2). Madsen refers, of course, to John Winthrop's "A Model of Christian Charity" delivered in 1630 aboard the *Arabella*, which contains the infamous statements "We must consider that we shall be as a city upon a hill" and "The eyes of all people are upon us" (101). In the sentences preceding these statements, Winthrop makes clear the ideology of exceptionalism when he declares, "The Lord will be our God, and delight to dwell among us as his own people, and will command a blessing upon us in all our ways" (101). Though overtly religious language does not characterize all forms of exceptionalism as it develops over time, the Puritans' assumption about their own status as people who are special, who have an important, world-changing mission to accomplish, and who are marked by success and supernatural blessing not only persists in American culture but is a defining feature of it. More specifically, Madsen identifies the Western story as a significant vehicle for the ideology of American exceptionalism. Drawing on Frederick Jackson Turner's "The Significance of the Frontier in

American History" (1894), she explains that "it was not the civilization of the Atlantic states but the Great West that best described the American nation" (123). Accordingly, "the Western is based on a story of individual heroism, where the individual is superior to the laws and institutions of the twentieth century," and this hero "represents the idealized American, living out the extreme significance of America's exceptional destiny" (124).

In the Border Trilogy, John Grady Cole, perhaps more than any other character, functions as a quintessential model of American exceptionalism, specifically the facet of the ideology promulgating that Americans have a special mission to accomplish in the world. For example, the passage in *All the Pretty Horses* when John Grady and his father ride horses together before John Grady leaves for Mexico indicates the extent to which this young character expresses the ideology of exceptionalism. Whereas John Grady's father looks over the country with despair, "See[ing] it as it had always been, would forever be," John Grady looks over the same country with different eyes (23). The following passage makes clear their ideological differences:

> The boy who rode on slightly before him sat a horse not only as if he'd been born to it which he was but as if were he begot by malice or mischance into some queer land where horses never were he would have found them anyway. Would have known that there was something missing for the world to be right or he right in it and would have set forth to wander wherever it was needed for as long as it took until he came upon one and he would have known that that was what he sought and it would have been. (23)

Here John Grady is presented as a character who has confidence in his vision of the world as amenable to his desires. His purpose is to ride horses and herd cattle, and in the narrator's hypothetical situation, he believes, whatever trials he faces, that his efforts to fulfill this purpose will result in success. After all, he rides with the confidence that he would find a horse in a world bereft of horses and singlehandedly set that world right. Further, he continues to believe in the rightness of his calling to be a cowboy even after grave disappointments, as he tells a shoeshine boy in *Cities of the Plain*, saying "I wouldnt be nothing else" when the boy presses him to explain his commitment to his work (95).

Sacvan Bercovitch, in his encounters with what he calls "the literature of westward expansion," illuminates John Grady's perspective when he describes "a country that, despite its arbitrary territorial limits, could read its destiny in its landscape, and a population that [...] could believe in something called an American mission, and could invest that patent fiction with all the emotional, spiritual, and intellectual appeal of a religious quest" (11). In *All the Pretty Horses*, John Grady's unshakable belief in his own purpose as a cowboy, combined with his pursuit of that life in Mexico, has all the energy, as Bercovitch suggests, of a "religious quest" (11). In Bercovitch's study of Puritan jeremiads, he consequently notes that John Grady's precursors do not question the validity of their quest or purpose but repeatedly ask, "When is our errand to be fulfilled? How long, O Lord, how long?" (11). John Grady acknowledges that, due to circumstances outside his control, such as his parents' divorce and his mother's resolve to give up on the ranch, he has no future as a cowboy in Texas. Nevertheless, he does not question whether his pursuit of the life of a cowboy is possible or legitimate. Instead, the passage above portrays him as pursuing this life with the belief that he will achieve it, that his efforts will yield success simply because he feels in his heart that it should be so.

John Grady's assumption that his errand will be successful additionally expresses his philosophical optimism, a powerful constituent of American exceptionalism. Louis B. Wright accordingly names "optimism" as "the most persistent" quality of Euro-American settlers in "the period of American territorial expansion" (18). He goes on to explain the mindset of the optmist when he asserts that "no hardships were so great that he could not overcome them with hard work and what he unsentimentally described as 'good luck,'" and "he rarely lost faith in an ultimate achievement of happiness and prosperity" (18). Terry Eagleton furthermore argues that "the United States is one of the few countries on earth in which optimism is almost a state ideology," which he describes as a "compulsive cheeriness" expressed with "I-can-do-anything-I-want rhetoric" (10). Like the optimists of Wright's study, John Grady acts according to the belief that his hard work and persistence will result in his achievement of the goods he seeks—such as the life of a cowboy; reconciliation with Alejandra; the recovery of his, Blevins's, and Rawlins's horses; and rescuing Magdalena and preparing a home for her. In the passage quoted above, John Grady wanders without having seen a horse but with the distinct sense that he seeks something that will make him whole. When he comes upon a horse, never having seen one, "he would have known that was what he sought and it would have been" (23). Although John Grady acts according to the principles of the optimist, he occasionally acknowledges the possibility of failure or a negative outcome. For example, Rawlins warns John Grady about the imprudence of stealing back Blevins's horse soon after their arrival in Mexico, which John Grady recognizes and yet concludes "I cant do it," meaning that he cannot leave Blevins to fend for himself (79). John Grady's commitment to his ideals compels him to undertake ill-fated missions, evincing his belief that somehow his acts contain meaning or will be rewarded. Hence, as these passages illustrate, the narrative of American exceptionalism is so compelling because it accentuates an individual's optimism—that one's feelings of desire or rightness have the power to bring about an outcome that is implausible or very difficult to achieve.

In contrast to John Grady's idealistic exceptionalism, McCarthy places the character's father's darker perspective, one that resonates with the nihilistic undercurrent in McCarthy's work, next to his son's.[5] Donald Crosby defines all forms of nihilism as having in common "an attitude of negation or denial" that "denies some important aspect of human life" (35). Crosby's description of "cosmic nihilism" may be the most apt for the present study, as this form of nihilism "disavows intelligibility or value in nature, seeing it as indifferent or hostile to fundamental human concerns" (35). For example, the father "look[s] over the country with those sunken eyes as if the world out there had been altered or made suspect by what he'd seen of it elsewhere. As if he might never see it right again. Or worse did see it right at last. See it as it had always been, would forever be" (23). Whereas the adherent of American exceptionalism could, in Bercovitch's words "read its destiny in its landscape," John Grady's father realizes that he had previously looked upon the Texas wilderness, and the world in general, as a place that would bend to his desires, that would make itself amenable to his purpose in the world. But as he looks over this familiar country with a lifetime of disappointment coloring his perspective, in which war and divorce are major features, he recognizes that the world has not changed but that he finally "see[s] it as it had always been, would forever be" (23).

Dismantling the myth of American exceptionalism entails, for John Grady's father, the recognition that the world was never amenable to the pioneer's conquest. It was not waiting for the pioneer to arrive and to bring his special errand to the land. John Grady's father therefore acknowledges American exceptionalism as a myth when he states, "We're like the Comanches was two hundred years ago. We dont know what's goin to show up here come daylight. We dont even know what color they'll be" (26–27). By likening pioneers and cowboys to Comanches, who in the nineteenth century lost land, power, and culture at the hands of Euro-American colonizers, the father acknowledges that his ancestors' conquest of the land he looks upon was neither the result of divine providence nor the favor of the world itself. Rather, their conquest was temporary. Moreover, it did not signify that they were exceptional. When he consequently "see[s] it as it had always been, would forever be," he not only confronts an unpleasant truth that revises a previously held belief that gave his life meaning but replaces it with a despair that holds much in common with cosmic nihilism—in Crosby's definition, he sees the Texas wilderness "as indifferent or hostile to fundamental human concerns" (35).

John Grady stands in contrast to characters such as his father and Dueña Alfonsa, who represent a much less idealistic view of the world. Although not a true nihilist herself, Dueña Alfonsa articulates, like John Grady's father, a version of cosmic nihilism, as a response to John Grady's optimism. She tells him, "In the end we all come to be cured of our sentiments. Those whom life does not cure death will. The world is quite ruthless in selecting between the dream and the reality" (238). She recognizes in him the optimistic belief, in the words of Thomas J. Elliott, that "a person with the right amount of energy and courage can always achieve personal 'salvation'" (123). In her philosophizing, Alfonsa makes clear that John Grady's "sentiments"—his desire to be a cowboy and to marry Alejandra—are a dream the natural world is not only unaware of but perhaps even hostile to. Alfonsa refers to the "world" as a ruthless entity for its complicity in perpetuating the reality that shatters one's dreams. She recognizes that there is a certain coldness in the fact that the world continues to circle the sun, impervious to the suffering of people living on it. Yet she accepts that "the world is quite ruthless in selecting between the dream and the reality," and that death will aid the coldly spinning world in disabusing people of their sentiments (238).

John Grady, however, does not let his sentiments die easily, and he is not "cured" of them, according to Alfonsa's perspective, until his death in *Cities of the Plain*. Alejandra, on the other hand, seems to have been handily cured of her sentiments through her dalliance with John Grady. When he meets her one last time in Zacatecas, he looks into her eyes and realizes that "he'd never seen despair before. He thought he had, but he had not" (251). Later, John Grady encounters his own temptation toward despair when he visits the cemetery after Abuela's funeral and grieves: "he said goodbye to her in spanish and then turned and put on his hat and turned his wet face to the wind and for a moment he held out his hands as if to steady himself or as if to bless the ground there or perhaps as if to slow the world that was rushing away and seemed to care nothing for the old or the young or rich or poor or dark or pale or he or she. Nothing for their struggles, nothing for their names. Nothing for the living or the dead" (301). Although John Grady ostensibly steadies himself, blesses the ground, or slows the world, the phrases that describe the coldly spinning world emphasize his losses and sorrows. He holds out his hands to slow the world due to his shock that, as Alfonsa tells him, the world "is quite ruthless in selecting between the dream and the reality" (238). John Grady's grief, therefore, is exacerbated by the coldness of this world that continues to revolve around the sun without a care for the "struggles" or "names" of people who are encountering its indifference and losing their dreams.

Billy Parham's Contact with Exceptionalism and Despair

In the second volume of the Border Trilogy, Billy Parham believes, like John Grady Cole, that he is called to a particular heroic task that resonates with Madsen's description of Puritans who "are charged with saving the world from itself" and Bercovitch's observation that their mission was imbued "with all the emotional, spiritual, and intellectual appeal of a religious quest" (Madsen 2; Bercovitch 11). In particular, Billy's quest to bring the wolf to safety has even more religious overtones than John Grady's expedition to Mexico.[6] In the first few pages of *The Crossing*, he has a spiritual experience as he exchanges recognition with a pack of seven wolves passing by his house in the night. Billy's awe and subsequent resolve not to speak of this encounter recalls the Virgin Mary's response to the miraculous, divinely ordained birth of Christ. Whereas shepherds who visit the holy family "made known abroad the saying which was told them concerning this child," Mary "kept all these things, and pondered them in her heart" (Luke 2:18–19).⁷ Similarly, after witnessing the wolves in the moonlight and having these creatures, in turn, look upon him, Billy keeps the experience to himself: "When he got back to the house Boyd was awake but he didnt tell him where he'd been nor what he'd seen. He never told anybody" (5). Billy's Mary-like response suggests his feeling that something exceptional and spiritual occurred between himself and the wolves, a feeling that expands as he undertakes his quest to bring a particular wolf—one wounded by a trap and pregnant—to the mountains of Mexico and ostensibly to safety.

Billy's refusal to collect the bounty for the wolf, as well as his explanation of his relationship to the animal, reveal how he gradually comes to believe that he is undertaking a spiritual mission. Prior to his capture of the wolf, Boyd wonders what Billy will do with her in the event of his success, and Billy responds that he will "collect the bounty, I reckon" (34). Likewise, once the wolf is in his possession, a man in a truck also questions Billy's intentions with the statement "I guess you'll collect the bounty. Sell the hide," to which Billy responds, "yessir" (60). However, Billy not only decides against collecting the bounty but refuses to sell the wolf when offered money, saying "she aint for sale" at the first offer and later, "he said that the wolf had been entrusted to his care but that it was not his wolf and he could not sell it" (70, 90). Billy does not specify who "entrusted" the wolf to his care, yet his repeated use of this phrase suggests the depth of his belief in its truth. Soon after Mexican deputies take the wolf from him, "The boy said that the wolf was not contraband but was property entrusted into his care and that he must have it back," and later he offers to earn her back with work, emphasizing that "he could not part with the wolf because the wolf had been put in his care" (99, 110). Finally, after the wolf fights vicious dogs in an arena for entertainment and Billy intervenes, "he said that he was custodian to the wolf and charged with her care" (118). Like the Virgin Mary, he speaks as if he has received a divine appointment to care for a vulnerable creature who will eventually suffer a brutal public death.

However, in contrast to Mary, there is no redemptive element in Billy's quest regarding the wolf. Following his ceremonious burial of the animal, the narrative declares, "doomed enterprises divide lives forever into the then and the now," and notes that Billy "thought to become again the child he never was" (129).⁸ Accordingly, Billy encounters multiple figures who present darker, more pessimistic ideologies as alternatives to exceptionalism, and who furthermore offer to explain why an enterprise such as the one he undertook with the wolf was doomed. For example, prior to his capture of the wolf, while seeking advice on how to trap the animal, an old man warns Billy that a wolf's knowledge points to a version of nihilism. He says, "that the wolf is a being of great order and it knows what men do not: that there is no order in the world save that which death has put there" (45).[9] Further, the man states that people, in contrast to wolves, are so deluded by their own view of the world and their place in it that they cannot see, in Crosby's words, that the world is "indifferent or hostile to fundamental human concerns" (35). The old man argues that people instead "see the acts of their own hands or they see that which they name and call out to one another but the world between is invisible to them" (46).

Given that this conversation occurs before Billy captures the wolf, it functions as a warning regarding his blindness toward the coldness of the world. Billy's experience with the seven wolves in the moonlight blinds him to the order of death, to the reality that the world continues to spin regardless of what he does with his life. The old man thus implies that what people "name and call out to one another" is merely a construction of their own perceptions, and Billy affirms this observation later when he insists that "the wolf had been entrusted to his care" and that "he was custodian to the wolf and charged with her care" (90, 118). According to the old man's logic, Billy is able to imagine himself as custodian of the wolf due in large part to the ideology of exceptionalism. What the old man calls "the world between"—in which Billy is neither custodian of the wolf nor the recipient of a divine appointment—remains "invisible" to him (46).

The old man, then, presents the dismantling of exceptionalism as a possible path to liberation from one's ideals. When the old man suggests that finding this place will help Billy, he is recommending that Billy accept that the acts of his own hands and that which he names are not what he thinks—they are neither as meaningful nor as effective as he assumes they are. As Dennis L. Sansom explains of the "teachers" of nihilism in the Border Trilogy, the old man espouses a view in which "no one can remove the despairing curse on all human efforts; no one can escape the senselessness of death, or the fact that their lives do not contribute to a grand moral or religious goal to human history" (75). Once Billy accepts this truth, he will be able to see the world as it is, saving himself from the startling realization that his "doomed enterprises" signify his own lack of agency and that the world is "indifferent or hostile to fundamental human concerns" (Crosby 35).

Other figures additionally echo the old man's pessimistic, somewhat nihilistic perspective, again presenting Billy with an ideology that eclipses exceptionalism. When he meets a blind man who lost his sight in the Mexican Revolution, the man tells him, "the world in which he made his way was very different from what men supposed and in fact was scarcely world at all," adding, "the light of the world was in men's eyes only for the world itself moved in eternal darkness and darkness was its true nature and true condition" (283). Finally, the blind man concludes with a question, "He said that he could stare down the sun and what use was that?" (283). By drawing attention to the movements of the world in darkness and the uselessness of a man staring down the sun, the blind man promotes the acceptance of darkness and the futility of human acts as the truth of existence. Similarly, Eduardo in *Cities of the Plain* reinforces the view of the old man who gives Billy advice about trapping the wolf and the blind man he meets following his failure to protect the animal. Eduardo tells him, "Men have in their minds a picture of how the world will be. How they will be in that world. The world may be many different ways for them but there is one world that will never be and that is the world they dream of" (134). Like Alfonsa when she refers to the difference between dreams and reality and John Grady's "sentiments," Eduardo warns Billy against the belief that a fantasy in his mind represents reality.

The world Billy dreams of that Eduardo insists will never be is a world in which the wolf is safe and free. Before he finds the wolf trapped and wounded, he daydreams of this world. As he tracks the wolf, "he closed his eyes and tried to see her. Her and others of her kind, wolves and ghosts of wolves running in the whiteness of that high world as perfect to their use as if their counsel had been sought in the devising of it" (31). Later, after he shoots the wolf and carries her body away for burial, he has another vision of a nonexistent world featuring the glories of the wolf. In this passage, Billy "closed his own eyes that he could see her running in the mountains, running in the starlight where the grass was wet and the sun's coming as yet had not undone the rich matrix of creatures passed in the night before her. Deer and hare and dove and groundvole all richly empaneled on the air for her delight, all nations of the possible world ordained by God of which she was one among and not separate from" (127). In both passages, Billy closes his eyes and has a dream of the kind to which Eduardo refers and is moreover narrated as a fantasy. In the first, the wolves behave as if the world is "as perfect to their use as if their counsel had been sought in the devising of it," and the second describes a "possible world ordained by God" (127). Both are presented as fantastical, hypothetical worlds that the reality of the story contradicts with the wolf's brutal death and Billy's helplessness to prevent it. In contrast to the world of which he dreams, the wolf is captured, abused, and tortured for entertainment. Further, Billy himself acts as her executioner rather than as a reverent witness to her majestic existence. Like John Grady at the end of *All the Pretty Horses*, Billy confronts the unpleasant possibility that the world itself "seemed to care nothing for the old or the young or rich or poor or dark or pale or he or she. Nothing for their struggles, nothing for their names. Nothing for the living or the dead" (301). Indeed, the world does not stand still for him; rather, it continues to spin after his doomed enterprise. At the end of the novel, "the right and godmade sun did rise, once again, for all and without distinction" (426). As Susan Kollin asserts, "Billy pays the price for his western dreams, with the western sun, indifferent to his sufferings, refusing to bestow its glory on him" (582).

Both John Grady and Billy acknowledge, at different points in the Border Trilogy, that the world is indifferent to their suffering. In a conversation between the two young men that occurs before John Grady's death, they even acknowledge to each other that the world is uninterested, perhaps hostile, to them. Billy tells John Grady, "The world dont know nothing about your judgment," to which the latter responds, "I know it. It's worse than that. It dont care" (219). Although both characters have moments in which they recognize their unexceptional, miniscule place in the world, they each appear incapable of internalizing exceptionalism as a myth and living with different assumptions regarding their relation to the world. Both men pursue a particular vision of the world that is strongly imbued with characteristics of the American Dream. For John Grady, in *Cities of the Plain*, that vision is domestic as he focuses on preparing a home and safe haven for himself and Magdalena.[10] John Grady consequently disregards Alfonsa's warning about pursuing an unattainable relationship, and her words function as a sort of prophecy that becomes clear after John Grady's death. As Alfonsa had promised, death would cure him of his sentiments if he did not let them go. Chasing after his sentiments—a domestic life with Magdalena—is what kills him.

Billy's moments of lucidity regarding his place in the world are also contradicted by his choices following those instances of recognition. At the end of *The Crossing*, he resolves to volunteer for military service in World War II, a patriotic impulse that reveals his desire to preserve the notion that Americans have a special mission to accomplish in the world. He makes three attempts to enlist in the army, telling the doctor during his last attempt, "I dont have anyplace to go. I think I need to be in the army" (341). He admits that he lacks direction, due to his loss of family, and so he expects military service to fill the void he feels and give himself purpose. He demonstrates a similar fidelity to his country when he defends, seemingly by default rather than passionate conviction, "good american whiskey" in a bar to a drunk man (361). Whereas John Grady places his hope in a domestic life, Billy looks for purpose through patriotism and the ideal of the nation itself. Despite the warnings both men receive, and offers of more pessimistic perspectives as alternatives to exceptionalism, they both are nevertheless incapable of living without this ideology. In the epilogue to *Cities of the Plain* in which Billy is an old man, he dreams of his dead brother and sister and when he wakes, he thinks of his siblings and that "in everything that he'd ever thought about the world and about his life in it he'd been wrong" (266). Given Billy's age in this scene, it is somewhat surprising that it is merely an echo of what he has circled back to at multiple points in this life: as he tells John Grady, "The world dont know nothing about your judgment" (219). His return, again and again, to the notion that the world is both cruel and indifferent to him, indicates that it is impossible for him to accept and that he grows old mourning the myth of American exceptionalism.

A Communal Ethic in *The Road* Challenges Exceptionalism and Despair

The constituents of American exceptionalism that are so compelling to John Grady and Billy in the form of the American Dream—such as the attachment to the cowboy's life and domesticity, the calling to care for a vulnerable animal, or the desire to serve in the armed forces—are images of fantasy that motivate them to continue striving for a state of satisfaction that is impossible to attain. In *Cruel Optimism,* Lauren Berlant discusses the kinds of fantasies that preoccupy John Grady and Billy, arguing that such "optimistic attachment" to certain dreams "involves a sustaining inclination to return to the scene of fantasy that enables you to expect that *this* time, nearness to *this* thing will help you or a world to become different in just the right way" (2). Although John Grady's dream of domesticity and the cowboy life was shattered in *All the Pretty Horses* with his arrest, Blevins's death, his own killing of a man, and his loss of Alejandra, he reappears in *Cities of the Plain* on a ranch in New Mexico, again pursuing the life of a cowboy and marriage to an unavailable woman. Billy's mission to save the wolf from harm fails, and yet he attempts to enlist in the army, fantasizing that perhaps "*this* time," as Berlant suggests, he will participate in a successful errand that will leave him feeling fulfilled rather than lost and empty. Berlant consequently argues that optimism becomes "cruel" when the fantasy "that ignites a sense of possibility actually makes it impossible to attain the expansive transformation for which a person or a people risks striving" (2). When John Grady and Billy are each tempted to despair as they encounter the myth of American exceptionalism, they briefly become aware of the fantasies that perpetuate their cycles of cruel optimism.

Neither character, however, is actually capable of living without the guidance of exceptionalism. Each continues to follow some version of the American Dream and to make optimistic decisions accordingly. John Grady thus dies a senseless death, and at the end of his life, Billy is a troubled sleeper, dreaming of the past and of the dead. Their outcomes seem to affirm the darker ideology that is continually offered to them as an explanation for their lives, pointing to the moral vision McCarthy develops and interacts with as he explores humanity's ways of relating to an indifferent, cruel world. In this moral vision, McCarthy's work aligns with Andrew Delbanco's, who argues in *The Real American Dream,* "hope has narrowed to the vanishing point of the self alone" (103). When a person's source of hope springs from the assumption that he is exceptional and appointed to a certain errand—such as protecting a wolf or being a cowboy—the cruel, indifferent world inevitably eradicates that hope. Consequently, this source of hope is unsustainable and leads to the despair with which many of McCarthy's characters wrestle. The Border Trilogy thus contains a trenchant critique of American exceptionalism, as well as where the ideology leads when it breaks down: a despair that often resembles nihilism.

The Road, however, offers a communal ethic that subverts both American exceptionalism and despair. The father in *The Road*, like John Grady Cole and Billy Parham, has his own startling encounters with the coldness of the world. In a situation wherein people can no longer see the sun, the man is yet aware of its presence and of the world's ambivalence toward the acts or desires of humans. This world is "populated by men who would eat your children in front of your eyes," and the man witnesses "pilgrims" who "sank down and fell over and died and the bleak and shrouded earth went trundling past the sun and returned again as trackless and as unremarked as the path of any nameless sisterworld in the ancient dark beyond" (181). Though the earth is covered in corpses that function as its burial clothes, it continues to roll on past the sun as it has every year and will continue to do so long after humans are extinct. The passage conveys the man's profound shock at this harsh reality. Several years of life in a postapocalyptic situation still has not inured him to the fact that the earth continues to revolve around the sun despite the unspeakable horrors it carries.

Some McCarthy scholars have consequently read *The Road* as ultimately nihilistic, scholars such as Tim Edwards, who calls it "a tale of nothingness," and John Cant, who writes that the novel affirms what is found elsewhere in the author's canon: "man's insignificance in a godless universe" (Edwards 59; Cant, "The Road" 185). Jacob M. Powning goes so far as to suggest that the outcome of *The Road*, in which the boy finds a new family, is actually the boy's "wishful dream" given that this turn of events is "discordant with the apparent nihilism of the rest of the book and McCarthy's previous works" (26). Other critics are sympathetic to such nihilistic or pessimistic readings of *The Road*, though in a more measured manner. For example, Erik J. Wielenberg writes that "there are hints of divine activity, but they are never more than hints," as he argues that "morality does not depend upon God for its existence or justification" (2, 1). Alan Noble calls the father's resolve to preserve his son's life evidence of an "absurd hope," and Matthew L. Potts similarly asserts that "the man on this road has something like faith" (Noble 97; Potts, "There is no god" 499). Lydia Cooper's assessment of the novel's ethical claims is also qualified. She writes that it "expresses a deep pessimism regarding humanity's self-destructiveness, but it concurrently proffers an affirmation of the individual's ability to experience a transcendent, and perhaps ultimately redemptive, empathic connection with others" (234). D. Marcel DeCoste provides an unreserved account of the novel's moral implications when he contends, "*The Road* offers not just a less than nihilistic study of virtue, but an explicitly Christian understanding of this term" (68). These readings, which encompass both philosophical and theological questions in the presence of nihilism, help illuminate ways in which *The Road* advances McCarthy's exploration of the relationship between exceptionalism and despair.

Similar to the novels in the Border Trilogy, *The Road* presents the father with Ely, a figure who conveys nihilistic ideas, though unlike John Grady and Billy, the father seems better equipped to engage Ely's ideas than the young men in the trilogy. Ely expresses nihilism when he says, "I knew this was coming" and "I always believed in it," as well as "people were always getting ready for tomorrow. I didnt believe in that. Tomorrow wasnt getting ready for them. It didnt even know they were there" (168). Ely's belief in the destruction of civilization builds to his argument, "There is no God and we are his prophets," and "Things will be better when everybody's gone" (170, 172). Although the father has no retort for Ely, his questions indicate that his faith lies elsewhere—in ideas that are neither exceptionalist nor nihilistic. The man does not deny that "tomorrow wasnt getting ready for them" or Ely's proclamation that "there is no God" (168, 170). The man halfheartedly agrees with Ely's statements about tomorrow with his response "I guess not," and to the argument "There is no God," he simply asks "No?" (169, 170). Similarly, the man phrases his own tenuous belief regarding the sanctity of his son as a question when he says to Ely, "What if I said that he's a god?" (172). The man's engagement with nihilism and despair, consequently, affirms the manner in which it debunks exceptionalism but nevertheless resists the denial of meaning that the ideology promulgates. As he parts from Ely, the man says, "You wouldnt understand" and "I'm not sure I do" when Ely wonders at the boy's benevolence (173). Likewise, the man admits, "I dont know what he believes in," and yet he affirms the legitimacy of the boy's faith when Ely says, "He'll get over it," and the man insists, "No he wont" (174). The father's hesitancy to deny God and to capitulate to meaninglessness, though he does not fully understand why, illuminates his ideological navigation through nihilism and to an affirmation of meaning without exceptionalism.

What enables the man to affirm meaning without embracing American exceptionalism, and thus what distinguishes his perspective from John Grady's and Billy's optimism, is a quality of hope that Eagleton differentiates from optimism. Eagleton argues, "Hope and temperamental optimism are at daggers drawn" (5). Further, hope involves "confess[ion] of how grave a situation is" while optimism "underestimate[s] the obstacles to tackling it" (11). Accordingly, John Grady and Billy both fail to recognize the gravity of the tragic situations in which they find themselves. John Grady attempts to free Magdalena from Eduardo though he does not have the resources to do so. Billy pleads with the *hacendado* who takes charge of the wolf to let Billy work to buy the wolf's freedom. The man in *The Road*, in contrast, acknowledges the dangers he and his son face every day and chooses to hope that they will live another day. In the passage containing his observation about the world's coldness toward the atrocities he and other humans have experienced, he recognizes that it is indeed a world "populated by men who would eat your children in front of your eyes" (181). At the end of his life, moreover, he chooses to hope, in the face of immense danger, that his son will survive after his own death. The man does not demonstrate the "compulsive cheeriness" common among optimists, but he intensely considers the possibility that his son will be killed and eaten by cannibals without his protection, and yet concludes, "Goodness will find the little boy. It always has. It will again" (Eagleton 10; *Road* 281).

The man's submission to his son's moral authority and subsequent recognition that the boy, rather than himself, is exceptional additionally provides a way for him to affirm nihilism's critique of exceptionalism and yet not to internalize nihilism itself and its guidance toward meaninglessness. Through the novel, the man's individualistic, survivalist mindset is in conflict with his son's communal ethic. The boy insists on an anti-exceptionalist perspective, in which he and his father share their resources and do not consider themselves entitled to survive at the expense of other people. The man fights against this impulse in his son, which culminates in the scene wherein a thief steals their shopping cart and the man forces the thief at gunpoint to strip naked and walk down the road with nothing on his body and nothing in his hands. When the boy protests that his father's treatment of the thief was fundamentally wrong, the man reveals his temptation to think of himself as exceptional when he tells his son, "You're not the one who has to worry about everything" (259). Allen Josephs refers to the boy's response, "Yes I am [...] I am the one," as "unmistakably religious language," and elsewhere I have argued that the boy's answer "rebukes the man for implying that he, rather than his son, is 'the one,' thus restoring himself as the moral authority to which the man should submit" (Josephs 138; Griffis 90). The boy's statement is the final word on the topic, and in the next scene, he and his father call out for the thief and eventually leave clothes in the road for the naked man. By submitting to his son, the man accepts the rebuke and thus eschews his tendency to think of himself as exceptional, as "the one." Unlike Billy, who names himself "custodian of the wolf," and who fixates on his own role on a noble errand, the man puts aside his own feelings of importance and allows his son to act as his guide.[11]

The ways in which *The Road* responds to and expands moral questions raised in McCarthy's earlier work, finally, indicate new directions in scholarship on this author. McCarthy himself admits in an interview with Richard Woodward that "books are made out of books," and Arnold explains that his "books speak to one another whatever their setting, and with each response, deepen and expand and give shape to McCarthy's overall artistic vision" (Woodward 31; Arnold, "The Mosaic" 17–18). Further, James Dorson notes that "theological readings [are] accruing around *The Road*" whereas nihilistic readings are more common for McCarthy's earlier works (121). Indeed, *The Road* is a text ripe for theological interpretation and should be read for its insights into the questions regarding despair, nihilism, and exceptionalism in the earlier novels. As a result, reading McCarthy's various works intertextually, as a long and deepening conversation with one another, may become not only a best practice of McCarthy scholarship but one of the most fruitful vehicles for understanding his work. Tracing the treatment of certain moral topics through McCarthy's work reinforces his proclivity to consider seriously diverse and contradictory answers to essential questions. In particular, by presenting readers with recurring images of the sun and the spinning world in both the Border Trilogy and *The Road*, McCarthy develops complex, multifaceted reflections on humans, meaning, and their relation to the world.

NOTES

1. Other studies in this vein argue that McCarthy debunks and invalidates the myth of the West in favor of a postmodern, centerless perspective (Messent 129; Owens 66; Saar-Hambazaza 192; Spencer 146; Spurgeon 42).

2. Many scholars have suggested that McCarthy's presentation of his characters' belief in their exceptionalism functions as a challenge to the United States's imperialism, as it is expressed both in Manifest Destiny and the Vietnam War (McBride 71; McGilchrist 128; Kollin 568).

3. Dianne C. Luce calls the Border Trilogy "an elegy for the evanescent world of the Southwest" ("The Vanishing World" 164). Trent Hickman, Mashid Younesi, and Hossein Pirnajmuddin have studied the nostalgic elements of the Border Trilogy. Hickman suggests that the stories demonstrate a way to honor characters of a lost tradition without slipping into nostalgia, and Younesi and Pirnajmuddin argue that the characters' attitudes about the loss of the Wild West contribute to their "wonder and terror when they happen to encounter nature's infinitude" (Hickman 162; Younesi and Pirnajmuddin 58).

4. Vince Brewton briefly mentions that "the novels of the trilogy propose an alternative to the Judge's nihilism," although this article does not account for the ways that John Grady and Billy are tempted by nihilistic perspectives (141).

5. The scholarly conversation regarding McCarthy's engagement with nihilism is one of the oldest among this author's critics. Vereen M. Bell's essay from 1983, in which he characterizes McCarthy's "metaphysics" as "no first principles, no foundational truth" is exemplary of this discussion (32). Bell later nuances this claim in *The Achievement of Cormac McCarthy* with the concession that "in the background of the novels there may be a residual yearning for ontological certainty," but "this nostalgia is subordinated forcefully to the opposing conviction, implied everywhere, that absolute certainty is always a form of unfreedom; that an administered world is, for the individual, a deprived one; that ideas and systems, the pursuit of essences and of first principles, are as dangerous and as reifying as imposed social orders" (8). In contrast, Edwin T. Arnold's response to Bell posits that McCarthy's novels contain "a profound belief in the need for moral order, a conviction that is essentially religious," as well as "the possibility of grace and redemption even in the darkest of his tales" ("Naming" 31). Similarly, Kim McMurtry suggests, "the need for human redemption is implied in the depravity" (144). The implications of the nihilistic elements of McCarthy's fiction have since functioned as an undercurrent in McCarthy scholarship, giving way to a variety of readings from philosophical, theological, economic, historical, environmental, and other perspectives.

6. As Petra Mundik argues, "Billy could never speak of the vision even if he wanted to because a mystical experience is impossible to convey in words and can only be experienced directly" ("All Was Fear" 10).

7. Theologian Edward Sri provides a gloss regarding this passage, explaining that others "'wonder' without pausing to keep and ponder the meaning of these events," which contrasts with Mary, who "is a person who reflects interiorly on the meaning of the events" (111, 112).

8. Charles Bailey argues that all three of Billy's border crossings result in "doomed enterprises," through which the novel illustrates the reality that "all heroic actions" are indeed doomed because they "rest on the hero's belief that he can control his fate" (65).

9. In his exploration of philosophical naturalism in *The Crossing*, Steven Frye reads this statement as meaning that "death itself is the agent of an order which does not necessarily emerge from any transcendent structuring principle such as God" (50).

10. In an essay wherein they explore John Grady's "longing for domesticity," Jay Ellis and Natalka Palczynski assert that many characters in the Border Trilogy inhabit roles similar to the chivalric code in Arthurian romances (105).

11. Regarding the conflict between the man's and the boy's perspectives, Rick Elmore and Jonathan Elmore explain: "The child's ethic becomes a powerful moral lesson to find community wherever one can by rejecting the impulse to hoard goods or to trade away a communal present for the promise of a solipsistic future" (145).

WORKS CITED

Arnold, Edwin T. "The Mosaic of McCarthy's Fiction." In *Sacred Violence: A Reader's Companion to Cormac McCarthy*. Edited by Wade Hall and Rick Wallach. Texas Western Press, 1995: 17–23.

———. "Naming, Knowing and Nothingness: McCarthy's Moral Parables." *Southern Quarterly*, Volume 30, number 4, 1992: 31–50.

Bailey, Charles. "'Doomed Enterprises' and Faith: The Structure of Cormac McCarthy's *The Crossing*." *Southwestern American Literature*, Volume 20, 1994: 57–67.

Bell, Vereen M. *The Achievement of Cormac McCarthy*. Louisiana State University Press, 1988.

———. "The Ambiguous Nihilism of Cormac McCarthy." *Southern Literary Journal*, Volume 15, number 2, 1983: 31–41.

Bercovitch, Sacvan. *The American Jeremiad*. University of Wisconsin Press, 1978.

Berlant, Lauren. *Cruel Optimism*. Duke University Press, 2011.

Brewton, Vince. "The Changing Landscape of Violence in Cormac McCarthy's Early Novels and the Border Trilogy." *Southern Literary Journal*, Volume 37, number 1, 2004: 121–43.

Cant, John. *Cormac McCarthy and the Myth of American Exceptionalism*. Routledge, 2018.

———. "The Road." *Cormac McCarthy: New Edition*. Edited by Harold Bloom. Infobase Publishing, 2009: 183–200.

Cooper, Lydia. "Cormac McCarthy's *The Road* as Apocalyptic Grail Narrative." *Studies in the Novel*, Volume 43, number 2, 2011: 218–36.

Crosby, Donald. *The Specter of the Absurd: Sources & Criticisms of Modern Nihilism*. State University of New York Press, 1988.

DeCoste, D. Marcel. "'A Thing That Even Death Cannot Undo': The Operation of the Theological Virtues in Cormac McCarthy's *The Road*." *Religion and Literature*, Volume 44, number 2, 2012: 67–91.

Delbanco, Andrew. *The Real American Dream: A Meditation on Hope*. Harvard University Press, 1999.

Dorson, James. "The Judeo-Christian Tradition." In *Cormac McCarthy in Context*. Edited by Steven Frye. Cambridge University Press, 2020: 121–31.

Eagleton, Terry. *Hope without Optimism*. University of Virginia Press, 2015.

Edwards, Tim. "The End of the Road: Pastoralism and the Post-Apocalyptic Waste Land of Cormac McCarthy's *The Road*." *Cormac McCarthy Journal*, Volume 6, number 1, 2008: 55–61.

Elliott, Thomas J. "Teaching Fiction in the Culture of Optimism." *College English*, Volume 42, number 2, 1980: 121–29.

Ellis, Jay, and Natalka Palczynski. "Horses, Houses, and the Gravy to Win: Chivalric and Domestic Roles in the Border Trilogy." In *Sacred Violence, Volume 2: Cormac McCarthy's Western Novels*. 2nd Edition. Edited by Wade Hall and Rick Wallach. Texas Western Press, 2002: 105–25.

Elmore, Rick, and Jonathan Elmore. "'You can stay here with your papa and die or you can go with me': The Ethical Imperative of *The Road*." *Cormac McCarthy Journal*, Volume 16, number 2, 2018: 133–48.

Frye, Steven. "Cormac McCarthy's 'world in its making': Romantic Naturalism in *The Crossing*." *Studies in American Naturalism*, Volume 2, number 1, 2007: 46–65.

Griffis, Rachel B. "Inverting the 'Gracelorn' Father: Augustinian Notions of Evil and Goodness in Cormac McCarthy's *Outer Dark* and *The Road*." *Literature and Theology*, Volume 36, number 1, 2022: 79–95.

Hickman, Trenton. "Against Nostalgia: Turning the Page of Cormac McCarthy's *Cities of the Plain*." *Western American Literature*, Volume 42, number 2, 2007: 142–63.

Holy Bible. King James Version. Thomas Nelson, 2017.

Jarrett, Robert L. *Cormac McCarthy*. Twayne Publishers, 1997.

Josephs, Allen. "The Quest for God in *The Road*." In *The Cambridge Companion to Cormac McCarthy*. Edited by Steven Frye. Cambridge University Press, 2013: 133–45.

Kollin, Susan. "Genre and Geographies of Violence: Cormac McCarthy and the Contemporary Western." *Contemporary Literature*, Volume 42, number 3, 2001: 557–88.

Luce, Dianne C. "The Vanishing World of Cormac McCarthy's Border Trilogy." In *A Cormac McCarthy Companion: The Border Trilogy*. Edited by Edwin T. Arnold and Dianne C. Luce. University Press of Mississippi, 2001: 161–97.

———. "'When You Wake': John Grady Cole's Heroism in *All the Pretty Horses*." *Sacred Violence, Volume 2: Cormac McCarthy's Western Novels*. 2nd Edition. Edited by Wade Hall and Rick Wallach. Texas Western Press, 2002: 57–70.

Madsen, Deborah L. *American Exceptionalism*. University Press of Mississippi, 1998.

McBride, Molly. "*The Crossing*'s Noble Savagery: The Wolf, the Indian, and the Empire." In *Sacred Violence, Volume 2: Cormac McCarthy's Western Novels*. 2nd Edition. Edited by Wade Hall and Rick Wallach. Texas Western Press, 2002: 71–82.

McCarthy, Cormac. *All the Pretty Horses*. Vintage, 1992.

———. *Cities of the Plain*. Vintage, 1998.

———. *The Crossing*. Vintage, 1994.

———. *The Road*. Vintage, 2006.
McGilchrist, Megan Riley. *The Western Landscape in Cormac McCarthy and Wallace Stegner: Myths of the Frontier*. Routledge, 2010.
McMurtry, Kim. "'Some Improvident God': Metaphysical Explorations in McCarthy's Border Trilogy." In *Sacred Violence, Volume 2: Cormac McCarthy's Western Novels*. 2nd Edition. Edited by Wade Hall and Rick Wallach. Texas Western Press, 2002: 143–57.
Messent, Peter. "'No Way Back Forever': American Western Myth in Cormac McCarthy's Border Trilogy." In *American Mythologies: Essays on Contemporary Literature*. Edited by William Blazek and Michael K. Glenday. Liverpool University Press, 2005: 128–56.
Morrison, Gail Moore. "*All the Pretty Horses*: John Grady Cole's Expulsion from Paradise." In *Perspectives on Cormac McCarthy, Revised Edition*. Edited by Edwin T. Arnold and Dianne C. Luce. University Press of Mississippi, 1999: 175–94.
Mundik, Petra. *A Bloody and Barbarous God: The Metaphysics of Cormac McCarthy*. University of New Mexico Press, 2016.
———. "'All Was Fear and Marvel': The Experience of the Sacred in Cormac McCarthy's *The Crossing*: Book I." *Southwestern American Literature*, Volume 36, number 1, 2010: 9–32.
Noble, Alan. "The Absurdity of Hope in Cormac McCarthy's *The Road*." *South Atlantic Review*, Volume 76, number 3, 2011: 93–109.
Owens, Barcley. *Cormac McCarthy's Western Novels*. University of Arizona Press, 2000.
Peebles, Stacey. "What Happens to Country: The World to Come in Cormac McCarthy's Border Trilogy." In *Sacred Violence, Volume 2: Cormac McCarthy's Western Novels*. 2nd Edition. Edited by Wade Hall and Rick Wallach. Texas Western Press, 2002: 127–42.
Potts, Matthew L. "'There is no god and we are his prophets': Cormac McCarthy and Christian Faith." *Christianity and Literature*, Volume 63, number 4, 2010: 489–501.
Powning, Jacob M. "'Dreams so rich in color. How else would death call you?': An Exploration of the Ending in Cormac McCarthy's *The Road*." *Cormac McCarthy Journal*, Volume 18, number 1, 2020: 26–36.
Saar-Hambazaza, Terje. "Reinventing the American West: Cormac McCarthy's *All the Pretty Horses*." In *North America: Tensions and (Re)Solutions*. Edited by Raili Põldsaar and Krista Vogelberg. Tartu Ulikooli Kirjastus, 2007: 191–99.
Sansom, Dennis L. "God, Evil, Suffering, and Human Destiny in the Border Trilogy: Learning from the 'Teachers.'" In *Cormac McCarthy's Violent Destinies: The Poetics of Determinism and Fatalism*. Edited by Brad Bannon and John Vanderheide. University of Tennessee Press, 2018.
Spencer, Andrew Blair. "A Cowboy Looks at Reality: The Death of the American Frontier and the Illumination of the Cowboy Myth in Cormac McCarthy's *All the Pretty Horses*." In *Western Futures: Perspectives on the Humanities in the Millennium*. Edited by Stephen Tchudi et al. Nevada Humanities Committee, 2000: 143–57.
Spurgeon, Sara L. *Exploding the Western: Myths of Empire on the Postmodern Frontier*. Texas A&M University Press, 2005.
Sri, Edward. *Rethinking Mary in the New Testament*. Ignatius Press, 2018.
Wielenberg, Erik J. "God, Morality, and Meaning in Cormac McCarthy's *The Road*." *Cormac McCarthy Journal*, Volume 8, number 1, 2010: 1–19.

Winthrop, John. "A Model of Christian Charity." In *The Norton Anthology of American Literature, Shorter Eighth Edition, Volume 1: Beginnings to 1865*. Edited by Nina Baym and Robert S. Levine. W. W. Norton & Company, 2013: 90–102.

Woodward, Richard B. "You Know about Mojave Rattlesnakes?" *New York Times Book Review*, 19 April 1992, page 28.

Wright, Louis B. "Historical Implications of Optimism in Expanding America." *Proceedings of the American Philosophical Society*, Volume 94, number 1, 1950: 18–23.

Younesi, Mahshid, and Hossein Pirnajmuddin. "Nostalgia and the Sublime in Cormac McCarthy's *The Border Trilogy*." *Journal of the Spanish Association of Anglo-American Studies*, Volume 40, number 2, 2018: 45–62.

"Whales and Men" and Its Echoes in the Border Trilogy

KATEŘINA KOVÁŘOVÁ

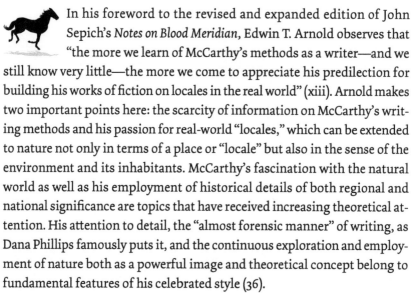 In his foreword to the revised and expanded edition of John Sepich's *Notes on Blood Meridian,* Edwin T. Arnold observes that "the more we learn of McCarthy's methods as a writer—and we still know very little—the more we come to appreciate his predilection for building his works of fiction on locales in the real world" (xiii). Arnold makes two important points here: the scarcity of information on McCarthy's writing methods and his passion for real-world "locales," which can be extended to nature not only in terms of a place or "locale" but also in the sense of the environment and its inhabitants. McCarthy's fascination with the natural world as well as his employment of historical details of both regional and national significance are topics that have received increasing theoretical attention. His attention to detail, the "almost forensic manner" of writing, as Dana Phillips famously puts it, and the continuous exploration and employment of nature both as a powerful image and theoretical concept belong to fundamental features of his celebrated style (36).

Since Arnold's remark, an important insight into McCarthy's writing methods has been provided by the opening of the archival materials in the Alkek B. Library in San Marcos, Texas. The access to the documents in the Wittliff Collections certainly has brought new and prolific impulse to the field of McCarthy studies. For the first time, the researchers have been (at least officially) able to study various drafts of the individual novels, notes, and correspondence of this otherwise somewhat reclusive author who refused to discuss his work.¹ Thus, the collection represents an exciting opportunity to study the development of McCarthy's individual novels and trace both literary and extraliterary sources of inspiration, as proved by Michael Lynn Crews's monograph *Books Are Made Out of Books*, published in 2017. For those interested in McCarthy's portrayal of American nature and his environmental sensitivity, an unpublished screenplay "Of Whales and Men," or "Whales and Men,"² is an important part of the collection now accessible to the public. Three versions of the text are housed at Wittliff: first (Folder 1), late (Folder 4), and final draft (Folder 5 and Folder 6). Moreover, the drafts contain holographic notes and corrections that are fascinating testaments of McCarthy's sources of inspiration and development of his texts.

Although the screenplay itself has not been published, it is instrumental for exploration of McCarthy's environmental imagery as it shares many features with the Border Trilogy, consisting of the novels *All the Pretty Horses* (1992), *The Crossing* (1994), and *Cities of the Plain* (1998). This essay thus examines the screenplay as an extremely valuable source of information on McCarthy's environmental sensibilities and explores the connections between "Whales and Men" and the Border Trilogy with particular focus on the second part, *The Crossing*, which shows important parallels both in its topics and the evolution of the text.³ Following the pioneering studies on "Whales and Men" by Dianne C. Luce, Jacqueline Scoones, Edwin T. Arnold, and James D. Lilley pointing out the connection of the whale and the wolf, this investigation takes a step further and analyzes the two iconic species to demonstrate the significance of the screenplay for the development of McCarthy's environmental and ethical concerns which play an important role in the rest of his novels that, as James D. Lilley observes, "engage issues of ecology and environmentalism in much more subtle ways" (158).

In his essay on "Whales and Men," Edwin T. Arnold notes the connection between the species: "The plight of whales is compared to that of wolves, for example, and the episode with the baby whale (with its obvious echoes of Hemingway's *The Old Man and the Sea*) is essentially a foreshadowing of the story of Billy Parham and the pregnant wolf" ("Cormac McCarthy's *Whales and Men*" 25). Yet the relationship between canines and cetaceans in McCarthy surpass simple substitution as both species show considerable parallels in McCarthy's texts. Firstly, they are both predators. While this might be quite obvious in the case of the wolf, McCarthy emphasizes the fact that the whale is a predatory species as well. Secondly, they both became symbols of environmental efforts and the ongoing ecological crisis since both species have been on the brink of extinction. Thirdly, they are highly social animals with rather iconic vocal capabilities and way of communication. And lastly, they both become symbols of human misunderstanding of the world and cruelty based on ignorance and fear.

While being McCarthy's most openly environmental work, the ecological appeals and concerns in "Whales and Men" are intertwined with references to Herman Melville's *Moby-Dick* (1851), other works of art, scientific data, and environmental texts. The core of the screenplay lays in images and speeches rather than a traditional plot or "action" as the majority of the scenes consist of monologues or dialogues elaborating on the whales, their representation and discussion about their possible, if not inevitable extinction. Other topics typical for McCarthy's work, such as the nature of language or nature of evil, are discussed in the script as well. As Arnold posits, "those who have read *Whales and Men* are in general agreement that, in its present state, it is not a filmable script. There are numerous examples of lengthy single-spaced monologues, anathema to conventional screenplays, and although the work does contain strong visual possibilities, it is concentrated much more on ideas than on actions" ("Cormac McCarthy's *Whales and Men*" 21). The actual implementation of the visual potential would certainly depend on the production; nevertheless, Arnold rightly points out that the screenplay is "obviously more philosophical and literary than cinematic" (22). In her book *Cormac McCarthy and Performance*, Stacey Peebles discusses the specific character of the screenplay further, also emphasizing that "many scenes consist of long, unbroken speeches and philosophizing" (56). She further observes that "the folder of notes on 'Whales and Men' also includes a few pages of notes labeled 'All the Pretty Little Horses,' indicating that the two projects probably had at least some overlap" (54). McCarthy worked on "Whales and Men" in the 1980s, in a period of transition from the South to the West. His letters to Howard Woolmer convey that in 1986 he made a trip to Argentina where he spent three weeks around whales with his friend, a whale biologist Roger Payne, and that he was working on a whale story ("McCarthy to Woolmer"). Furthermore, McCarthy started to write an early draft of *The Crossing* in October 1987, which means that he began his work on the novel at the same time or right after writing "Whales and Men." In addition, the third part of the trilogy, *Cities of the Plain*, originated as a screenplay that McCarthy wrote in the early 1980s (Arnold, "Cormac McCarthy's *Whales and Men*" 29). As suggested above, the screenplay is reminiscent of a closet drama and/or a thinking exercise exploring ideas that would be used in McCarthy's later works (Arnold, "Cormac McCarthy's *Whales and Men*" 21). While no information is available on why McCarthy abandoned the project to which he had devoted a significant amount of time, in the current state its main significance is in its open and straightforward exploration of environmental ethics, material reality of nature, and spiritual relationship between humankind and nature. All these topics appear to various degrees not only in the Border Trilogy but also in the southern novels. Nevertheless, as mentioned above, the most obvious connection is between "Whales and Men" and *The Crossing*, especially in the use of two rather emblematic animal species, a wolf and a whale. In one of his dialogues with a marine biologist Guy Schuler, John Western elaborates on the predatory species, emphasizing the link between whales and wolves:

> Having to kill in order to eat has brought the predators into a much more elaborate relationship with the world. They not only have to be quicker and stronger than the animals they eat, they have to be smarter. And they have to understand each other. They share in the work of hunting and they share in the kill. Cooperative society among grazing animals scarcely exists. Hemingway said that hawks dont share. But of course hawks do share. It's rabbits that dont share. And of course it's also the grazing animals that fight to the death. If you're a hunter you have to learn to control your aggression. Wolves dont kill each other. (McCarthy, "Whales and Men" 87)

McCarthy's fascination with predatory species recurs throughout his literary career, from hawks and cats in *The Orchard Keeper* to Malkina's pet cheetahs in *The Counselor*.[4] However, he does not focus necessarily on their hunting skills and aggression, which is usually the basis of their cultural representation, but rather emphasizes their intelligence, self-control, and a sense of community that is not usually associated with predators (the cultural stereotype of a lone wolf speaks volumes). Revisiting *Moby-Dick* and various representations of wolves in literature, such as Ernest Thompson Seton's "Lobo, the King of Currumpaw" or Jack London's *White Fang*, McCarthy attempts to alter the view of predators as natural-born killers that are a nuisance more than they are an integral part of the ecosystem.[5] While "correcting" the reputation of the wolf as a loner, he also offers a different perspective on the whale, representing it as a predator, a fact that tends to be suppressed in its cultural or environmental imagery.[6] Again, the aim of it is not to amplify the creature's aggression but rather to emphasize its intelligence and social bonds and potentially to repair the common misconception and provide scientifically more accurate representation. In the above-quoted speech, John Western attempts to restore the negative connotations of predatory species as misunderstood with the emphasis on their "much more elaborate relationship with the world."

In the 1970s and 1980s, when McCarthy worked on these texts, the wolf and the whale both became symbols of the nascent environmental movement and the ongoing ecological crisis, and serious concerns with the possible loss of whole ecosystems were extended to marine animals and began to replace the notion of the sea as a vast and inexhaustible reservoir of resources. As Lawrence Buell observes, "few episodes in the history of modern environmentalist consciousness have been more dramatic than this late twentieth-century awakening to the awareness that three-quarters of the globe, hitherto thought virtually immune from human tampering, might be gravely endangered" (201). The gravity of a situation when each specimen killed might mean a death sentence for a whole species and the discouraging skepticism of Guy Schuler, who is convinced that the whales are beyond the point of saving, are manifestations of the bleak reality accessible only to a rather small community of scientists.[7] Furthermore, both texts contain historical details on systematic hunting and near extermination of both wolves and whales. The first part of *The Crossing* is set in the 1930s when the wolves were basically extinct in the American Southwest (Robisch 401), a fact that is reflected several times in the novel. The historical connection with the systematic wolf extermination at the beginning of the twentieth century is emphasized by the mention of W. C. Echols, one of the best wolf trappers in the 1920s (Robisch 405).[8] Similarly, in "Whales and Men" Guy speaks about a pirate whaling ship, *Sierra*, and Japanese whalers who constantly violate the international conventions designed to protect the remaining whales.

The hunting equipment, or instruments of destruction of the two species, are also described in length and detail, along with the process of the hunt itself. Arguably, the trapping of wolves still possesses some romantic qualities as a combat of the wit of the trapper and the wolf; however, the wolf/dog fighting to which the she-wolf is subjected in the end is a cruel theater with no other purpose than to amuse the audience. The bloodshed in "Whales and Men" is further echoed in a detailed scene of the hunt of the wild dogs in *Cities of the Plain*. Since the dogs cannot be trapped, the men use hunting dogs and destroy the wild pack in a rather brutal manner, dragging them behind horses. A "religion of utility" mentioned by Guy Schuler in "Whales and Men" is preached through use of a whale's body and absence of the predatory wolf or wild dog, and these become what Wallis R. Sanborn calls "a metaphor for man's careless appetite for control over the natural world," meaning he "controls the animals he can, and he kills those animals he cannot" (131, 134). Since the puppies in *The Cities of the Plain* can be controlled and domesticated, they can be spared, unlike the adult dogs, who are doomed just like the wolves before them. Being in their essence a human creation, the wild dogs also symbolize the transformation of nature towards civilized land, a process that begins at the end of McCarthy's fifth novel, *Blood Meridian or The Evening Redness in the West* (1985).

The reality of the extermination of the wolf in the United States in the 1930s portrayed in *The Crossing* is quite similar to the situation of the whales facing near extinction later in the century. The 1980s were also the time of the efforts to reintroduce the wolf in America, which adds yet another dimension to the second part of the Border Trilogy since the reintroduction program has been a subject of controversy and opposed by many.[9] In this context *The Crossing* carries a powerful ethical message warning against repeating the mistakes of the past suggested by the lyrical ending of the first part where Billy Parham mourns the dead she-wolf:

> He squatted over the wolf and touched her fur. He touched the cold and perfect teeth. The eye turned to the fire gave back no light and he closed it with his thumb and sat by her and put his hand upon her bloodied forehead and closed his own eyes that he could see her running in the mountains, running in the starlight where the grass was wet and the sun's coming as yet had not undone the rich matrix of creatures passed in the night before her. [...] He took up her stiff head out of the leaves and held it or he reached to hold what cannot be held, what already ran among the mountains at once terrible and of a great beauty, like flowers that feed on flesh.

What blood and bone are made of but can themselves not make on any altar nor by any wound of war. What we may well believe has power to cut and shape and hollow out the dark form of the world surely if wind can, if rain can. But which cannot be held never be held and is no flower but is swift and a huntress and the wind itself is in terror of it and the world cannot lose it. (131)

"Whales and Men," similarly to the Border Trilogy, is a critique of treating animals and nature in general as a commodity or a mere resource without any respect. As Guy Schuler puts it, "We want everything to be for something. We're prisoners of a religion of utility. That's why the whale is doomed. He has to be for something too" (94). Killing a highly developed species to harvest blubber, exterminating all the predators to avoid losses in livestock, and hunting mindlessly without understanding the impact on the whole ecosystem are only a few examples of McCarthy's critique of mankind's treatment of nature that recurs throughout his work. The texts then reflect a moral outrage of a nature enthusiast who wants to prevent the catastrophe of the irreversible disappearance of these species, employing the proven conservationist method of aesthetic appeal, portraying creatures "at once terrible and of a great beauty" that "the world cannot lose."

What brings whales and wolves even closer is the notion of their strong social bonds, a depiction based on real-world scientific observations rather than cultural symbolism. Animals in McCarthy generally exceed simple symbols or metaphors and their corporeality is always emphasized as well as the vulnerability and materiality of their bodies and the fragility of the ecosystem they belong to. As Julius Greve posits in his 2018 book *Shreds of Matter*, "for McCarthy, nature is always material" (3). While somewhat mystical and mythical creatures, their pressing bodily presence impedes purely symbolical reading. Furthermore, their social ties and their physical existence are closely connected in the works. James D. Lilley elaborates further that "what whales and wolves [. . .] have in common is an inbuilt and immediate compassion for the suffering of others: whales and wolves will put their own bodies in danger in order to assist a member of their community; they take care of their dead and dying" (156). A testament of this is the scabbed wound on the she-wolf's flank inflicted by her mate when she refused to leave him caught in a trap with hunters approaching. When she is about to leave Hidalgo County, where she came to search for her kin in the first place, she is attracted by the scent left by Billy's father near one of the traps, which leads to her tragic fate. Her socialness becomes her downfall. In "Whales and Men" the most evident representation of the social ties of the whales is the opening scene of a cetacean stranding. In the first draft seven pilot whales[10] and in the final draft seventeen of them appear on the beach, creating arguably one of the most powerful images in the whole script. Among the gathering crowd Guy Schuler painfully watches the animals' slow and inevitable death. When he proceeds to sedate the whales to prevent other whales gathering in water from coming, he is confronted by a girl who does not understand why they cannot be towed back in the ocean, to which he replies, "Don't you see them out there? They wont leave. As long as there is one whale alive on this beach they will not leave. They will continue to try to come to its aid until it is dead. By Thursday there could be three hundred animals dying here" (2).

When writing this apocalyptic opening image, McCarthy might have been inspired by one of the largest cetacean strandings in history that took place on June 16, 1979, in Oregon, with forty-one sperm whales dying on the beach. This event is thoroughly explored in Barry Lopez's essay "A Presentation of Whales," first published in *Harper's Magazine* in 1980. McCarthy's screenplay shows striking similarities to Lopez's description of that event. Scientists who wanted to obtain samples were denied access to the still-living whales and their actions were probably perceived as rather cynical by the onlookers and police. However, it soon became obvious what the scientists had known—there was no hope for the whales (Lopez 697–98). "A belligerent few in the crowd shouted objections as the first syringes appeared,[11] and yelled at scientists to produce permits that allowed them to interfere in the death of an endangered species" (699). Whether McCarthy was inspired by Lopez's essay or not cannot be confirmed since there is no mention of it in his notes. Nevertheless, he certainly was familiar with the author since his notes include comments on Lopez's book *Arctic Dreams* from 1986 (Crews 266). Another Lopez book, *Of Wolves and Men*, had an impact on McCarthy's portrayal of the wolf in *The Crossing* (and potentially on the name of the screenplay).[12] Stranding is not the only example of animals dying *en masse* in McCarthy's fiction. A brief echo of this traumatic image appears in *All the Pretty Horses*: "Bye and bye they passed a stand of roadside cholla against which small birds had been driven by the storm and there impaled.

Gray nameless birds espaliered in attitudes of stillborn flight or hanging loosely in their feathers. Some of them were still alive and they twisted on their spines as the horses passed and raised their heads and cried out but the horsemen rode on" (75). McCarthy employs another similarly powerful image in *Blood Meridian*, drastically rewriting the picturesque Old West romantic panorama: "Dead animals scattered over the grounds [...] and the tandem wagons groaned away over the prairie twenty and twenty-two ox teams and the flint hides by the ton and hundred ton and the meat rotting on the ground and the air whining with flies and the buzzards and ravens and the night a horror of snarling and feeding with the wolves half crazed and wallowing in the carrion" (334). All these scenes possess a certain apocalyptic quality and all these phenomena have been scientifically or historically documented, meaning they are not mere creations of McCarthy's imagination. However, while the birds are killed by a thunderstorm, the bison carnage is humankind's doing and this image is yet another graphic accusation of man's cruelty and irresponsibility toward nature. The cetacean stranding, on the other hand, is even more fascinating because its causes remain unknown, adding to the mysteriousness of whales. Nonetheless, it represents a successful strategy to evoke sympathy in the readers/viewers by presenting the whales as extremely vulnerable, not to mention its cinematic potential. The vulnerability of the whales is also emphasized in the scene of a brutal slaughter of a group of blue whales later in the script, which, besides its alteration in *Cities of the Plain*, also echoes the bison carnage briefly depicted in *Blood Meridian*. The orphaned whale calf subsequently wandering to *Albion* attracted by its motors is the most explicit symbol of the whale's vulnerability. The lone individual with no chance to survive is an antithesis of the mass death and yet the single animal's pending death appeals to the reader's emotions in a very similar manner. In this sense, the scene translates into the description of the trapped she-wolf, which is remarkably absent of any sign of aggression:

> She was caught by the right forefoot. [...] The wolf crouched slowly. As if she'd try to hide. Then she stood again and looked at him and looked off toward the mountains. [...] When he approached her she bared her teeth but she did not growl and she kept her yellow eyes from off his person. White bone showed in the bloody wound between the jaws of the trap. He

could see her teats through the thin fur of her underbelly and she kept her tail tucked and pulled at the trap and stood. (McCarthy, *The Crossing* 54)

The she-wolf is also extremely vulnerable, being "trapped, pregnant, wounded, and at the mercy of man in the environment where she is undesirable. Her most prominent feature is not her white strong teeth, a common image in wolf literature, but an exposed white bone surrounded by blood and metal jaws of the trap, at once indicating that she is in pain and putting the man in the position of the merciless predator" (Kovářová 62). In both "Whales and Men" and *The Crossing*, the inflicted pain is represented indirectly through the image of blood and damage done to the body, accentuating the physicality of the creatures and the susceptibility of their bodies to pain. The psychological effect is similarly powerful: the animals are defenseless and doomed; there is no Melvillian pathos of the fight against a symbolic enemy.

The loneliness of both the she-wolf and the whale calf represents yet another layer of their vulnerability. As social species whales and wolves are highly vocal animals who use sound to communicate with their kin. As Lawrence Buell observes, "cetaceans have remarkably sophisticated and acute vocal and auditory capacities that allow some species to communicate acoustically thousands of miles away by a process still not fully understood" (203). The extent and even the mechanics of animal communication are in many aspects still a mystery for humankind. In Guy Schuler's words, "if you want to know about whales you have to listen. They're almost completely dependent on sound for making their way in the world. Among other things they are enormous moving sonar stations. Much more sophisticated than any we've devised" (McCarthy, "Whales and Men" 25). In "Whales and Men," the fact that the whales are distinct from human beings and their world based on sound rather than vision, making it a strange world altogether, is emphasized several times. As Guy Schuler puts it, "What we think about is the world and the whale's world is not ours" (93). Silence or isolated calls then become a motif of loss, of loneliness and disappearance. In the end of the scene of the stranding "we can hear the calls of the whales intermittent and very lonely" (3). Later in the text, Guy Schuler points out that he does not want to think about the last survivors roaming the seas in silence.[13] Similarly, in *The Crossing* the absence of the wolf is manifested mainly through the silence, as observed by the old gentleman whom Billy meets on his way to Mexico: "When we used to bring cattle up the valley from down around Ciénega Springs why first night we'd generally hit in about Government Draw and make camp there. And you could hear em all across the valley. Them first warm nights. You'd nearly always hear em in that part of the valley. I aint heard one in years" (62). Dianne C. Luce notes that "when Billy wakes to the sound of wolves howling in his first winter in Hidalgo County, he is hearing the remnant of a nearly extinguished species" (174). This is later confirmed by another old man in *Cities of the Plain* who describes the wolves he saw hanging on a fence when he was a boy, concluding "I aint heard a wolf in this country since [1917]. I suppose that's a good thing. They can be hell on stock" (127).[14]

While the sense of hearing (and of smell in the case of the wolf) is designated as the most important, in terms of physiology, McCarthy pays more attention to an eye. The images of the animals' eyes, be it horse, wolf, or whale, appear frequently in his works. However, they are not windows to the soul, but rather mirrors of the soul, as people are not able to see through them but see themselves in the reflection: "Some older people have gathered about one of the dying whales. He opens his eye and looks at them. Reflected in the eye the people are distorted of face and figure. They lean closer. Then the eye closes again" (McCarthy, "Whales and Men" 3). Similarly, the eye is a significant motif in *The Crossing*: "The wolf sat on her haunches below him in the draw and watched him with her intractable eyes so red in the firelight" (75).[15] In both cases the eye symbolizes the impenetrability of the animal's mind, adding to the completely different experience of its world from the human one. McCarthy's fascination with the whale's eyes is also clear in his letter to Albert Erskine: "They are huge and in the middle of this great wall of living (presumably) material is an eye—not all that large, maybe the size of a tennis ball. And this eye is watching you" (qtd. in Peebles 54). The eye of a cetacean is similar and yet different from the human one, an image evoking both the sense of uncanny resemblance and opening the question of an anthropocentric perspective.

While the differences between humans and the other species are emphasized in both texts, the characters experience uncanny moments when the similarities appear. John Western has a book with an illustration of whale anatomy including the bone structure hidden in the flippers. When Kelly comes and puts her hand on the illustration, they are of the same size and presumably of similar shape.[16] Similarly, when Billy Parham tastes the blood of the wolf, it tastes "no different than his own" (McCarthy, *The Crossing* 129). These moments represent an unstable boundary between human and non-human and possibly McCarthy's sensitivity to the transformation of imagination accompanying the growing environmental consciousness. Buell explains that "whales anciently seemed to partake of ocean's mysterious, radical, ambiguous otherness: to symbolize divine power, whether benign or threatening. Today whales still seem uncannily other, but with the uncanniness increasingly seen to reside in the 'fact' that despite dramatic differences in scale and anatomy and habitat they are so much like us" (203). The whale is no longer a leviathan, a sea monster; it is an intelligent being capable of grief and, as suggested in "Whales and Men," love.

The cetacean stranding, which may or may not be caused by human-related factors, and the whale calls are integral parts of McCarthy's whale imagery, together with the suggested mysterious knowledge of the universe and other inexplicable phenomena connected to the whale. While he is very realistic in the descriptions of the physiognomy and behavior of the animals, his imagery is far from pure realism. Julius Greve offers a very precise observation that "[the] realist tone, however, is generally counterbalanced by the mythical depth of McCarthy's work, and as many scholars have remarked, it is this tension between lyrical mythography and stark realism that defines the unique character of McCarthy's storytelling techniques" (3). Both wolf and whale are shrouded in mystery and myth in terms of what they evoke in us as human beings, as well as in the way they are represented in literature and other art. Instead of trying to replace the myth with scientific facts, McCarthy creates a new, potentially harmless mythology of both wolf and whale based on respect to the fact that we indeed do not know a whole lot about them, an attitude that links him to both Lopez and Payne, who emphasize this fact in their books. While describing the she-wolf with an unprecedented accuracy, McCarthy does not pretend to know what she might think. We see her body language and its interpretation is the only clue we as readers get. The wolf is made in the same way the world is, mysterious and not readily knowable and nameable, which aligns the environmental notion of respect to McCarthy's philosophical materialism. In "Whales and Men," Guy Schuler speaks in length about various scientific theories of whales' way of communication or the function of their brain. While we may be able to understand how they communicate, we do not understand why or to what extent. Guy even suggests that they might contemplate the universe and possess some knowledge inaccessible to human beings, challenging the prevalent notion of human superiority: "Suppose God came back from wherever it is he's been and asked us smilingly if we'd figured it out yet. Suppose he wanted to know if it had finally occurred to us to ask the whale. And then he sort of looked around and he said: By the way, where are the whales? And we said: Well, we uh... —And he said: Yes? And we said: Well. We used some of them for axle-grease and fertilizer and the rest of them we fed to the dogs" (23–24) In "Whales and Men" the impenetrability of other species' mind, thought, and way of seeing the world, or the mere idea that someone in this world may possess knowledge we do not seems to provoke humankind so much that we aim to destroy what we cannot understand and then assimilate. A very similar comment appears in Roger Payne's book *Among Whales*, and Payne himself is being considered a source of inspiration for Guy Schuler:

> What we do with whales (or with other large mammals with the potential to inspire us) takes the measure of our souls. When we turn them into meat and oil, we demonstrate that we have no souls (or only little, wizened souls). We reveal what we aren't up to the challenge of whales—that our ignorance of that they offer humanity and our prejudice against nonhuman life are too profound. When we kill off populations of any large mammal it is the same; it makes no real difference whether we are destroying giraffes, or rhinoceros, or elephants, or whales. It is the same crime. It requires exactly the same shortfall of imagination to mount a rhinoceros on a wall as it does to turn a whale into cat food. (336)

In this aspect, McCarthy's imagery is closer to nonfictional environmental books, such as Lopez's *Of Wolves and Men* and Payne's *Among Whales*. Payne's extensive monograph on his experience and study of whales is dedicated to McCarthy, and it is very similar to "Whales and Men" in emphasizing the respect to animals we know so little about. As Payne claims, "the study of whales is a kind of a trial by fire in which one learns eventually (and at a non-inconsiderable cost) that it is enough to be a part of life on earth, rather than trying to control it" (111), a comment that could have easily appeared in McCarthy's screenplay, where the question of control is further infused with the discussion about language and evil. Peter Gregory elaborates on his mistrust of language: "What had begun as a system for identifying and organizing the phenomena of the world had become a system for replacing those phenomena. For replacing the world" (McCarthy "Whales and Men" 57). This outlook is translated into the Border Trilogy, and *The Crossing* in particular, not only in the end of the first part quoted above, but also in the speech of the Quijada later in the book: "The world has no name, he said. The names of the cerros and the sierras and the deserts exist only on maps. We name them that we do not lose our way. Yet it was because the way was lost to us already that we have made those names. The world cannot be lost. We are the ones. And it is because these names and these coordinates are our own naming that they cannot save us. That they cannot find for us the way again" (398). Both of these passages emphasize the disconnection of humans from the rest of the world.

The transformations of the topics, motifs, and individual images are manifested not only across the individual works but also between individual drafts, demonstrating, for example, the impact of "Whales and Men" on the evolution of *The Crossing*. In the first draft of "Whales and Men," Guy Schuler watches the beached whales and the whole crew leaves on a plane leaving the orphaned whale calf behind. In the final draft, however, he injects the beached pilot whales with panabarbitol, a tranquilizer that will kill them, to save other whales that gather in the water nearby and who would throw themselves on the beach in an attempt to help their kin. He also tranquilizes the baby whale later in the screenplay to spare it suffering from being torn apart by sharks that start to attack it. In the early versions of *The Crossing* (labeled "early draft" and "first draft" in the collection), the first part has a different ending than the published version. Billy Parham trades the she-wolf for his rifle while she is still alive, though terribly wounded after being forced to fight with the dogs. He tries to tend her wounds with an ointment and takes her to the mountains, where he continues to take care of her until the morning when "she gave a great sigh and her breath ran out and she quivered and was still. He knelt forward and reached to touch her. Hold that back, what could not then or ever be held. What ran among the mountains. What blood and flesh was made of and not the other way around. [. . .] But which could not be held and it was no flower but was swift like a hunter and the wind was in terror of it and the world could not lose it" (McCarthy, "The Crossing—early draft" 131). For comparison, the same passage in the first draft:

> He leaned and touched her and he thought that in her dreams she was running in the mountains. [...] Her legs ran slowly in the leaves and he held his hand against her heart and her heart beat and then it did not beat and that was all. [...] He knelt forward and lifted up her head. He reached to hold what cannot be held. [...] But which cannot be held never be held and is no flower but is swift and a huntress and the wind is in terror of it and the world cannot lose it. (McCarthy, "The Crossing—first draft" 168)

The most notable difference is in the transformation of the tense in the last sentence, which becomes a generalization and, in the context of the reintroduction programs, supposedly a moral appeal not to lose the wolf yet again. The last sentence from the first draft is identical with the final version of the novel, where Billy takes his rifle and shoots the she-wolf in the pit. Then he trades his rifle for her dead body, refusing to accept the bounty economy that values the animal's hide as a proof of it being killed. He keeps his promise to bring her home and carries the dead animal and buries her in the mountains. Both Guy Schuler and Billy Parham are thus transformed from passive observers or witnesses of the animals' deaths to the final executors/bearers of their death. They both kill what they love to spare the creatures further suffering. However, the fate of the whale calf and the she-wolf was sealed long before. In the context of utilitarian anthropocentrism and irresponsibility to nature the killing of the individual creature ironically signifies both a failure to protect (since each and every whale might be the turning point leading to extinction and the pregnant wolf would bring new specimens to the world) and an act of mercy.

"Whales and Men" offers the most open and clear version of McCarthy's attitude to nature, anthropocentrism, and environmental ethics, topics recurring throughout his literary career. A critique of mindless exploitation of nature and warning to what end it may lead, and a vision of Earth under total control of humankind is also suggested in the first draft of the screenplay, by Peter Gregory: "When we have slaughtered and poisoned everything in sight and finally incinerated the earth itself that black and lifeless lump of slug will revolve in the void forever" (McCarthy, "Of Whales and Men" 10P). This vision evokes the ultimate destruction in *The Road* (2006). In the end, the future of not only wolves and whales but of the whole planet depends on the relationship between the human and nonhuman, one of the fundamental topics of Cormac McCarthy's fiction. The whales and wolves then become not only ambassadors of their species and representatives of nature as a whole, but the creatures that can assist us in challenging the anthropocentric perspective and suggesting more humble and respectable views of the world.

The parallels between "Whales and Men" and other McCarthy's works help to "decipher" some more obscure motifs and references in McCarthy's novels. While the environmental readings of Arnold and Lilley focus more on the relationship of the human to the nonhuman, this essay has made a step toward the nonhuman, pointing out the mutuality of the relationship and importance of an analysis of the nonhuman elements, such as wolves and whales. While both species have a rather long and rich history of cultural representation, McCarthy does not use them as mere symbols, and it has been demonstrated above that he provides a more scientifically accurate imagery of these creatures. They are not just mirrors of humans; they exist as individual entities that are caught in the human-nonhuman relationship, which has fatal consequences for them. There is no sense of victory over the natural world but rather a sense of tragedy rooted in the failed responsibility of humans in general, which cannot be overturned by the individual characters' attempts. The speeches and attitudes of the characters toward the nonhuman are important, yet both the wolf and the whale are represented as equally, if not more, important than the human characters. The complexities of human-nonhuman relationships have also been extensively studied by Lydia R. Cooper in her recent monograph *Cormac McCarthy: A Complexity Theory of Literature*. Similarly, as the nonliterary concepts can enrich reading McCarthy, the archival materials, which certainly harbor more treasures and fascinating details on McCarthy's writing methods, might enable us to better understand the development of his imagery and shed new light on various aspects of his published works. A step toward the nonhuman already has and will continue to extend our understanding of this author so deeply fascinated with the material world and its physical, philosophical, environmental, and ethical dimensions. McCarthy's ability to describe in this case two animal species with scientific precision and yet with enough humbleness that he does not pretend to know everything about them is in itself a demonstration of respect for their otherness. This combination of knowledge, curiosity, and humility creates natural imagery both original and worth exploring.

NOTES

1. This notion is slightly contested by the recent Dianne C. Luce and Zachary Turpin's paper "Cormac McCarthy's Interviews in Tennessee and Kentucky, 1968–1980," published in the *Cormac McCarthy Journal* in 2022.

2. "Of Whales and Men" is the title of the first draft, which was altered to "Whales and Men" in the final draft. I follow the consensus and refer to the text as "Whales and Men." The title "Of Whales and Men" is used only to refer specifically to the first draft and thus differentiate between the two versions.

3. In her essay "The Road and the Matrix: The World as Tale in *The Crossing*," Dianne C. Luce points out thematical parallels between the works and the concurrence of their origin (205).

4. There is an interesting if marginal link between "Whales and Men" and *The Counselor*. At the beginning of "Whales and Men," the tennis and yacht club organize an auction of a lion cub, which is bought by John Western for Kelly to basically save it and provide it with a decent life, supposedly at a sanctuary. In the first draft, the scene is accompanied by a handnote, "Chateau Thoiry," a famous French zoo and botanical garden. The irresponsible and ethically questionable captive breeding of the large felines in the United States has been a concern for several decades now. The whole scene adds another layer to the screenplay's exploration of the troublesome relationship between humans and their environment as the cub becomes a commodity to be monetized, even though in a different way than the whales. In *The Counselor*, Malkina owns two cheetahs who are one of the symbols of her status since cheetahs are very difficult to breed in captivity and thus extremely expensive in comparison with other large felines.

5. I explore the relationship between McCarthy and these authors in more detail in "A Vulnerable Predator: The Wolf as a Symbol of the Natural Environment in the Works of Ernest Thompson Seton, Jack London and Cormac McCarthy," in *Mediating Vulnerability: Comparative Approaches and Questions of Genre*, edited by Anneleen Masschelein, Florian Mussgnug, and Jennifer Rushworth, UCL Press, 2021, 52–67.

6. The gentle giant stereotype tends to be the basis of its portrayal except for an orca. Lawrence Buell explores the position of the whale in the environmental imagery, claiming that "all large creatures have the potential to become environmental icons" (201), and

also mentioning Faulkner's Old Ben in *The Bear*. The whales are perfect candidates for such icons considering their size, intelligence, difference from humans, and rarity (Buell 203).

7. Guy Schuler's skeptical and defeated attitude is reminiscent of older Billy Parham at the end of *The Crossing* where he chases away a desolate stray dog, an antithesis of the magnificent wolf in the first part of the book. Young Billy is in his attitude much more similar to Kelly McAmon from "Whales and Men," portrayed as rather naive and immediately forming an attachment to the whale calf. In his insistence on saving the she-wolf, young Billy also resembles Ahab's madness and single-mindedness turned upside down. Where Ahab wanted to kill the whale, Billy wants to save the wolf. His determination to get her to the mountains persists even after her death when he trades her for his rifle and buries her as the ultimate rejection of what Guy Schuler calls "a religion of utility," which creates another parallel with Kelly, who attempts to protect the calf from sharks in this similar paraphrase of *The Old Man and the Sea*, as mentioned above by Edwin T. Arnold.

8. For more information on the timeline of the wolf extermination, see *The Wolf in the Southwest: The Making of an Endangered Species*, edited by David E. Brown, University of Arizona Press, 1983.

9. McCarthy knew about the reintroduction program and discussed it with Edward Abbey shortly before Abbey's death in 1989 (Woodward 30).

10. Unlike the brutal theater of the beached whales, *The Crossing* begins with a dreamish scene when Billy sneaks out to watch seven (as in the first draft "Of Whales and Men") wolves hunting in the snow, woken up by their calls almost as if they were calling him. This image seems to impact his actions later in the novel when he decides to transport the she-wolf to Mexico, envisioning her future on the basis of this encounter. It is also significant that even though Billy is very close to the wolves, there is no sign that he could be in danger, further challenging the traditional imagery of wolves as merciless killing machines.

11. While it is not completely clear, the syringes were most probably for drawing blood of the living specimens at that point. The idea to euthanize the surviving animals came, according to the text, on the next morning, yet the notion might have been the mixture of the two. In any case, the image of the stranding bears noticeable resemblance to the final draft of "Whales and Men" where Guy Schuler injects the whales with a tranquilizer, while a girl objects to his action. The rupture in the sentiment of the public and the scientists is present both in Lopez's essay and McCarthy's screenplay.

12. Lopez and McCarthy knew each other, and Lopez mentions McCarthy as one of the authors who influenced him (e.g., in his interview with Michael Shapiro for *Michigan Quarterly Review*). In his book *Science and Literature in Cormac McCarthy's Expanding Worlds*, Bryan Giemza confirms that McCarthy contacted Lopez when he was writing *Of Wolves and Men* and they stayed in touch (102).

13. This image translates directly into *The Crossing*, when the she-wolf roams around the Animas Plains: "Before sunrise she was off the plain and she would raise her muzzle

where she stood on some low promontory or rock overlooking the valley and howl and howl again into that terrible silence" (26).

14. This brief comment is yet another testament of the general ignorance and utilitarian mentality toward the environment often present in McCarthy's characters.

15. The image of the eyes of the she-wolf is usually connected with a previously mentioned scene, when her "eye turned to the fire gave back no light and he closed it with his thumb," which can be compared to Aldo Leopold's famous essay "Thinking Like a Mountain": "We reached the old wolf in time to watch a fierce green fire dying in her eyes" (130) and the subsequent epiphany that led to the transformation of his view on the protection of predators. While McCarthy mentions Leopold directly in one of his notes in an early draft of *The Crossing*, his wolf mythology is much more elaborate than Leopold's (Crews 234–35). For extensive discussion on Leopold and McCarthy, see Dianne C. Luce's essay "The Vanishing World of Cormac McCarthy's Border Trilogy."

16. The similarity of the bone structure of a human hand and the bone structure of a flipper is also mentioned in *Moby-Dick*, in the description of "the side fin, the bones of which almost exactly answer to the bones of the human hand, minus only the thumb" (208). When asked about his interest in whales, John Western mentions the recapitulation theory based on the belief that "ontology recapitulates phylogeny." When he sees a whale fetus in a glass vial, it looks like a human fetus. He further elaborates: "I had an uncanny sense that we were somehow included in the whale's history. That we were what the whale might have been. And that he was what we would never be" (McCarthy, "Whales and Men" 95). Julius Greve also points out the substitution of the word "ontogeny" with "ontology" in John's replica, which might be either a mistake or a reference to Lorenz Oken (171–72).

WORKS CITED

Arnold, Edwin T. "Cormac McCarthy's *Whales and Men*." In *Cormac McCarthy: Uncharted Territories*. Edited by Christine Chollier, Presses Universitaires de Reims, 2003, 17–30.

———. Foreword. *Notes on Blood Meridian: Revised and Expanded Edition*, by John Sepich. University of Texas Press, 2008, xi–xvii.

Brown, David E., ed. *The Wolf in the Southwest: The Making of an Endangered Species*. University of Arizona Press, 1983.

Buell, Lawrence. *Writing for an Endangered World: Literature, Culture, and Environment in the U.S. and Beyond*. Belknap, 2001.

Cooper, Lydia R. *Cormac McCarthy: A Complexity Theory of Literature*. Manchester University Press, 2021.

Crews, Michael Lynn. *Books Are Made Out of Books: A Guide to Cormac McCarthy's Literary Influences*. University of Texas Press, 2017.

Giemza, Bryan. *Science and Literature in Cormac McCarthy's Expanding Worlds*. Bloomsbury Publishing, 2023.

Greve, Julius. *Shreds of Matter: Cormac McCarthy and the Concept of Nature*. Dartmouth College Press, 2018.

Kovářová, Kateřina. "A Vulnerable Predator: The Wolf as a Symbol of the Natural Environment in the Works of Ernest Thompson Seton, Jack London and Cormac McCarthy." In *Mediating Vulnerability: Comparative Approaches and Questions of Genre*. Edited by Anneleen Masschelein, Florian Mussgnug, and Jennifer Rushworth. UCL Press, 2021, 52–67.

Leopold, Aldo. *A Sand County Almanac and Sketches Here and There*. Oxford University Press, 1949.

Lilley, James D. "Of Whales and Men: The Dynamics of Cormac McCarthy's Environmental Imagination." In *The Greening of Literary Scholarship: Literature, Theory, and the Environment*. Edited by Steven Rosendale. University of Iowa Press, 2002.

Lopez, Barry. "A Presentation of Whales." *American Earth: Writing since Thoreau*. Edited by Bill McKibben. Library of America, 2008, 696–711.

Luce, Dianne C. "The Road and the Matrix: The World as Tale in *The Crossing*." In *Perspectives on Cormac McCarthy*. Edited by Edwin T. Arnold and Dianne C. Luce. University Press of Mississippi, 1999, 195–220.

———. "The Vanishing World of Cormac McCarthy's Border Trilogy." In *A Cormac McCarthy Companion: The Border Trilogy*. Edited by Edwin T. Arnold and Dianne C. Luce. University Press of Mississippi, 2001, 161–97.

Luce, Dianne C., and Zachary Turpin. "Cormac McCarthy's Interviews in Tennessee and Kentucky, 1968–1980." *Cormac McCarthy Journal*, Volume 20, number 2, 2022, 108–35.

McCarthy, Cormac. *All the Pretty Horses*. 1992. Picador, 2010.

———. *Blood Meridian or The Evening Redness in the West: 25th Anniversary Edition*. Vintag International, 1992.

———. *Cities of the Plain*. 1998. Picador, 2010.

———. *The Crossing*. 1994. Picador, 2010.

———. "The Crossing." Typescript, early draft beginning dates October 1987. Heavily corrected. Irregular pagination. Cormac McCarthy Papers Box 55, Folder 6, Southwestern Writers Collection, The Wittliff Collections, Texas State University, San Marcos.

———. "The Crossing." Typescript, first draft, [1991]. Heavily corrected. Irregular pagination. Cormac McCarthy Papers Box 57, Folder 2, Southwestern Writers Collection, The Wittliff Collections, Texas State University, San Marcos.

———. "Of Whales and Men." Unpublished screenplay. Typescript with holograph corrections in pencil. Cormac McCarthy Papers Box 97, Folder 1, Southwestern Writers Collection, The Wittliff Collections, Texas State University, San Marcos.

———. "Whales and Men." Unpublished screenplay. Photocopy of printout draft with holograph corrections in pencil. Cormac McCarthy Papers Box 97, Folder 6, Southwestern Writers Collection, The Wittliff Collections, Texas State University, San Marcos.

McCarthy to Woolmer, 27 August 1986, Woolmer Collection of Cormac McCarthy Box 1, Folder 6, Southwestern Writers Collection, Texas State University, San Marcos.

Melville, Herman. *Moby-Dick: An Authoritative Text, Contexts, Criticism.* Edited by Hershel Parker. Third Norton Critical Edition. W. W. Norton & Company, 2018.

Payne, Roger. *Among Whales.* Scribner, 1995.

Peebles, Stacey. *Cormac McCarthy and Performance: Page, Stage, Screen.* University of Texas Press, 2017.

Phillips, Dana. "History and the Ugly Facts of *Blood Meridian.*" In *Cormac McCarthy: New Directions.* Edited by James D. Lilley. University of New Mexico Press, 2002, 17–46.

Robisch, S. K. *Wolves and the Wolf Myth in American Literature.* University of Nevada Press, 2009.

Sanborn, Wallis R. *Animals in the Fiction of Cormac McCarthy.* McFarland & Company, 2006.

Scoones, Jacqueline. "The World on Fire: Ethics and Evolution in Cormac McCarthy's Border Trilogy." In *A Cormac McCarthy Companion: The Border Trilogy.* Edited by Edwin T. Arnold and Dianne C. Luce. University Press of Mississippi, 2001, 131–59.

Shapiro, Michael. "The Big Rhythm: A Conversation with Barry Lopez on the McKenzie River." *Michigan Quarterly Review,* Fall 2005.

Woodward, Richard B. "Cormac McCarthy's Venomous Fiction." *New York Times Magazine.* 19 April 1992, 28–31.

Cormac McCarthy's Idea of Race

JOHN VANDERHEIDE

 From his earliest novels, Cormac McCarthy was constructing essential links between ideas of race and nation, figuring certain white supremacist racial categories as foundational elements of America's material and semiotic being, its social or political ontology. While biological notions of race are evoked in it in ironic or humorous ways, McCarthy's fiction consistently treats race as a social idea, one entangled inextricably with certain economic and theological ideas also defining the nation's being. The Anglo-Saxon America that emerges from across McCarthy's novels is thus one isomorphic with bell hooks' powerful conception of Western society as a "white supremacist capitalist patriarchy" (hooks 22). Similar to hooks's work, McCarthy's fiction finds entangled in American social and political ontology white supremacist ideas about race with capitalist economic ideas about debt and work, patriarchal ideas about gender and sexuality, as well as Anglo-Saxon theological ideas about salvation and damnation. As elaborated in what follows, in his earlier novels of the Appalachian South such as *Child of God*, McCarthy constructs the idea of race and especially the racial difference between white and Black as a social and metaphysical problem without solution. The novel turns Blackness into an allegorical sign of the white protagonist's ontologically antagonistic standing with his community and society, making clear the entanglement of that society's white supremacist racial ideas with its core economic and theological beliefs. In later, outlier southern works such as *The Stonemason* as well as those set in the borderlands of the American Southwest and northern Mexico such as *The Crossing*, race is shown even more clearly to be a problematic social idea, but these works also pose solutions to the problem, with racialized characters evoking figures meant to reconcile and transcend racial difference. Whether these symbolic solutions falter or fail, there remains much for McCarthy scholars to unpack in his consistent engagements with the problem.

Of course, many excellent studies related to the issue of race in McCarthy's works have already been written. Especially informing my present approach are two recent essays from 2014 and 2020: Jennifer A. Reimer's essay "All the Pretty Mexican Girls: Whiteness and Racial Desire in Cormac McCarthy's *All the Pretty Horses and Cities of the Plain*" and Noemí Fernández Labarga's "No gray middle folk did he see": Constructions of Race in *Suttree*." Both Reimer and Labarga pursue rhetorical analyses of the racialized tropes and figures McCarthy deploys, and both focus their analysis on only one racial difference: Reimer on the racial differences of Mexicans to whites in McCarthy's Border Trilogy, and Labarga on those of Blacks to whites in the late Appalachian novel *Suttree*.

Even in her singular focus on the racial othering of Mexicans (especially Mexican women) in McCarthy's Border Trilogy, Reimer presumes more broadly that McCarthy's America represents "a world system that *must* mark the limits of the nation and the race through a violent process of racial and gendered othering and exploitation" (Reimer 429). The racial othering of Mexican women characters in the Border Trilogy is from Reimer's perspective an instance of a broader systemic process that would by necessity affect, however differently, Black, Indigenous, or other women of color as well. In her rhetorical analysis of the intersection of race and gender in Mexican characters such as Alejandra and Magdalena, Reimer adapts the Africanist lens developed by Toni Morrison in *Playing in the Dark: Whiteness and the Literary Imagination*. Morrison's Africanist lens provides a theoretical overview of recurrent rhetorical strategies in American literature that affirm an Anglo-Saxon racial hierarchy with white men at the top and Black women at the bottom. Reimer applies Morrison's rhetorical tools to her own analysis of the Mexican tropes in the Border Trilogy; and Labarga, acknowledging Reimer, follows suit in applying Morrison's Africanist lens to *Suttree*'s Africanist tropes. While she too finds what Morrison calls metonymical displacement, metaphysical condensation, and fetishization in McCarthy's crowning Appalachian work—involving Black characters such as Ab Jones and Mother She—Labarga ultimately concludes that "*Suttree's* caricatured Africanist presence acts as a way to reveal that white literary identity is as constructed, as exaggerated, and as unnatural as marginalized identities" (145). In short, the constructedness of race (whiteness and Blackness) and its hierarchies reveals the unnaturalness of the social ontology that requires them to exist and function in the first place. As whiteness becomes de-universalized, so the social ontology guaranteeing its supremacy becomes denaturalized. While *Suttree* may not propose any ostensible or positive solutions to the problem of race, it at least affirms its social essence in its denaturalizing figurations of racial difference.

My own approach follows Reimer and Labarga, acknowledging that in McCarthy the Anglo-Saxon idea of race cannot be separated out from the larger idea of the nation itself, its own social or political ontology. Over the course of his career, McCarthy's fiction came to present two sets of racial differences—Black to white, and Indigenous to settler—as especially essential to Anglo-Saxon America's historical idea of itself. To illustrate more clearly McCarthy's consistent approach to these differences, I juxtapose it throughout with the theoretical work of bell hooks, but also the works of Frank Wilderson III, Saidiya Hartman, and the Afropessimist movement more broadly. In *Red, White & Black: Cinema and the Structure of U.S. Antagonisms*, Wilderson provides a materialist conception of American political ontology in which the nation's larger social machine, in part by material force or constraint and in part by semiotic or linguistic strategies, confers different "ontological" statuses—of varying degrees of capacity and incapacity—to white, Black, and Indigenous populations (49). Not unlike bell hooks's threefold conception of the white supremacist capitalist patriarchy, Wilderson's work conceives American political ontology as originating in three primary "ontological" positions, determined by these three "races," which differ in kind and are irresolvable to one another: the "Red" (Indigenous), the white, and the Black. Accordingly, in American political ontology the white is the "Human," the Indigenous is the "Savage" (who can become human), and the Black is the nonhuman "Slave." If all three racial positions are different in kind, that of the Black thus differs in kind from the other two even further, being barred from the human constitutively. (The "Savage" can become "human" but only if completely assimilated to Anglo-Saxon culture/genocided as to their own culture.) As Wilderson's work draws especially upon the works of Saidiya Hartman and Orlando Patterson, the three writers have been associated together as Afropessimists: the name reflecting their pessimism in regard to any prospect of change in "ontological" position for Black people in American society, even if "ontically" many may enjoy social success, wealth, security, and/or fame. For Wilderson, while the ontic level of immediate experience may have changed in some respects for the better, the ontological level of long experience, the experience of social nonbeing, persists. Even in contemporary Hollywood films with Black protagonists, played by famous and successful Black performers, the "fungibility" that originally defined African Americans as nonhuman Slaves appears to have remained an unconscious social norm, expressed not only in dialogue but also in the form of the narrative action. As elaborated below, the pessimism of McCarthy's own diagnosis of the social problem of race in America as a structural problem resonates in significant ways with the Afropessimist overview of race relations in America.

The Idea of Race in *Child of God*

In his 1997 book *Cormac McCarthy*, Robert Jarrett argues that race generally plays only a marginal role in McCarthy's Appalachian novels, which, as he puts it, "does not necessarily suggest an absence of racial prejudice on the part of the Appalachian South, but it does point to the forces that structure this region in a cultural pattern distinct from the larger South" (26). In favor of Jarrett's nuanced reading, it does seem that most of the critical works on the issue of Blackness in McCarthy's Appalachian novels, such as Labarga's, concentrate on *Suttree*, set in Knoxville, which by far has the most variety of representations of interracial encounters, interactions, and relationships. Taking Jarrett's point that it plays a marginal role in the narrative action of the Appalachian works (with few and often only passing interracial encounters), I still contend that race plays a significant role in *Child of God*'s figurative meaning. Formally speaking, McCarthy is an allegorist. His allegorism shapes the realist narrative action of his works, allowing a field of figurative meaning to detach from that literal action and enter into an interrogative correspondence with it. Even if *Child of God* has little "literally" to do with race, McCarthy employs various figurative or allegorical strategies at crucial turning points to cryptically affirm its meaningfulness in relation to the theological and economic underpinnings of the Appalachian society it depicts.

Race is indeed evoked directly in the narrative's first description of Ballard, which deftly links the biological conception of race with a Protestant theology of judgment and a capitalist economy of debt. As McCarthy writes: "He moves in the dry chaff among the dust and slats of sunlight with a constrained truculence. Saxon and Celtic bloods. A child of God much like yourself perhaps" (4). Ballard is thus firstly declared of both "Saxon" and "Celtic" "bloods," the primary and secondary forms of "whiteness" in McCarthy's America, which in their own historically hierarchical difference (e.g., between the English and Irish) suggest a similar imbalance in Ballard. The affective division between his "truculence" and his "constrain[t]" seems tied to these racial markers also (Saxon constraint and Celtic truculence), foreshadowing the uniqueness of Ballard's eventual focused mania (the fixed wrath he serially pursues). Moreover, in this introductory passage the transition from the ethological and biological to the theological is swift, evoked immediately in the biblical phrase "Child of God." One of the biblical sources of the phrase is 1 John 3:10, where it is placed in opposition to its obverse: "In this the children of God are manifest, and the children of the devil: whosoever doeth not righteousness is not of God, neither he that loveth not his brother" (KJV Online, n.p.). Given its binary pairing with its obverse, "Child of God" should thus be understood not as an isolated descriptive term but as a judgment. In the structure of judgment, good implies evil, innocence guilt, salvation damnation. Indeed the other theologically charged term in the opening sentences of *Child of God*—"chaff"—immediately raises the specter of damnation for the biblically literate. The term in its literal sense is scenically appropriate, given at that moment of narration Ballard is in his barn. But in relation to the self-buffering theological register of the writing, Ballard's proximity to "chaff" figuratively poses his own damnation, even if his tentative status as a "Child of God" of "Saxon and Celtic bloods" suggests the opposite possibility.

At the beginning of the novel, Ballard's theological status is thus called into question. How is the reader to make their first judgment about it? For Ballard, it is not his race that serves as an outward sign of his inward damnation; it is the repossession of his family estate. In Ballard's more Saxon Protestant than Celtic Catholic Appalachian society, theological damnation is primarily signaled if not confirmed, at least for (white) males of Saxon and Celtic bloods, in economic damnation. Ballard's tragedy indeed originates in his criminal reaction to his objective economic damnation. Rather than seeking economic and theological atonement or redemption through work—a state ostentatiously showcased by the character of the blacksmith, who lovingly explains his trade to Ballard's great boredom—Ballard is driven by a perverse wrath to confirm his damnation absolutely, morally as well as economically, ontologically as well as ontically, through a series of escalating crimes. As he begins the irreversible descent into serial murder, rape, and necrophilia that socially and metaphysically confirms his guilt and damnation, Ballard twice encounters a Black figure, both times in the opening part of the novel. In the repetition, Blackness takes on a figurative meaning in relation to Ballard's descent, illuminating as it does the theological-political ontology of Anglo-Saxon Appalachian society.

The first encounter with Blackness is actually a non-encounter, resulting from a racist misperception of Ballard's own making, when he discovers a parked car on the Frog Mountain turnaround and mistakenly thinks he is witnessing an interracial sex scene: "A pair of white legs sprawled embracing a shade, a dark incubus that humped in a dream of slaverous lust. It's a [n—], whispered Ballard" (20). He repeats this statement again, only to be disabused when he sees clearly the man in the car is white. Given that Ballard's subsequent discovery of a parked car at the same turnaround is the inaugural scene of his actual criminal transgression of necrophilia, this initial racist fantasy of witnessing the cultural transgression of interracial sex creates an association between the sexual perversity of necrophilia which Ballard will pursue and that of "slaverous" interracial sex, which Ballard only briefly imagined. "Slaverous" appears to be a McCarthy coinage; in any case, it evokes, in its tying of interracial sex to "slave," "slaver," and "lascivious," racist (and sexist) fantasies of the Black slave's hypersexuality and their seduction of the "morally weak" white slaver (Hartman 88). In the ostentatious yet esoteric portmanteau of "slaverous," the novel thus allegorically figures a relationship between Ballard's systematic lust for corpses and the systematic lust for Black bodies in the white slave-holding South, the latter the allegorically signified of the former. Like a slave, a corpse is both a person and not one. Like the sexual abuse of a slave, the sexual abuse of a corpse can be viewed as the defilement of chattel or property, sex with a thing that only appears (ontically) human, or sex with a thing that (ontologically) belongs or belonged to another human. In both cases, an ontological line is crossed. If signifying nothing else, Ballard's attempt to ontologically antagonize his "Saxon and Celtic" Appalachian society for the sake of his own wrath ends up repeating in analogy an antagonistic racial injustice allowed by that society's very ontological structure. Ballard's association with Blackness is thus complex: he is identified abjectly with the antagonistic nonhumanity of an incarcerated Black man (modern analogue of the Slave). But at the same time, he is also identified as a perverse fulfillment of the white slaver, using power and gender-based violence to make other people his victims and property.

Ballard's association with Blackness is repeated and reconfirmed the second time when, shortly after the first incident, he is arrested and incarcerated in Sevier County jail for attempted sexual assault. Behind bars, Ballard encounters a Black prisoner in the cell next to him. As if to emphasize this character's own damnation in Lester's world, the narrative itself deploys the n word in introducing him, melding in a free indirect discourse with Lester's own racist speech: "They had a [n—] in the cell opposite and the [n—] used to sing all the time. He was being held on a fugitive warrant" (53). Lester himself will soon become a fugitive to the law, and his life will soon be wanted by his own Saxon and Celtic race, so this encounter with the archetypal paradigm of the eminently killable fugitive in the Anglo-Saxon imaginary—a Black man—seems significant. In juxtaposition, the figure of the brutally named "[N—] John" signifies an additional meaning about Lester, something that makes them akin: being completely given over to social death. As [N—] John sings "Flyin home / Flyin like a motherfucker / Flyin Home," the aptly named Sheriff Fate informs him, as Ballard listens and watches, that the only place he will be "flyin" to is "home to [his] maker" (54). The ontological antagonism in Fate's attitude toward the incarcerated Black man is not hard to detect; an analogous kind of ontological antagonism will develop as Fate finds himself pursuing and seeking to incarcerate Ballard. Blackness in this second instance thus once again functions as an allegorical sign of Ballard's own fateful consignment to ontological damnation.

Writers associated with the Afropessimist canon from Orlando Patterson to Saidiya Hartman and Frank Wilderson III take for granted that, in the social and political structure of Anglo-Saxon America, Black bodies have, just by virtue of their racialized difference, been consigned (and continue to be consigned) an ontologically different place than the whites in that structure, even the ones like Ballard who are abjected, "damned," or otherwise given over to other kinds of social death. The persistence of this difference of ontological position for Black Americans attests to what Saidiya Hartman in *Scenes of Subjection* (1997) calls "the impossibility of instituting [for Black people] a definitive break between slavery and freedom, compulsion and consent, and terror and discipline" (130). As Hartman argues, many of the same constitutive features of Black slavery survive in some form in the social and political structuring of Black lives to the present day. Her powerful analysis of the ambiguous transition from slavery to freedom for African-Americans elaborates upon and extends the three constituent features of slavery in the South which Orlando Patterson detailed in his influential 1982 work *Slavery and Social Death*: generalized violence, natal alienation, and generalized dishonor, each of which in their own complexity helps define American slavery as *"the permanent, violent domination of natally alienated and generally dishonored persons"* (Patterson 13). For Hartman, Emancipation did not overturn the ontological position of the Black as vulnerable, natally alienated, and dishonored nonhuman; it merely allowed, in restrictive and rigged ways, for some always reversible ontic gains to be made through the vagaries of work and opportunity.

Beyond his two encounters with Blackness, unreal and real, Ballard suffers forms of violent domination, natal alienation, and generalized dishonor through what befalls him and through his reactions. Like many other McCarthy (anti)protagonists, Ballard is more or less orphaned and kinless. But this orphanhood represents only a relative kind of "natal alienation"; though existentially bereft of kinship relations, Ballard still has a known and transmissible history of kinship, indeed one that links his family to the "White Caps," a Klan-like anti-Black white supremacist association (*Child of God* 165). The natal alienation of Black slaves was incomparably more absolute, for they were separated from their histories, cultures, and languages: bereft not only of kinship and national relations, but also any knowledge of those relations. Even after the end of slavery, Black people in America are, from the Afropessimist outlook, still consigned to an ontological state of "fungibility" (Wilderson 49). From this perspective, Ballard's own objective and subjective undoing can only approximate this ontologically distinct state of the

Black nonhuman, even ending as it does in the utter abjection of his autopsy: "[Ballard's] head was sawed open and the brains removed. His muscles were stripped from his bones. His heart was taken out. His entrails were hauled forth and delineated" (194).

Relating the theological and economic dimensions of Ballard's damnation and social death through the racial sign of Blackness, the novel figures race as an essential part of the theology of American commercial society, the theology of its Anglo-Saxon white supremacist capitalist patriarchy. The Afropessimists find the problem of race so deep and intractable as to harbor no hope for any kind of remedial solution, in whatever reforms or amendments. For not only must white supremacy fall for solutions to racial hierarchizations to become possible, but capitalism and patriarchy would have to fall along with it, so inextricably intertwined are the three. The pessimism of *Child of God* with respect to these matters appears raised to a similar degree of intensity. In ensuring the irreversibility of his social damnation through the serial chain of his crimes, Ballard is able to bring into clearer focus the ontology of the society from which he is abjected and self-abjects: an ontology that requires the absolute otherness of Blackness to determine its own furthest limits, and to ground its most far-reaching social and metaphysical judgments. Ballard's psychopathic line of flight betrays the entanglements American Anglo-Saxon social ontology establishes between ideas of race, theology, and economics. His horror story denaturalizes that ontology, denaturalizing race, but neither Ballard in his line of flight nor any other character in the novel provides a positive figure of an alternative form of social assemblage. The novel even seems to cast the overwhelmingly white Saxon/Celtic chorus of locals witnessing Ballard's actions throughout the novel, inoffensive as they are, as but parts of the "race that gives suck to the maimed and the crazed, that wants [Ballard's] wrong blood in its history and will have it" (156). The pessimism of *Child of God* thus strongly resonates with that of the Afropessimists in their similar convictions that the problem of social ontology—of its machinic assembling of passions, bodies, and goods and its semiotic assembling of events and ideas—have not been determined fully enough yet for any kind of solution to be posed. The narrative knows that race is a social idea, but it does not know how that idea might be overcome socially.

The Stonemason's Failed Resolution to the Problem of Race

In Labarga's analysis of *Suttree*, Black figures appear as Africanist caricatures, but the whiteness of white figures also appears grotesque, so racial difference becomes denaturalized, understood as a social fantasy. My own reading of *Child of God* moves backward in McCarthy's corpus but follows a similar analytic path and comes to a similar conclusion. In its symbolic over-identification of Ballard and Blackness, the novel allegorically figures essential relationships between racial difference, economic hierarchies, and theological judgments, but it stops short in providing symbolic resolutions to them. This "stopping short" may reflect an aesthetic or ethical choice on McCarthy's part, a humility before the complexity of the problem or a demonstration of the writer's control over the allegorical method, which on its own has no inherent limit on extension, including extending from the allegorical description or figuring forth of a problem to that of a solution.

Like *Child of God*, and *Suttree*, *The Stonemason* can be considered a southern work, and I also consider it generically as allegorical. But it is also unlike those works not just because it is a play rather than a novel, and not even because its central protagonist is Black rather than white. It is unlike them in that it is not content just to denaturalize race by linking it to questions of theology and economics, but attempts to provide a figure that transcends race altogether, a figure thus indexing a transformed or different kind of social ontology. Unfortunately, the more an allegory figures a solution to the problems it simultaneously poses, the more moralistic or ideological it becomes. *The Stonemason* in this sense appears much more crudely "allegorical" than a novel like *Child of God* precisely because of the overtness of its moralistic intention, its pretension for attempting to fold the racial otherness of Blackness into something common to all, regardless of race.

In the definitive critical anatomy of the play, Peter Josyph cites the play's moralism as one of the key factors in its not holding up as a work of theatrical art. As he writes, *The Stonemason* is a play "determined to make a point" (137), a work of "studied and relentless moralizing" (138). Interestingly, Josyph suggests the moralizing is a consequence of McCarthy's attempting to "novelize" when he should rightfully have been attempting to dramatize, finding the initial stage instructions McCarthy provides at the beginning of Act I, Scene I, particularly telling as a novelist's ignorance of actual stagecraft. In his splitting of the stage, McCarthy betrays, as Josyph writes, a "deeper fault of stagecraft" in asking the audience to set "Ben 1" outside of the play, since "no measure of high-blown caution [...] will keep the audience *from integrating, or trying to integrate,* the figure of Ben 1 with the action of Ben 2, or alternately, from willing him off the stage" (139, emphasis added).

In his novelistic allegorism, McCarthy would not presume the audience should integrate the Ben on the podium (Ben 1) with the Ben on the stage (Ben 2). Rather he would presume the audience, readers of allegory, should relate the two Bens figuratively, in terms of promise and fulfillment, problem and solution, passing judgment between them. Indeed, the stage directions in the published version of the text state theologically that Ben 1 has "an agenda which centers upon his own exoneration, his own salvation" (McCarthy, 6). These theological terms, moreover, can easily translate into economical ones: Ben 1 is in a relation of (moral) debt to Ben 2: the audience is thus asked to judge whether Ben 1's "Chautauqua" has value enough to redeem the debts incurred, or fulfill the promises made, in the dramatic action enveloping Ben 2. As the stage instructions suggest, the "audience may perhaps be also a jury" (ibid.). Outside these initial stage instructions, the entanglement of theological, juridical, and economic ideas with that of race persists. For whatever other kind of salvation Ben 1 seeks in his "Chautauqua," it is also the salvation from the idea of racial difference (Black to white in particular) as any kind of determinant regarding the physical and metaphysical fulfillment of human life.

For Ben as well as for his papaw, the one determinant for life's fulfillment, regardless of race, is work. *The Stonemason*'s solution to the problem of white supremacy is a respiritualization of work, the reclamation of it from its alienated form of wage labor (working to live later) to its vocational form (living through working), in which the reward for work is both sufficiently material, providing intergenerational familial stability, as well as sufficiently spiritual, providing the worker a unique wisdom gained from their mediated experience of what lies beyond the sphere of individual concern—the common, the cosmic, and the true.

Ben 1 grounds his salvific vision of work on the authority of the Christian Bible, or his deeply Protestant reading of it. To authorize this reading, he cites Old Testament passages on prohibited and proscribed forms of stone working: "There is no historian and no archaeologist who has any conception of what stonework means. The Semitic God was a god of the common man and that is why he'll have no hewn stones to his altar. He'll have no hewing of stone because he'll have no slavery" (66). In this racially complex passage, the white (Irish Catholic) McCarthy makes his Black protagonist racialize his presumably Christian God as Semitic (Jewish/Arab), thus asserting the reconciliation of not just two but three racial types in a religion that historically was introduced to Black slaves by white slavers, who, as descendants of European Christendom, also had a history of entertaining centuries-long internal and external warfare against both Jewish and Arab "Semites." But here Ben reclaims the God of American Christianity for "the common man," a figure who reconciles all the aforementioned races within itself, ending their social antagonism. If their enslaved ancestors had retooled the Saxon Semitic religion that was forced on them into something for themselves, Papaw and Ben have likewise retooled it somewhat anew in their "gospel of the true mason" (10). For the same sacred Book, the Christian Bible, that white Americans used to justify Black slavery, Ben calls a "handbook for revolutionaries" (65), penned by a God that forbids all slavery, a God who would only have everyone, of whatever race, working freely in common with others at whatever freely desired trade or art.

For Ben 1 and Papaw, the way forward (to undoing white supremacist racial hierarchies) is thus a way back to a deeply subjective form of Saxon Protestantism, with faith their refined Abrahamic theology will prove accommodating enough to reconcile racial if not religious differences in its race-transcending figure of the "common man." In stereotyped dialogue, Papaw explicitly dismisses the importance of race as a matter for human concern, stating, "There aint nothing triflin about God. He made everbody the color He wanted em to be and He meant for em to stay that way. And if that suits Him its got to suit me too, else I's just a damn fool" (47). Neutralizing racism theologically, Papaw sounds somewhat theologically essentializing about race. Nonetheless since racial difference is as God willed, it should be of no concern, no conflict, and certainly no ontological antagonism, among people. A reorientation to life's "vertical" axis through vocational work is to solve any conflicts along the less important "horizontal" one of material social relations.

Ben 1's theological-political figure of the "common man" extends an earlier discussion Ben 2 has with Maven in which he argues: "You cant separate wisdom from the common experience and the common experience is just what the worker has in great plenty" (38). Accumulating "common experience," the reflective worker comes closer to God, gaining tolerance for others. But this "common experience" is acquired only through work: "a laborer who thinks, well, his thought seems more likely to be tempered with humanity. He's more inclined to tolerance. He knows that what is valuable in life is life" (38). For Papaw, too, racism is a problem that is solved by work, even as work is acknowledged as a medium for racist conflict. As he says, "Stone aint so heavy as the wrath of a fool and I worked for white men and I was subjugated to that wrath many a time and I become very dissatisfied about my lot in this world. The peculiar thing was that the very thing that brought me to that pass was what led me out of it and since that time I've come to see that more often than not that's how the Lord works" (48). The (Black or white) common man can be "led out" of "the pass" of (anti-Black, white supremacist) racism, but only by a love of work.

Unfortunately, Ben and Papaw's purification of the Protestant work ethic is unable to rid their Protestantism of a need for judgment, and thus a need for damnation as much as its opposite. Balancing the material and spiritual rewards doled out to Papaw and Ben, McCarthy's drama grimly visits material and spiritual punishments upon Big Ben (Ben's father) and Soldier (Ben's nephew, whose given name is also Ben). Both of these fungibly named secondary characters are portrayed, in counterpoint to Papaw and Ben, as idle pleasure seekers: with Big Ben an adulterer and eventual suicide, and Soldier a drug addict and eventual overdose victim. These characters especially appear as Africanist caricatures, shiftless sex and drug-addicted Black men. But their inclusion in the dramatic action seems necessitated theologically and economically. Ben and Papaw treat race as an "ontic" problem, solvable and transcendable by immersion into work. Big Ben and Soldier's deaths silently contradict that conclusion, showing that Black social death remains an "ontological" requirement in a capitalist economy.

Indeed, in the suffering, damnation, and necessary sacrifice of these characters, *The Stonemason* echoes Reconstruction-era primers written by white writers to newly freed Black slaves, enjoining them to work. In *Scenes of Subjection*, Saidiya Hartman examines primers like the 1864 *Advice to Freedmen* written by I. W. Brinkerhoff as white America's early attempts to revise its racial myths to accommodate the newly "freed" Black, exchanging the figure of the slave for that of the self-possessed individual worker "burdened" with a freedom understood economically as the freedom to become indebted. As Hartman states: "The mantle of individuality effectively conscripted the freed as indebted and dutiful workers and incited forms of coercion, discipline, and regulation that profoundly complicated the meaning of freedom" (121, 122). Informed by Hartman's analysis, the meaning of freedom that Ben provides in his "Chautauqua" becomes complicated, given the punishment visited upon his father and nephew, cautionary figures appearing to function only to coerce, discipline, and regulate the will to work. For Ben, work guarantees that racial difference is just an ontic accident, with no deeper roots, nothing "ontological" about it. In Afropessimist terms, however, insofar as Big Ben and Soldier's deaths appear dramatically necessary, *The Stonemason* reaffirms rather than repudiates the ontological difference of Blackness as nonexistence in the theology of America's white supremacist capitalist patriarchy. Ben's purified singular figure of the "common man" fails as a symbolic resolution to racial differences and hierarchies because the "common experience" that the figure is said to accumulate is in the end a false universal. The dramatic necessity of Big Ben and Soldier's deaths ironically reveals a "common experience" common only to Black characters, the experience of one's death as something socially demanded. *The Stonemason* betrays the "pessimism" of earlier works such as *Child of God* in providing a symbolic resolution to the racial difference they affirmed as inscribed into America's social or political ontology. But the betrayal is not worth it in the end, as the resolution falls back into the logic of the social ontology from which it wanted to escape. In asserting that racial difference and hierarchization are mere ontic "conflicts" rather than ontological "antagonisms," McCarthy's Black protagonist fatally undermines his vision of the common experience of the cosmic or divine in vocational work, disavowing the ontological nature of racial antagonisms, and thereby failing to achieve a truer sense of what is common.

The Crossing's Alternative Resolution to the Problem of Race

Published in the fall of 1994, only months after the release of *The Stonemason*, *The Crossing* was the much-anticipated second installment of the Border Trilogy, as well as the third novel set in the border regions of the American Southwest and northern Mexico, beginning with *Blood Meridian or The Evening Redness in The West*. As mentioned above, Jennifer Reimer's work demonstrates how the Border novels traffic in racially othering Mexicans through their use of caricature and stereotype (such as the animalization and fetishization of the Mexican woman). For Reimer, the rhetorical use of Mexican caricatures is one way McCarthy's white American male protagonists can confirm their own racial, gendered, and national identity. Reimer focuses on one of these protagonists exclusively, John Grady Cole, and his two doomed Mexican loves, Alejandra and Magdalena, from *All the Pretty Horses* and *Cities of the Plain* respectively. But the problem of race is not only articulated in a white-centered racial othering of Mexicans. After *Blood Meridian*, a historical novel spanning the years 1833–1878 which follows a gang of genocidal mercenaries operating in the border regions of Mexico and the U.S., *The Crossing* is also deeply invested in interrogating problematically the Indigenous figure in its confrontation with the corresponding figure of the European-descended settler (American and Mexican alike).

In "*The Crossing*'s Noble Savagery: The Wolf, The Indian, and The Empire," Molly McBride argues that if "Native Americans play an important though not predominant role in McCarthy's Southwestern fiction" (71), it is because their very presence illustrates the genocidal success of European settler colonialism's own imperialist will to limitless expansion. The novel establishes a metonymical connection between the Indigenous figure and the figure of the wolf as different near-genocided objects of that will's aggression. As McBride writes: "The Indian and the wolf are not only coconspirators, they are mirror figures: both are drifters, both take food from the rancher, both are considered feral by the Anglo settlers who invaded their territory from the east and north, and both must kill to survive. Wolf and Indian are adversely affected by colonization and its impact on the environment" (73). In the Africanist lens adapted by both Reimer and Labarga, the noted conflation of "Indian" and "wolf" might appear to signal the possible animalization of the racial other, the erasure of the other's humanity that Toni Morrison calls "metaphysical condensation." But for McBride, rather than animalizing the Indigenous figure, the association between the wolf and the "Indians" in *The Crossing* links Indigenous genocide and the equally methodical extermination of wolves as two consequences of a settler colonial society's desire for its own growth. Put in Afropessimist terms, McBride's argument demonstrates how *The Crossing* reflects the relationship between white (Saxon and Celtic) settlers and Indigenous people as ontologically antagonistic rather than merely ontically conflictual.

McBride also notes that the novel makes use of racial caricature, especially in the construction of the figure she refers to as "the Indian," though in fact in the novel the initial *i* is never capitalized. In his first appearance in the narrative action, we thus read: "The indian Boyd passed crouching on his heels did not even raise his eyes so that when he sensed him there and turned the indian was looking at his belt and did not lift his eyes even then until he'd stopped altogether" (McCarthy 5). As McBride suggests, the stealthy or treacherous "indian" is a caricature common to Western fiction. But equally for her, the caricatured aspect of the character is immediately undermined by the similarity of his clothing and dialect to those of Boyd and Billy. As she concludes, "Thus, McCarthy's Indian is no noble savage. His situation in 1940s America is one of destitution and homelessness as a result of a century's advancement from 'savagery to civilization'" (McBride 72). Granted, any pity a reader may wish to project upon *The Crossing's* "indian" is obstructed by the possibility that he may be the murderer of Boyd and Billy's parents. But as the Cherokee writer Thomas King notes in *The Inconvenient Indian*, there are other Indigenous caricatures than just "the noble savage": as he writes, "There was [also] the bloodthirsty savage, [...] and the dying savage" (40). If McCarthy's "indian" may not be a noble savage, he may be a treacherous and bloodthirsty one. When Billy finds out about his parents' murder, he asks the sheriff, "Were they Mexicans?" The sheriff responds, "They was indians. Or Jay Tom says they was indians" (167). However, the sheriff is uncertain, and the accusation is only based on secondhand hearsay. Boyd is the only witness, and he does not explicitly confirm that one of the murderers was "the indian." All this supports McBride's argument that the figure of "the indian" is not a racist stereotype, but a critical deconstruction of one.

For Thomas King, the noble savage and the bloodthirsty savage were both really just iterations of the third figure of the dying savage, which in some sense is the central Indigenous figure that America's white supremacist capitalist patriarchy uses to explain itself. As King writes, "Dead Indians are the only antiquity that North America has. Europe has Greece and Rome. China has the powerful dynasties. Russia has the Cossacks. South and Central

America have the Aztecs, the Incas, and the Maya. North America has Dead Indians" (76). It is not surprising then that *The Crossing*'s "indian" is not only coded as potentially bloodthirsty, but also as dying or dead, as belonging to the past. Upon their first encounter, Boyd looks into "the indian's" eyes, which were "so dark" that Boyd sees himself reflected in them twice over and feels as if he were looking at "some cognate child to him that had been lost who now stood windowed away in another world where the red sun sank eternally. As if it were a maze where these orphans of his heart had miswandered in their journey in life and so arrived at last beyond the wall of that antique gaze from when there could be no way back forever" (McCarthy 6). McBride thinks this passage confirms him as the eventual murderer of the Parhams, but the very fact that the passage comprises an extended simile casts doubt on that conclusion. In any case, the simile makes "the indian's" gaze "antique," and coming from "another world where the red sun sank eternally," descriptions that figure him quite ostentatiously as a Dead or Dying Indian, with the redness of the sun invoking both the color and the "setting/dying" attributed to Indigeneity in historical discourse. Whether "the indian" killed the Parhams is actually textually irresolvable, but at the very least, this early encounter with a Dead or Dying "Indian" seems retroactively to foretell of Boyd's own eventual vanishing and death, not to mention his subsequent transformation into a generic legend. As McCarthy associates his tragic Saxon-Celtic protagonists with Blackness in his Appalachian works, so in *The Crossing*, he associates his ill-fated European-descended (American, but also Mexican) settler-colonial protagonists with Indigeneity. Their social deaths once again reveal, this time from the analogue of an Indigenous perspective, the theological and economic underpinnings of America's white supremacist capitalist patriarchy, and possibilities of other forms of life.

In *Manifest Manners: Narratives on Postindian Survivance*, Anishinaabe cultural theorist Gerald Vizenor argues not just the obvious, that the name "Indian" is of European linguistic derivation, an "occidental" or "colonial" invention (11 and 24), but that it is best understood generally as a simulation, a fiction capable of producing material effects. In this case, what the simulation (re)produces is the ongoing material "dominance" of American Anglo-Saxon settler society over the Indigenous peoples and nations whose lands it has stolen and turned into property. As Vizenor writes: "The word Indian, and most other tribal names, are simulations in the literature of dominance" (10). In a later work, *Native Liberty: Natural Reason and Cultural Survivance*, Vizenor places the notion of "the indian" (now written in the lowercase) in an oppositional relationship to that of "the native," writing: "The indian, of course, has no real referent, no actual native ancestors. The simulation of that name is a colonial enactment. The indian is the absence of natives. The name is an ironic noun, a simulation of dominance that transposes native memories, imagic moments, and stories of survivance" (NL 162). In "the indian" *The Crossing* presents its first Indigenous character as a caricature and "simulation of dominance." For McBride the novel deconstructs the caricature in part by juxtaposing the figure of "the indian" with the figure of the wolf, aligning both as populations targeted for genocide by American capitalist imperialism. However, while she cites another important Indigenous figure in the novel, Quijada, she does not dwell enough on the significant relationship the novel establishes between Quijada and "the indian," which turns out to be an oppositional one, like Vizenor's antagonism between simulations of dominance and survivance.

Quijada first appears to mediate the nonviolent release of the Parhams' stolen horses back to Billy and Boyd. He addresses the boys, and at Billy's request, writes a receipt for the returned horses, and ensures they leave unharmed. His second appearance is near the end of the novel when, heralded by a "red sun that burned in the broad gap of the mountains," he is visited by Billy at his "small weatherboard cabin" (McCarthy 383). To say the least, the return of the "red sun" imagery signals the scene's allegorical prescription of reading Quijada in relation to "the indian," and as himself Indigenous. In this late scene, Quijada tells Billy what he knows about the circumstances of Boyd's death, advising Billy to leave Boyd's remains in Mexico, saying to him that "[his] brother is in that place which the world has chosen for him. He is where he is supposed to be. And yet the place he has found is also of his own choosing. That is a piece of luck not to be despised" (387, 388).

From his two brief appearances, Quijada appears a complex portrait of Indigenous survivance. Not only in contrast to "the indian" does Quijada enjoy a proper name, occupation, personality, and the sketch of a history; the character is based on a historical person. As Steven L. Davis shows,[1] McCarthy drew the character of Quijada from the Southwestern folklorist J. Frank Dobie's recollections of Lupe Quijada, a "Yaqui" (Yoemem or Yoeme or Hiaki) man who indeed worked as a superintendent at the American magnate-owned Babícora ranch during the time period in which *The Crossing* is set. Dobie relates that the real Quijada studied French and Greek at an American college but that his pride "was not Mexican. It was far more that of the Indian" (Qtd. in Davis 55). The first time Billy and Boyd encounter him, Quijada discerns that they are American and immediately addresses them in English, suggesting he is likely trilingual at the least: speaking English, Spanish, and his mother tongue, Yoeme. In this first encounter, Billy and Boyd are too preoccupied with getting their horses back to notice or reflect on Quijada's fluent English in speaking and writing, or the likelihood he learned it to work for the American that currently owned "property" set in the place his people had chosen and had been chosen by, prior to any Mexican or American presence.

Even in their second encounter, Billy seems too self-absorbed to appreciate Quijada's difference. Telling Billy he cannot know the "soul of Mexico" since anyone who claims to know it "is either a liar or a fool" (385), Quijada tersely conveys to Billy the state of epistemological deficit he is in with respect to the nonhuman agency of the place he has come to. Mexico's soul is older than both the Spanish-descended Mexicans and the Anglo-Saxon-descended Americans, and it had other names before its current one. Quijada tells Billy that "[the] Yaqui have long memories" (385), implying that it is the Yaqui, rather than the Americans or Mexicans, who know most about the place and its agency. When Billy thus asks Quijada how he can work at an American-owned ranch so hated by the Mexicans, Quijada replies "I am not a Mexican. [. . .] I dont have these loyalties. These obligations. I have others" (385). These other obligations, which he refuses to elaborate on further, are neither to the Americans nor to the Mexicans, whose presences he must nonetheless mediate. Rather, they are to his own nation and to the place itself, the land around them that comprises his nation's traditional territory.

Quijada's concepts of place and world invoke a critique of language that McCarthy pursued in other contexts, including his nonfiction article "The Kekulé Problem," in which language is conceived as operating in distinction to the organism's "biological unconscious" (n.p.). In *The Crossing* Quijada opposes language to the world in a similar way: "The world has no name. [. . .] The names of the cerros and the sierras and the deserts exist only on maps. [. . .] And it is because these names and these coordinates are our own naming that they cannot save us" (McCarthy 387). As "the world" cannot be contained in human language, language cannot be used to denote the experience of the world. Language is unable to convey directly the nonhuman agency of a given place, not to mention the experience of this agency, which may be common to some in the place but not all. Boyd's acceptance by the "soul of Mexico" is signaled in the corrido sung of him. As Quijada explains, the corrido itself predates Boyd but nonetheless accommodates him retroactively, as one who abandoned himself to the land. When Billy asks Quijada if he thinks the corrido tells of Boyd, Quijada replies: "Yes, it tells about him. It tells what it wishes to tell. It tells what makes the story run. The corrido is the poor man's history. It does not owe its allegiance to the truths of history but to the truths of men" (386). Opposing the discursive truths of the Western idea of history to the biological and social truths of human beings as they have experienced them, Quijada also happens to echo Sioux writer Vine De Loria Jr.'s critique of the West's notion of history and his assertion that "ceremonies, beliefs, and great religious events of the tribes were distinct from history; they did not depend on history for their verification. If they worked for the community in the present, that was sufficient evidence of their validity" (102). It seems for Quijada the corrido is one of the "poor man's" ceremonies for celebrating place and world outside of history.

The "poor man" is thus *The Crossing*'s alternative to *The Stonemason*'s "common man." As I argued above, Ben's "common man" reduced the ontological antagonism of Black and white in American society to an ontic conflict surmountable through a religious devotion to freely chosen work. But *The Stonemason*'s conception of experience was too monolithic to achieve its goal of overcoming the problem of race, ultimately falling back on the ontological necessity of Black nonexistence in its caricatured depictions of the deaths of Big Ben and Soldier. Almost as if to correct *The Stonemason*'s approach, Quijada presents the alternative weakly utopian figure of the "poor man." Enacting a kind of disenchantment in Billy if not the reader also, the poverty of Quijada's "poor man" is in part epistemological: the poor man's poverty of knowledge about the world, but also the world's poverty of knowledge about the poor man, who lives and dies beneath the notice of history. This epistemological impoverishment is presented in the novel's linear movement from "the indian" to Quijada: from a racial stereotype masquerading as an object of knowledge to a historically based figure that refuses to be one, from a simulation of dominance to one of survivance. In his resistance to be known to Billy, Quijada maintains an ontological antagonism between Billy's culture and his own. In such a state of "poverty," disenchantment, and epistemological deficit, Billy learns of worlds outside of his own national and cultural history, worlds where white supremacist ideas of racial difference dissolve, alongside certain economic ideas of debt and certain theological ideas of judgment.

Conclusion

The Stonemason and *The Crossing* do not give isolated treatments of unrelated racial problems; they both project a broader vision of America's social or political ontology as it is, and give signs of emergent utopian alternatives. Whatever these emergent social forms, their solution to the systemic structure of white supremacy in American social ontology must involve an attitude of epistemological poverty in the search for what is truly common. Even though *The Stonemason* deals exclusively with the racial otherness of Black people to white people, and *The Crossing* deals predominantly with the racial otherness of Indigenous people to European settlers, and of Mexican people to white Americans, the approach to racial difference in both cases betrays the same allegorical vision of an Anglo-Saxon idea of race essential to American political ontology, an idea of Anglo-Saxon superiority which is troubled especially (though not exclusively) by the racial otherness of Black and Indigenous peoples, those they enslaved and those they genocided and colonized to bring their own commercial society into being.

Indeed, a self-conscious triangulation of the Black (Africanist), "Red" (Indigenous), and white (Saxon/Celtic) positions as irreducible to American social ontology is already apparent in McCarthy's 1985 novel *Blood Meridian or The Evening Redness in the West*. Cornered and defeated at the climax of the novel's narrative action, the character Glanton refers to the Yuma leader about to execute him as a "mean red [n—]" (286). And near the end of the novel, a similar rhetorical fusion occurs when the "kid" (now "man") encounters an orphan named Elrod and his crew. Showing them his "scapular" of dried ears, Elrod and the others mistake them at first for the ears of runaway Black slaves:

> [n—] ears, by god.
> They aint [n—]
> They aint?
> No.
> What are they?
> [I—]. (333)

In these and other rhetorically racist fusions of Indigeneity and Blackness, *Blood Meridian* suggests an "ontological" connection between the distinct but inseparable events of Black slavery and Indigenous genocide at the origin of the nation. As such briefly outlined examples show, there is more for McCarthy scholarship to make of his consistent treatment of race as a social idea.

NOTE

1. See Davis's "Mining Dobie: Cormac McCarthy's Debt to J. Frank Dobie in *The Crossing*." *Southwestern American Literature*, Volume 38, number 2, Spring 2013.

WORKS CITED

Davis, Steven L. "Mining Dobie: Cormac McCarthy's Debt to J. Frank Dobie in *The Crossing*." *Southwestern American Literature*, Volume 38, number 2, 2013.

De Loria, Jr., Vine. *God Is Red: A Native View of Religion*. Fulcrum, 2003.

Hartman, Saidiya. *Scenes of Subjection*. Oxford University Press, 1997.

hooks, bell. "Eating the Other." In *Black looks: Race and Representation*. South End Press, 1992.

Jarrett, Robert L. *Cormac McCarthy*. Twayne Publishers, 1997.

Josyph, Peter. "Older Professions: The Fourth Wall of *The Stonemason*." *Southern Quarterly*, 1997.

King James Bible online. https://www.kingjamesbibleonline.org/

King, Thomas. *The Inconvenient Indian*. Anchor Books, 2013.

Labarga, Noemí Fernández. "'No gray middle folk did he see': Constructions of Race in *Suttree*." *Cormac McCarthy Journal*, Volume 18, number 2, 2020.

McBride, Molly. "*The Crossing*'s Noble Savagery: The Wolf, the Indian, and the Empire." In *Sacred Violence, Volume 2, Cormac McCarthy's Western Novels*. Edited by Wade Hall and Rick Wallach. University of Texas at El Paso Press, 2002.

McCarthy, Cormac. *Blood Meridian or The Evening Redness in the West: 25th Anniversary Edition*. Vintage International, 1992.

———. *Child of God*. Vintage International, 1993.
———. *The Crossing*. Vintage International, 1995.
———. "The Kekulé Problem." Published in *Nautilus,s* April 17, 2017.
———. *The Stonemason*. Vintage International, 1995.
———. *Suttree*. Vintage International, 1992.
Reimer, Jennifer. "All the Pretty Mexican Girls: Whiteness and Racial Desire in Cormac McCarthy's *All the Pretty Horses* and *Cities of the Plain*." *Western American Literature*. Volume 48, number 204, 2014, 422–42.
Patterson, Orlando. *Slavery and Social Death*. Harvard University Press, 2018.
Vizenor, Gerald. *Manifest Manners: Narratives on Postindian Survivance*. Bison Books, 1999.
———. *Native Liberty: Natural Reason and Cultural Survivance*. University of Nebraska Press, 2009.
Wilderson III, Frank B. *Red, White & Black: Cinema and the Structure of U.S. Antagonisms*. Duke University Press, 2010.

The Black and White Jacksons
Nonarbitrary Racial Conflict and the Resonance of the Racial Sign in Faulkner and McCarthy

PETER LURIE

 The following essay's approach to *Blood Meridian* finds it grounded in a fraught sociohistorical context, one in which the novel's oft-remarked violence depicts a racial animus that reverberates across its regional workings and through an intertextual dynamic with Faulkner's Yoknapatawpha. The latter, as we know, is a fictive space marked by anti-Black bias and one Faulkner shapes with a language that painfully voices the South's deep scars. My discussion thus positions itself against some of the most notable and important critical approaches to McCarthy we have, some of which define his work as uniquely abstracted from the tensions that animate Faulkner and literary studies generally that concern themselves with race.

Dana Phillips, for example, in his encompassing article "History and the Ugly Facts of Cormac McCarthy's *Blood Meridian*," sees its events—including if not especially its most violent acts—as mundane doings in a scenario marked by indifference and "human failure" (447). One example for Phillips is the random burning of a man in a pitcher of aguardiente outside a bodega. Despite a belated and inept attempt to help, the scene's onlookers arrive to discover only the man's "blackened shriveled [body] in the mud like an enormous spider" (McCarthy, *Blood Meridian*, 280). Referring to the characters' detachment from what they witness, Phillips writes that the tendency of human action "to be other than brutal" here and throughout the novel "is not treated [. . .] as a departure from the ordinary course of events. It is just another event" (447). Phillips cites Lukács in suggesting that the novel is not a version of epic; yet he avers elsewhere that McCarthy is in fact neither writing historical fiction in the strictest manner. "Neither the history of the American West nor natural history is put forward in *Blood Meridian* as the last vestige of the mysterious or lyrical," he writes. "Natural history makes the provisional quality of all human interpretations of events [...] painfully apparent" (448–49). Provocatively, Phillips claims that aspects of the novel preclude such interpretations: "Once psychology, morality, and politics come to be seen as mere languages," a fact Phillips attributes to McCarthy's characters' opaque speech, "propriety becomes a highly relative question, even an uninteresting one" (449). (By "propriety" here, Phillips seems to refer to a Lukácsian sense of the purview of history as mediated by the literary.) Steven Shaviro's widely cited essay "'The Very Life of the Darkness': A Reading of *Blood Meridian*" pursues a similar nonpolitical or, we might go so far as to say, amoralistic approach. Shaviro calls the book's powerfully nonreferential language a prose he describes as "in intimate contact with the world in a powerfully nonrepresentational way" (153). He appears to agree with Phillips when he claims the novel offers a version of characterization in which "there is no subjectivity." Finally, David Holloway, one of McCarthy's most formidable formalist critics, refers to the "steady accumulation of detail [that] drips a logic of *différance* relentlessly into the text" of *Blood Meridian* (193), including the ways the two eponymous characters of this essay, the white and Black Jackson, are "tabernacled [...] in exchange and so on in an endless complexity of being," as Judge Holden puts it (147).[1]

Yet the words of McCarthy's text are not quite empty signifiers. In genuine deference to Holloway and others' powerfully attentive deconstructive readings, we should allow that words and their sound have meanings that register differently in various interpretive contexts. As one example, and perhaps outside the views of the scholars cited above, stands the singular moment in the book of the white Jackson's murder by his counterpart, the Black Jackson. I say "singular," for the event is unique for its clear motive in and response to racial animus. The Black John Jackson (who shares a first name as well as a surname with his white counterpart, a point to which I'll return) kills the white Jackson in response to the latter insulting him by forcing him from his vicinity at one of the Glanton gang's camps. In what follows, I do not mean to subvert the powerful rendering of the novel's strangeness in what I provisionally call apolitical readings by the likes of Phillips, Shaviro, and others. Their attention to the prodigious force of McCarthy's writing is crucial to McCarthy studies and our sense of the writer's accomplishment. Rather I build on their work to trace a powerfully resonant sounding—both figurative and otherwise—of a racial politics that suggests a link to Faulkner, one we may not have yet acknowledged and that deepens our sense of what McCarthy says about the West, American racial history, and his work's contiguity with the earlier writer.

Blood Meridian's narrator introduces the two Jacksons the chapter before the gruesome murder in a manner both offhand and portentous. Chapter 7 begins with the typically detached voice stating, "In this company there rode two men named Jackson, one black, one white, both" in a further coincidence, "forenamed John" (85). Immediately, however, the narrative tone shifts when the narrator states, "Bad blood lay between them," before he goes on to describe how the white John Jackson "would fall back alongside the other and take his shadow for the shade that was in it and whisper to [the black Jackson]" (85). Despite our learning that "the white man laughed and crooned things [...] that sounded like the words of love," the fact that the Black Jackson "would check or start his horse to shake [...] off" his antagonist indicates that such "crooning" he hears is not an expression of affection (85).

And sure enough, twenty-odd pages later the "bad blood" manifests in violence. The narrator says nothing of the fuller history that lies behind these two riders, men whom Glanton, we learned earlier, "simply reckon[ed] [...] among his number" (85). Yet for events that take place in 1849 we do not have to speculate much as to the cause for racial conflict. A free Black working among Glanton's white crew would not have been impossible in Texas; it was predominantly a slave state at the point when the novel's events occur. Yet the vast Mexican Cession territory through which the Glanton gang travels was not settled territory nor within a particular slave or free "jurisdiction." Glanton may have reckoned these two men among his numbers while being indifferent to their race. The two Jacksons themselves, however, are not.

Obviously the history of enslavement is enough to comprise the mutual "bad blood" they feel. Yet several elements of this portion of the novel and the episode of the white Jackson's murder are notable. One is McCarthy's only seemingly arbitrary naming of them. "John Jackson" is an only slight variation on Jack Johnson, the African American boxer who, McCarthy surely knew, became the first Black heavyweight champion in 1908 by beating the white Tommy Burns. The event was years in the making and enjoyed extensive media coverage, including by the adventure writer Jack London, who, like many American observers, saw the fight as a window onto racial definitions of character.[2] The bout was among the first sporting events to be recorded by the fledgling medium of film—a recording that stopped, notoriously, at the moment when Johnson's victory was secured. In mentioning Jack Johnson, I do not mean to suggest the boxer as a source for McCarthy's rendering of the two Jacksons in his novel. Yet I also cannot see his use of naming or the sounds of the forename/surname of his characters to be wholly arbitrary. "John Jackson," the same name shared by these two men in *Blood Meridian*, and "Jack Johnson" are very close as verbal signifiers.[3] As such, they echo the history of both sportive and social conflict the early prizefight occasioned. The echoic re-sounding of such conflicts is a principle of my reading of this event in McCarthy's novel and across the regional and textual spaces he shares with Faulkner. Following a wager placed by Bathcat, the Welshman who joins the company and challenges Toadvine to a bet about "which Jackson would kill which" (86), we see his prescience in declaring a few pages later "the blackie will do for him" (91).

After a tense encounter with a juggler and a fortune teller who reads Jackson's card, one depicting a "fool in harlequin and a cat" or "El tonto," as the fortune teller reads (97), only a few nights later the enmity between the two Jacksons erupts. This is presaged by the meeting with the juggler and the blind "seer"; though blindfolded, she also intuits that this card had been drawn, as she says, by "El negro" (97). When she speaks further in Spanish about the card's meaning and its bearer's fortune, Jackson demands to learn what she says. Only the judge can respond: "I think she means to say that in your fortune lie our fortunes all" (97).

That fortune is first revealed—or the first part of it realized—in the following chapter. After Glanton murders an aged native woman in a town square who'd been injured during an attack at another camp, the company spends the night near a cantina where they find the proprietor's son bleeding from a wound during a card game. When they move on to another campsite, the narrator presages the outcome of both Bathcat's bet and the fortune teller's untranslated words, declaring "the murder that had been reckoned upon took place" (111). What follows is an act that stands out in the novel for many reasons. To begin, notwithstanding the extreme, pervasive violence toward and between natives and the white bounty hunters that defines the world of *Blood Meridian*, this act alone is prompted by an instance of personal racial hate. In McCarthy's rendering of the white Jackson's death, we also find an uncanny reverberation of several acts of racial violence in Faulkner. In the case of McCarthy's novel, these echoes are augmented by the curious use, as well as peculiar non-use, in *Blood Meridian* of the racial epithet for Black people.[4]

The Black Jackson's long-simmering anger galvanizes at the campsite when he tries to sit among the white Jackson and the other white men of the company. There were two fires at the camp, one of which was attended by the Delaware scouts Glanton had recruited along with other newcomers to the gang. The narrator makes clear the putatively egalitarian nature of social relations within the larger group: "There were two fires in the camp and no rules real or tacit as to who should use them" (111). For reasons that McCarthy does not make explicit—but which become the more audible for that—the white Jackson sees fit to break those rules on this particular night. Noting the other(ed) campfire gathering, when the Black Jackson "threw down" his saddle blanket and sat down, the white Jackson repels him: "with a gesture and a *slurred oath* he warned the black away" (my italics 111).

McCarthy's always resonant language in describing what follows suggests much about what lies beyond this scene. By which I mean both the larger world the novel encompasses—as well as what lies beyond its own historical context—and the moments from Yoknapatawpha it recalls. Moving immediately from the white Jackson's "slurred oath" and what I will suggest is a slurred but yet-audible (racial) curse, the narrator offers in the next sentence a Judge Holden-like decree: "Here beyond men's judgments all covenants were brittle" (111). What is perhaps not clear is the nature of these "brittle covenants" nor, perhaps, what the narrator refers to as "here." That spatial designation may well be the camp and the borderland where the novel's events take place. The covenants he mentions, though, could be any, as it appears that all agreements between people are brittle in a world defined by earlier McCarthy scholars by wanton, destructive violence and its barely pecuniary motives (such as those that the Glanton gang pursue). What is clear here is that the white Jackson has rendered a judgment of personal bias based in race.

In response the Black Jackson ultimately withdraws from his place by the fire. He first opposes the white Jackson, declaring, "Any man in this company can sit where it suits him," but his antagonist threatens him with his pistol, declaring "You dont get your black ass away from this fire I'll kill you graveyard dead" (112). The Black Jackson glances at Glanton, also seated nearby, who merely watches in typical indifferent silence. He then gives the white Jackson a last challenge, asking "Is that your final say?," to which he responds, "Final as the judgement of God." Following this fatal pronouncement the Black Jackson relents. But in recompense he will return moments later and will calmly, and as the narrator states, "ceremony[iously]" (112) stave off the white Jackson's' head with a bowie knife.

Before the Black Jackson leaves the campfire to, then, return, the narrator describes the light that emanates from it. And he does so tellingly. "About that fire were men whose eyes gave back the light like coals socketed hot in their skulls," McCarthy writes, "and men whose eyes did not" (111). Jackson's eyes stand in a different relation to both the light and to time hence that will follow these doings: as the narrator states, "But the black man's eyes stood as corridors for the ferrying through of naked and unrectified night from what of it lay behind to what was yet to come" (111). After his following, final exchange with his white counterpart and leaving the refracted firelight in the other men's eyes, Jackson leaves and then comes back to emerge "out of the darkness bearing the bowieknife in both hands like some instrument of ceremony" and "with a single stroke swapt off [the white Jackson's] head" (112). Following this ritualistic act, "Two thick ropes of dark blood and two slender rose like snakes from the stump of his neck and arched hissing into the fire" (112).

This passage and what surrounds it stand as a conjunction of the resonant nexus between Faulkner's and McCarthy's texts. At its center is the role in both writers' works of a word that, as we've seen, is muted or "slurred" here, but that features audibly and at key moments as the engine of similar violence in Faulkner. Additionally, this recursion serves to extend meaningful acts of racial confrontation in Yoknapatawpha and their own "ferrying through" of "what was yet to come" in McCarthy's novel and in both men's fiction—as well as in the world beyond.[5]

As we know, much of the violence that occurs in Faulkner's oeuvre does not hinge on the racial epithet. Racial animus runs deep in his world, whether or not his characters give voice to it. Yet as recent scholarship in digital humanities has shown, the epithet's use by white men (in particular, though not exclusively) tracks across particular intersectional conflicts of race and class.[6] And as our students have taught us, the clamor of this term can be felt loudly—it can resonate—well beyond its immediate sounding. (I refer to the fact that no one utters this word in the classroom. Even when we encounter it in reading from the works in question or in others).[7] Sound itself figures prominently in the white Jackson's murder. As does an equally vivid visual imagery. As I show, their conjunction and interplay bodies forth in McCarthy's text similar acts of racial confrontation in Faulkner.

It is worth noting first, however, the immediate reaction to the Black Jackson's action. Or, we should say, nonreaction. The white Jackson's unmitigated racism, which prompts the murder, is not common among the other men. No one among the company does or says anything about the Black Jackson's action. Despite what appears their shared bias against native people throughout the book—whom they consistently use the epithet for Black people to describe—they do not object to a free Black person in their midst acting out a version of racial recompense against one of their own. That indifference and the Black Jackson's racial rage seem far from the apolitical climate that Phillips and others attribute to the novel.

That in fact deeply political act owes its textual meaning as well as some of its effects— and affects—to McCarthy's debt to Faulkner. As I mentioned, sound figures powerfully in the author's rendering of the campfire scene—of any of the novel's "scenes," including other lyrical or stylized accounts of horrific violence. Here McCarthy insists on readers *hearing* the prose that describes the white Jackson's murder. After he has been struck by the bowie knife, we read, "Two thick ropes of dark blood and two slender rose like snakes from the stump of his neck." The assonance of "ropes" and "rose" are taken up in the next sentence, as we learn that "the head rolled to the left." The sibilance of the blood "hissing" in the fire extends the "s" that sounds when "the black [had] stepped forward and with a single stroke swapt off his head." This auditory property, along with the passage's strikingly imagistic quality (about which more in a moment), ensures we hear the prose that relays the event.

What such aural prominence lends the scene, I suggest, or among the reasons for McCarthy adopting it, is its bodying forth of the "sound" of racism that is elsewhere not voiced in the text. The racial epithet is never uttered in the passages that describe the Black and white Jacksons; we never hear the white Jackson's sinister whisperings as he rides alongside his antagonist or the "slurred oath" with which he "warned the black away" at the fire. Yet that word appears in the novel's opening pages. And it does so in close connection with a clear evocation of enslavement as well as with Toadvine, a character who figures importantly in this connection owing to certain physical features as well as what we glean are his own racial proclivities.

When in the book's first chapter the kid leaves home and crosses Tennessee heading west as "a solitary migrant on that flat and pastoral landscape," the narrator includes in that setting "Blacks in the field, lank and stooped, their fingers spiderlike among the boils of cotton. A shadowed agony in the garden" (5). Clearly an image of the enslaved in Tennessee, these figures' "shadowed agony" in the "garden" of the rural south in 1849 evokes the social terrain of the plantation and that, we can readily surmise, subtended acts like the white Jackson's and marks them and the peculiar institution as biblical taintings. Nothing in the novel suggests any Edenic innocence in the American "garden," among the reasons that McCarthy's irony here may be so ringing. As though to emphasize the link of slavery's racism to the appearance of the white Jackson much later, McCarthy uses the word "anchorite" here—his only other use of it in the novel—to describe both him and earlier, in chapter 1, the crazed hermit the kid meets after burning the hotel. Important to this connection is the hermit's confession to the kid that before living alone in his squalid prairie dwelling, where he harbors a "n—'s [dried] heart," he'd formerly "come from Mississippi," where he'd been a slaver (16).[8]

This passing reference to African sufferance ("Blacks in the field") does not figure in the kid's travels, which lead, on the same page, to his entering, first, Saint Louis, then New Orleans, and finally riding a boat from thence to Texas. Here the major action of the novel will take place over its next three hundred pages. "Only now," arriving in that contested borderland, "is the child finally divested of all that he has been," the narrator claims portentously (5). "His origins are become as remote as is his destiny and not again in all the world's turning will there be terrains so wild and barbarous to try whether the stuff of creation may be shaped to man's will or whether his own heart is not another kind of clay" (6). An echo of the "garden" in which the enslaved toil in Tennessee, "the stuff of creation" in which the entire novel shows its male characters' willful exertions, the fact that the human heart is indeed another kind of "clay" than any that scripture imagined—this passage and all that it presages may be said to encompass—or to resonate with—the fact of African "agony" in the South's cotton fields. This passage may mark the shift from McCarthy's Appalachian to his Western phase. But that shift carries with it the southern scenario that links him to Faulkner and in ways in which this novel, the first of his Western books, echoes Faulkner deeply.

Among the first of those instances is the description of the white Jackson's death. As I mentioned, that event is marked aurally by McCarthy's prose in relaying it and in a manner, I suggest, that bears the mark of the novel's other sounds and their contexts. In a moment we will see affinities between the white Jackson's death and Faulkner's account of Joe Christmas's dying moments in *Light in August*, a novel that itself resounds with both racial violence and a near-incantatory textual sounding of the racial epithet or "sign." That word appears at several points in *Blood Meridian*. Significantly, its first utterance is by the narrator. Still in the first chapter, after the novel's introduction of Judge Holden in the tent revival meeting, this passage is animated by the presence of another of the novel's main characters, Toadvine. The kid and Toadvine had met the night before near the "jakes" outside a saloon, where in their first encounter they fight in a typically bloody, muddy contest (9). The next morning, however, they become better acquainted, and Toadvine will accompany the kid in his wanderings with the Glanton gang for nearly the entirety of the novel. Two details from Toadvine's first description recur in the account of the white Jackson's murder; a third figures provocatively in how we might hear the others and their textual resonance with other sonic and semantic emanations.

When the kid and Toadvine commence fighting, the latter "threw down the bottleneck" with which he attacks the kid "and unsheathed an immense bowieknife from behind his neck. His hat had come off and his black and ropy locks swung about his head" (10). The bowie knife later returns as the Black Jackson's weapon of vengeance, and we noted the "ropy" streams of blood that issue from the white Jackson's neck when he is killed. By this I do not mean to suggest that Toadvine's introduction and its mention of the knife as well as his ropy hair prefigure the later event, precisely. While these lexical details do return—or re-sound—they do so by way of an odd feature of Toadvine's physiognomy. The morning after his and the kid's nearly fatal fight, as they make peace the narrator notes that in addition to the letters

"H," "T," and "F" branded into Toadvine's forehead, "the kid could see that he had no ears" (11).

Only a few lines later the novel pronounces the racial epithet for the first time. Toadvine and the kid have wandered into a dramhouse where they will seek a man named Sidney. When they entered the room, "There were no patrons. The barman looked up when they entered, and a n— that had been sweeping the floor stood the broom in the wall and went out" (12)—rightly so, for what ensues is Toadvine's act of arson when he sets fire, first, to the door to Sidney's room and then to the whole building. The episode recalls Faulkner's "Barn Burning" in several ways, including the fact that, before the kid and Toadvine mount the stairs to Sidney's room, they "leav[e] varied forms of mud behind them on the floor" (12).

What is striking about this conjunction of details is their configuration. We hear the first use of the epithet in the novel a few pages after its reference to slavery, but on the same page in which McCarthy points to a character who "had no ears." In addition to adding to Toadvine's appearance as a grotesque, this strange lack of appendage does not seem to affect his hearing; he can converse freely with others. Yet the blockage or stop on hearing that it connotes implies the odd vacuum into which the epithet's expression will somehow be swallowed up—only to recur or resonate obliquely and in other registers across the book's pages. A few moments later, for example, after the whole hotel is aflame and the kid rides past a group of men "standing around watching it" (15)—similar to the group of onlookers in *Light in August* attending the spectacle of Joanna Burden's house's fire (*LiA* 196)—we hear that the kid's mule "kept shaking his head sideways as if it had something in its ear" (14). That "something" ringing troublingly in this nonhuman auditory canal is the redounded sound of the n-word, a lingering impact that extends through the novel in its bizarre application to non-Black characters like the American Indian and in the not fully suppressed "oaths" and curses of men like the white Jackson.

Light in August furnishes perhaps the most immediate precursor in the Faulkner corpus for the white Jackson's death. Yet the resonance of the oft-cited passage involving Joe Christmas and Percy Grimm is different from that which, I suggest, suffuses *Blood Meridian*'s internal aural vibrations. As we've seen—and the register I stress here is visual—the white Jackson dies when his head is cut off. There are beheadings in Faulkner, including Joanna

Burden's at the hands of another rightly angered racial subject in Yoknapatawpha. A similar incision to the one that the Black Jackson performs also occurs in *Go Down, Moses*, when Rider elegantly severs the cheating dice dealer Birdsong's neck in "Pantaloon in Black." I trace a line from this novel's several acts of black-on-white violence forward to *Blood Meridian* shortly.

The moment of Joe Christmas's death has been read widely. What I hope to stress newly here are the ways in which its imagery and its meanings made a particular impact on McCarthy and the intertextual dynamic I've been tracing. "Books are made out of books," critics are fond of quoting McCarthy stating (Phillips 436).[9] The echo I find in the instance of black-white conflict I've cited, and which shows a distinctly nonarbitrary action and more than a Derridean play of signs, is, first, visual. When Joe lies dying on Gail Hightower's kitchen floor, after Grimm's grisly acts of shooting and then castrating him,

> he looked up at them with peaceful and unfathomable and unbearable eyes. Then his face, body, all, seemed to collapse, to fall in upon itself, and from out the slashed garments about his hips and loins the pent black blood seemed to rush like a released breath. It seemed to rush out of his pale body like the rush of sparks from a rising rocket; upon that black blast the man seemed to rise soaring into their memories forever and ever. They are not to lose it, in whatever peaceful valleys, beside whatever placid faces of whatever children they will contemplate old disasters and newer hopes. (513)

While we cannot say this of Grimm or his descendants, surely McCarthy and others who view (or read) this scene "are not to lose it." It "soar[s]" into a common memory and into informed, subsequent acts of writing like McCarthy's and the acts of violence they describe. Like Joe's blood here, the "ropes" of the white Jackson's blood "rose," as we've seen earlier, "and arched" into the Glanton camp's fire, from which "a gray cloud of smoke rose" and produced "columnar arches of blood" (112). The visual emphasis on rising; the repetition, in McCarthy's passage, of the assonantal repetition in Faulkner—these elements are pronounced ("unfathomable . . . unbearable; seemed . . . seemed; black blast"). When the white Jackson's head falls "from the stump of his neck," it "came to rest at the expriest [Tobin's] feet where it lay with eyes aghast" (112). Different from Joe's "unfathomable and unbearable eyes," Tobin's eyes in McCarthy nevertheless repeat an expression and a mode of address we've seen in Faulkner and one attending an act of acute racial violence.[10]

Importantly for this analysis, the celebrated passage in *Light in August* ends with a direct reference to sound. Or rather, to the extinguishing of the siren that approaches the Hightower house but which, as the chapter ends, "pass[es] out of the realm of hearing" (513). There was shock or alarm sounded in the text at the rise of Joe's blood "like the rush of sparks." But, like the memory of Christmas's eyes contemplating his murderer, this note is suppressed or sealed up within a textual break—here, the chapter's end. This enveloping is then completed in the following chapter, which presents our last view of Hightower and turns toward a visual rather than auditory rendering of the scene in its opening line: "Now the final copper light of afternoon fades; now the street beyond the low maples and the low signboard is prepared and empty" (514).

The significance for my argument of this abrogating of sound at Joe's death and beyond it is its impact on what Julie Beth Napolin, in her reading of Faulkner and Walter Benjamin, calls "The Fact of Resonance." She points to the stunning coincidence of Benjamin asking Adorno in 1940, in one of the final letters of their celebrated correspondence, if he had read Maurice Coindreau's translation of *L'umière d'août*. She uses Benjamin's remarks about sound recording in the 1930s to posit that "Faulkner's propagative technique of working with voices and sonorities continually indicates the social and historical constraints of physical perception in the present, but also the possibility that perception, [and] the forms of recognition and intimacy it admits, might become otherwise" (172). She points to Benjamin's 1932 radio address about the great 1927 Mississippi flood, one in which he cites the testimony of a survivor and ends with a warning to his German audience of the dangers of the Ku Klux Klan. In her rendering of this caution, Napolin maps the temporal movement of sound and silence across both Benjamin's text here and in *Light in August* in ways that redound to my effort to perform what she calls "Faulknerian listening," a mode of hearing that allows "stories [to] release their affective potency after a long time" (172). That time, traced here, includes the span across the writing of Faulkner's and, then, McCarthy's later text. As Napolin says of Benjamin's warning about the Klan, and that is apposite to the intertextual dynamic I trace here: it was "a haunting echo of what is to come" (174).

This is the siren's echo that re-sounds in McCarthy's novel. Yet it is a sound which, appearing in a later work, pointedly attends events that took place long before those that occur in the historical context of *Light in August* as well as in Faulkner's other major works I treat here. This is the recursion or resonance of my essay's title, the signal appearance—as well as telling suppression—of the racial sign, the epithet for Black people, as well as the hatred and rage it subtends, that recurs in such oddly configured ways in *Blood Meridian*. The racial violence at the heart of *Light in August*, Faulkner's most violence-saturated novel, was itself a warning. And one that echoes *back* to the South's and the country's history, a history that encompasses that of the extended 1840s scene of McCarthy's book as well as forward to his writing it. Faulkner's muting the siren at Christmas's death does not, that is, prevent it from being audible at other points, among them in the later scenario of McCarthy's writing and the events he depicts. And the scenario of our reading them. Napolin traces the complex ways in which, in *Absalom, Absalom!*, Rosa Coldfield's voice (acousmatic, as Napolin describes, a sound emanating from no clear source) as well as her body act as a medium for the resonance of the gunshot that kills Charles Bon.[11] "It is the form of inaudible content," Napolin says of Rosa's voice; "it finds its ground in residual auditory acts" (180). One of those acts is Quentin and Shreve's sustained renarrating of Rosa's story in the novel's closing chapters. I suggest this "residual auditory act" includes not only the acts of other characters within Faulkner, but by way of his fiction's interlocutors, those of readers like McCarthy. Such examples of Faulkner's words that resonate in *Blood Meridian* do so by way of their affinity, for example, with the white Jackson's murder but also, as I've been describing, in how the novel amplifies the discordant note of the racial "sign" in Faulkner's corpus.

Joe Christmas spends his life being called the n-word. The dietitian uses it in the passage when she discovers him in her closet; in the same scene she refers to the other children using the term, potentially at the instruction of Doc Hines. Joe's struggle over his identity's external designating is precisely what Napolin calls "inaudible content." Joe—and the reader—continually hears this word applied to him. But we never "hear" Joe's internal musing or reflection on its meaning. We hear what he hears externally, and we note key words and their repetition. In addition to those mentioned above are Joanna Burden's sexualized fetish of the pronouncement "Negro! Negro! Negro!," an utterance that resonates across Joe's psyche and informs his act of silencing her. We know of the Christian catechism that McEachern forces Joe to memorize and Joe's evasion of its precepts. We understand that these acts of forced listening sear a racialized and religious "scar" on Joe's internal hearing and his incapacity to express what any of it means to him. Napolin refers to Benjamin's essay "News of a Death" to make an important point about the overlaps between Benjamin's optical and acoustical apperceptive models. Referring to the well-known visual emphasis in the "Work of Art" essay, the "optical unconscious" that Benjamin saw motion pictures animate, she suggests an "acoustical unconscious, an incomplete counterpart to his optical theory that nonetheless resounds across [Benjamin's] writings and fragments" (180). Joe's experience in *Light in August* is thoroughly visualized, as others have detailed, particularly around cinematic and photographic tropes.[12] The imagistic quality to his death that I describe above also attends the key passage that opens Chapter VI, when the novel turns the temporal movement of the narrative back to the orphanage. "Memory believes before knowing remembers," the chapter famously opens, before the narration describes the "sootbleakened" "big long cold echoing building of dark red brick [. . .] set in a grassless cinderstrewnpacked compound surrounded by smoking factory purlieus [and . . .] the bleak windows where in rain soot from the yearly adjacenting chimneys streaked like black tears" (131). Into, or rather from within this visualized prose will erupt the dietitian's shrill exclamation only pages later when she discovers Joe: "'You little rat! You little n— bastard!" (135).

Her accusing voice will stay with Joe for the rest of his life, fusing with those of others such as Joanna Burden and Percy Grimm. As such, this voice and the word it hurls at Joe affects him in the manner Napolin shows Benjamin to claim: "Shouldn't we speak of events which affect us like an echo— one awakened by a sound that seems to have issued from somewhere in the darkness of past life?" (Benjamin 206, quoted in Napolin 180). The overlap of the verbal and the visual here is what, after Napolin, I mean to stress in referring to a Benjaminian "acoustical unconscious" in Joe that harbors knowledge of—and unhealed injury from—"events which affect [him] like an echo."

The temporal displacement here is key. And it will allow me to turn to other Faulkner moments that, I argue in closing, make McCarthy's links to Faulkner more "audible" or explicit. Joe's murder of Joanna Burden is one example of his effort to articulate (or voice) a resistance to others' treatment of him. If I suggest that the Black Jackson's murder of his own white counterpart offers a later instance of a writer showing a similar outcome to characters' use of a racial sign, I do not mean to overstate the connections between Christmas and McCarthy's characters. Other moments appear in Faulkner, however, that more readily link to the Black Jackson. Their own resonance within Faulkner's corpus, moreover, allows me to connect them to McCarthy more fully and to draw the lines of my argument together.

Elsewhere I have written about the way events in *Go Down, Moses* recur within the novel's temporal and narrative workings so as to show their links and their progressive change.[13] When Lucas Beauchamp threatens his cousin Zack Edmonds by holding a knife to his throat in "The Fire and the Hearth," he does not ultimately kill him. Later, however, in "Pantaloon in Black," we see Rider follow through on an act of racial self-assertion when he cuts Birdsong's neck during a dice game. Prior to Rider entering the shed where the game takes place, the narrator describes him "crossing the junctureless backloop of time's trepan" (114). The temporal "backloop" Faulkner enacts across the novel brings Rider's action back to Lucas's, or it echoes and repeats it, here with a meaningful difference. (Rider follows through on an act Lucas doesn't finish.) Part of my discussion of the novel emphasizes its links to classical cinema, the silent film of Faulkner's upbringing which, like events in *Go Down, Moses*, draws on the workings of contingency or chance to imply a temporal openness rather than a narrative form or a sense of history—and therefore of the future—that is predetermined or closed. That is to say: Rider's act links back to Lucas's progressively. I cannot here elaborate fully the terms of my earlier argument about the novel's ending and the role in its stories of the indexical mark that film captures and which, as the theorist Mary Ann Doane elaborates, allows for the impression of contingency and play.[14] What I can do is extend the interior model of *Go Down, Moses* forward to McCarthy. The Black Jackson, like Rider, acts with a racial purpose that some critics overlook in *Blood Meridian*. Contrary to some readings that stress a metaphysics of violence in the novel, I describe how McCarthy's characters enact their own deeply motivated meanings or response to events. And their occurring bodies forth an echo marked across a shared textual and narrative "sounding" of a kind of racial confrontation at the heart of both Yoknapatawpha and *Blood Meridian*.

The most ringing echo of Faulkner sounding in the two Jacksons' conflict arrives by way of a key moment in *Absalom, Absalom!* Rosa Coldfield and Clytie do not share a surname, as McCarthy's characters do. Yet they do reside together in the Sutpen home for a long period, and they share an interracial bond that Rosa herself describes as a kind of sisterhood (116). Like the Black and white Jacksons in *Blood Meridian*, they are also engaged in a sustained conflict, one that reaches a crescendo in an act of physical force. When Rosa arrives at the mansion after learning of Bon's murder, she races up the stairs to try to get to Judith and see her lover's corpse. Or rather, she tries to do so before she's arrested in her urgency by Clytie's "*untimorous*" hand (115).

Julian Murphet concludes *Faulkner's Media Romance* with this moment and an extended reading of what follows. To Murphet the scene and the verbal exchange it engenders between the two women stands out for several reasons, above all the way it serves as a block to the romance materials that otherwise furnish the basis for the Sutpen narrative and on which, to Murphet, Faulkner draws—but refashions by way of incorporating the period's mass communications media. Murphet's gambit is that Faulkner's modernism can be defined by this odd conjunction of old and newer aesthetic forms. The moment with Clytie is significant in his analysis because of the patent failure of Rosa's objection to being touched by her Black antagonist, expressed in her shrill demand to Clytie's obstacle: "Take your hand off me, n—!" (115).

I cite this moment for all of its reverberations. Rosa's insult fails, as Murphet points out, because it appears in Rosa's monologue in a passage that is followed by the long period in which, after Bon's death, Rosa moves into the mansion and lives peaceably and productively with Clytie and Judith in what she calls a "*convent*" (128). Rosa's earlier use of the epithet with Clytie performs initially as a shibboleth, as a marker of what Murphet cites Derrida to describe as a place where "one must pronounce a *shibboleth* properly in order to be granted the right to pass" (Derrida, "Shibboleth: For Paul Celan," cited in Murphet 275). Marc Redfield comments on Derrida's essay in ways that are helpful here: "But *shibboleth* poses singular complications. [...] It is less, more, and other than a word; and to the extent that it is one, no language can properly claim it. It owes these complications to a narrative that made it unusually mobile, capable of traveling from one end to the other of recorded history, and across any number of languages" ("*Shibboleth* 1" np). I will return to the sense of a word, a shibboleth such as the epithet, that is "unusually mobile" across and within Faulkner's and McCarthy's texts, "capable of traveling" across vast historical spans. That word in *Blood Meridian*, as we've seen, is also "other than a word," appearing or registering in realms it should not (e.g., a nonhuman ear or in the presence of a character like Toadvine, who lacks the organ for hearing). As Murphet elaborates on the crucial passage from Rosa above, and in ways that will resonate with my claims about McCarthy, that shibboleth for Rosa falters; it does not grant her access to the "closed door" (121) beyond which lies Bon's body. "Something is missing here [in chapter 5 of *Absalom, Absalom!*]," Murphet avers, which is, namely, "that unpronounceable word whose meaning would matter less 'than, let us say, its signifying form once it becomes a password'" (Derrida cited in Murphet 275).

That shibboleth for Rosa is the term for Clytie she uses as an imperative: "Take your hand off me [...]!" Yet as Murphet argues, it fails to operate as the meaning-making word she intends. Because Rosa utters it too late. It follows and, I will say, blends with what Murphet calls the echo of the "last shot" of the Civil War: the sound of Henry shooting Charles Bon at the Sutpen's Hundred gate (274). This is the echo Napolin traces through Rosa's attenuated hearing, the resonant sound that exists in fact outside of its source, which Rosa is too far away in Jefferson to have heard when it happens. The "fall of eggshell shibboleth of caste and color too" (115) that Rosa had declared before she inveighs against Rosa is what allows the eight-month period of the women waiting for Sutpen to be the communal experience which, in McCarthy's novel, never occurs: a found, shared endeavor and space that ignores racial difference. Faulkner wrote *Absalom* fifty years before McCarthy published his magnum opus. But the echo of Faulkner's work and the ugly signifier it uses at key moments is audible in the later writer's return to an earlier historical period.

Napolin is at pains to show how Faulkner's narrative "grammar" works alongside his sonic treatment to fashion a particular kind of space for characters and readers alike. The bells that chime in the Jefferson church, for example, that had done so in 1833 when Thomas Sutpen arrived repeat their ringing to Quentin's ear in 1909. She notes the curious "detuning" of the bells' chime between the two dates, a fact that Faulkner's description includes and which allows Napolin to claim that the otherwise unifying impact of this localizing sound displaces the hearer: there is a gap in audition, she claims, for "the sound is not the same, though it is reiterative" (182–83). In connection to this "gap" Napolin finds a "desubjectivizing" or "de-substantiating" on the part of Faulkner's characters. Pointing to Faulkner's stylistic and formal attenuating, she claims that "narrative [in his case] has put the subject as a coherent substance into question" (183).

This is a similar claim to that of McCarthy criticism with which I began this discussion. According to some readers, there is little in *Blood Meridian* to merit traditional novelistic analysis such as considerations of psychology, subjectivity, or motive. The moment of the white Jackson's murder, though, operates precisely as such an instance of human identity and subjecthood. One of the values of sound studies like Napolin's is the way her work allows us to see—or to hear—the singular importance of the Black Jackson's act as piercing, like Barthes's *punctum*, an otherwise "silent" textual working. As we've seen, there are sounds and particularly fraught words that appear at key junctures in the book's workings. Their auditory register, or rather their displaced audition into other sections of the narrative and as echoes of events, not only from earlier in *Blood Meridian* but also from the works of another writer, allows them to make an even more urgent claim.

"Who hears?," Napolin asks, in her discussion of the bells in the *Absalom* church, pointing to "an atmospherics of the past, one that haunts the written word as it struggles to predicate its own subject" (183). She offers this after she has posited the de-, and then "re-substantiating," of the subject of Faulknerian narrative occasioned by Faulkner's syntax and the "frustrating grammar of the narrative" in *Absalom*. Pointing to the subtle shift in the paragraph that opens *Absalom*'s chapter 2 and that traces the history of the church bells' chiming, Napolin claims that an "immanent object of sound [by which she means the reader or "hearer"] moves the prose forward" (183). By way of the passage's shift from the past tense of "heard" to the present progressive of the bells' "ringing" in June 1909, she shows how the reader is, or rather is placed, "there" in the Jefferson town center. "Narrative in Faulkner is a more sensitive device for perceiving reality, more sensitive than the sense perception of its characters," Napolin claims. "Narrative perceives a sound that is not identical to narrative form (183)."[15]

I'd like to expand the sense of narrative that Napolin posits here and attributes to the "story" of reading, and of reading-as-listening in *Absalom, Absalom!*, or even our reading Faulkner's whole corpus. In light of Napolin's claim that "there is an atmospherics of the past, one that haunts the written word as it struggles to predicate its subject," I refer to the past of Faulkner's fiction as he wrote it and its anterior position to McCarthy's writing. The racial epithet, appearing in Faulkner as a written word for Black characters, is one that sounds throughout Faulkner's canon but is also one that, when it recurs and "struggles to predicate its own subject" in the present (our contemporaneousness with McCarthy and his writing act), resonates with different and new meanings and subject formations. "Narrative perceives a sound that is not identical to narrative form" as Napolin puts it because, as Faulkner's novel illustrates and a later writer like McCarthy reveals, "the act of hearing that registers [sound] exceeds the physical capacity of audition *only if* that act is understood as contemporaneous and identical with itself (to hear is here and now [only])" (183). We hear much in Faulkner reading him today. As did McCarthy. We also re-hear or hear again the de- and re-formation of what particular words mean when, like the Jefferson church bells, they sound across time and the space of these separate but related novelists.

Napolin's essay itself operates as a kind of echo or resonance, that being Carolyn Porter's example of what we might call an early or proto-version of sound studies. Porter is not interested in mass media, radio, or the cinema in her important book *Seeing and Being*. Yet her tracing the role of sound in 1932's *Light in August* in general, and in particular by way of the church bells in Jefferson, may well be said to resound in Napolin's work. The contemporary context to the earlier novel's events places it at an historical moment beyond that of *Absalom* and the latter's turns to 1909, 1833, and points between. When Faulkner wrote of those same bells in 1932 in a novel whose action is determined by Jim Crow, the "professionals who control" the church "have removed the bells from the steeples" (487 *LiA* cited in Porter 246). Commenting on their absence, Porter writes, "the bells which ring the hours, ordering man's days in accord with a redemptive organization of time, are gone" (246), and she goes on to equate Hightower, Percy Grimm, and the church community's devotion to a soundless, static, and lifeless realm of belief. As she puts it, "as the roles of [adherents like] Joanna Burden, McEeachern, and Doc Hines make clear, the Protestant church supports and enforces that commitment to the rigid distinction between black and white which imprisons and destroys Joe Christmas" (246). This is the same church and commitment to which the white Jackson appeals in *Blood Meridian* when he imposes a rigid distinction between racialized spaces in the novel, a fact made clear when, after cursing the Black Jackson and ordering him away from the shared fire, the latter confronts him and asks, "'Is that your final say?,'" to which the white Jackson responds, "'Final as the judgment of God.'" Reading what McCarthy's whole novel "says"—and how it says it—shows that the Jefferson bells' removal occurred long before events in Yoknapatawpha. But as we can see and still hear today, their absence allows another ringing: that of the "say[ing]" of words and false human judgements across and within Faulkner and McCarthy's intertextual world.

Like Murphet, Napolin ends her essay with the echo of the shot and Rosa's effort to pass Clytie on the stairs just before she hurls her failed command. Napolin points to the role of an earlier version of Clytie in "Evangeline," who appears in the story as "Raby" and who, like Rosa, hears more than she should. Lines of Raby's recur verbatim in *Absalom* and function as a continuation not only in Rosa's monologue but then again later in Quentin's retelling parts of the same story and scene. They repeat in Quentin when he too "recalls" hearing the "running feet on the stairs" (129). Describing this process, Napolin claims that "sounds in Faulkner's work remain resurrected, incomplete, and not fully treated or uncontained, not only for the characters who hear, but also for the writer [Faulkner] who continually returned, echoically, to a series of sounds" (184). Other writers, too, return to these sounds. And to their effects. "There are consequences for form as Faulkner sees it in the fact of resonance," Napolin puts it piquantly. "Such form [...] fluctuat[es] and move[s] across works, to soften the otherwise ossified boundaries between individuals and works themselves" (184–85). This is, finally, the *acoustical democracy* that extends from Faulkner to McCarthy, a complement to the "optical democracy" (247) of perception in one of *Blood Meridian*'s most celebrated passages, a circumambience of sounds that includes the most hateful sound we know today. We do not utter certain words such as these anymore. Yet they remain significant, and we hear them and their effects anyway, sadly. McCarthy heard them surely. If his novel's singular example of personal racial animus recalls or continues Faulkner's scenes, it is because as they appeared—or sounded—in Yoknapatawpha, they were never meant to cease their ringing.

NOTES

1. By "différance," Holloway refers to Derrida's notion of verbal play and the "endless" linkage between signifiers in a text. I make much of this textual property in what follows. Yet I link it to *Blood Meridian*'s powerful rendering of meaning that is real and importuning—not deferred in a Derridian capacity.

2. See Fusco.

3. Jack Johnson won the heavyweight title by defeating Burns and, in so doing, received worldwide acclaim as the first African American champion. Yet the social impact of such accomplishment was met with intense resistance and even retribution, as Johnson's later arrest on charges for violating the Mann act attest. As I discuss below, the two Jacksons' conflict has an importantly different impact and outcome.

4. As we know, the term is nearly ubiquitous in Faulkner's Yoknapatawpha. Recent Digital Humanities work shows the extent to which the epithet appears in the fiction, most often used by the working-class white men who were most threatened by the racial equity Faulkner saw the South lacking and whose opposition he critiqued. As I mean to show, McCarthy's use is revealing in its suggestiveness and selectivity.

5. Faulkner's fiction is rife with the kind of violence I trace here, often also keyed to the use of the same epithet as I suggest prompts the Black Jackson's action. His 1931 "Dry September" describes a lynching that is initiated in a barber shop punctuated by its white patron's near-incantatory repetition of the word in question. Joe Christmas in *Light in August* is defined by a childhood experience of being labeled such by other children and the dietitian at an orphanage; his adult life is haunted by his troubled racial identity and, I suggest, the indelible impact of others' appellation.

6. See Johannes Burgers' account of this work in the *Norton Critical Absalom, Absalom!*: "*Absalom, Absalom!* and the Digital Humanities: Charting Characters, Events, and Language."

7. I refer here also to the fact that as scholars we don't admit the word's use generally. Please see Catherine Kodat's discussion of the importance of a judicious approach to citing the epithet in the closing pages of *Faulknerista*. She there refers to my declared policy as the Editor of the *Faulkner Journal* encouraging authors in this regard (224).

8. See Catherine Kodat's and my editorial colleague Nathan Grant's statements about the racial epithet, who maintain there are reasons to cite it when we point to a particular character's use of it as a harbinger of their racial bias. Grant cited in Peter Lurie, "Editorial Note" (*Faulkner Journal* 32.1 [Spring 2019]).

9. Phillips cites McCarthy's remark in Richard B. Woodward's 1992 *New York Times Magazine* article, "Cormac McCarthy's Venomous Fiction" (19 April 1992).

10. The ambiguity attending Joe's racial identity that in Grimm's hateful view signifies Blackness absolutely, we can say, shows the hardening across time and fictive (and post-Reconstruction) historical space of the seeming acceptance of the Black Jackson among Glanton's gang.

11. Napolin mentions Michel Chion in this context and his coining of the model of the *acousmêtre*. See *La voix au Cinéma*. Paris: Cahiers du Cinema, 1984.

12. See Burgess, Lurie, Morrell, and Murphet.

13. "'Crossing the Junctureless Backloop of Time's Trepan': Freedom, Indexicality, and Cinematic Time in *Go Down, Moses*," in *William Faulkner in the Media Ecology*, edited by Julian Murphet and Stefan Solomon. Louisiana State University Press, 2015.

14. See Doane, *The Emergence of Cinematic Time: Modernity, Contingency, and the Archive*. Harvard University Press, 2002.

15. By "narrative" here Napolin means more than the Sutpen story—both its creative telling and its auditors' listening in the book. She also means something more than the formal workings of the modernist novel.

WORKS CITED

Benjamin, Walter. "The Storyteller." In *Illuminations*. Trans. Harry Zohn. Shocken Books, 1968.

Burgers, Johannes. "*Absalom, Absalom!* and the Digital Humanities: Charting Characters, Events, and Language. In *The Norton Critical* Absalom, Absalom! Edited by Susan Scott Parrish. Norton, 2023.

Burgess, Miranda J. "Watching Jefferson Watching: *Light in August* and the Aestheticization of Gender." *Faulkner Journal*, Volume 7, number 1 and 2, 1991 and 1992: 95–114.

Chion, Michel. *La voix au Cinéma*. Cahiers du Cinema, 1984.

Doan, Mary Ann. *The Emergence of Cinematic Time: Modernity, Contingency, the Archive*. Harvard University Press, 2002.

Faulkner, William. *Absalom, Absalom! Novels 1936–1940*. Library of America, 1990. [1936.]

———. *Light in August: Novels 1930–1935*. Library of America, 1990. [1932.]

Fusco, Katherine. *Silent Film and U.S. Naturalist Literature: Time, Narrative, and Modernity*. Routledge, 2016.

Halloway. David. "'A False Book Is No Book at All': The Ideology of Representation in *Blood Meridian* and the Border Trilogy." In *Myth, Legend, Dust: Critical Responses to Cormac McCarthy*. Manchester University Press, 2000.

Kodat, Catherine G. *Faulknerista*. Louisiana State University Press, 2022.

Lurie, Peter. "Cinematic Fascination in *Light in August*." In *A Companion to William Faulkner*. Edited by Richard Moreland. Blackwell Press, 2006.

———. "'Crossing the Junctureless Backloop of Time's Trepan': Freedom, Indexicality, and Cinematic Time in *Go Down, Moses*." In *William Faulkner in the Media Ecology*. Edited by Julian Murphet and Stefan Solomon. Louisiana State University Press, 2015.

McCarthy, Cormac. *Blood Meridian or The Evening Redness in the West: 25th Anniversary Edition*. Vintage International, 1992.

Morrell, Sascha. "Kodak Harlot Tricks of Light: Faulkner and Melville in the Darkroom of Race." In *William Faulkner in the Media Ecology*. Edited by Julian Murphet and Stefan Solomon. Louisiana State University Press, 2015.

Murphet, Julian. *Faulkner's Media Ecology*. Oxford University Press, 2017.

Napolin, Julie Beth. "The Fact of Resonance: An Acoustics of Determination in Faulkner and Benjamin." *Symplokē*, Volume 23, numbers 1 and 2 (2015).

Phillips, Dana. "History and the Ugly Facts of Cormac McCarthy's *Blood Meridian*." *American Literature* Volume 68, number 2, 1996: 433–460.

Porter, Carolyn. *Seeing and Being: The Participant Observer in Emerson, James, Adams, and Faulkner*. Wesleyan University Press, 1981.

Redfield, Marc. *Shibboleth: Judges, Derrida, Celan*. Fordham University Press, 2021.Shaviro, Steven. "'The Very Life of the Darkness': A Reading of Blood Meridian." In *Perspectives on Cormac McCarthy*. Edited by Dianne C. Luce and Edwin Arnold. University Press of Mississippi, 1999.

Unsettling Testimony

Settler Law and Native Persistence in *Blood Meridian*

ALEX HARMON

Cormac McCarthy's 1985 apocalyptic Western novel, *Blood Meridian*, is largely set in the U.S.-Mexico borderlands between 1849 and 1850, just after the official end of the Mexican-American War with the treaty of Guadalupe-Hidalgo and the annexation of Texas. The novel centers on the wanderings of a central character (though critics rarely call him a protagonist, I will argue that he becomes one in the final third of the novel) who is known only as "the kid." The kid drifts between bands of mercenaries who move between towns on the Texas-Mexico border, murdering North American Native people and Mexican nationals and collecting scalps to be sold to the governor of the state of Chihuahua. *Blood Meridian* is a novel of the frontier, but its frontier is a markedly indeterminate one: national borders are never demarcated clearly in the novel, and it is likewise unclear which of the novel's scenes of brutal violence depict implicitly government-sanctioned violence, and which acts are explicitly extralegal. The novel's obfuscation of legal and illegal killings reflects a violent reality of the time and place it depicts; in the wake of the Mexican-American War and with a federal government unable to regulate its own agents, killings and scalpings for profit were commonplace. Profiteers need not have worried whether the scalps they collected were those of legitimate enemies of the United States— it is impossible to determine ethnicity or national affiliation from a patch of skin and hank of hair.

Following and adding to the critical reading of violence and myth in McCarthy studies, I suggest that the novel, particularly through its Native characters, *bears witness* to the mythologizing of the West and the ways in which that mythologization was achieved, both in the physical space of the west itself (particularly in the final third of the novel, when McCarthy leaves historical sources behind and the judge begins to build his own malevolent mythology) and through the sociopolitical processes that justify violence in the service of ideology. More particularly, I examine the intervention of law into the "lawless" spaces inhabited by the Glanton Gang as the mechanism through which the transformation of the west from mythic space to historical place, confined by the strictures of law, is achieved. As I will argue, this transformation corresponds to the conversion of Indian land into western property; thus, it will be necessary to contextualize the novel's action and rhetoric within the twinned apparatuses of federal foreign policy and federal Indian law.

A number of McCarthy scholars have called attention to the novel's "demythologizing" of the West through depictions of brutal violence and unplotted movement. Jonathan Pitts, for example, has called the novel demythologizing and even "devisionary"—a critique of American mythmaking and vision itself through the novel's motif of "optical democracy," and Sarah Spurgeon has called the novel "a sort of antimyth of the West" (20). Since the grounding narrative of the novel is the story of men out to hunt Indian scalps for profit as filibusters and mercenaries, these critics are right to suggest the importance of interpreting the brutality of the novel not as the mythic violence of the "wild West," where lawlessness is a central and romantic part of the narrative, but instead as historically situated within a particularly violent U.S. colonial project. This is perhaps why many critics insist that the novel demythologizes the West. It is also why the novel is read as an overtly revisionist Western: it aggressively dismantles many of the foundational myths of U.S. expansion. As Rick Wallach puts it, the novel reveals that "the American Dream, which posits our collective social being, has been a nightmare of genocidal appropriation involving the effacement of oral cultures" (134). Neil Campbell similarly argues that "*Blood Meridian* is an excessive, revisionist, and contradictory narrative of the American West which rewrites both the myths and histories of the West inherited from Frederick Jackson Turner. [. . .] Part of what is being revised in McCarthy is a whole tradition of historiography [. . .]

predicated upon a narrative told by the victor in which the dominant story is represented as a triumphal procession" (218–19).

These critics argue that by dwelling on violence in a space of "optical democracy," the novel teases apart history and myth at a crucial juncture and re-inserts the violence that has been effaced in the United States's nationalist historiographical tradition. A reading that claimed that *Blood Meridian* "unveiled the hidden violence" attendant to mid-nineteenth century claims of Manifest Destiny would accord with these antimythology readings, but would not, ultimately, fully account for its historicism or its relationship to the motifs of testimony, witnessing, and confession (Sedgwick and Frank 140). Jay Ellis explains the novel's historicity as a function of its demythologizing impulse, claiming that the novel occurs at the moment when "antinomian space" becomes "historical place"; that is, the last moment in which the "ageless violence" of the Glanton Gang could exist before becoming simultaneously domesticated by history and transmogrified into myth (170). Yet the violence of *Blood Meridian* is difficult to classify as antinomian in the sense that Ellis uses the term, as "opposed to the obligatoriness of moral law," precisely because of the novel's historical and legal situatedness and the function of witnessing in the text. In fact, the novel seems less interested in the workings of "moral law" than it is in an apparent contradiction in that term when applied to the historical context of U.S. settler colonialism (OED). In his book *Cormac McCarthy: American Canticles*, Kenneth Lincoln points out that "McCarthy's violence is never voyeuristic prurience. In an ancient classic tradition, his fiction would expose evil for what it is, face up to God's wrath, speak honest truth to corrupt power, and witness atrocity without moralizing. [. . .] War marks a constant in Western history, along with lawlessness, racism, sexism, slavery, injustice [. . .] the deadly sins plus a few" (22).

If indeed the novel "expose[s] evil for what it really is," its Native characters become particularly troubling and compelling. Though described as belligerent, cannibalistic, and as a "legion of horribles," they are most often figured as the witnesses of the atrocities of the novel rather than its perpetrators (McCarthy 55). Thus a reading such as Jay Ellis's, which claims that "McCarthy's description of Indians [. . .] amounts to xenophobia, a caricature of the racial other as having no identity beyond that of animals dressed in the garb of colonial violence," is perhaps too simple an understanding of the novel's Native characters (174). In fact, this sort of reading and others that interpret the novel's Native characters as both monstrous and pitiful run the risk of recapitulating the kind of colonial violence that I will suggest the novel works against insofar as they pull McCarthy's Indians out of time and understand them ahistorically. What is needed is a reading that unites the novel's historico-legal critique of settler violence with its depictions of Native people.

The Law as a Settler Expedient

Specific legal structures are rarely mentioned in *Blood Meridian*, and when they are they act explicitly as the engines and justificatory mechanisms of settler colonialism. Although the kid spends the vast majority of the novel traveling with a fictionalized Glanton Gang, whose historical counterparts raided communities and hunted scalps along the border between Sonora and New Mexico and Arizona, his first foray into organized violence occurs under the aegis of the United States military, and specifically under a fictional army officer, Captain White, whose willful disregard of the war's end and liberal interpretation of the Monroe Doctrine combine to produce a particularly hawkish perspective on the uses of military violence. White heads a military filibuster at the U.S.-Mexico border, operating at the fraying edge of federal regulation. Though White's actions are unauthorized, he retains, for the first part of the novel, his military rank and deploys unchallenged the military chain of command. As a result, he both flouts and represents federal law, embodying the liminal space produced by aggressive settler policies in the wake of the Treaty of Guadalupe-Hidalgo.

Those policies enliven the famous violence of the novel. *Blood Meridian* is set in the very midst of intense U.S. expansion and border fortification just after the end of the war with Mexico, a few years after the Monroe Doctrine and at the time of the federal government's policy of Indian removal and relocation, twenty years after the Indian Removal Act and twenty years before Congress halted the practice of treating with tribes in 1871. During the same time, the western gold rushes of the late 1840s and early 1850s brought unprecedented numbers of European American settlers west, seeking out land that had been allotted for reservations. *Blood Meridian* proposes that fledgling federal law not only enabled but produced the settler violence that structures the novel. The kid, who begins the novel as a child in Tennessee and is pushed—seemingly without agency—westward with an inchoate wave of settlement, is given his first sense of purpose from his chance encounter with Captain White and his military filibuster. White takes a sense of permission for ongoing violence despite the end of the Mexican-American War, from the Monroe Doctrine's rhetoric of national fortification. In turn, his men reflect a concocted ideological amalgam of Christian religious fervor and mercenary capitalism—a dyad that recurs persistently through the novel's most devastating scenes of violence. The kid's recruitment to the filibuster is typical of the pairing:

> What about wages?
> Hell fire son, you won't need no wages. You get to keep ever-thing you can raise. We goin to Mexico. Spoils of war. Aint a man in the company wont come out a big land owner. How much land you own now? (32)

And a few lines later: "I've been in Texas since thirty-eight. If I'd not run up on Captain White I dont know where I'd be this day. I was a sorrier sight even than what you are and he come along and raised me up like Lazarus. Set my feet in the path of righteousness. I'd done took to drinkin and whorin till Hell wouldn't have me. He seen somethin in me worth savin and I see it in you. What do ye say?" (32). No contradiction between the language of righteous Christianity and a kind of conquest capitalism is apparent to either the recruiter or the kid. While much criticism surrounding *Blood Meridian's* religious universe centers on the unknowability and effacement of God in mystic traditions,[1] this conversation demonstrates the novel's perhaps more forceful examination of Christian creed—the mutability it demonstrated toward capitalist aims in the era of Manifest Destiny. Manifest Destiny is, in fact, the ideological outgrowth of the complicity of religion and capitalism as two fundamental structuring principles of settler colonialism.

The novel characterizes the relationship between settler ideology and settler law as an ambivalent but mutually enabling one. The kid meets Captain White and his company just as they have seamlessly transitioned from war under color of law to a military filibuster, acting strictly against the laws of the nation but nominally for the aim of securing its territory and subjugated its recent enemies. White, in fact, sees the purpose of filibuster to defend the nation when its own government has betrayed it: "We fought for it. Lost friends and brothers down there. And then by God if we didn't give it back" (35). The captain's interest is baldly self-motivated—"And we will be the ones who divide the spoils," he tells the kid—but they are cloaked in the rhetoric of the civilizing mission (35). The Mexicans, he says, are: "a race of degenerates. A mongrel race, little better than n—s. And maybe no better. There's no government in Mexico. Hell, there's no God in Mexico. Never will be. We are dealing with a people manifestly incapable of governing themselves. And do you know what happens with people who cannot govern themselves? That's right. Others come in to govern for them" (36). Along with offering a rationale for the depredations of the filibuster, White's language of progress and civilization reveals the fundamental anxiety of the settler colonial nation. His statement that those who cannot govern themselves will be governed by others serves as a justificatory framework for colonization, but also as an anxious reflection of the tenuous hold the United States maintained over its territories at a moment when westward settlement was outpacing governmental control and challenges to U.S. territorial expansion were mounting from the New World and Europe alike. Indeed, White concludes his speech by making that connection explicit, saying to the kid, "And mark my word. Unless Americans act, people like you and me who take their country seriously while those mollycoddles in Washington sit on their hindsides, unless we act, Mexico—and I mean the whole of the country—will one day fly a European flag. Monroe Doctrine or no" (37).

This mention of the Monroe Doctrine and an oblique reference to the Treaty of Guadalupe-Hidalgo (referenced only as "the treaty") are the novel's only references to the specific legal frameworks that underpin and animate its action. As I have been arguing that Captain White's account of the mechanisms of settler colonialism structure the novel's critique of the same, his glancing reference to the Monroe Doctrine as a reasonable policy in need of defense by "people [. . .] who take their country seriously" merits closer attention.

The Monroe Doctrine and Manifest Destiny

The list of scholars who have linked *Blood Meridian* to the mythologies of the frontier and the quasi-religious dogma of Manifest Destiny is long and varied. Most recently, Lauren Brown has written that the novel reconsiders the novel's violence to emphasize its political effects, which has the effect of decentering the power of the judge's rhetoric of all-encompassing power (Brown 73).[2] However, few of these scholars have attended to the specific legal mechanisms that structure and enable the novel's violence, focusing instead largely on the ideological climate that permitted it to go unchecked and uncriticized.

The Monroe Doctrine, written by John Quincy Adams under the authority of then President James Monroe, is an 1823 statement of U.S. foreign policy that marked a shift away from the United States's previous isolationism in order to actively oppose European colonization in the western hemisphere. Its terms dictated that any intervention into the political affairs of the Americas by European powers would be understood as an act of aggression toward the United States. While scholars agree that the already-strained U.S. military could likely not have sustained an attack from a European country had there been one, the policy was nevertheless a formidable statement of U.S. sovereignty and a signal that the nation saw itself as a growing imperial power on par with European colonizers. Captain White's simultaneous approval of the document's aims and anxiety about its enforceability invite *Blood Meridian's* readers to consider the violence of the novel, which is almost exclusively border violence, not only from the perspective of the social-cultural realities that underpinned the mechanisms of Manifest Destiny, but also the legal instruments that structured it.

The Doctrine itself is couched in friendship with Europe predicated on geopolitical equality and the understanding "that the American continents, by the free and independent condition which they have assumed and maintain, are henceforth not to be considered as subjects for future colonization by any European powers" (Monroe Doctrine). The document arose out of concern that Europe would ally to restore Spain's former colonies in Latin America and was strictly unenforceable from the standpoint of U.S. military capability. Thus it is often read as an embodiment of ideology of Manifest Destiny that pervaded national sentiment in the early nineteenth-century United States.

In other words, the Monroe Doctrine was mostly nationalist bluster at the time of its declaration, and had it been tested it would have proved an empty threat. Perhaps that is why White's mention of it has not garnered more scholarly attention. However, though its contemporaneous import was largely political rather than legal, the Monroe Doctrine—as an indication of the attitude of the federal government regarding settlement and national boundary fortification—is crucial for creating the legal conditions in which the novel's violence proliferates. These conditions are evident in the very existence of Captain White's filibuster. The official end of the Mexican-American War, combined with a federal government that was both eager to defend U.S. territory and global standing and too feeble to enact robust federal oversight, produced a liminal border space of quasi-legality, in which violent raids and killings by filibusters and gangs like the Glanton Gang were officially censured but effectually tolerated. The novel's rendition of the frontier, then, is responsive not only to the ideological and social climate produced by Manifest Destiny but instead to the legal and historical predicates that produced that ideology in the first place.

The turn to a reading attendant to federal law and policy, then, shifts the responsibility for the violence of the novel away from its perpetrators, who are in any case almost uniformly rendered obliquely and without much internality or self-reflexiveness, and onto the settler systems of law and governance that facilitated such violence. The novel reflects a nation uninterested in administering its own laws in the face of the settler imperatives of territorial expansion and defense. The novel's often indistinguishable violence on both Mexican and Native American people reflects an equally indistinguishable entanglement of domestic and foreign policy in the early nineteenth century—just as legal precision and caution was subsumed by the ideological banner of settler colonialism, making foreign policy and Indian policy two sides of the same coin, the novel's massive violence ignores legal categories of national borders and treaty statuses as it proceeds indiscriminately across landscapes considered hostile to the settler colonial project.

The Monroe Doctrine, *Johnson v. M'Intosh*, and the Justification of Settler Violence

A reading that emphasizes the novel's settler violence through the mechanism of law also permits and even necessitates an analysis of the legal instruments that underpin that violence even if they are not directly mentioned in the novel. Though in the early scenes of the novel the Monroe Doctrine is central, in order to catch the full force of the imperial ideology that animates the novel, that doctrine must be read alongside the Supreme Court case *Johnson v. M'Intosh*, which was decided the same year that the Monroe Doctrine was declared. If the Monroe Doctrine sought to stabilize the United States's external boundaries by prescribing action if those boundaries were violated, *Johnson v. M'Intosh* performed the same labor for what some were worried were *internal* boundaries in the United States with foreign nations—Indian tribes. *Johnson v. M'Intosh* began the crucial nationalist project of eroding those boundaries, even as the nation's external boundaries were being reinforced. The Marshall Court, in other words, instantiated the ideological frame through which the violence of the novel's filibuster and later the Glanton Gang was sanctioned. In turn, the novel's depiction of the hellish brutality of that violence enacts an implicit critique of the foundational tenets of federal Indian law: the seemingly benign translation of Indian title into the right of occupancy.[3]

The case is, notably, one in which no Native people were involved as litigants and no Native people gave testimony—a fact which will become important for my analysis. The Native characters in the novel become witnesses not only to the ferocious violence that saw them dispossessed of land, culture, and often life, but also to the colonial discourse that created from that violence a coherent narrative of conquest and inevitable demise. This narrative, embodied succinctly in *Johnson v. M'Intosh*, is so pervasive in federal Indian law and legislation that by the time of the 1954 *Tee-Hit-Ton v. U.S.* decision the stereotypes generated by *Johnson v. M'Intosh*—that "the tribes of Indians inhabiting this country were fierce savages, whose occupation was war, and whose subsistence as drawn chiefly from the forest" (590)—were echoed with the preface "As every schoolboy knows."

Though never mentioned in the text, Marshall's decision in *Johnson*, which barred private citizens from purchasing lands from Native peoples by drawing a distinction between aboriginal and absolute title, provides the backdrop for the brutal colonial violence of McCarthy's novel. Yet the novel has never yet been read in the context of the case, decided just twenty-six years before the action of the narrative begins.

Background of the Case

Johnson v. M'Intosh is the foundational case of federal Indian law, as well as a foundational case of property law in the United States. The case, as legal scholar Robert Williams has put it, "ensured that future acts of genocide would proceed on a rationalized, legal basis" (*The American Indian* 317). That assertion is supported by the narrative structure of the case, which attempts to assure that genocide would never become the dominant interpretation of Native extermination. Marshall achieves his hermetic interpretation by writing, in dicta, a thoroughly revisionist history in which Native people were always already ghosts—destined to recede as a natural consequence of westward expansion by Anglo settlements. Of course, Marshall did not create this version of history (and perhaps did not even support it), but the opinion was the lynchpin that secured it to the canon of U.S. law. Marshall's decision in favor of M'Intosh draws heavily on both English Property Law and on the so-called "doctrine of discovery," and finds its constitutional basis in the Commerce Clause (Article 1, § VIII, ¶ 3). Legal scholar Jedidiah Purdy describes the much-examined contradictions of *Johnson v. M'Intosh*, writing that the case "has long been a puzzle, both in its doctrinal structure and in long, strange dicta which are both triumphal and elegiac" (Purdy 329). The terms act dialectically for Purdy, expressing the fundamental contradictions at the heart of the case and opening interpretive space for a reading of Chief Justice Marshall's ambivalence. Alongside the opinion's much-studied ambivalence, I would like to consider the coherence (in a nationalist context) of a position that embodies—in reference to the dispossession of Native people—both the triumphal and the elegiac, and in fact the necessity of that position to the nationalist project leveraged by the opinion. The majority opinion in this case is a profoundly nationalist utterance. The Doctrine of Discovery, the originary concept that produces the court's decision, performs the conceptual labor of disappearing Indians—demographically and culturally—from the precolonial North American landscape to shore up U.S. colonial claims to territory. Marshall's opinion, in fact, rehearses a whole historical fantasy of colonialism on U.S. soil, of which the primary fiction is the inevitable disappearance of Native people.

Marshall elucidates the discovery doctrine this way: "On the discovery of this immense continent, the great nations of Europe were eager to appropriate to themselves so much of it as they could respectively acquire. Its vast extent offered an ample field to the ambition and enterprise of all; and the character and religion of its inhabitants afforded an apology for considering them as a people over whom the superior genius of Europe might claim an ascendency" (543). The opinion continues, "The potentates of the old world found no difficulty in convincing themselves that they made ample compensation to the inhabitants of the new, by bestowing on them civilization and Christianity, in exchange for unlimited independence" (543). Here he further stresses the inevitability of conquest through the notion of compensation, nodding to earlier (and less controversial) law that claimed preemption for the federal government in the purchase of Indian land.[4] However, compensation itself becomes abstracted here, so that "bestowing [...] civilization and Christianity" are posited as "ample compensation" for Indian land. In other words, religious conversion—itself the forerunning apparatus of European colonialism in the "New World"—both prepares the way for settler colonialism and acts as recompense for its violence. Although the language is ironic (of course the potentates of Europe, who were hungry for new land, "found no difficulty in procuring it"), the translation of religion into compensation performs the rhetorical labor of suggesting that Indigenous people in the Americas had already been "paid" for their lands, while abstracting that payment in terms that pave the way for the full articulation of the Discovery Doctrine.

Marshall then pairs the notion of compensation with that of preemption: "The exclusion of all other Europeans, necessarily gave to the nation making the discovery the sole right of acquiring the soil of the natives, and establishing settlements upon it. It was a right with which no Europeans could interfere" (572). Preemption, however, is not the paradigm under which the opinion operates. Instead, Marshall shifts from claiming for Europeans the right of preemption to the right of title itself. Just before the passage above, describing the Doctrine of Discovery, he writes: "This principle was, that discovery gave title to the government by whose subjects, or by whose authority, it was made, against all other European governments, which title might be consummated by possession" (572).

Though the notion of preemption may have been largely accepted in 1823 (as evidenced by positive law including the Virginia Declaratory Act of 1779), Marshall's extension of preemption into title is of his own devising. The opinion reinforces the European claim to Native land further by relying on a largely fictional account of Native people to reiterate an old saw (even in 1823) that American Indians were fated to disappear. The dicta achieve the rhetorical disappearance of Native people first by asserting (over and over) the right of discovery in spite of Native occupancy,[5] a move that simultaneously affirms Native existence and rejects Native agency or presence in a way that would affect European historical claims. And finally, Native people are absent even in the configuration of the case, which is a property dispute between two European American disputants, with no representation from the Piankashaw. Any culturally specific referents (including queries that could have affected the case's outcome, such as how the land was used by the Piankashaw[6] and how, culturally, territory was defined) are evacuated and replaced with typecast barbarians: "But the tribes of Indians inhabiting this country were fierce savages, whose occupation was war, and whose subsistence was drawn chiefly from the forest. To leave them in possession of their country, was to leave the country a wilderness; to govern them as distinct people, was impossible, because they were as brave and as high spirited as they were fierce, and were ready to repel by arms every attempt on their independence" (590). This passage is a particularly salient example of the tone that Jedidiah Purdy describes as both "triumphal and elegiac." The (entirely fictional) Indians of the passage must be fierce savages because to claim the essential rightness of colonialism the court must make reference to both a civilizing mission and a necessity of just war, the two of which intertwine to spin a remarkably strong nationalist thread by creating a common antagonist in Native Americans. That thread is then interwoven with a eulogizing impulse to describe the Indians as "brave and high spirited" to produce a tapestry of nationalist feeling: at once triumphant in victory over the savages and regretful that it simply had to be that way—that there must inevitably be those trampled in the march toward civilization.

Reading Native Nations in *Blood Meridian*

It is precisely this march of historical time that *Blood Meridian* dismantles. *Blood Meridian* is set in the very midst of intense U.S. expansion and border fortification, a few years after the Monroe Doctrine and at the time of the federal government's policy of Indian removal and relocation, twenty years after the Indian Removal Act and twenty years before Congress halted the practice of treating with tribes in 1871. During the same time, the western gold rushes of the late 1840s and early 1850s brought unprecedented numbers of European American settlers west, seeking out land that had been allotted for reservations.

I propose three related frameworks under which we might begin to undertake an analysis of the Native characters in the novel that demonstrates that, far from racialized colonial projections of the Other, they are instead resistant and persevering witnesses to the entwining of violence and mythmaking on North American soil. First, I explain the work of the court (and the Glanton Gang, whom we will come to understand as the court's functionaries), in terms of Lauren Berlant's concept of "slow death." I attach the idea of slow death to Robert Cover's view of the Supreme Court's primarily jurispathic function. And finally, I note *Blood Meridian's* complicated portrayal of testimony and witnessing in order to illustrate the ways in which the Native characters that inhabit the novel become more than simply figures for repressed American guilt or shadowy postmortem phantoms of North American Native peoples.

There are no named Native characters in the novel, only spectral processions of unidentified Native peoples on the move, some the victims of policies of Removal and some taking advantage of the postwar instability of territorial governments to conduct predatory raids.[7] All are poor, many are refugees of removal and the quarry of the government-sanctioned Indian killers. They have been robbed of all defining features and retain no tribal or clan affiliations beyond the broadest terms (Comanche, Apache, Yuma). They are often described using only the generic title of "Indian drovers." In one scene, before a violent encounter, they are described at length. It is the lengthiest description of the Indian characters in the book and bears reproducing at length:

> A legion of horribles, hundreds in number, half naked or clad in costumes attic or biblical or wardrobed out of a fevered dream with the skins of animals and silk finery and pieces of uniform still tracked with the blood of prior owners [. . .] death hilarious, all howling in a barbarous tongue and riding down upon them like a horde from a hell more horrible yet than the brimstone land of christian reckoning, screeching and yammering

and clothed in smoke like those vaporous beings in regions beyond right knowing where the eye wanders and the lip jerks and drools. (McCarthy 55)

This visceral, excessive description is uncommunicative in telling ways. No cultural specificity is noticed or noted; rather, the Indians are "attic or biblical"—descriptors that allude to fallen civilizations as well as to the wanderings of the Israelites in the Old Testament. The passage establishes the interpretive model through which the Glanton Gang implicitly glosses both their mission and their enemy: as extensions of a Western mythohistorical tradition in which history is written by the victors.

Accordingly, the "Indian drovers" passage's description of clothing "attic or biblical" draws on western cultural logic, but not on Native cultural specificity; the "costumes" have been stripped of everything outside western history. Western dress—particularly that dress associated with colonization or war—is legible, if fantastical: the armor of a conquistador, "frogged imperial jackets," the "coats of slain dragoons." Yet despite the grounding in western narratives, these figures are incommensurably other, and essentially savage. They are ragged and fundamentally bereft of law or institution, a point which is emphasized by their nakedness or half-nakedness under their partially westernized attire, as well as by the general chaos of the picture they present. As a result, the narration can only cobble together an image of them embedded in Western institutions and imaginings; in fact, the Indian drovers (despite their fearsomeness) are implanted into Western history so seamlessly in the passage that colonial domination seems garishly inevitable: their very aspect is that of "death hilarious."

The passage—the first in which the kid encounters Indians—is, in this sense, a vividly drawn picture of the American racial imagination. It combines—often in dissociative, uneasy ways—myths of genesis and social evolution. It appeals to the repressed psychosocial idea of the savage, along with religiously grounded notions of the ignorant unbaptized awaiting salvation through civilization. In this reading, the drovers are the embodiment of the manipulative possibilities of the discourse of savagery, which might equally be cast as debased or possessed of an essential and "pure" nobility.

Yet the novel's Delaware, Apache, and Comanche, however overdetermined as avatars of western cultural history, are never fully eliminated from the landscape, acting as a trace of Native communities that the U.S. government has eradicated or hopes to eradicate. And it's important to note as well, that they are not what Robert Williams has called "the vanquished, vanishing, doomed Indian savage [that] is a stock character in nineteenth-century American literary classics, dime novels, and Wild West Shows" (*Like a Loaded Weapon* 35). Because of the flattening effect of a novel so devoid of psychology, they are nearly indistinguishable from their counterparts whose charge is to murder them. They become witnesses of the colonial violence wrought under the auspices of federal Indian law, just as the Glanton Gang is depicted as the instrument of that violence. The Glanton Gang are the primary agents of willed disappearance or ghosting in the novel, particularly—as Phillip Snyder notes—within the "larger sociopolitical context of frontier colonization through the annihilation of indigenous peoples" (133). They are the agents of what Jacksonian-era bromides called "Removal." Reading McCarthy's Glanton Gang this way, it becomes impossible to see them as other than bound up in the legal configurations represented by the Monroe Doctrine and, more immediately, *Johnson v. M'Intosh*.

We can imagine McCarthy's Indians in *Blood Meridian* being held in the unsettling present of the crucial historical moment engendered by *Johnson v. M'Intosh*. One way to understand *Blood Meridian*'s critique of coloniality is Lauren Berlant's concept of "slow death." Berlant writes that "the phrase *slow death* refers to the physical wearing out of a population in a way that points to its deterioration as a defining condition of its experience and historical existence" (95). For her, this points up a development in the ways we conceptualize contemporary historical experience, especially where that experience is simultaneously at an extreme and in a zone of ordinariness, where life building and attrition of human life are indistinguishable, and where it is hard to distinguish modes of incoherence, distractedness, and habituation from deliberate and deliberative activity, as they are all involved in the reproduction of predictable life (96). We might understand the Native presences in *Blood Meridian* as witnesses to "slow death" in the process of becoming; that is, as witnesses to the very discursive practices that create slow death by producing the narrative foreclosures that such a death entails. Passages such as the Indian drover passage produced above are silent and described in terms of their "deterioration as a defining condition." Unexpectedly, though, it is precisely through the novel's insistence on incoherence and violence as a mode of habituation that space in the novel for active resistance is created;

while one might expect Native life to dissolve or disappear beneath the continuous onslaught of excessive violence, the historical and literary fact of the novel is that Native peoples engaged that violence and resisted it.

The distinction Berlant makes between the quotidian and the historical is important, and it is the same distinction (and connection) I want to draw between the events of *Blood Meridian* and the *Johnson v. M'Intosh* decision. For Berlant, "the current discussion of sovereignty [is] as a condition of and a blockage to justice [which] recapitulates the widespread contemporary projection of sovereignty onto events of decision making" (96). And yet this formulation "masks in a discourse of 'control' the wide variety of processes and procedures involved historically in the administration of law and of bodies" (96). In other words, Berlant seeks to decenter moments of legal/administrative decision making as the critical junctures of sovereignty. She is describing an alternative to the critical genres of crisis and interpretation through attention to the time and space of "ordinariness" rather than the moment of the event. For this reason, Berlant sees slow death at work not in traumatic events but instead in "temporally labile environments whose qualities and whose contours in time and space are often identified with the presentness of ordinariness itself" (100).

Berlant's determination to look closely at the everyday and to turn away from the rhetoric of crisis holds rich potential for understanding the ways in which McCarthy's Native characters might unmoor from more traditional, symptomatic readings. McCarthy, often to shocking effect, moves violence into the realm of the everyday. Not just "enemy combatants," or even adult people, are casually killed: babies, donkeys, cats, and chickens are shot in descriptions that are all the more brutal for their ordinariness. As a result, the time and space of the novel are stretched; rather than a massacre acting as an "event" that takes place in a given material "environment," massacre becomes the basic condition of life in the novel. The world of *Blood Meridian* is one in which "death seemed the most prevalent feature of the landscape" (42).

McCarthy's Indians then, complicatedly situated as they are as victims, drovers, enemy armies, and Indian hunters themselves, pull *Johnson* and the Monroe Doctrine out of the rhetorical tradition of single events that shaped history and into the unfolding time and space. This move is significant because it signals a durability of narrative presence, of a living through that might be held aside from the event of *Johnson v. M'Intosh,* or the event of

Removal (as a time-bounded policy). That is, it suggests that these figures, elusory as they are, are not extinguishable in the very ways that Indian law and policy of the time would have wanted to extinguish them. Their wraith-like appearance in this work of American fiction is not a recapitulation of their removal from American land in literature, but rather a resistance to that removal via the act of witnessing its violence, which the reader witnesses alongside them.

Death itself, suffused throughout the novel, might be read politically in these terms. Pheng Cheah provocatively began his 2003 book *Spectral Nationality* with the sentence, "Nationalism has almost become the exemplary figure for death" (1). Though Cheah is imagining a far more multifarious vision of nationality than the one I am dealing with here—nationality in the age of global cosmopolitan challenges to the form—the statement is apt. The nation-building impulse that suffused the zeitgeist of the mid-nineteenth-century United States puts Marshall in the position of eulogizing a group of cultures that are not actually dead, in an attempt to narratively kill them off. A potentially transformative way of understanding this gesture is thinking it through what legal scholar Robert Cover has called the "jurispathic function" of the court, which he claims acts not to create law but to kill it, and to kill narrative along with it. That is, the creation of new law actually entails the winnowing of multiple possible futures (legal outcomes) to one precedential decision, foreclosing other narrative and legal possibilities. Cover has written that judges are essentially "people of violence. Because of the violence they command, judges do not characteristically create law, but kill it" (Cover 53). Robert Williams extends Cover's claims regarding the jurispathic, attributing this function most particularly to Supreme Court justices and arguing that the jurispathic court "play[s] a critical role in sanctioning and perpetuating racism against certain groups. The stereotypes or images that the Court has thus legitimated and expanded can now be used to legally justify a rights-denying, jurispathic form of racism against those groups. [. . .] In other words, the justices have the legal authority in our society to tell people that it's not only reasonable to act in a racially discriminatory and hostile way, it's perfectly legal as well" (Williams 21).[8] In other words, we can understand *Johnson v. M'Intosh* producing a colonial narrative by "killing" all other possible narratives (and potential legal interpretations) that would produce other, less teleological narrative possibilities. We can think of the jurispathic action of "killing" alternative interpretations or narratives, and of the ghosts this action produces as the stubborn traces of those other narratives. Constituted this way, the otherwise pitiful Native characters exude real resistant—and even potentially reparative—possibility.

An example of how these concepts work together: Marshall avers that federal land patents can be obtained from Indians either through purchase or just war. Part of McCarthy's intervention is to demonstrate the absurdity of the justice of war by depicting its violence and its illegalities often on the minutest level. If *Johnson v. M'Intosh* operates on the level of decision making, the actors and events of McCarthy's novel represent the historical processes of sovereignty as it plays out in embodied form: that is, how the law touches the lived bodies of actors on both sides of the ideological and legal conflict it creates.[9] This connection is particularly important because it addresses a conceptual gap between the legal workings of the court and the extralegal movements and actions of the Glanton Gang. Once the court invokes a version of slow death—which it does quite explicitly in sentences such as, "As the white population advanced, that of the Indians necessarily receded"—it becomes impossible, from a national standpoint, to see disappearance otherwise than as a defining condition of Native existence. Therefore the strong sovereignty this assertion allows the court to exercise also becomes the implicit sense of permission that permeates the actions of the novel's Indian hunters and filibusters. Though not associated with the law, the Glanton Gang (and White's filibusters before them) operate under the auspices of the discourse of sovereignty as expressed by a deeply nationalist court.

Judge Holden, Justice Marshall, and the Legal Work of Ghosting

Of course this might at first blush seem to be a nihilist or (a favorite word of McCarthy fans) apocalyptic reading that accords with Judge Holden's own ideas about the futile nature of existence, much less history. I read it differently, though. In a famous scene, Judge Holden delivers a lecture on geology. He includes in his discourse, which he frames as a natural history, some description of the remains of Anasazi life around them. I place special importance on this scene because that trace of a precolonial existence is precisely what Judge Holden would destroy in this scene, and likewise exactly the target of the language of savagery in *Johnson v. M'Intosh.*

Among the "ruins of an older culture," Judge Holden spends a day collecting artifacts of Indian culture and colonial occupation (145). The scene is narratively significant because it is the first glimpse of the all-consuming power of the judge's book (a subject to which I will return in a moment). Taking first slings and potsherds, then the relic of a Spanish breastplate, Holden, described here as "a draftsman as he is other things," sketches them into his book. When asked why he records the objects, the judge replies, "that it was to expunge them from the memory of man" (147). The judge's book obviates the old chestnut "history is written by the victor" with a more radical claim. Who gets to tell the narrative of colonialism is a negative conceptual field: there can be no countervailing claims to history if there is no history at all. The judge's book functions to wipe out narrative possibility, to erase the whole history of colonialism. Holden completes the narrative foreclosure with two statements, one as grandiose a claim about history as one could wish, and one suggesting a localness so immediate as to be colloquial.

The latter is his announcement that the Anasazi "quit these parts," a statement notable for its departure from his usual portentous language (152). He then expounds that idea into a lengthy speech that acts as a denial of the possibility of Anasazi memory:

> They quit these parts ages since and of them there is no memory. They are rumors and ghosts in this land and they are much revered. The tools, the art, the building—these things stand in judgment on the latter races. Yet there is nothing for them to grapple with. The old ones are gone like phantoms and the savages wander these canyons to the sound of an ancient laughter. In their crude huts they crouch in darkness and listen to the fear seeping out of the rock. All progressions from a higher to a lower order are marked by ruins and mystery and a residue of nameless rage. So. Here are the dead fathers. Their spirit is entombed in stone. It lies upon the land with the same weight and the same ubiquity. (McCarthy 152)

Both of these statements, the colloquial and the grand, are attempts to sanitize the violence of the colonial project by couching it in the discourse of inevitability (a discourse that the judge takes further on the following page when he claims that "[man's] meridian is at once his darkening and the evening of his day" (153). More radically, the second statement is an attempt to extirpate even the memory of the precolonial. His claim that "of them there is no memory" is a willful attempt to force that forgetting, much the way Marshall forecloses political potentialities in *Johnson* through the rhetorical foreclosure of *narrative* or historical potentialities other than the inevitability of conquest. That is, in *Johnson* as in Judge Holden's book, history is erased rather than written, creating space for the wholesale mythologization. The difference is that in the world of the novel, such foreclosure is made impossible by the witnessing—especially the Indigenous witnessing—of the daily condition of violence.

The Anasazi whose materiality is written out of existence in Judge Holden's book exemplify the legacy of the jurispathic function of the court. However McCarthy's judge sanitizes violence by embracing it—and he does so in a multitude of ways (through discourses on the cyclicity of time and the inevitability of destruction, through committing senseless violence to strip it of narrative possibility, through embracing it via the language of war)—he is not, ultimately, successful. Though attempting to write the subjects of his book out of existence, the paradox of the judge is that everything he attempts to eradicate is recorded in the novel itself.

Like Holden, Chief Justice Marshall inhabits and relies on a deep-seated colonial narrative, though also like Holden he is deeply implicated with that narrative's shaping. When Marshall claims in the *Johnson v. M'Intosh* opinion that "conquest gives a title which the courts of the conqueror cannot deny," he accedes to the power of that narrative: the narrative of conquest that will cut the path for all of federal Indian law still to come (588). The statement has been read as evidence of Marshall's ambivalence, a reading to which I give credence. Here, though, I'd like to suggest—through a comparison to Judge Holden—that its ideological attempt, like Holden's, is to "expunge" the history of coloniality "from the memory of man." The opinion achieves this in several ways. It both insists on the inevitability of Native disappearance and instantiates the legal mechanism for that disappearance by translating land into property and preemption into title.

In one of *Blood Meridian*'s most painful passages, the Glanton Gang led by Judge Holden stalk and hunt a group of Indian men, cornering them in the cavity of a defunct volcano. Holden then begins shooting wildly, and when he stops a voice calls out to him for mercy, in English and Spanish (the languages of the two "conquerors" at the North American border). The judge says only "Gentlemen. Then [...] he drew [his pistols] one in each hand and he is as either-handed as a spider, he can write with both hands at a time and I've seen him do it,[10] and he commenced to kill Indians. We needed no second invitation. God it was a butchery. At the first fire we killed a round dozen and we did not let up" (140). The scene so traumatizes the kid that he can only repeat, as in a litany, "What's he a judge of? [...] What's he a judge of? What's he a judge of?" (141). It marks the moment in the narrative when the kid begins to begrudge his membership in the Glanton Gang, an ideological betrayal for which the judge will murder him at the novel's end. As such, the passage is no mere slaughter but instead functions as condensed ideology, foundational to the sociopolitical (and sociopathic) educations of the Glanton Gang.

Similarly, in spite of Marshall's apparent ambivalence, *Johnson v. M'Intosh* is both an act of foundational violence and a statement of commitment to an organizing ideological narrative of conquest. Though the case seems straightforward enough—a property dispute in which the court was charged with deciding whether or not private citizens could legally buy land from Indian tribes—the decision is generalizing and far-reaching. Of the avenues available to interpretation, Marshall self-consciously grounds the case in the European Law of Nations. It is conceivable that Marshall could have grounded his opinion solely in the Commerce Clause, which designates to federal government the power "To regulate Commerce with foreign Nations, and among the several States, and with the Indian Tribes" (Article I, Section 8, Clause 3), and the Indian Non-Intercourse Acts. However, Marshall goes further. His statement is mostly dicta, and that dicta works to create a teleological narrative of discovery and conquest that Marshall goes on to support with reliance on international law. The tension between the narrative of discovery and the reality of a peopled continent forces Marshall to distinguish between "aboriginal title" and absolute title, claiming priority for the latter.

There is a moment, however contrived, in which Holden might have shown mercy. He walks to the rim of the volcano waving a white flag. It is, of course, a ruse, and the chicanery serves to further ironize Holden's title of judge (hence the question that arises for the kid, again and again, "What's he the judge of?"). That irony extends to Marshall's opinion as well, in which the "court of the conqueror," through the colonial logic of discovery, acts as a handmaiden to the political exigencies of conquest. Like Holden's white flag, Marshall's opinion is a false olive branch. Like Holden, Marshall "writes with both hands," as the following passage exemplifies. Here Marshall simultaneously avers that Native people have the right to "retain possession" of the soil, but then evacuates that possession of meaning by reasserting the right of Europeans to "exclusive title."

They were admitted to be the rightful occupants of the soil, with a legal as well as just claim to retain possession of it and to use it according to their own discretion, but their rights to complete sovereignty as independent nations, were necessarily diminished, and their power to dispose of the soil at their own will, to whomsoever they pleased, was denied by the original fundamental principle that discovery gave exclusive title to those who made it (574).

In the penultimate scene of the novel, the offense for which the kid dies is his rejection of the logic of conquest and his sympathies for the Native peoples whom he has been hired to kill. In the final chapters of the book, the kid is no longer a pursuer but instead pursued by the judge, who tells him "You alone were mutinous. You alone reserved in your soul some corner of clemency for the heathen" (312). Later, coming upon the kid in a jail cell (a quality of the judge is his totalizing omnipresence) he tells the kid, "You came forward [...] to take part in a work. But you were a witness against yourself. You sat in judgement on your own deeds. You put your own allowances before the judgements of history and you broke with the body of which you were pledged a part and poisoned it in all its enterprise" (319). In the judge's particular teleology, man was made for war and war was made for history: this is the "work" to which this passage refers. The history of "man" is a history of conquest, and that is his purpose in joining the Glanton Gang (rather than for the more contingent, materialist purposes of accumulating wealth in which the other members were engaged). His dedication to conquest is what figures the Indians as savages. When the kid begins to witness the violence in terms of human cost, sitting "in judgment on [his] own deeds," he broke not only with the "body" of the gang, but with the conjoined bodies of history and law to which the judge and, implicitly, the gang, are "pledged." The kid's ambivalence has no place in the ideology of violence the judge espouses. Sympathy or humanizing is a betrayal of the cause.

When the judge finally does kill the kid, he achieves it not with the outright violence of the rest of the book, but with an embrace. The kid approaches the jakes and opens one, to find the judge inside. He "rose up smiling and gathered him in his arms against his immense and terrible flesh and shot the wooden barlatch home behind him" (347). In a novel so nearly fanatical in its descriptions of brutal and ceaseless violence, this is the only description we are offered of the protagonist's demise.[11] The kid, who has in effect become a traitor to the colonial project simply through an unspoken internal conflict (never does the kid show outward sympathy toward a Native character), is simply swallowed up or smothered by the judge. Figuratively, his resistance is smothered by the "immense and terrible" discourse of colonialism.

A resistance to expansionism, in the world of the novel, is intolerable even at the level of thought or consideration. In the last encounter between the judge and the kid in which the kid actually speaks, his anticolonial stake becomes clear. The chapter is a study on the extended metaphor of "the dance" as participation in history and therefore, inevitably, violence. The kid claims (making his position clear for the first time), "I ain't studyin no dance" (340). Nonparticipation means death, and most importantly, death without a trace. As the judge tells the kid (shortly before killing him): "Hear me, man, he said. There is room on the stage for one beast and one alone. All others are destined for a night that is eternal and without name. One by one they will step down into the darkness before the footlamps. Bears that dance, bears that dont" (345). There are two bears in the novel: the grizzly that attacked the Delaware scouts, and the dancing bear that, in the scene described above, was shot in a scene of grotesque and gory violence. Both participate in the dance as the judge figures it, because the logic of conquest is pervasive and all encompassing: whether the wild bear disappears or is tamed and finally killed is the same in the judge's imperial understanding.

There is no description of the kid after death, and he has no last words. As the kid's part in the narrative diminishes, the judge begins to take up more and more space, both narratively and, it seems, physically, as his already massive figure dances through the final pages, finally "towering over them all" (348). "Huge and pale and hairless," his head becomes a "lunar dome" (348–49). As resistance is erased, the judge "will never sleep [...] will never die" (349). Though perhaps a quotidian comparison given the mythic tone of the final pages, the way in which the judge (as the personified form of colonial logic) might never die is in the continual enactment of colonial violence in the maneuverings of a colonial body of law (the judge's book, with which he seeks to erase everything other than conquest from both the pages of history and the understanding of the present).

Blood Meridian, though, is not the judge's book. In that book, it is true that the kid acts as a "witness against himself." As we have seen, though, whatever the strength of colonial discourse, McCarthy's Indians stand witness to a whole history of violent and racist colonial Indian law that begins with the court's unanimous decision in *Johnson v. M'Intosh*. Like the Supreme Court's function, Judge Holden's role is jurispathic: he records in his book in order to wipe the traces of previous cultures from human memory. By writing in his book he is in fact erasing: the essence of jurispathy. Finally, he kills the kid, too; though he claims that he acted as a "witness against himself," the kid must be killed because he has betrayed the killing function of nationalist discourse with fleeting moments of sympathy for both Indian and Mexican people. The novel's end leaves the judge triumphant, but, as we have already seen, he is not the author he purports to be. The sketches in his book are not erased or erasable, because they have been recorded in a book not of his own making, a novel in which Native people bear witness to the bloody crimes of Manifest Destiny, in spaces both legal and extralegal. The judge cannot kill the proliferation of meanings that arise from this bearing witness.

By suggesting this, I don't mean to impose a redemptive reading on a novel that offers no such redemption. Rather, I mean to draw attention to the way the novel refuses either to obscure or to apotheosize the violence of the colonial project. As I have suggested, violence is the medium through which all the novel's actions play out, and its brutality resists an easy translation into nationalist jingoism or mythmaking. The novel tracks the way in which dissociation from the foundational myths of American nation building and affiliation with Native people, however slight, constitute a "bearing of witness against oneself." But the novel does exactly that labor of dissociation by producing witnesses to mythmaking. The kid only becomes the protagonist of the novel once he becomes the enemy of the judge, an event that coincides with the end of the historical material from which the plot is drawn; in other words, the kid finds affinity with the Indian witnesses to the violence of colonialism at the very moment that the judge's mythmaking detaches from historical record and takes on a life of its own. Like the Delaware scouts, his testimony ("I ain't studyin' no dance") does not simply articulate a demand to be seen or recognized as a victim of violence or history, but rather bears witness to "a pathos beyond recognition." I would like to end by discussing a possibility suggested in this essay's title: the notion that the witnessing performed in the novel by the kid, by the ghostly Natives, and by the reader (all of whom have affinity by the novel's end) constitutes a kind of "unsettling." By this I mean, certainly, an uneasiness in colonial discourse and an inability to fit the ordinariness of bloodshed, as depicted in *Blood Meridian*, into that discourse. But I also want to at least suggest a more literal meaning: a kind of un-settling of the spaces of settler colonialism. This, then, is the payoff of the novel's famous "optical democracy" passage: a possibility of a radical spatial/narrative democracy in which the violence witnessed by Native people can be situated side by side with, rather than under or buried by, the narrative of U.S. settler colonialism.

NOTES

1. For some of the most well-known and pertinent scholarship along these lines, see Petra Mundik, "'Striking the Fire Out of the Rock': Gnostic Theology in Cormac McCarthy's *Blood Meridian*" (*South Central Review*, volume. 26, number. 3, 2009: 72–97).

2. See, for example: John Dean, 74–104; Julius Greve, 23–62; Petra Mundik, 71–100.

3. See Cheyfitz in both "Savage Law" and *The Poetics of Imperialism* for a reading of the translation of Indian land into property for the precise purpose of divesting Indians of it: Eric Cheyfitz, "Savage Law: The Plot against American Indians in Johnson and Graham's Lessee v. M'lntosh and The Pioneers," in *Cultures of United States Imperialism* by Amy Kaplan and Donald E. Pease (Duke University Press, 1993: 109–28), *and The Poetics of Imperialism: Translation and Colonization from the Tempest to Tarzan* (Oxford University Press, 1991).

4. See *Fletcher v. Peck* (10 U.S. 87).

5. For example, "They were the rightful occupants of the soil" (574); "a country, every acre of which was then claimed and possessed by Indians, who maintained their title with as much persevering courage as was ever manifested by any people" (586); "This territory, though claimed by both nations, was chiefly in the occupation of Indians" (587).

6. In a particularly egregious example of the refusal to consider cultural specificity, Marshall claims the following: "According to every theory of property, the Indians had no individual rights to land; nor had they any collectively, or in their national capacity for the lands occupied by each tribe were not used by them in such a manner as to

prevent their being appropriated by a people of cultivators" (570). The Piankashaw, part of the larger tribal affiliation of Miami Indians, were a Mississippian agricultural society (Emerson and Lewis 17).

7. While the white characters in the novel never learn the tribes of many of the Native people they encounter throughout the text, the reader learns their tribes through the headings that precede each chapter. For example, after the first violent encounter with Indian cattle drovers, the kid asks a companion if he knows "What kind of Indians was them?" Though "I don't know" is the reply (59), the headings inform the reader that they had been attacked by Comanche. Historically this makes sense, since Comanche took advantage of the weakened state of military forces along the border of Texas and Mexico to conduct raids. Here again is the distinction between history/teleology, which makes a kind of narrative sense, and its embodiment in a moment, which often doesn't.

8. Cover elaborates on the social function of jurispathy as well: "A community's acquiescence in or accommodation to the judge's interpretation reinforces the hermeneutic process offered by the judge and extends, in one way or another, its social range" (21). This of course, begs the question of what community is being referred to. Not, one must assume, Indian communities. I am reminded of Vine Deloria: "Indians have not accepted the mythology of the American past which interprets American history as a sanitized merging of diverse peoples to form a homogenous union. The ties to tribal heritage are too strong, the abuses of the past and present too vivid, and the memory of freedom too lasting for many Indians" (Deloria 2).

9. Contrast this with law professor Eric Kades's 2000 study entitled "The Dark Side of Efficiency: *Johnson v. M'Intosh* and the Expropriation of American Indian Lands," which argues that Marshall's decision was rendered to maximize efficiency in government acquisition of Indian Land. He writes, "The thesis of this Article is that colonists established rules to minimize the costs associated with dispossessing the natives. If it had been cheaper to be more brutal, then Europeans would have been more brutal. Such brutality, however, was not cheap at all. Likewise, if it had been cheaper to show more humanity, the Europeans would have exhibited more, such as extending Indians full rights to sell (or keep) their land" (1071). Such a reading demonstrates one benefit of reading literature alongside legal scholarship; while the language of Marshall's decision may not have been "brutal," assuredly violence and brutality toward Native people were a result.

10. This is one of the rare instances in which the effaced narrator of the novel reveals himself, speaking in first person. The use of the first person here is of particular interest because the narrator is so hidden. At times it seems that the narrator cannot possibly be human, at others that he must be part of first Captain White's deployment and then the Glanton Gang. Here first person only doubles the effect of the judge's mysterious power: as in a rumor, *someone* has seen the judge writing with both hands at once, but the source of that knowledge is always unknowable.

11. This is not quite true. The death is treated obliquely in the chapter's subheadings in two short phrases: the jakes and what was encountered there—Sie müssen schlafen aber Ich [*sic*] muss tanzen. The German translation, "You must sleep, but I must dance,"

suggests not only the kid's death at the hands of the judge, but also that the judge has invaded even this level of the narrative, which has until this last chapter been exclusively third person. So this heading also prefigures the complete ascendency and diffusion of the judge's ultraviolent worldview.

WORKS CITED

Adair, James. "The History of the American Indians." Oliver's Bookshelf. n.p., 24 Apr. 2008. Web. 24 Aug. 2015.

Berlant, Lauren. *Cruel Optimism*. Duke University Press, 2011.

Brown, Charles H. *Agents of Manifest Destiny: The Lives and times of the Filibusters*. University of North Carolina Press, 1980.

Brown, Lauren. "Existing without Consent: American History and the Judge in Cormac McCarthy's Blood Meridian." *Cormac McCarthy Journal*. Volume 16, number 1, 2018: 73–94.

Byrd, Jodi A. *The Transit of Empire: Indigenous Critiques of Colonialism*. University of Minnesota Press, 2011.

Campbell, Neil. "'Beyond Reckoning': Cormac McCarthy's Version of the West in Blood Meridian or The Evening Redness in the West." *Critique: Studies in Contemporary Fiction*. Volume 39, number 1, 1997: 55–64.

Cheah, Pheng. *Spectral Nationality: Passages of Freedom from Kant to Postcolonial Literatures of Liberation*. Columbia University Press, 2003.

Cheyfitz, Eric. "The Colonial Double Bind: Sovereignty and Civil Rights in Indian Country." *University of Pennsylvania Journal of Constitutional Law*. Volume 5, number 2, 2003: 223–40.

———. *The Columbia Guide to American Indian Literatures of the United States since 1945*. Columbia University Press, 2006.

———. *The Poetics of Imperialism: Translation and Colonization from the Tempest to Tarzan*. Oxford University Press, 1991.

———. "Savage Law. The Plot against American Indians in Johnson and Graham's Lessee v. M'lntosh and The Pioneers." In *Cultures of United States Imperialism*. Edited by Amy Kaplan and Donald E. Pease. Duke University Press, 1993: 109–28.

Cover, Robert. "Nomos and Narrative," *Harvard Law Review*. Volume 97, number 1, 1983.

Dean, John E. How Myth Became History: Texas Exceptionalism in the Borderlands. University of Arizona Press, 2016. https://search.ebscohost.com/login.aspx?direct=true&db=mzh&AN=2016380755&login.asp&site=ehost-live.

Deloria, Vine. *Behind the Trail of Broken Treaties; an Indian Declaration of Independence*. Delacorte, 1974.

Dole, Charles F. "The Right and Wrong of the Monroe Doctrine." *The Atlantic*, Atlantic Media Company, 19 June 2017.

Emerson, Thomas E., and R. Barry Lewis. *Cahokia and the Hinterlands: Middle Mississippian Cultures of the Midwest*, University of Illinois Press, 2000.

Ellis, Jay. "'What Happens to Country' in Blood Meridian." *Rocky Mountain Review of Language and Literature*. Volume 60, number 1, 2006: 85–97.

Gordon, Avery. *Ghostly Matters: Haunting and the Sociological Imagination*. University of Minnesota Press, 1997.

Greve, Julius. "'Another Kind of Clay': On Blood Meridian's Okenian Philosophy of Nature." *Cormac McCarthy Journal*. Volume 13, number 1, 2015: 27–53.

Guillemin, Georg. *The Pastoral Vision of Cormac McCarthy*. Texas A&M University Press, 2004.

Johnson and Graham's Lessee v. William M'Intosh. 21 U.S. 543. Supreme Court of the United States. 1823. HeinOnline. 3 May 2015.

Kades, Eric. "The Dark Side of Efficiency: Johnson v. M'Intosh and the Expropriation of American Indian Lands." *University of Pennsylvania Law Review* 148, number 4, 2000.

Lincoln, Kenneth. *Cormac McCarthy: American Canticles*. Palgrave Macmillan, 2009.

McCarthy, Cormac. *Blood Meridian or The Evening Redness in the West: 25th Anniversary Edition*. Vintage International, 1992.

Mundik, Petra. *A Bloody and Barbarous God: The Metaphysics of Cormac McCarthy*. University of New Mexico Press, 2016.

"'On Indian Removal' (1830)." OurDocuments.gov. National Archives and Records Administration, 25 Aug. 2015.

"Peter Burnett: 1851 State of the State Address." Governors of California. California State Library, n.d. 21 Sept. 2015.

Pitts, Jonathan. "Writing On: 'Blood Meridian' as Devisionary Western." *Western American Literature*, Volume 33, number 1, 1998: 6–25.

Purdy, Jedediah. *Property and Empire: The Law of Imperialism in Johnson v. M'Intosh*. George Washington Law Review 75, 2007, 329–71.

Rives, George Lockhart. *The United States and Mexico, 1821–1848; a History of the Relations between the Two Countries from the Independence of Mexico to the Close of the War with the United States*. C. Scribner's Sons, 1913.

Robertson, Lindsay Gordon. *Conquest by Law: How the Discovery of America Dispossessed Indigenous Peoples of Their Lands*. Oxford University Press, 2005.

Scott, James C. *Seeing like a State: How Certain Schemes to Improve the Human Condition Have Failed*. Yale University Press, 1998.

Sedgwick, Eve Kosofsky., and Adam Frank. *Touching Feeling: Affect, Pedagogy, Performativity*. Duke University Press, 2003.

Snyder, Phillip A. "Disappearance in Cormac McCarthy's Blood Meridian." *Western American Literature*. Volume 44, number 2, 2009, 127–39.

Spurgeon, Sara L. *Exploding the Western: Myths of Empire on the Postmodern Frontier*. Texas A&M University Press, 2005.

Wallach, Rick. "Twenty-Five Years of Blood Meridian." *Southwestern American Literature*. Volume 36, number 3, 2011.

Williams, Robert A. *The American Indian in Western Legal Thought: The Discourses of Conquest*. Oxford University Press, 1990.

———. *Like a Loaded Weapon: The Rehnquist Court, Indian Rights, and the Legal History of Racism in America*. University of Minnesota Press, 2005.

Wood, James. "Red Planet: The Sanguinary Sublime of Cormac McCarthy." *New Yorker*. Conde Nast, 25 July 2005.

U.S. Const. art. 1, sec. 8, cl. 3. Print.

The Frailty of Everything Revealed at Last

Cormac McCarthy and Radical Atheism

DAVID DEACON

This essay will explore the manifestation of atheistic thinking in Cormac McCarthy's writing, with a primary focus on *The Road*, though connections will be made with *The Sunset Limited* as well. Associations between McCarthy and a religious or spiritual structure of feeling are numerous, from Tom Ryan's proposition of a "Catholic sensibility" in *The Road* (13), to Broncano's systematic mapping of religious symbolism across his published works (2013). Edwin T. Arnold maintained the following: the question of whether or not "Cormac McCarthy is a writer of the sacred should be beyond dispute" (215). In contrast to this, I will argue that McCarthy's veneration of life is indeed demonstrable, though its predication on the sacred and transcendent is often ambiguous and even questionable. This is not to suggest that the author's literary style dwells in nihilism. Rather I claim that his later works contemplate a form of radical atheism, a position developed by Martin Hägglund in response to the so-called religious turn in Jacques Derrida's philosophy. This atheistic framework enables us to read McCarthy against both a straightforward embrace of theological revelation and nihilism. This false dichotomy distracts from the way in which McCarthy grounds his work in the flawed nature of both totalities. For Hägglund, the revisionist impression of Derrida's aesthetic, style, and concern around religiosity was a misreading. At the basis of Derrida's writing, Hägglund contends, lies a radical and irreducible atheism that recognizes the contradictory nature of sacralization and transcendence. *The*

Road, I argue, contains a similar revelation. This position will be developed with due regard to the cultural and political climate of the twenty-first century, as I view both *The Road* and *The Sunset Limited* as documents reflective of the post 9/11 era.

McCarthy often presented his political, economic, and theological affiliations in ambiguous ways—where he divulged them at all. Catholicism, however, does form a symbolic register in his published novels, alongside other metaphysical positions like Gnosticism.[1] Despite his aversion to media attention, the topic of atheism became an unlikely point of public elucidation for the author in 2013. McCarthy chose to appear in a documentary entitled *The Unbelievers*. It charts the journey of both Richard Dawkins and physicist Lawrence Krauss on a global lecture tour in which they promulgate the natural sciences as a tonic for the irrationality of religiosity. The director, Gus Holwerda, also chose to include interviews with various notable artists and personalities (Cameron Diaz and Woody Allen among them) who identified with the message of New Atheism and its evangelical mission—they appear to be literally spreading the evangelical truth of atheism in the documentary's narrative.[2] McCarthy's appearance is minuscule, played during the final credits. He states simply: "[Is science] the last word on what the physical world is? I don't know, but if it's not the last word it's at least the best word" (*The Unbelievers*). While publicizing the documentary, Holwerda (2014) stated that McCarthy is "kinda undecided" on the god question, while many of the rest were "quite outspoken" when it came to their nonreligious identity. This public coyness was not unusual for McCarthy, who often avoided promotion of his novels until the 1990s—only a handful of interviews ever appeared in print until the early 2000s. His appearance on Oprah to promote *The Road* was his only appearance on camera until that point; *The Unbelievers* was his second. At the very least we can say that the topic of atheism and how it is discussed is something he takes seriously.[3] Until now, scholars have been largely interested in the religious themes and references throughout his prose. Atheism has received comparatively little attention.[4] Quite often atheism is understood as a proxy for nihilism, positivism, or a one-dimensional naturalism. The heart of Hägglund's framework of radical atheism is to differentiate between the veneration of immortality and transcendence on religious terms and the desire for such a thing, which is ultimately an untenable and contradictory position. Hägglund finds in Derrida's project of deconstruction a wish to engage theological vocabulary and ideas to interrogate them and the desires they portend to satiate. The desire for religion and the sacred is a psychological and ontological position that is crucial to Derrida's philosophical project in Hägglund's reading, such that the true objects of faith (transcendence and the actualization of immortality) are rendered illusory and undesirable. What emerges is a philosophical logic of survival that tries to navigate fragility and radical contingency. It is this logic which I suggest is profitable in a reading of late McCarthy too. It accounts for the presence of religious taxonomies insofar as they describe a desire or yearning for stability which cannot, and arguably should not be fulfilled. The extremities explored in *The Road* and foreshadowed in *The Sunset Limited* are navigated within a framework of atheistic survival—as per Hägglund's methodology—as opposed to a theological imperative.

The Sunset Limited, 9/11, and the Politics of Atheism

The format of *The Sunset Limited* (*TSL*) is often debated within McCarthy's body of work. It was not his first piece of theatrical writing. Prior to its publication he had released *The Stonemason*, a text that struggled to gain critical recognition alongside his novels. *TSL* was largely written in tandem with *The Road* throughout 2004–2005, and was eventually published in two versions. One was intended for stage production, and the other appeared with the curious subtitle of "A Novel in Dramatic Form." It proceeds as a dialogue, Beckettian in style, between two characters known only as "Black" and "White." White has attempted to throw himself in front of a train known as "the Sunset Limited" on a New York subway platform. Black has saved his life and sets about convincing him that the God of the Bible planned this action. White—a nihilistic college professor—is dismissive of this notion and systematically undermines Black's religious arguments in the ensuing dialogue. It is essentially a problem play grounded in competing determinisms, with Black giving credence to the omniscient guiding hand of a transcendent deity, while White subscribes to rationally deduced principles of physical and cultural entropy. His attempted suicide is, accordingly, not an act of revolt, but rather one of resignation to what O'Connor calls the knowledge of a "brutally indifferent reality of the material universe" in this era of

McCarthy's writing ("Anti-Matters" 3). The illusion of a deity, and everything we have summoned up to replace it, has lost its effervescence.

Tyburski has previously proposed some thematic similarities between *TSL* and *The Road*, stating "McCarthy demonstrates that, where there is no apparent evidence of the divine, we will create 'a naked intent toward God,' even out of abomination and ash" (127). Tyburski follows in the critical approach of Arnold, who asserted that the "ambiguous nihilism"—a term associated with Vereen Bell's pioneering scholarship—of McCarthy's early writing receded with the coming of the 1990s Border Trilogy. This notion of a generally humanistic stance (in congress with religiosity) in the author's work has persisted, though some critics like Dorson (in Counternarrative Possibilities) and O'Connor are among a growing body to gently dispute this in a variety of ways.[5]

A pedestrian reading of the character White would place him in an existential crisis or mode of perpetual melancholia, induced by the stubborn entropy O'Connor sees as a structuring tenet of the landscape in *The Road*. When queried on his reasons for choosing to end his own life by Black, who remains incredulous, he says that "I cant speak for others. My own reasons center around a gradual loss of make-believe. That's all. A gradual enlightenment as to the nature of reality. Of the world" (120). This "gradual enlightenment" has led him to believe the following: "the world is basically a forced labor camp from which the workers—perfectly innocent—are led forth by lottery, a few each day, to be executed. I dont think that this is just the way I see it. I think it's the way it is. Are there alternate views? Of course. Will any of them stand close scrutiny? No" (122). In White we see a symbolic articulation of disenchantment. Its source is relatively unambiguous also. He asserts that "the things I believe in dont exist anymore. It's foolish to pretend that they do. Western Civilization finally went up in smoke in the chimneys at Dachau but I was too infatuated to see it. I see it now" (27). White proposes that the Holocaust represented a definitive moment or event that ruptured a narrative of humanistic progression, something that he aligns with the momentum of Enlightenment thought and tradition.

TSL operates as a journey through modern atheistic thought, from the optimism of the Enlightenment through to Nietzsche's tragedy of the "death of God," and finally to postwar existentialism. When the character of Black pleads with White to reconsider his plan to take his own life on the basis of religious determinism, he asserts, "I dont believe in God. Can you understand that? Look around you man. Cant you see? The clamor and din of those in torment has to be the sound most pleasing to his ear. And I loathe these discussions. The argument of the village atheist whose single passion is to revile endlessly that which he denies the existence of in the first place" (125). White's frustrations align with the "lateness" of style that Boxall diagnosed as a discernible development in early twenty-first century fiction. In our era, he argues:

> Many of the senses by which we orient ourselves have failed, or seemed to fail, leaving us uncertain both of our whereabouts, and of our heading. [...] The grand historical narratives of western modernity, which led us to believe that we were a venerable people, a people with most of our history behind us, seem suddenly to have yielded to the realization that we are still young, a culture at the beginning of a new era, for which we have no measure, and no chronological apparatus. (19)

It is this sense of disorientation, malaise, and crisis structuring *TSL*, which makes it a significant complementary piece to *The Road*. Aside from the practicalities of being written in tandem with one another, both texts share a concern for the existential and total raisons d'être as they relate to religious modes of living. The disagreement between Black and White in *TSL* highlights the eroded state of the latter in McCarthy's literary project. This negative imagination has also been highlighted by Dorson, who argues that McCarthy's writing has always constituted counternarratives to different hegemonies—social, political, economic, and cultural—and it is clear from the interplay between texts here that metaphysical, theological, and even atheistic determinisms are being scrutinized.

The sociopolitical and cultural context of *TSL* is significant and unusual in the McCarthy canon. It marked a departure from the rural, southern, and sparse locations of his earlier career. What is more, situating the dialogue in a tenement apartment in New York City signifies a shift in perspective if the text is read in congress with his preceding works. To center such a discussion in an urban metropolis while imbuing it with an interrogation of social class—the setting acts as a dislocating one for the comparatively well-heeled character of White—invites questions concerning location, space, and literary strategy. Likewise, the recent alignment of McCarthy's late writing with the post-9/11 epoch should not be overlooked here. Richard Gray argued for *The Road*'s inclusion in the post 9/11 canon more than ten years ago, suggesting that the book's ennui, apocalypticism, and hunger for redemption was emblematic of the effect the years after the World Trade Center attacks had on the public imagination. The propensity to consciously or subconsciously invoke the myth of the fall, Gray argues, was omnipresent in the narrativization of those years. Holloway places *The Road* within the structure of feeling or emotional framework shaped by these years, suggesting that the hegemonic narrative of perpetual threat against the United States provided justification for aggressive foreign policy. The fortification of the U.S. "homeland" employed quasi- and often openly religio-political tropes, a sense of endurance, and spiritual vindication. This served to consolidate a purposefully ambiguous notion of terror,[6] and Holloway notes that this affective framework is one shared by *The Road*. McCarthy's positioning of *The Sunset Limited* in New York during this time also resonates with this reading of the author's environment and sociopolitical imagination. It is the site of trauma and loss, one that White struggles to overcome, countered by Black's sense of determinism and zeal. Michael Lynn Crews has explored McCarthy's affinity for Oswald Spengler's infamous narrative of Western decline, and this too is detectable in White's rhetoric. It compounds the notion of a cultural precipice or looming void tied to discussions about civilization and its vulnerability. Spengler's thesis resonated with Samuel P. Huntington's influential re-incantation of the *Clash of Civilizations* debate prior to 9/11—a rallying call of sorts for neoconservative rhetoric in the months and years following the WTC attacks. The political unconscious of *TSL* is alive with the emotional and affective post-9/11 features outlined by Holloway in relation to *The Road*, and alluded to by Cooper (2011) before him.

 I outline the sociopolitical and cultural debates surrounding both *The Road* and *TSL* as I consider McCarthy's presentation of religious and atheistic discourse to be reflective of and connected to these contextual features. The emergence of New Atheism during these post-9/11 years—despite claims toward scientific objectivity and positivism—was also deeply political.[7] McCarthy's participation in *The Unbelievers*, along with his characteristic ambiguity casting doubt over the central thesis of the documentary, suggests that he was engaged with and cognizant of this body of discourse. Its religio-political basis overlaps with McCarthy's in his contemporaneous fictional endeavors, though he does not share their methods or zeal. Rather, I will argue, the binary ideological opposition in *TSL* is complemented by the manifestation of a different kind of atheistic thinking in *The Road*. While Tyburski deems the connection between both texts to be grounded in spiritual sustenance, I see it as one of atheistic rumination. McCarthy attempts to think beyond an antireligious atheism and begins by interrogating our desire for religion in a philosophical mode. Martin Hägglund's concept of radical atheism develops this, and will be applied to the novel in due course, after I outline the methodology below.

Reading Radical Atheism

"The debate between philosophy and literature begins over the question of desire" (Hägglund, *Dying for Time* 1). With this sentiment, Hägglund opens his study of literary modernism, particularly the work of Proust, Woolf, and Nabokov. The modernity these authors sought to articulate and wrestle with had not yet overcome the fundamental tragedy of mortality nor envisioned a way beyond it. The propensity to elevate art to a surrogate for grand metanarratives in a secularizing cultural climate was merely retreading what Hägglund sees as the chrono-libidinous struggle to survive. Facing mortality and the fate of tradition imparted to these celebrated modernist writers was something which was far more eternal than the notion of an enduring religious culture or theology. It was the desire for these things that was most pressing. The modernist canon, Hägglund argues, chronicles the logic of survival under modernity. This is ultimately a struggle to comprehend and function within a secular temporality. Hägglund frames this around "Socrates' demarcation of poetry from philosophy. Poetry engages the desire for mortal life that can always be lost. In contrast, the task of philosophy is to convert the desire for the mortal into a desire for the immortal that can never be lost" (2). McCarthy's reverence for Greek tragedy is well-established, and the tension between the poetic and philosophical instinct is tangible at the heart of the narrative in *The Road*. What is more, *The Sunset Limited* is based on a dialectic between these two intuitions and can thus be read as a reduction of these principles in McCarthy's vernacular.

For Hägglund much of what we call modernist literature is underpinned by these two forces: observing how technology can align our lived or imagined realities with one principle or another, for example, or considering the degree to which our consumption and indulgence in the trappings of modernity might accelerate one or the other. As such the antimetaphysical sensibility that a cursory reading of postmodernism would suggest was banished in the mid-late twentieth century may have found renewed application. A certain degree of this is also tangible in *The Road*, a text that reifies anxieties about the ability of our environment to sustain even the most basic of existences. The prospect of a child for the character of Ely (or the character best described as Ely), for instance, is an apparition to begin with. The idea of the world as it is in *The Road* is not welcoming of such promise and may even form a new kind of tragedy, one in which the boy's generation might not wish for survival at all.

Hägglund suggests this fraught nexus of philosophical and poetic drives underpinned modernist endeavors and became the basis of Derrida's trouble with the stability of truth and enchantment—a quandary McCarthy shares. To navigate it, Hägglund (in *Radical Atheism*) argues that Derrida crafted a "logic of survival" that begins to explain our desire for religion, immortality, and transcendence without ultimately submitting to it. He does so by establishing Derrida's philosophy as one built on a radical atheism. This contradicts much of the so-called religious turn that supposedly manifested in Derrida's later writing. John D. Caputo is a primary figure in these religious appraisals of Derrida, arguing that deconstruction in fact correlates with a conception of theological practice known as "weak thought" (*Prayers and Tears*), an approach celebrating the weakness of God, or a deconstructed and therefore less institutionalized theology. Caputo's position was an influential one, but Hägglund's more recent intervention has not only demanded a reappraisal of Derrida's commitment to sacred ontology but also the way in which his work articulates a form of atheism that is at once antimetaphysical and attentive to the poetic/philosophical binary outlined above. He explains the position as follows:

> In short, radical atheism seeks to demonstrate that the temporal finitude of survival is not a lack of being that we desire to overcome. Rather, it is because of temporal finitude that one cares about life in the first place. If life were fully present in itself—if it were not haunted by past and future, by

what has been and what may be—there would be no reason to care about life, since nothing could happen to it. That is why I argue [. . .] that the so-called desire for immortality is contradicted from within by a desire for survival. If one did not desire to survive, one would not fear death and dream of immortality. For the same reason, however, an immortal state of being cannot even hypothetically appease the fear of death or satisfy the desire to live on. Rather than redeeming death the state of immortality would bring about death, since it would put an end to the time of life. Given the desire for survival, the timelessness of God or immortality is thus undesirable, since it would eliminate the possibility for anything to happen and anyone to survive. ("The Radical Evil of Deconstruction" 133)

His critical stance seeks to distance atheism from its positivistic stance as a finely tuned rationalistic vehicle for the refutation of God's existence. For Hägglund—and as he views it, for Derrida—it should question "the desire for God and immortality" (*Radical Atheism* 1). He argues that scientific metaphysicians—those who feel that a deity's existence can be disproven by reason alone—operate on an ironic fallacy, in that "mortal being is still conceived as a lack of being that we desire to transcend" (1). He formulates a conception of ontology bound by Derrida's concept of the trace, that which allows us to experience the past in a present moment and preserve it through to some radically unknown future. Life is intrinsically dependent on temporality, and it is our experience of this that creates a conscious appreciation for the fragility, and thus the value, of life in all its radical contingency. Hägglund considers this a mode of living cognizant of the "radical finitude of survival" (1)—it is not something to be overcome, as this would equate to a yearning for immortality, which he likens to our thirst for God. To hunger after or desire a life beyond this radical finitude we are persistently open to in our everyday lives would be to neglect the very essence of what makes life so precious to begin with. In Hägglund's model of atheism, "the finitude of survival opens the chance for everything that is desired and the threat of everything that is feared" (2).

His core argument arises from what he sees as a misunderstanding of Derrida's employment of religious terminology, and its overall goal of theorizing some kind of absolute, though flawed (or weak) overarching goodness. He posits that this notion of something that is absolute, and unscathed by evil or error (in Derrida's lexicon), is intrinsically antipodal to Derrida's most basic of concepts at the heart of deconstruction. Hägglund's reappraisal of his work focuses on the paradoxes of immortality, purity, and idealism that Derrida's work consistently sought to problematize and subvert. For Hägglund, his corpus develops a radically atheistic "logic of survival," in that it acknowledges the irreducible facticity of atheism but will not be reduced to this negation as a condition of human survival.

The Road contains what Watkin calls an "anthropotheistic" sentiment wherein the man deifies his son.[8] The flawed and desperate nature of this strategy is apparent from early on, however, given the sheer contingency of their existence in the world that remains. I contend that McCarthy's novel is ultimately one of reckoning with the time of (atheistic) life. It employs religious motifs, symbols, rituals, and reference points, but what is actually rendered in so doing is the desire for religion and immortality, such that the man can survive in the harsh and disorientating remains of the world. He "cobble[s] together [a] passable ghost" (58–59)—on the advice of his partner before her presumed surrender to the bleak circumstances—and yet his desire for such perfection has often been read as a sacred revelation.[9] On the contrary, I propose that *The Road* constitutes an examination of care and hospitality grounded in the desire for life and immortality and recognition of its limits, such that the novel submits to the (radically atheistic) time of life. There is precedent for applying Derrida to McCarthy. Skrimshire uses Derrida's interpretation of messianism to appraise the promise and thirst for redemption amid disaster, arguing it to be a novel of "simultaneous resistance and mourning" (13). This resistance is fueled, for Skrimshire, by a force bearing many similarities to Derridean messianism. The application of Hägglund's ideas expand on this and enable a consideration of how these contradictions (resistance-mourning) might ultimately lead to an atheistic temporality and space in McCarthy's landscape.

The Road and Radical Atheism

The Road begins by displacing its characters in terms of temporal orientation in a space beyond clock time. We are told that the "clocks stopped at 1:17" (54). The referential points of time circle only around the bare ingredients of survival. Time is measured in proximity to sustenance and that which would present danger to these fundamentals of endurance. This enforced reduction of existence reorientates the protagonists toward the time of life as something defined by the sheer vulnerability of mortal life. Their temporality or experience of time is not dictated by anything beyond base-level survival, underscored by the sparsity of luxury, commodities, and security. Hägglund's radical atheism elementally acknowledges frailty as a mutually recognizable trait from which an intersubjective ethics can grow. When the fragility of the landscape and the protagonists' ability to interpret it with linguistic referents are seen to be equally vulnerable, the reader is presented with the following passage; a monologue from an omniscient narrator: "He'd had this feeling before, beyond the numbness and the dull despair. The world shrinking down about a raw core of parsible entities. The names of things slowly following those things into oblivion. Colors. The names of birds. Things to eat. Finally the names of things one believed to be true. More fragile than he would have thought. How much was gone already? The sacred idiom shorn of its referents and so of its reality. Drawing down like something trying to preserve heat. In time to wink out forever" (51–52).

I will consider this "sacred idiom," bearing in mind what sacredness is within the context of Hägglund, and thus Derrida's logic: "the very movement of sacralization is contradicted from within by a constitutive autoimmunity. To hold something to be sacred is to seek to immunize it, to protect it from being violated or corrupted. Yet one cannot protect anything without committing it to a future that allows it to live on and by the same token exposes it to corruption. The immunization of the good must therefore 'take in trust'—as Derrida puts it—'that radical evil without which good would be for nothing'" ("The Radical Evil of Deconstruction" 132). The narrator alludes to the "world shrinking down around a raw core of parsible entities" (*The Road* 51). The term "parsible" here is notable, in that it alludes to the analysis of a system in fragmentary form (often linguistic systems) in order to uncover an underlying meaning or logic. I focus on it here as McCarthy is persistently interested in the idea of a logos—some originary animating force that brings order to a world. McCarthy's fiction is efficient at interrogating various interpretations of logos—be they religious, positivistic, scientific, political, economic, or otherwise. In *The Road*, the divine lens through which the man views the child is further consolidated in the following passage:

"The boy sat tottering. The man watched him that he not topple into the flames. He kicked holes in the sand for the boy's hips and shoulders where he would sleep and he sat holding him while he tousled his hair before the fire to dry it. All of this like some ancient anointing. So be it. Evoke the forms. Where you've nothing else construct ceremonies out of the air and breathe upon them" (77). The care of his child is bound up in forms tied to religiously inclined models of devotion, as though a divine creation or embodiment is the only sense that can be made of the boy's unyielding hopefulness for his life to come. I propose here, against theological and postsecular interpretations of the text, that McCarthy is not evoking the forms of old to sustain the world in a religiously imbued sense with a view to reigniting a divine metaphysics. Rather, I understand this drive of evocation as something synonymous with Derrida's (and by extension Hägglund's) employment of faith. It is not subservient to a deconstructed divinity, as faith is not the same as "the religious ideal of absolute immunity (or 'the unscathed')," as Hägglund ("Radical Evil of Deconstruction" 132) puts it. McCarthy himself acknowledged this distinction between faith and its object—or the lack of necessity for a divine object to worship—in his interview with Oprah Winfrey. Asked about the religious undertones of *The Road* and their centrality to the theme of perseverance, McCarthy responded that "sometimes it's good to pray. I don't think you have to have a clear idea of who or what God is to pray. [In fact] you can be quite doubtful about the whole business."[10]

McCarthy's focus on method or utility of ritual as opposed to the substance of divinity or object of deification suggests that there is something about the concept of performative discourse he finds attractive, giving further credence to his affinity with poststructuralism, while also applying it directly to the idea of divinity. His aversion to such an idealism or totalizing metaphysics can be understood through his disinclination toward the idea of perfectibility. Beyond this being a mere injunction against a metaphysical deity, the author has suggested in previous interviews that he is suspicious of utopian projects of the human, asserting: "I think the notion that the species can be improved in some way, that everyone could live in harmony, is a really dangerous idea. Those who are afflicted with this notion are the first ones to give up their souls, their freedom. Your desire that it be that way will enslave you and make your life vacuous" (McCarthy in Woodward 29). The "vacuity" of existence is reminiscent of the double bind Hägglund describes at the heart of religious desire. Humans, for McCarthy, exist and develop like the pragmatist model of the self,[11] utterly contingent, and at the whim of a contemporaneous social order, which in itself represents a contingent and imperfect disunity. Therefore the prospect of perfectibility is anathema to McCarthy. The status of the unscathed is contradictory in his literary universe, and it would appear, in his general outlook. Hägglund defines the unscathed as:

> [The] pure and the untouched, the sacred and the holy, the safe and sound. The common denominator for religions is thus that they promote a notion of the unscathed—regardless of whether the unscathed is posited as transcendent or immanent and regardless of whether it is called God or something else. As Derrida puts it, 'every religion' holds out a 'horizon of redemption, of the restoration of the unscathed, of indemnification.' Accordingly, the religious promise of the good would be the promise of something that is unscathed by evil. The good may be threatened from the outside—by corruption, idolatry, misunderstanding, and so on—but in itself it is exempt from evil. ("The Radical Evil of Deconstruction" 129)

This idea of something that is pure—an irreducible good—is evocative and useful when interpreting *The Road*. The father-son relationship does appear to rest upon the man's steadfast belief that within his son there resides an unscathed goodness; something intangible, but worth protecting with his life. In fact, it is so imperative that the boy's essential essence remain unscathed by evil that his father instructs him in the most efficient manner to end his own life, should the man be killed in the process of finding food or protecting the boy. In a memorable scene the man wonders whether or not he could take the boy's life if it meant sparing him the grim reality of death at the hands of the cannibalistic marauders: "He watched the boy sleeping. Can you do it? When the time comes? Can you?" (28). The idea of protecting his child through such radical means is grounded in a belief that the boy is representative of radical, absolute goodness—therefore, the extinguishing of his fragile material ontology would in some perverse way protect the essence of unscathed goodness in his eyes. That is to say a conception of this goodness is necessary for his perseverance—similar to Metcalf's proposition (via Dewey's pragmatist philosophy) of a balance between idealism and the actual. Early in the novel the man's partner (the boy's mother) decides to abandon the family, exiting their temporary shelter with a lack of supplies (even basic clothing), surely equating to death by exposure. Her logic for abandonment—which the man later condones—is as follows:

> Sooner or later they will catch us and they will kill us. They will rape me. They'll rape him (the boy). They are going to rape us and kill us and eat us and you wont face it. You'd rather wait for it to happen. But I cant. I cant. . . . The one thing I can tell you is that you wont survive for yourself. I know because I would never have come this far. A person who had no one would be well advised to cobble together some passable ghost. Breathe it into being and coax it along with words of love. Offer it each phantom crumb and shield it from harm with your body. As for me my only hope is for eternal nothingness and I hope it with all my heart. (58–59)

The man later describes his duty to protect his son as one "appointed [. . .] by God" (80). So far it is not difficult to understand the application of the unscathed to the text. It provides us with a method of understanding the intersubjective dynamic between father and son in a way that surpasses standardized accounts of intergenerational relations. It also demonstrates the sensibility of "eternal nothingness" that the mother longs for. She espouses that there is no naturally existing counterbalance to the evil now pervading the landscape, and as such one who wishes to survive must "cobble together some passable ghost" in order to endure it. This gesture, I argue, is central to the affinity between the man's sense of mission and a form of "radical evil" that he cannot escape from.[12]

Snyder proposed that Derrida's ideas of hospitality "may have just the philosophical structure we need to construct a productive model through which we can interrogate hospitality's ethical dilemma in *The Road* and reveal its pervasiveness throughout the novel" (3). If hospitality is built upon the intersubjective relationship between a known agent and an other—in the case of *The Road*, this is usually a father and son motif, though other characters like Ely do emerge—then it is also a productive lens through which to view the embrace of vulnerability and its presentation in the novel. Hägglund's assertion about Derrida's embrace of fragility is crucial—the welcoming of another person bears within it the possibility of both good and evil, and this is precisely the recipe of life Hägglund suggests Derrida has in mind as the basis of his "logic of survival," one which is simultaneously aware of its mortality and averse to sacralizing it in order to place the former beyond reach. Survival in Hägglund's interpretation of Derrida proceeds from a radical openness to finitude and hence a radically atheistic point of origin. The wish to embrace the timelessness of God is in fact undesirable, as it is a contradiction—"If one did desire to survive, one would not fear death and dream of immortality" (131). This fear of death stems from the fact that "it is because of temporal finitude that one cares about life in the first place. If life were fully present in itself—if it were not haunted by past and future, by what has been and what may be—there would be no reason to care about life, since nothing could happen to it" (131). I maintain that *The Road* exudes a similar proposition of meaning and how it is obtained. The man is haunted by the real prospect of violence and finitude; its inescapability is manifest in daily living. The text consequently offers a vision of a fragile future. Boxall speaks of a sense of "late culture" in his overview of twenty-first-century fiction—the new millennium brought with it a sense of an ending, like the closing of a cycle, and is arguably tied to fears of environmental vulnerability (12). The latter, too, is a discernible theme in McCarthy's rendering of an indeterminate period in America's future. Many ecocritical readings of the novel have taken place, but I would argue that this too falls into the remit of McCarthy's presentation of life as being bound to an absolute vulnerability and contingency, thus rendering the cause of the ecological disaster secondary to its endurance.[13] This is not something to be mourned so much as understood in the context of its basic animating feature—the only real alternative to it is an immortality grounded in timelessness, usually represented or presided over by a deity or animating spirit. The man's installment of his son as a "god" in *The Road* is a fallacy the environment and his own material frailty betray by the novel's closure.

Snyder's contention that hospitality in a rendering of America that would seem to warn against it is, I agree, a productive mode of interrogating the text. His interpretation, however, stops short of proposing the heightened focus on the dangers of hospitality. One of the most memorable encounters in the novel is with an aging man who remains as weary of his hosts as the man is of his motives. He calls himself "Ely," but later admits that this is a pseudonym. He is otherwise referred to as the "old man," but for ease of differentiation he will be referred to here as Ely. When the man and boy encounter him, he recoils in fear, inviting the pair to look through his things, assuring them that "I dont have anything. You can look if you want," assuming the pair are "robbers" (172). Having established that neither side intends any immediate harm—though the man remains wary of Ely—the child seems to insist on their welcoming of him: "He's just scared papa" (172). A curious utterance is issued when the man finally accepts his duty to entertain Ely, at his son's behest: "Damn, he whispered. He looked down at the old man. Perhaps he'd turn into a god and they to trees. All right, he said" (173). As their conversation continues, the man inquires into the length of Ely's wandering in the wilderness. He responds: "I was always on the road. You cant stay in one place" (179). Ely suggests that he "knew [the event] was coming" (180), extinguishing stable localities and standard models of existence, rendering him a form of (potentially sophistic) prophet. He insists that he did nothing to prepare for the apocalyptic event, however. A reluctance with which the man agrees: "People were always getting ready for tomorrow. I didnt believe in that. Tomorrow wasnt getting ready for them. It didnt even know they were there" (179). The man's postulation of undetermined temporality dissolves narratives of redemption both in relation to futurity, and by extension a glorious past. In this sense, he finds agreement with Hägglund's temporal vision and model for contingent ontology. This recognition voices, for O'Connor, an "anti-conservative message" in the novel's revelation: "one cannot satisfactorily retrieve the past, there is no golden age, and any attempt to construct memory, to fortify it, to make it immune from contamination, is automatically negated. "The father acknowledges as much when he sees the boy as alien. The reason it is essential that the father is differentiated from the boy, like all fathers, is that the son comes from a future world, one that is as alien and monstrous as another planet" (23). This resonates with the status of such fallacies in the context and framework surrounding both *The Road* and *The Sunset Limited*. Not only does the man's logic here acknowledge an elemental contingency in the world he navigates, but it also speaks to the desire for such fallacies to begin with. Within the post-9/11 epoch the vulnerability of the U.S. homeland—the dreadful potential for its destruction is represented by the scorched earth and ubiquitous ash—and the lionization of glorious pasts and invocations of sublime futures maintains an implicit critique of the ideological employment of such ideas in a time where the management of existential anxiety so often embraced religio-nationalistic fervor akin to this rhetoric. That is to say, the quest or journey narrative McCarthy crafts frequently resonates with the political surroundings of these years, and as Dorson argued, forms a counternarrative. I suggest that the religious symbolism and mythology woven into the novel should also be read as such, underscoring the critical potential and utility of an atheistic reading.

Conclusion

Existing perspectives on *The Road*—as well as *The Sunset Limited*—tend to operate within a religious-secular (or materialist) binary. Where atheism is considered within this dynamic it is often aligned with nihilism and resignation to the cruelty or indifference of the environment. Religious allegory, symbolism, and ritual are similarly presented as indicative of an underlying spiritual basis of hope and endurance. The argument I have presented speaks to the ambiguity and pragmatism that characterizes much of McCarthy's writing. The narrative is attuned to the time of life, which for Hägglund requires a necessarily atheistic appreciation of radical contingency and fragility. The moral basis of the novel's trajectory is directed, sustained, and undermined by the man's alternating zeal and pragmatism. The abiding truth of his legacy is the contingency of their ontology, and this establishes a radically atheistic angle on the novel's quest.

In the same way that *Blood Meridian* constitutes a counternarrative to the foundational mythos of the United States, and particularly the romance of benevolent domination in the Western, I suggest that McCarthy's post-9/11 writing can be viewed in a similar way. The presentation and focus on religious, antireligious and (a)theological rumination between *The Sunset Limited* and *The Road* is a fertile space for new potential in our grasp of McCarthy's response to the sociocultural and political context of these novels too, in both conscious and subconscious ways. The logic of survival that emerges in *The Road* around an atheistic appreciation of temporality and endurance speaks to the diversity of McCarthy's philosophical endeavors, but also to his social, cultural, and political imagination, given the rhetorical fusion of religio-political language, taxonomy, and import in his contemporaneous surroundings. The employment of religious motifs and language is not merely reverential or indeed political, but a way of mapping McCarthy's efforts to think beyond theology and the desire for its rewards. This is the fulcrum of Hägglund's addition to this method of interpretation—God is not merely silent, omniscient, or monstrous for McCarthy. Rather, the prospect may simply be undesirable. The contingency of the human world as it is rendered may encourage a thirst for immortality and divine intention beyond the protagonists' perception, but its delivery would negate their knowledge, experience, and even motivations to begin with. The man's love for his child, for example, exceeds the vessel of religious ritual and language and is even rejected by the boy, who—despite his father's insistence—is not unscathed or immune to the dangers of the world or even subverting moral expectations of his own accord. Taking the atheistic potential of his literary evolution seriously may also help us to interrogate some historical assumptions about the McCarthy canon and revisit his appreciation of the natural world in its both malignant and wondrous capacities, alongside how we navigate them. This is not to position McCarthy as an atheist on a personal level, though I venture to say that we should seriously consider the potential of his writing in its capacity to explore atheistic approaches to ontology, culture, historicization, rhetoric, and narrative.

NOTES

1. Beyond Broncano's extensive mapping of McCarthy's religious allusions, Watson also suggests a productive use of Catholic sacraments and symbolic registers in *Suttree*. O'Gorman describes McCarthy's affinity with Flannery O'Connor's writing, and indeed the southern Gothic tradition more broadly as a likely basis for Catholicism's productive stylistic capacity in his work. Mundik's comprehensive *A Bloody and Barbarous God: The Metaphysics of Cormac McCarthy* outlines Gnostic allusions in *Blood Meridian* among numerous other metaphysical perspectives on the McCarthy corpus.

2. New Atheism refers to a publishing phenomenon and cultural movement in the early 2000s. Sometimes understood as British in nature, its impact was quite considerable in the United States. Richard Dawkins's *The God Delusion* was kept from reaching number one on the Amazon Bestsellers chart in 2007 in Britain only by a celebrity chef's cookbook and the final two installments of the Harry Potter series. It charted within the top fifty titles in the United States in the same year. Christopher Hitchens's *God Is Not Great: How Religion Poisons Everything* achieved number twenty-five in the United States. The first text to create sizeable impact, Sam Harris's *The End of Faith*, was released in 2004. He has explained that composition began on September 12, 2001, perceiving the terrorist attacks on the United States to be grounded in religious thinking more

generally, though this latter assertion was made in defense against subsequent claims of Islamophobia. Accusations of the latter were commonplace regarding most figures of New Atheism, and the movement is now often understood as a product of the post-9/11 era, wherein the rationalistic and positivistic stances of key figures was presented as a tonic against the irrationality of a crudely reduced notion of "religion." See LeDrew's *The Evolution of Atheism* for more.

3. McCarthy did participate in the Science Friday podcast with host Laurence Krauss and film-maker Werner Herzog in 2016. His relationship with Krauss seemed to endure with another podcast appearance for the Origins series in 2022 before McCarthy's death.

4. Nietzschean perspectives on McCarthy have been explored by Woodson. These encapsulate a tendency toward existentialism in the author's work and its associated body of critique, spanning back to the formative insights from Bell. More recently O'Connor's focus on the antimetaphysical basis of *The Road* has added significant depth to post-theological readings of McCarthy, culminating in the recent monograph *Cormac McCarthy, Philosophy and the Physics of the Damned*.

5. O'Connor's proposition (in "Anti-Matters") of *The Road* being grounded in a recognition of intensifying scarcity (both material and cultural) as it relates to forces of entropy, linked to McCarthy's proximity to the discipline of physics in recent years, provides a crucial exploration of moral ethics in the father-son relationship through an antimetaphysical lens.

6. Dick Cheney, for example, asserted on September 14, 2001, that "the theme that comes through repeatedly for me is that 9/11 changed everything. It changed the way we think about threats to the United States. It changed about our recognition of our vulnerabilities. It changed in terms of the kind of national security strategy we need to pursue, in terms of guaranteeing the safety and security of the American people. [. . .] From our perspective, trying to deal with this continuing campaign of terror, if you will, the war on terror that we're engaged in, this is a continuing enterprise. The people that were involved in some of those activities before 9/11 are still out there ("Transcript for September 14").

7. See LeDrew's *The Evolution of Atheism* (2015).

8. Watkin explains that anthropothecisms, which include secularisms, "merely [replace] 'God' with a supposedly atheistic placeholder such as 'Man' or 'Reason,' explicitly rejecting but implicitly imitating theology's categories of thinking, changing merely the terms in which those categories are articulated" (2).

9. Pudney argues that the novel invites both Judeo-Christian and atheistic perspectives, but crucially depicts atheism as an absence of God's light: "McCarthy's novel is clearly preoccupied with very similar ideas about the place of humanity in a godless, or at least seemingly godless, universe" (298). Atheism, then, exists as a dark foil of enchantment. Metcalf offers an engaging reading of McCarthy's adoption of "religiousness" in the pragmatist tradition of John Dewey, asserting that what "we see in McCarthy's novel [is] the religious faith that Dewey describes as a devotion to the ideal while manifesting 'piety toward the actual'" (147). I view the novel's devotion to the

ideal as more problematic and difficult to counterbalance, and as such account for it as something which is hollowed out or bankrupted, demanding a repositioning within something more akin to Hägglund's atheistic temporality.

10. No official transcript of this interview exists, but it can be viewed here: https://www.youtube.com/watch?v=y3kpzuk1Y8I

11. Here I refer specifically to Richard Rorty's description on the social imperative of the self, outlined most succinctly in *Contingency, Irony, and Solidarity*.

12. "Radical evil" is a tenet of Kantian philosophy Derrida readily drew inspiration from. Furthermore, Hägglund uses it to support his logic of radical atheism. It recognizes the irreducible presence of evil in every interaction that welcomes the good. The thirst for pure goodness is self-negating in this perspective.

13. See Estes, De Bruyn, and Gruber Godfrey for example.

WORKS CITED

Arnold, Edwin T. "McCarthy and the Sacred: A Reading of *The Crossing*." In *Cormac McCarthy: New Directions*. Edited by James D. Lilley. University of New Mexico Press, 2014: 215–38.

Bell, Vereen M. *The Achievement of Cormac McCarthy*. Louisiana State University Press, 1988.

Boxall, Peter. *Twenty-First Century Fiction: A Critical Introduction*. Cambridge University Press, 2013.

Broncano, Manuel. *Religion in Cormac McCarthy's Fiction: Apocryphal Borderlands*. Routledge, 2013.

Caputo, John D. *The Prayers and Tears of Jacques Derrida*. Indiana University Press, 1997.

Cheney, Richard B. "Transcript for September 14 2003." NBC News, September 2003.

"Cormac McCarthy Interview on the Oprah Winfrey Show," YouTube, uploaded by Mohammad Farooq, 2014.

Cooper, Lydia R. "Cormac McCarthy's *The Road* as Apocalyptic Grail Narrative." *Studies in the Novel*, vol. 43, no. 2, 2011, pp. 218–36.

Crews, Michael Lynn. *Books Are Made Out of Books: A Guide to Cormac McCarthy's Literary Influences*. University of Texas Press, 2017.

Dawkins, Richard. *The God Delusion*. Bantam Books, 2006.

De Bruyn, Ben. "Borrowed Time, Borrowed World and Borrowed Eyes: Care, Ruin and Vision in McCarthy's *The Road* and Harrison's Ecocriticism." *English Studies*. Volume 91, number 7, 2010: 776–89.

Dorson, James. *Counternarrative Possibilities: Virgin Land, Homeland, and Cormac McCarthy's Negative Imagination*. University of Chicago Press, 2016.

Estes, Andrew Keller. *Cormac McCarthy and the Writing of American Spaces*. Rodopi, 2013.

Gray, Richard. *After the Fall: American Literature since 9/11*. Wiley, 2011.

Gruber Godfrey, Laura. "'The World He'd Lost': Geography and 'Green' Memory in

Cormac McCarthy's *The Road*." *Critique: Studies in Contemporary Fiction.* Volume 52, number 2, 2011: 163–75.

Hägglund, Martin. *Dying for Time: Proust, Woolfe, Nabokov.* Harvard University Press, 2012.

———. *Radical Atheism: Derrida and the Time of Life.* Stanford University Press, 2008.

———. "The Radical Evil of Deconstruction: A Reply to John Caputo." *Journal for Cultural and Religious Theory.* Volume 11, number 2, 2011: 126–50.

Harris, Sam. *The End of Faith: Religion, Terror, and the Future of Reason.* W. W. Norton & Company, 2004.

Hitchens, Christopher. *God Is Not Great: How Religion Poisons Everything.* Atlantic Books, 2007.

Holloway, David. "Mapping McCarthy in the Age of Neoconservatism, or the Politics of Affect in *The Road*." *Cormac McCarthy Journal.* Volume 17, number 1, 2019: 4–26.

Holwerda, Gus. "Stephen Colbert Featured in '*The Unbelievers*.'" Colbert News Hub, 14 March, 2014.

Huntington, Samuel P. *The Clash of Civilizations and the Remaking of World Order.* Simon & Schuster, 1996.

Krauss, Lawrence, host. "From the Origin of Art, to the End of Humanity." *Science Friday*, Science Friday Initiative, 1 January 2016, https://www.sciencefriday.com/segments/from-the-origin-of-art-to-the-end-of-humanity/#segment-transcript.

———. "Dialogue with Cormac McCarthy about Science, on the occasion of his newest book releases." *Origins Podcast*, 9 December 2022, https://www.youtube.com/watch?v=wfYr5zF-0Ns.

LeDrew, Stephen. *Evolution of Atheism: The Politics of a Modern Movement.* Oxford University Press, 2015.

McCarthy, Cormac. *Blood Meridian or The Evening Redness in the West: 25th Anniversary Edition.* Vintage International, 1992.

———. *The Road.* Alfred A. Knopf, 2006.

———. *The Sunset Limited: A Novel in Dramatic Form.* Random House, 2006.

———. *Suttree.* Random House, 1979.

Metcalf, Robert. "Religion and the 'Religious': Cormac McCarthy and John Dewey." *Journal of Speculative Philosophy.* Volume 31, number 1, 2017: 135–54.

Mundik, Petra. *A Bloody and Barbarous God: The Metaphysics of Cormac McCarthy.* University of New Mexico Press, 2016.

O'Connor, Patrick. "Anti-Matters: Moral Ethics in Cormac McCarthy's *The Road*." *European Journal of American Studies.* Volume 12, number 3, 2017.

———. *Cormac McCarthy, Philosophy and the Physics of the Damned.* Edinburgh University Press, 2022.

O'Gorman, Farrell. "Violence, Nature and Prophecy in Flannery O'Connor and Cormac McCarthy." In *Flannery O'Connor in the Age of Terrorism: Essays on Violence and Grace.* Edited by Robert Donahoo and Avis Hewitt. University of Tennessee Press, 2010: 143–68.

Pudney, Eric. "Christianity and Cormac McCarthy's *The Road*." *English Studies.* Volume 96, number 3, 2015: 293–309.

Rorty, Richard. *Contingency, Irony, and Solidarity.* Cambridge University Press, 1989.

Ryan, Tom. "*The Road* by Cormac McCarthy." *National Catholic Reporter,* May 4 2007.

Skrimshire, Stefan. "'There is no God and we are his prophets': Deconstructing Redemption in Cormac McCarthy's *The Road.*" *Journal for Cultural Research.* Volume 15, number 1, 2011: 1–14.

Snyder, Phillip A. "Hospitality in Cormac McCarthy's '*The Road.*'" *Cormac McCarthy Journal.* Volume 6, number 1, 2008: 69–86.

The Unbelievers. Directed by Gus Holwerda, featuring Richard Dawkins, Lawrence Krauss, and Cormac McCarthy, Black Chalk, 2013.

Tyburski, Susan J. "'The Lingering Scent of Divinity' in '*The Sunset Limited*' and '*The Road.*'" *Cormac McCarthy Journal.* Volume 6, 2008: 121–28. Watkin, Christopher. *Difficult Atheism: Post-Theological Thinking in Alain Badiou, Jean-Luc Nancy and Quentin Meillassoux.* Edinburgh University Press, 2011.

Watson, James. "'The only words I know are the Catholic ones': Sacramental Existentialism in Cormac McCarthy's *Suttree.*" *Southwestern American Literature.* Volume 62, number 5, May 2013.

Woodson, Linda. "'The Lighted Display Case': A Nietzschean Reading of Cormac McCarthy's Border Fiction." In *Philosophical Approaches to Cormac McCarthy.* Edited by Chris Eagle. Routledge, 2017: 126–41.

Woodward, Richard B. "Cormac McCarthy's Venomous Fiction." *New York Times Magazine,* April 1992: 28–31.

The Darker Picture and the Ghost of Culture

The Sunset Limited

TREVOR JACKSON

> It is through story that we devise ways of living bearably in time.
> —CHARLES TAYLOR, *The Language Animal*

> Death is the major issue in the world. For you, for me, for all of us.
> It just is. To not be able to talk about it is very odd.
> —CORMAC MCCARTHY, "Cormac Country"

When *The Sunset Limited: A Novel in Dramatic Form* first appeared just a month after *The Road* in 2006, Dianne Luce observed that both works provided a "disturbingly realistic contemplation of the loss of the world in a future that reinscribes the terrain of McCarthy's personal and writerly beginnings," harkening back to the nihilism first detected by Vereen Bell in *The Achievement of Cormac McCarthy* ("Beyond the Border" 6). Lydia Cooper similarly remarks that the play leans "precariously in the direction of a nihilism not seen in McCarthy's work since *Blood Meridian*," both signaling a new orientation for McCarthy studies after the Border Trilogy and sketching a picture of its particularly bleak outlook (1). This is not to say that readers have not found redemptive or spiritual elements in McCarthy's latest works that gesture toward the positive. Indeed, as we shall see, while many scholars acknowledge the grimness of the play, they have also sought to wrestle the dialogic contest away from White and generally validate Black's position or find the play ambiguous in its outcome. I would like to suggest an interpretation in which White wins the staged debate and where, despite this, Black survives by recourse to language—it is, after all, only the words he says he lacks to express the absent presence, to give representation to that apparently ineffable thing that typifies his faith. By recognizing the constitutive aspects of language, the aspects that allow Black to retain his reason for existence or construct his faith anew around an absent present, we can transform this grim outlook into one that can sustain life, both individual existential life and collective social life.

As Nicholas Monk claims, modernity is the "background" that supplies the force to McCarthy's work as a whole: a modernity that is "imperialist, Eurocentric, scientific, rational, and technological" (1). *The Sunset Limited* can be read fruitfully—and frighteningly—with this background in mind, and I follow such a perspective that draws on the wide concerns of modernity and the current globalized situation and existential predicament in which the Western world finds itself. With the consequences of modernity in mind, Monk goes on to say that "over the large part of his work, McCarthy has shown us the ultimate destination for the present direction of human travel both for us as individuals, and for our systems of government and social interaction" (xiii). If *The Sunset Limited* and *The Road* are representative of the direction of human travel, alarm is appropriate. If McCarthy's work operates "at the level of consciousness-raising," as Monk argues it does, then "there is hope that at least the *direction* of the dialectic of modernity might be altered and its coercive force weakened" (15). My purpose in reevaluating White's perspective is to put into relief the wider consequences of modernity and the urgency with which McCarthy regards the fundamental questions of human existence in the contemporary world. This essay does seek a reevaluation of White's perspective, which scholars have been quick to dismiss or distance themselves from. White's assessment of the world is one that Black recognizes (he's looking at it every day, he says), and not enough attention has been paid to the weight of White's claims as they concern contemporary social life: Black's tenement apartment as the Everywhere of the world; White's disillusion with human culture as a stable, life-sustaining entity (and religion is clearly part of human culture); Black's likening White's condition to an addictive illness; and White's assertion that the world is a forced labor camp. In what follows, I'll address each of these moments in the play and provide analysis situating that urgency. Before reassessing White's outlook, the first section of this essay gives an extensive review of the positions that scholars have taken on *The Sunset Limited*. This is intended, first, to provide a context that includes the variety of arguments evolving out of the play and their relations to one another and, second, to highlight the manner in which scholars tend to validate Black's perspective or maintain an ambiguous interpretation of the play. Such a review of the scholarly writing also allows the core themes of the play to rise to the surface.

Dianne Luce offers an initial reading of the play that underlines audience involvement, writing that the "capacity of the characters for making us care about and identify with them is key to the emotional life of *The Sunset Limited*, which is inescapably intimate and deeply personal to the audience" (13). Subtitled "A Dialogue of Life and Death," Luce's review of the play's Chicago production focuses on its existential aspects that she says "pertains to actual people" rather than abstract ideas (13). She remarks how the play moves in one direction, from Black dominating the discussion and argument to White doing so by the end, a movement "from faith to despair," but she also holds that the play "represents humankind's eternal dialogue with self, and with God" in the fashion of Dostoevsky (16). She characterizes Black as the "gnostic messenger from the alien good God" who delivers a "largely Christian message" that involves connection to God and to one's fellow human beings, and White as unable to relinquish his "intellect or his exceptionalism" despite the fact that he "recognizes that his devotion to culture has contributed to his misery" and "partly agrees with Black that his education is pushing him toward suicide" (16 and 18). Finding that the play ends with the "mysterious silence of God," Luce admits that while "White's anger has won him the argument" and "Black has lost his gambit to help this special case," Black has "not decisively lost his faith in God and his own mission" (20).

Unlike Luce, John Vanderheide views *The Sunset Limited* as an allegorical battle where Black and White vie in "relative symmetry and stasis" (still an ambiguous position) and emphasizes the demonic unfreedom that each character embodies (108).[1] Vanderheide argues that the point of the play is not that Black save White, but that "if anything, God arranged the encounter with the express purpose of curing Black's daemonism" and Black "fails to recognize this" (116). Black "misinterprets the significance of the event" in his demonic obsessions with helping and saving others and is left bereaved at the end, and Vanderheide writes that the "allegorical battle that Black wages with all his rhetorical force against his pale 'brother' falters and comes to nothing" (118). At the same time, however, and after seeming to yield ground to White, he writes of the play as a "collision of incompatible and opposing discourses that ends in an impasse," equalizing the play and arguing that the point is not the elevation of a victor and the desecration of a vanquished but the recognition of the self-destructive problems of a daemonic outlook (110).

Dividing reason and divinity into two modes of "apprehending reality" that constitute the "core" of the play's debate, Susan Tyburski acknowledges that the play strips the "human condition to its bones" (121). White is aligned with reason and the intellect, attempting to "convince Black that his instinctive faith is based on fantasy," while Black is aligned with the "scent" of divinity, which is not attainable through reason but is "something more basic and elemental, even sensual" (121). Tyburski argues that because White "cannot look beyond his disillusionment and pain, he is trapped in darkness and driven to self-destruction" (124). Black on the other hand finds that the "lingerin scent of divinity" (*TSL* 13) is what can "keep us reliably grounded in the world of the living" (122), what Tyburski calls the "surviving spiritual spark" or a "human hunger" for that very scent of divinity (121). We, the audience, are apparently left "breathing in desperation on the remaining embers of our faith" just like Black at the end of the play, and Tyburski argues ultimately that McCarthy "demonstrates that, where there is no apparent evidence of the divine" we will create it "even out of abomination and ash" (127), a perspective that works well for Black but does not fit White, taking for granted as it does the backdrop of faith in Christian culture and the apparent drive to rekindle it that is neither universal nor guaranteed.

Taking up both the overt and covert literary allusions of the play—Tolstoy, Gibbon, Kafka, Beckett, the Bible, Goethe—William Quirk gives most emphasis to Nietzsche and the oppositional forces of the Apollonian and Dionysian expounded upon in *The Birth of Tragedy*.[2] Isolated from others and vesting his belief in the beautiful illusion of cultural things, Quirk aligns White with the "Apollonian figure in extremis" (41). Black, then, becomes the Dionysian figure who tells stories, offers food, and engages White in all kinds of ways such that much of the play is Black drawing White into a variety of conversations. While "White wants the release in the destruction of individuation as death," Black "proposes a reunion with the 'unity of being' by finding some sort of community with which White might feel at home" (42). Because there are moments in which "periodic relaxations of the tension[s]" between the two characters take place—Black's jailhouse conversion story, anecdotes about alcoholism, the sharing of a meal—Quirk argues that "far from triumphant, White's nihilism has been tempered by a furtive Dionysianism, oddly minimalist but decidedly life-affirming in the end" (53–54). Quirk does not show, however, how these temporary relaxations of the tensions render the entirety of the play life-affirming (other than to say that they do) and such an account does not seem to take White's position into perspective. The play may be somewhat life-affirming for Black, but this is not the case for White.

Following Quirk's investigation of literary references in *The Sunset Limited*, Lydia Cooper examines Samuel Beckett's influences upon McCarthy's play.[3] The play's conclusion for Cooper is "not so much a conclusion as it is a trenchant rejection of any comforting sense of resolution" (1). Indeed, she argues that finding a resolution is not so much the point as is "contending with the questions" brought up in this "dichromatic, claustrophobically static, and silence-haunted play" (3).[4] In the tenuous discussion of two competing conceptions of life, Black's perspective stresses the inherent value of human life based on the "human capacity to create and experience *divine* significance through linguistic acts," language being the entity that allows human beings not only to communicate with one another but also to transcend the temporal limits of human life (7). On the other hand, White's perspective recognizes the "absurdity of such claims of meaning in a world in which the arbitrary nature of human conditions and the ubiquity of death annihilate such consolations" (7). Cooper points to Artaud's defense of suicide as the logical conclusion wrought by the conditions of the postmodern world (7). Employing both stasis and silence for its Beckettian effects, and despite highlighting White's claims, Cooper finds that when Black and White depart one another they do so "without resolution," while at the same time permitting the "audience to confront both possible and justifiable interpretations of an authentic life" (12).

Considering the frequency with which McCarthy evokes the sacred and Christianity in his works, Mary Brewer draws a distinction between the author's novels, which "foreground how dominant cultural values and practices do not represent a humane order," and the plays, which "express a spiritual world view" and show McCarthy to be a "deeply moral writer who is fundamentally concerned with spiritual aspects of human existence" (40).

The Stonemason and *The Sunset Limited* both, according to Brewer, reveal a "distinct lack of ambivalence concerning the question of God's existence" on the part of key characters (42). Black is obviously invested in a belief in God and the afterlife, and Brewer points out that his existential Christianity is of a Kierkegaardian hue that elevates the central message of Jesus—love—above the regurgitation of dogma so that one does not need even to have read the Bible to be saved (42). Brewer finds a "sense of stability attached to the spiritual self" and claims that the "imagined world of the drama offers us an authentic accounting of God and faith" (43).[5] Black becomes a "literal fisher of men" intent on imitating the life and deeds of Jesus (48). White, on the other hand, for Brewer, can "only identify with others in abstract terms" (48). She cites White's desire not to visit his dying mother, his lack of friends, his "over-investment in things," and his maledictions uttered against his fellow humans as evidence that despite his revulsion of the Holocaust and the current breakdown of human civilization his "claims to be moved by larger crimes against humanity ring hollow" (48–49)—an assertion that I do not believe holds up when we consider the severity of White's claims. She even speculates that White may not go on to commit suicide once he departs the apartment, a claim that is absurd in the context of the play itself. For Brewer, in the end, Black remains confident and retains his faith, the "silent but palpable presence of the divine finally endorsing Black's ticket to salvation" (50), echoing again a world that works well for Black but does not fully consider White's perspective.

In his *Cormac McCarthy: American Canticles*, an overview of McCarthy's work, Kenneth Lincoln advances one salient point concerning race in *The Sunset Limited* that foregrounds the social and historical circumstances that lend credence to White's argument: that "from 6 to 10 million Afro-American [*sic*] slaves were brought to our shores in chains by privileged prodigal Puritans looking for a new life" and the "country may not want to hear this over, but White Man's Burden and oceanic slave trade hyperrealize American history to this day" (156–57). He adds the specter of Manifest Destiny and the long eugenics movement in the United States to the concerns to contemplate when we look at White's apocalyptic perspective, and writes that in the end the "white man is left with the strange fruits of his own racial guilt and dubious material success, the suburban spoils of his toxic mind, greedy pockets, and affluent suffering" (161). More useful for identifying the vertiginous social issues springing from a reading of *The Sunset Limited* than an accurate picture of White's character, Lincoln reminds us of the tremendous inequalities, savagery, and violence that have been perpetrated in the name of civilization.

Rather than the reflecting the minimalism of Samuel Beckett, Robert Wyllie argues that *The Sunset Limited* is a "philosophical dialogue, the minimally literary genre closely associated with Plato and neglected by philosophers since the Enlightenment" (186). Like "Plato's early aporetic Socratic dialogues," Wyllie also finds *The Sunset Limited* "ultimately inconclusive" (187). Nevertheless, he writes that the play "does not become White's diatribe" and that it remains "a two-sided philosophical dialogue in which Black's position must be taken seriously" (187). Wyllie argues that McCarthy sets Kierkegaard on one side of this philosophical dialogue, associating him with Black, and on the other situates Schopenhauer whose ideas are embodied by the figure of White. Drawing from *The Sickness unto Death*, where Kierkegaard speaks extensively of suicide, Wyllie writes that "White inhabits what Kierkegaard calls a *self-inclosing reserve* of despair" wherein the greatest danger becomes suicide and which Black attempts to "interrupt" by references to the outside world (190). Against White's intellectualism, Black "argues for powerful religious feelings that he cannot articulate" and "raises the existential possibility of the Christian's radical cosmic optimism" (188–89). This, of course, works well for Black's perspective but not for White's. According to Wyllie, White's "belief in the primacy of the intellect leaves no room for wonder" and where Black's experience of divinity is "beyond understanding," for White what "cannot be understood is not worth understanding" (195): Black attempts to convince White that his is not an "intellectual solution to a hypothesis, but rather a passionate leap of pride or envy" (201). White's suicide, however, short of being an act of escapism, has "philosophical grounds" (200): White "repeats some of the core tenets of Schopenhauer's pessimism: death is the purpose of life, existence is a process of constant dying, existence is pervaded by suffering" (197). Wyllie admits that White is even more dangerous than Schopenhauer when it comes to the maintenance of human life, but, again, finds the dialogue, while dark, inconclusive, writing that any "hope or despair must come from outside of the text" (202).

Deepening this engagement with Schopenhauer, Russell M. Hillier examines the play in light of the philosopher's ethical system, claiming that as the play comes to resemble a "daunting compendium of Western philosophy" understanding Schopenhauer's moral philosophy better situates "Black's altruism as well as White's egoism and solipsism" and allows us to "re-read the play's ambiguous conclusion" (106). Considering Schopenhauer's ethical system, "White's ostensibly Schopenhauerian perspective can be seen to lack substance and credibility," while Black's ethical conduct makes him not only a "virtuous man" but places him "on the path toward Schopenhauerian sainthood" (107). The Schopenhauerian individual is one who "sets himself or herself apart from and superior to everyone and everything else" and regards "all phenomena about the self as objects to fulfill one's own will," which turns out to be "illusory and delusional" because it harms others (109). For Hillier this accurately describes White, whose misanthropy and hermetic isolation from others "prevents the possibility of coming to know himself through conversation with others" such that his seclusion "cuts off the possibility of self-reflection" (110). Because Schopenhauer classifies suicide as a "self-obsessed expression of the Will-to-Live," Hillier sees White's attempt as a "further manifestation of his egoism" and argues that in such light "suicide is a betrayal of life and an offense to those who heroically endure the sufferings of this world" (112–13). Black, however, follows an altruistic or saintly ascetic and as a "reformed Cain" (119) has "risen from a more depraved and benighted moral condition" than White and seeks redress for his former mistreatment of his fellow men (117). Hillier argues that the entirety of the play's drama is "built upon Black's untiring ingenuity in trying to open White's eyes to the truth of the oneness and identity of all with all" (122), a unitary perspective assuming a "fellowship of pain" goes on to produce a "moral imperative for a fellowship of compassion" (119). White, however, does not acquiesce to Black's rhetoric, instead electing to remain within Schopenhauer's *"principium individuationis"* (125). Of the two monologues that close the play, Hillier dismissively calls White's "a noisy jeremiad scornful of the ideas of God and human fellowship" that is "ultimately closed, self-contained, and self-involved" while Black's closing monologue—delivered to an empty stage—is "prayerful, open, and provisional, recognizing the presence of a covenant with God and others and the value of his continuing altruistic purpose and endeavor" (128). Concluding that the play "denies us a middle ground or a comfortable seat on the fence" and emphasizing White's "troubled egoism" and Black's "saintly altruism," Hillier still finds that it "requires its readers and spectators to choose which moral path is worth the candle" (130).

As I demonstrate, *The Sunset Limited* is a rich and richly debatable text. This essay has also highlighted the ways in which ambivalence toward the ending and a tendency to favor Black's position have pervaded readings of the play. Except for a few instances that I have foregrounded in the above, criticism thus far has not adequately dealt with White's position, calling for a revaluation that I begin below. One purpose of reframing the discussion around *The Sunset Limited* in favor of White's claims—or at least his victory in the play's debate—is to bring greater urgency to and increased consciousness about the legacy and effects of modernity at large.

From the very first line of the play—"What am I supposed to do with you, Professor?"—*The Sunset Limited* begs questions of ethics (*TSL* 3). The second line—"Why are you supposed to do anything?" (3)—transitions the question into the existential, and the play at large deals with the approaching death that all human beings must face up to in one way or another. That the play makes itself relevant by confronting the looming specter of death cannot be overstated, and while the play seems small scale and sparse enough—two men in a minimal room—the discussion is expansive and so wide ranging as to include the concerns of all human beings. It is this very scope that is all-inclusive, leading Dianne Luce to recognize that the play takes place in "the eternal present" (14). Despite being set in a "tenement building in a black ghetto in New York City" (*SSL* 3), the play remains "in its way, just as barren as the cadaverous world of *The Road*" (Tyburski 122), for "seemingly no world lies beyond Black's apartment" (Wyllie 190), the two characters enclosed behind a strange set of locks. Engaging as he does a range of philosophical issues pertaining to death, McCarthy reminds his "everyman and everywoman readers that their philosophical heritage and the issues of life and death that heritage entails do not belong on the dusty shelves of libraries, garrets, or ivory towers as the preserve of an elite" (Hillier 105). The play and the content it covers, in other words, belong to all who will one day die. McCarthy himself has even said that "that stage, that room, is the world" (quoted in Peebles 87). For the reader, "White's suicides and Black's salvations are extreme versions of the mini-dramas enacted by ordinary people every day" (Cooper 12) such that the world of the play becomes all-encompassing: ideas of verisimilitude aside, as Peter Josyph points out, suicidal depression and the notion of God are both powerful forces (80).

Not only, then, are the play's concerns those of everyman and everywoman, but the location of the play is set in an everywhere space that equates itself with the world. That world is identified with the carceral, with the prison, and more properly, as modernity. I will have more to say about modernity later, but for now it bears stressing that *The Sunset Limited* extends its everyperson applicability to the environment and conditions of modern society. The world of the play is both contemporary and carceral. When Black refuses to let White go his own way and leave the apartment, White alludes to this fact by saying "So what am I, a prisoner here?" (31). Black's response—that White was a death row prisoner before he ever arrived in Black's apartment—reinscribes White's meaning into the realm of the metaphorical, but does not dispel the sense of captivity that is a major theme of the play and which hovers over both characters (31). Black admits to being a murderer (36), indicates that he might be "just condemned" to trouble (38), and points out that he has spent time incarcerated. "I done seven years hard time," Black tells White, "and I was lucky not to of done a lot more" (37). Soon after this, when White asks how long he has been in the apartment, Black responds in similar manner, with a similar amount of time that serves to equate prison with the apartment: "Six years. Seven, almost" (39). Though the stage directions do not specify the number of locks on the door of Black's apartment, Diane Luce observes seven in the play's first performances at Steppenwolf's Garage Theater in Chicago, and Rick Wallach ties these to the Seven Seals of Revelations ("Dialogue" 15). The several sevens notwithstanding, Black makes one direct statement that confirms the commensurability of the apartment not only with the carceral but with the aforementioned everywhere of the modern world: when asked why he lives where he does, Black says: "Well, I'd say this pretty much is anywhere" (39).

The subsequent scene turns attention to Black's environment for the first time in the play, and we hear "I could live in another building I reckon. This is all right. I got a bedroom where I can get away. Got a sofa yonder where people can crash. Junkies and crackheads, mostly. Of course they goin to carry off your portables so I dont own nothin. And that's good" (39). Black's professed optimism—"And that's good" (39)—remains somewhat at odds with his own description, as he goes on to highlight the following points:

that the junkies Black endeavors to help prevent him from having appliances and music, that he can "get away" from the main room of his apartment and the junkies he hosts only by retreating to his bedroom, and that he needs a steel door for that bedroom, which he is saving up for, before he can have music again because the junkies would presumably steal whatever music-playing device he obtains. Still, Black seems to look upon his situation as normal, opposed to White who finds the place "terrible" and the kind of life "horrible" (40).

Black also offers the space of the apartment as everywhere in another way: "You want to help people that's in trouble," he says, underscoring his larger mission of bringing the word of God to the seemingly godless and depraved, "you pretty much got to go where the trouble is at" (38). And Black—"I aint a late sort of person" (22)—believes himself to be where he is supposed to be and that it would make little difference if he were in a separate building because again, in his words, this "pretty much is anywhere" (39), which is to say, everywhere.

For his part, White wants to know what "would be the difference between a building that was morally and spiritually vacant and one that was just plain empty" (77) and does not "see how you can feel safe" (75) in such a location as Black's apartment (Black agrees), calling it, and by extension the world, an unsalvageable cesspool. Black believes that "you [are] responsible for your brother" and adamantly—"I don't believe *think* quite says it" (77)—considers himself to be his brother's keeper. However, the efficacy of Black's practice, of his ministry, is radically called into question as White queries:

> WHITE: Have you ever stopped any of these people from taking drugs?
> BLACK: Not that I know of.
> WHITE: Then what is the point? I dont get it. I mean, its hopeless. This place is just a moral leper colony. (75)

Black provides one perspectival, personal response to White's query earlier in the play when he states that he enjoys a challenge:

> WHITE: You must know these people are not worth saving. Even if they could be saved. Which they cant. You must know that.

> BLACK: Well, I always liked a challenge. I started a ministry in prison fore I got out. Now that was a challenge. Lot of the brothers'd show up that they didnt really care nothing bout it. They could care less bout the word of God. They just wanted it on their resumé. (40–41)

In both instances—the ministry in prison and the work he is doing with junkies and crackheads in the tenement building—Black's admissions are those of failure: he has not stopped any of the junkies and crackheads from taking drugs, and he has not necessarily had any measures of success in prison ministering to convicts. Later in the play, as the contents of his "trick bag" wane and White begins to exercise his own rhetorical power, Black admits that he has never dealt with a suicide before:

> WHITE: You dont know what to offer a man about to board the Limited.
> BLACK: No. I dont. I feel like I'm about traded out.
> WHITE: Maybe you are. Have you ever dealt with suicides?
> BLACK: No. You the first one. (129)

Black's answer here in the negative adds to a string of seeming defeats and failures. Soon after this another, similar exchange:

> WHITE: Maybe you just need to accept that you're in over your head.
> BLACK: I do accept it. It dont let me off the hook though. (134)

And again, earlier in the play:

> WHITE: Why cant you people just accept it that some people don't even *want* to believe in God.
> BLACK: I accept that.
> WHITE: You do?
> BLACK: Sure I do. Meanin that I believe it to be a fact. I'm looking at it every day. I better accept it. (53)

Together these instances begin to craft an image of Black that reveals the depravity in which he lives and even the potential illusion of his ideas. For

White, happiness is "contrary to the human condition" (54), and this is an inevitable part of human culture: "We were born in such a fix as this. Suffering and human destiny are the same thing. Each is a description of the other" (55). White's is a sobering look at some of the basic facts of human life—that the "shadow of the axe hangs over every joy. Every road ends in death. Or worse. Every friendship. Every love. Torment, betrayal, loss, suffering, pain, age, indignity, and hideous lingering illness. All with a single conclusion. For you and for every one and every thing that you have chosen to care for" (137–38). "Everything you do," he says earlier, "closes a door somewhere ahead of you. And finally there is only one door left" (131): death. However we wish to dress up and respond to White's assessment with the concealing clothing of various culture apparatuses—from the religious to the philosophical and the literary, all of which may be ways to keep this reality at bay—he no doubt lays bare a chief existential reality of life.

That is to say, the responses to death, the myriad ways of confronting or avoiding it (including the conception of an afterlife that attempts to nullify death, as well as ritual and religious responses developed over thousands of years), are part and parcel of human culture. White finds in human culture the responses to daily and worldly trauma that make up so much of the social field of modern life, and it is important to understand his predicament, which Black ultimately relates to an addictive illness.[6] Black diagnoses White as a "culture junky" (27) because White says he values "cultural things," "books and music and art" and other "things like that," which are—or were—the "foundations of civilization" (25). These, however, have lost their value, frail and fragile as they are: "The things I believed in dont exist any more. It's foolish to pretend that they do. Western Civilization finally went up in smoke in the chimneys at Dachau but I was too infatuated to see it. I see it now" (27). If culture had been a life-sustaining entity for White, it no longer holds the power that it once did. Moving through the compendium of Western civilization that is *The Sunset Limited*, as already stated, Quirk has identified a number of the play's references to German literature and culture, including Kafka, whom McCarthy has White mention by name (135). Kafka is a herald of modernity par excellence, and both his stories "A Hunger Artist" and "In the Penal Colony" are referred to in the play (Quirk 38–40). Both stories evince the breakdown of meaning and the confusion of law and custom in the modern world, the former with a kind of artist alienated from his craft and the latter with an elaborate torture implement that is both a writing machine and an execution device. At large, as Quirk notes, in the "play's exploration of nihilism of the West, German literary tradition and culture has a certain centrality, in particular because of the terrible paradox that German culture presents" (Quirk 39). More narrowly and in the words of Walter Benjamin, Kafka's writing—and the sense of the modern subject I am trying to establish here—revolve around the "modern citizen who knows that he is at the mercy of a vast machinery of officialdom whose function is directed by authorities that remain nebulous to the executive organs, let alone to the people they deal with" (Benjamin 141). This is another way of underlining the alienation of modern life, especially considering the development and implementation of the Nazi concentration camps whose horrors stretch over all of Western civilization. White underscores this with his mention of Dachau, the prototype or pilot Nazi concentration camp that would house all manner of people and function as a slave-labor and death camp.[7] But the camp is both older and more ubiquitous than we often acknowledge, not an exclusively German phenomenon. As Michael A. Peters observes, the presence of the camp in the modern world is pervasive and diverse: "labor camps, concentration camps, extermination camps, death camps, reservations, immigrant camps, and camps for seemingly more benign purposes such as school, health, or scout camps" (1165) all abound with examples, from the American Indian Removal Act of 1830 to the British Boer War, to the German Herero genocide, to the Nazi concentration camp, as well as the Soviet gulags and Japanese internment camps to more contemporary instances (1166). Even this abbreviated list should give us pause when we consider the shared landscape of the modern world in which we live.

What counts in the last analysis, Giorgio Agamben tell us, is that the camp is the "place in which the most absolute *conditio inhumana* that has ever existed on earth was realized" (166). "Today," Agamben writes, "it is not the city but rather the camp that is the fundamental biopolitical paradigm of the West," a claim that "throws a sinister light on the models by which social sciences, sociology, urban studies, and architecture today are trying to conceive and organize the public space of the world's cities without any clear awareness that at their very center lies the same bare life [. . .] that defined the biopolitics of the great totalitarian states of the twentieth century" (181). All of this will "lead us to regard the camp not as a historical fact and an anomaly belonging to the past" but rather as the "hidden matrix and *nomos* of the political space in which we are still living" today (166).

In much the same way does White articulate his own vision of the world. Just after Black proclaims that "you must love your brother or die" (*TSL* 121) in a crystallization of his own position, White is urged to talk about the "world you know" (122):

WHITE: You dont want to hear.
BLACK: Sure I do.
WHITE: I dont think so.
BLACK: Go ahead.
WHITE: Alright. It's that the world is basically a forced labor camp from which the workers—perfectly innocent—are led forth by lottery, a few each day, to be executed. I dont think that this is just the way I see it. I think it's the way it is. Are there alternative views? Of course. Will any of them stand close scrutiny? No. (122)

White's use of the labor camp is instructive here, since this can be used to describe the condition of modernity as we have just seen, where one has few alternatives for living than to participate in the labor market in one way or another. Differing levels of comfort and income aside, White and Black are both participants in the labor system and the notion of work and identity is one tightly wound through American history—labor continues to have a powerful hold on any subjectivity. In the Western world, the near-compulsory aspects of work in modern life are difficult to miss and need little emphasis. So too with global inequalities, wealth disparities, and the colonial legacy of modernity. Considering Agamben's emphasis on the contemporaneity of the camp and Peters's variety of cases, Western civilization, which is the globalized form of colonial modernity, appears as a brutal history of exploitation and subjection. White extends this principle to the earliest times of history, issuing a major claim that "the darker picture is always the correct one. When you read the history of the world you are reading a saga of bloodshed and greed and folly the import of which is impossible to ignore. And yet we imagine that the future will somehow be different. I've no idea why we are even still here but in all probability we will not be here much longer" (112). White's claim is reminiscent of Walter Benjamin's famous statement in his seventh thesis on the philosophy of history: "For without exception the cultural treasures [the historical materialist] surveys have an origin which he cannot contemplate without horror. They owe their existence not only to the efforts of the great minds and talents who have created them, but also to the anonymous toil of their contemporaries. There is no document of civilization which is not at the same time a document of barbarism. And just as such a document is not free of barbarism, barbarism taints also the manner in which it was transmitted from one owner to another" (Benjamin 256). The connection to Benjamin allows us to ask whether White has, in fact, an idealized notion of culture, one that implicitly assumes that reality cannot be different than it currently stands. This is an assumption that, for Benjamin, would fail to appreciate the fact that there is nothing natural or necessary in the cultural development of capitalist modernity. However, White would surely be wise to this as an intellectual, and it is not so much that the project of modernity has failed in its formulations as that it has been successful in its culminations. By this, I mean the tools of management and coercion, the "imperialist, Eurocentric, scientific, rational, and technological" (Monk 1) project that persists to this day and which is mentioned in the opening of the essay. Culture could have flowed in a different direction than the darker picture that White propounds, but it didn't. The idea that culture "tends to contribute to human misery," that the "more one knows the more unhappy one is likely to be," may seem at first contrary to a definition of culture, which might involve the flourishing of human creative capacities and intellectual achievements, but which cannot be separated from the paradoxical overflow of violence and cruelty that exists alongside, and even conditions, our notions of a civilized world (110). Just as suffering and human destiny are mutually defining terms, so too are civilization and barbarism, one, as Benjamin writes, tainted by the other in an incommensurable way. "It's the first thing in that book there," White tells Black of the Bible in a similar vein, "The Garden of Eden. Knowledge as destructive to the spirit. Destructive to goodness" (111). The withholding of the trees of knowledge and of life in Genesis are certainly provocative, if not indicative of what White advances here.

Culture seems to be the fluid through which barbarism is inevitably transmitted, and violence taints every aspect of culture. As Lydia Cooper sees it,

> Both Black and White, in other words, fail to differentiate effectively between those things which grant meaning to life and death and those things which void human existence of merit. *Violence has completely infected their worldviews.* White no longer finds consolation in art or other indications of cultural vitality because of the real-world atrocity that has devastated the human race, making the aesthetic forms produced by these vicious creatures incapable of alluding to "higher" values. Black, on the other hand, unproblematically links violence to redemption in a theology that, because of its fusions of death and life, cannot provide a functional rationale for survival. (my italics 9)

If culture had been a life-sustaining entity for White it had been so through the "dreams or illusions" (136) that attend culture, things that "have been slowly emptied out. They no longer have any content. They are shapes only. A train, a wall, a world. Or a man. A thing dangling in senseless articulation in a howling void" (139). White's reason for suicide, he says, "center around a gradual loss of make-believe. That's all. A gradual enlightenment as to the nature of reality. Of the world" (120). These are what Black calls "worldly" or "elegant" reasons for White's decision to take his own life (120), reasons that align White's "pain and the world's pain [as] the same pain" (128). The broad view is important to keep in mind because White's dismay at the world is a dismay born from a sober, reasoned, elongated engagement with the intellectual tradition and with cultural history.

In his final monologue, where he coldly proclaims that he does not believe in God, White issues several claims, the first of which seeks to put any theodicy to rest when he says the "clamor and din of those in torment has to be the sound most pleasing to [God's] ear" (137). From here, White moves on to repetition, indicating at last that he loathes "these discussions" between the atheist and the man of faith, which they have been engaged in and that White has clearly worked through before (137). Both Cooper (13) and Quirk (50) speak of "endlessly repeated reenactment" and of the play "carrying out a continual, though not necessarily exact repetition of itself" respectively. Indeed, repetition and rehearsal seem to be an important part of the play, but it is clearly not endless as the play does come to an end with White's departure. White's repeated attempts to leave the apartment are repetitious, certainly, but perhaps more telling is when Black remarks that the bludgeoning of a fellow inmate in the chow hall is "really just the introduction to the actual story" of his hearing the voice of God (48); or that he "can come back to this" part about the alcoholic's dilemma because "I aint going to lose my place" (58); or the claim that "that's my story, Professor" once Black has revealed that crux of his jailhouse tale where he had to ask for help of divinity laying in the hospital bed after being stabbed many times (107). All indications are that Black has rehearsed and performed the central points of his theology before, presumably delivering his monologues to the crackheads and junkies he hosts and hopes to help. What he has not encountered before, as I have already pointed out, is White. For his part, White has already attended therapy (82) and attempted medication (83) for his existential ailments, all in vain, and his suicide is not some frivolous error so much as a calculated, contemplated choice. Both characters, clearly, have had debates, have run through the arguments and ideas, concerning the nonexistence of divinity—a fact that must be true for any reader of *The Sunset Limited*—and in the final analysis it is Black who is outmatched not just by the erudition of White, but by the weight of his claims.

White goes on in his final monologue to say the following about Black's theological community: "Your fellowship is a fellowship of pain and nothing more. And *if that pain were actually collective instead of simply reiterative* then the sheer weight of it would drag the world from the walls of the universe and send it crashing and burning through whatever night it might yet be capable of engendering until it was not even ash" (my italics 137). To make this point plainly, if all the pain of the world—of history and civilization—were experienced collectively (that is to say, all at once) rather than iterated in multiple individual installments as it is, then the weight of that pain would be ultimately devastating. It is through recourse to repetitions—your ministry, White accuses Black, "prepares one only for more life"—for "dreams and illusions and lies" that the actual collective pain is obfuscated and parceled into individual iterations of loss and suffering.

While White's ultimate fate remains clear (he departs the stage after Black has reluctantly unchained the door and goes out to his death), what of Black? Black survives. His first impulse is that of denial—"I know you dont mean them words" he calls after White (141)—and the hope, equally negligible, that White will again be on the subway platform awaiting Black: "I'm goin to be there in the mornin" (141). Now alone in an empty room, his second impulse, also of denial, is to speak to God in some kind of appeal, perhaps on behalf of White: "He didnt mean them words. You know he didnt. You know he didnt" (142). His next impulse is to turn to the self, to his own failure and his faith in God but also to language: "I dont understand what you sent me down there for. I dont understand it. If you wanted me to help him how come you didnt give me the words? You give em to him. What about me?" (142). Weeping on his knees by this point, his next impulse is self-reassurance, with an emphasis on language: "That's all right. That's all right. If you never *speak* again you know I'll keep your *word*. You know I will. You know I'm good for it" (my italics 142). Finally, he questions his own plan of endurance upon the emptiness of the stage—"Is that okay? Is that okay?" (143)—and the play concludes with a palpable sense of irony, as we are left to question Black's state of mind. What is important to emphasize here at the end is the degree to which language is being invoked and emphasized: everything is about words (keeping one's word, the meaning of words) or speech. Literally chasing the word of God, Black at one point tells White that "I'm hopin he might speak to me" again rather than to White (125). With "The Kekulé Problem: Where Did Language Come From?" (April 2017) and "McCarthy Returns to the Kekulé Problem: Answers to Questions and Questions That Cannot be Answered" (November 2017), McCarthy provides a new interdisciplinary directive to scholars to consider language and its development in the light of the scientific rather than that of the sacred or the mysterious.

In the latter of these two essays, he writes at one point that language is a "human invention, and human inventions are magical in that they give life to what heretofore had no existence," insisting that our "good working ideas have the capacity to direct our lives in a manner indistinguishable from any other reality." Charles Taylor's *The Language Animal: The Full Shape of the Human Linguistic Capacity* similarly claims that language does not only describe the world, but it in fact constitutes the world and shapes human experience. The importance of the words, and of their power to constitute reality (that is to say, to create and develop gods and religious systems, hypotheses and theoretic discourse, poetry and literature, modern epistemology) are of paramount importance not just to McCarthy, but also for calibrating the civilization of the future. The point that language is constitutive reminds us that the world need not be taken as it is given, that the entanglements and coordinates of modernity need not persist down the road that McCarthy has necessarily displayed and can be ruptured. This will hopefully be for the better, but the current direction of Western civilization will not be easily derailed. Tyburski writes that Black "spins his prison tale to keep White from walking out the door for another suicide attempt" (122), endeavoring to use language to preserve human life, if only for a short time, and Luce says that the "Scheherazade-like" Black "spins stories to save his brother's life," both acknowledging the relationship of language to what Luce calls "strategies to help him value his life" ("Dialogue" 16–17). Indeed, Cooper writes that "only words can prevent the imminent suicide but those words are so sonically charged that their very sense-making ability is thrown into question" (5). When Black speaks about the truth "wrote in the human heart," which "was wrote there a long time ago and will still be wrote there a long time hence" (68), the "deep bottom of the mine where the gold is" and the accommodating shape of Jesus Christ that must have existed before Christ himself, he alludes to language, that "forever thing" that only humans possess and that, because of this possession, has shaped us separately from all other creatures. In this view, language, rather than God or divinity, becomes an essential coordinate for McCarthy and further an instrument for interrupting the course of modernity that he has charted throughout the body of his work.

I opened this essay suggesting that Black survives by recourse to language—the words, he emphasizes repeatedly, are imbued with a sense of the sacred—but I would like to shift that focus, as McCarthy seems to want to do, to the scientific and the social. The problem that presents itself with any meditation on the constitutive power of language is how, indeed if, it can transform culture without carrying forward the barbarism that seems inherent in culture. Language, after all, for all its wondrous capabilities, can also be an instrument of violence. It is this very contingency of language that makes the task of recalibrating the direction of modernity so daunting. It is important to remember, however, that language has introduced "much greater flexibility, a capacity to change, even transform ourselves, which has no parallel among other animals" (Taylor 339): language has the ability to change, and has changed, the human organism. Charles Taylor highlights several capacities that are key in this unparalleled human flexibility. One is cultural: while humans everywhere appear to have similar instincts, they have engendered from one society to another vastly different cultures that are capable of changing in succeeding generations (399). Another is the development of a universalist ethic, which includes human rights, ideas of equality, and the pursuit of humanitarian action (340). A third is the possibility of a radical evil "aroused in us by the rejection of the good itself," the excitement of destruction that comes in "tearing down what the ethic of universal benevolence has tried to build" (341). It is this second thing—the development of a universalist ethic—that I would draw attention to. "The mystery" of such a universalist ethic, Taylor writes, "is that it was ever adopted, and comes more and more to be endorsed" (340). Taylor calls this mysterious because the universalist ethic often contrasts with local and instinctual concerns—such as, for instance, loyalty to the group and solidarity with insiders, which often translates to and requires hostility to outsiders and their exclusion from the group. Carrying out this ethic, Taylor says, involves a "kind of transcendence in relation to the instincts which the first humans inherited from their evolutionary ancestors" (340). This "ability to transform and transcend the instinctual heritage of nascent humanity" (341) is propelled by the incredible flexibility that language enables and is arguably a result of the emergence of language. In light of this, we might come to understand culture, as the origin of the word implies, as something that grows or is cultivated over time and transmitted through learning, something that undergoes development and develops ontologically. There is no human culture without language. Culture, if it is to be redeemed from the fatalism that White has articulated, becomes the resistance to and overriding of our instincts, the ability to deny or rechannel the tendencies that come to us naturally. The deprogramming of instinct is at once the opening to radical freedom, but also to a greater awareness of the contingency of the human meanings we have developed. Where White finds the evolutionary apparatus has brought "life ultimately to an awareness of one thing above all else and that one thing is futility" (136), it can equally be said that life ultimately needs sustaining narratives, what White has, in a critically dismissive way, called dreams and illusions. Such sustaining narratives—be they mythic, religious, scientific, or related to the universalist ethic—might not be so much illusions as projections, postulations, and principles to externalize and follow. The good life, clearly, is by no means guaranteed. It must be conceived, developed, and spread through the conscious processes of culture in order to be actualized. This related idea, that capitalist modernity need not be the way the world is, remains essential to any attempt to reject the notion of McCarthy as pure pessimist. In this essay, I have sought a reevaluation of White's perspective, which we might view as a warning for the future direction of Western civilization.

NOTES

1. For Vanderheide, this "ostentatious unfreedom" that characterizes demonism—where a character is represented by a singular trait that seems to be monomaniacal—"defines the opposing parties" of the play, where Black and White both have no choice but to embody the polar oppositions they argue for throughout (111). Neither White nor Black is a "memetic representation of a human being, but a personified complex of signs bearing iconographical meaning for the culturally initiated" such that, on the allegorical level, their very names signify a flight into the abstract (112). Drawing a connection between White, Melville's *Moby-Dick*, the Book of Job (which is the only book of the Bible mentioned in the play by name, the only part of it White says he has read), and ultimately a connection to the biblical Leviathan, Vanderheide aligns White's character with Leviathan and Black's with Job. In the Book of Job, Vanderheide argues that "Leviathan's function is singularly clear: to cure Job of his daemonic single-mindedness," to "free Job from his obsession before it leads to a fatal encounter with an overwhelmingly greater demonic force" (115). This liberation from daemonic obsession "entails the unfixing of Job's identity—a difficult and painful process for a daemonic agent" (115).

2. Where the Apollonian is the "state of individuation" represented by the tragic hero of Greek theater, primarily connected with sculpture, with contemplation and appreciation at a distance and "with its orientation around beautiful appearances," the Dionysian involves the more engaged "call to song, dance, and the fullest enjoyment of the senses," a state of "intoxicated, musical jubilation" represented by the chorus in Greek tragedy (40).

3. The "play's simplistic stage dialogue in which the meaning of life and definitions of human courage and ethics are distilled into the barest parsable linguistic entities" warrant comparison to Beckett (3). For Cooper, *The Sunset Limited* is similar to Beckett's "under-populated stage worlds in which characters trapped in physical stasis argue philosophically through dialogue that play on the meaningless of disconnected, unproductive language (1)."

4. Finding that White and Black are not two separate entities but "two parts of a dramatic whole," Cooper sees the play as a "wryly meta-textual 'play' at human connection" and the holding together of community with language (5–6). As both characters "play up the absurdity of the *content* of language that is devoid of meaning, their very verbal engagements demonstrate the irreducible connection that they experience" such that neither character can quite quit the other (6).

5. She also foregrounds race, claiming that *The Sunset Limited* "notably tests the concept of white masculinity as a stable essence, specifically the white American man's status as God's chosen," White obviously seeming quite far from divinely elected (45), and Black's ability to "perceive spiritual truth" Brewer relates to his "marginal status in American society" due to his race (46).

6. See pages 56–62 of the play for a discussion of the alcoholic's dilemma. Black tells a second story and alludes to Alcoholics Anonymous, finally figuring "out that what was true about AA was probably true about a lot of other things too" (62). Gregory Bateson puts alcoholism and addiction into cybernetic terms, finding that in an "unusually disastrous variant of the Cartesian dualism" (313) the alcoholic's dilemma "is not a matter of revolt against insane ideals around him but of escaping from his own insane premises, which are continually reinforced by the surrounding society" (311). Sounding much like Black, Bateson writes that the "errors of the alcoholic" are, in the words of AA's Big Book, the same as the "forces which are today ripping the world apart at its seams" (334). Bateson asserts that the "nonalcoholic world has many lessons which it might learn from the epistemology of systems theory and from the ways of AA. If we continue to operate in terms of a Cartesian dualism of mind versus matter, we shall probably also continue to see the world in terms of God versus man; elite versus people; chosen race versus others; nation versus nation; and man versus environment. *It is doubtful whether a species having both an advanced technology and this strange way of looking at its world can endure*" (my italics 337).

7. Kenneth Lincoln notes Adorno's assertion that after Auschwitz art is barbaric and lists some of the artists who died by suicide: "Hart Crain jumping ship, Paul Celan drowned in the Seine, Papa Hemingway with shotgun barrels to his temple, Virginia Woolf stone-weighted in the river, Primo Levi broken down the stairwell, Sylvia Plath placing her head in the oven" (156). Lincoln queries: "Has overcivilized humanity seen enough misery?" (156). We may add Walter Benjamin to this list as well.

WORKS CITED

Agamben, Giorgio. *Homo Sacer: Sovereign Power and Bare Life*. Translated by Daniel Heller-Roazen. Stanford University Press, 1995.

Bateson, Gregory. "The Cybernetics of 'Self': A Theory of Alcoholism." In *Steps to an Ecology of Mind*. University of Chicago Press, 1972.

Bell, Vereen M. *The Achievement of Cormac McCarthy*. Louisiana State University Press, 1988.

Benjamin, Walter. *Illuminations: Essays and Reflections*. Edited by Hannah Arendt. Schocken Books, 1968.

Brewer, Mary. "'The light is all around you, cept you dont seen nothing but shadow': Narratives of Religion and Race in *The Stonemason* and *The Sunset Limited*." *Cormac McCarthy Journal*. Volume 12, number 1, 2014: 39–54.

Cooper, Lydia. "'A Howling Void': Beckett's Influence in Cormac McCarthy's *The Sunset Limited*." *Cormac McCarthy Journal*. Volume 10, number 1, 2012: 1–15.

Hillier, Russell M. "Two Men in a Trickbag: White, Black, and the Operation of Schopenhauerian Ethics in Cormac McCarthy's *The Sunset Limited*." *Cormac McCarthy Journal*. Volume 16, number 2, 2018: 104–32.

Josyph, Peter. "Now Let's Talk about *The Sunset Limited*: An Exchange With Marty Priola." *Cormac McCarthy Journal*. Volume 9, number 1, 2011: 66–86.

Lincoln, Kenneth. *Cormac McCarthy: American Canticles*. Palgrave McMillion, 2009.

Luce, Dianne C. "Beyond the Border: Cormac McCarthy in the New Millennium." *Cormac McCarthy Journal*. Volume 6, number 1, 2008: 6–12.

———. "*The Sunset Limited*: A Dialogue of Life and Death (A Review of the Chicago Production)." *Cormac McCarthy Journal*. Volume 6, number 1, 2008: 13–21.

McCarthy, Cormac. *The Sunset Limited: A Novel in Dramatic Form*. Vintage, 2006.

———. "The Kekulé Problem: Where Did Language Come From?" *Nautilus*. April 20, 2017.

———. "Cormac McCarthy Returns to the Kekulé Problem: Answers to Questions and Questions That Cannot Be Answered." *Nautilus*. November 27, 2017.

Monk, Nicholas. *True and Living Prophet of Destruction: Cormac McCarthy and Modernity*. University of New Mexico Press, 2016.

Peebles, Stacy. *Cormac McCarthy and Performance: Page, Stage, Screen*. University of Texas Press, 2017.

Peters, Michael A. "The Refugee Camp as Biopolitical Paradigm of the West." *Educational Philosophy and Theory*. Volume 50, number 13, 2018: 1165–1168.

Quirk, William. "'Minimalist Tragedy': Nietzschean Thought in McCarthy's *The Sunset Limited*." *Cormac McCarthy Journal*. Volume 8, number 1, 2010: 34–54.

Taylor, Charles. *The Language Animal: The Full Shape of the Human Linguistic Capacity*. Cambridge, Belknap Press of Harvard University Press, 2016.

Tyburski, Susan J. "'The lingering scent of divinity' in *The Sunset Limited* and *The Road*." *Cormac McCarthy Journal*. Volume 6, number 1, 2008: 121–28.

Vanderheide, John. "Sighting Leviathan: Ritualism, Daemonism, and the Book of Job in McCarthy's Latest Works." *Cormac McCarthy Journal*. Volume 6, number 1, 2008: 107–20.

Wyllie, Robert. "Kierkegaard Talking Down Schopenhauer: *The Sunset Limited* a Philosophical Dialogue." *Cormac McCarthy Journal*. Volume 14, number 2, 2016: 186–203.

Woodward, Richard B. "Cormac Country." *Vanity Fair*. August 2005: 98, 100, 103–4.

Chaos, Law, and the Materiality of McCarthy's Language

VERNON W. CISNEY

"If you wanted me to help him how come you didnt give me the words? You give em to him. What about me?" (McCarthy, *The Sunset Limited* 142). These desperate lines are among the final ones spoken by the character known only as "Black" in Cormac McCarthy's 2006 dramatic work, *The Sunset Limited*. They follow a substantive philosophical conversation in Black's dilapidated and sparsely furnished New York City apartment, between Black and the character designated as "White." The occasion for their encounter has been Black's last-second rescue of White, just as he is about to leap in front of the Sunset Limited, the famous transcontinental train that, for much of its history, ran from New Orleans to Los Angeles. That White has decided to kill himself on the morning of his birthday is, to him, mere coincidence. But as one might imagine, Black's interruption of White's suicide attempt provokes an exploration of the meaning of life, coupled with the question as to whether it is, after all, worth living. But as Black's words also indicate, by the story's conclusion, he has failed to speak convincingly to White and he is, as Steven Frye notes, reduced to silence (151). The terrain of language, and the rationality that undergirds it, has proven futile in Black's attempt to argue in defense of life. White leaves Black's apartment, presumably in order to complete the self-destructive task that Black had earlier interrupted, leaving Black alone on the floor, kneeling, dejected, and pleading despairingly with an unresponsive God.

This incapacitation of Black's words points to a broader theme throughout much of McCarthy's writing, the theme of the word itself and its relation to questions of law and order, reason and justice, as well as chaos, violence, and destruction. In what follows, I will be tracing this thread through three of McCarthy's works—*Blood Meridian* (1985), *No Country for Old Men* (2005), and *The Sunset Limited* (2006). In the order of their publication, this progression demonstrates an apparent deepening of the divide between the laws of order and the principles of chaos, so as to highlight the deeper point that both terms of this complementarity are held together by the tool of language and its organizing principle—rationality. Language and reason can just as easily sanction slavery as they can emancipation, murder as healing, or genocide as justice. They can declare by fiat that a biological human being of a specific race or ethnicity counts only as a fraction of a human, or something less than human. They can mangle the definition of 'torture' to the point of unrecognizability, so as to justify the deliberate infliction of harm within the putative letter of the law. Language, then, is woefully inadequate when it comes to resolving the most pressing concerns of human existence, and in its stead, McCarthy will lean more and more on the unconscious, which he designates the "machine for operating an animal" (McCarthy, "The Kekulé Problem").

In his *Nautilus* piece on the origins of language, "The Kekulé Problem," McCarthy claims that "it's hard to escape the conclusion that the unconscious is laboring under a moral compulsion to educate us," and he further argues that the counsels of the unconscious are metalinguistic, likely because the unconscious antedates our linguistic capacities by a few million years. Perhaps this is why the tiny flickering embers of hope that often appear in the conclusions of McCarthy's stories are not inherent to their narratives proper but are left as open gestures. In place of the dispassionate morality of duty for duty's sake, or the enlightened self-interest of *homo economicus*, we are left with only whispers of love, the groundless upsurge of care, affirmation, and hope, eschewing rationality and the narrow concerns of self and offering up everything on the altar of absolute risk. In place of the covetous, rapacious, and idolatrous man of culture, we are left with the hope, receptivity, and openness of the child.

See the Child

Blood Meridian tells the story of America's founding violence through the historical narrative of westward expansion, with the ninety-eighth meridian, the novel's namesake, being the border of the frontier that opens onto the unconquered world of nature. The ubiquitous brutality of this literary landscape is deftly juxtaposed with the "optical democracy" (McCarthy, *Blood Meridian* 259) that objectively paints it. Here, in the frontier town of Nacogdoches, we meet the novel's protagonist, a sixteen-year-old boy known only as "the kid," echoing a commonly employed trope in the American Western mythos (Billy the Kid, the Sundance Kid, the Two-Gun Kid, etc.). Nacogdoches is pivotal, as the site of the introduction of Judge Holden, the novel's compelling villain.

While McCarthy's description of Holden closely resembles the description given in Samuel Chamberlain's *My Confession*, little is known about Judge Holden and his provenance, outside of his unusual and imposing physical appearance, his expansive catalog of knowledge across a wide variety of disciplines, his fluency in a number of languages, and his status as the philosophical anchor of the Glanton Gang. Led by ex-military figure John Joel Glanton, the Glanton Gang was a brutal band of murderous mercenaries, scalp hunters for hire charged with settling border disputes involving the indigenous tribes to the west and the Mexicans to the south.

Holden's philosophical constitution is often characterized in the scholarly literature as Nietzschean in nature (Monk 11; Lincoln 89; Frye 82–84), but more closely resembles what could be described as a reductive Heracliteanism, based on the ancient Ephesian thinker of becoming, who famously posited that one cannot step twice into the same river (Heraclitus et al. 35). While Thales had argued that water was the principal element underlying all things, and Anaximenes had followed with the assertion of air, Heraclitus had argued for fire, unique among the four classical elements in its dynamic insubstantiality (25). Fire is, only in its transfiguration and its movement. It binds together things even as it fundamentally alters their natures. Human beings have forever reveled in the mystical nature of fire, perhaps without being entirely aware they were doing so, inasmuch as the fire is the anchor of a campsite, the centerpiece of the home's hearth, the source of heat, sustenance, and life.

Blood Meridian, employing a motif that will become increasingly prevalent in McCarthy's work, addresses this mystical multiplicity: "The flames sawed in the wind and the embers paled and deepened and paled and deepened like the bloodbeat of some living thing eviscerate upon the ground before them and they watched the fire which does contain within it something of men themselves inasmuch as they are less without it and are divided from their origins and are exiles. For each fire is all fires, the first fire and the last ever to be" (McCarthy, *Blood Meridian* 255). McCarthy here draws attention to the flowing and ebbing, the subtle expansions and contractions, of the embers' glows, resembling, as they do, the very repetitions of life itself, connecting this elemental image to the macroscopic life activities of human beings who cannot survive without this sustenance. Just as all live by the spirit that God breathed into the dust in the Garden, Prometheus's purloined offering to humanity engenders every imperceptible pulsation of motion that sustains us.

Moreover, just as fire can both harden wood and temper steel, and can also utterly reduce the most durable human structures to ash, the cosmic principle contains within it the apparent contradictoriness of nature's binary opposites—night and day, life and death, good and evil, etc. This inherent duality and complementarity are constantly negotiated and renegotiated by way of an ongoing struggle, a cosmic strife, *polemos;* but a war that is also not devoid of jubilation and frivolity; eternity, Heraclitus writes, is child's play (37). This is echoed by the judge when he claims that the cosmos is defined only by its infinitely variable possibility, that the only "order" to creation is in the interpretive web we cast over it: "The universe is no narrow thing and the order within it is not constrained by any latitude in its conception to repeat what exists in one part in any other part. Even in this world more things exist without our knowledge than with it and the order in creation which you see is that which you have put there, like a string in a maze, so that you shall not lose your way" (McCarthy, *Blood Meridian* 256).

But the "order" of the universe, such as it is, is defined by war: "Before man was, war waited for him," and "War is the ultimate game because war is at last a forcing of the unity of existence. War is god" (261). This, too, echoes Heraclitus: "War is father of all, and king of all" (Heraclitus et al. 37). God is violence, the cosmic dice game wherein each roll reconfigures the rules anew. Heraclitus will identify an organizing principle, operating beneath this principle of strife, that of the *logos:* reason, account, language, word, etc. (11). Like Heraclitus, Judge Holden will imbue the *logos* with a power independent of human subjectivity. Speaking of Sergeant Aguilar, he claims, "Words are things. The words he is in possession of he cannot be deprived of. Their authority transcends his ignorance of their meaning" (McCarthy, *Blood Meridian* 89). But unlike Heraclitus, Holden will understand this power as one that certain human beings can master. The only victor in the cosmic game of war, as Holden understands it, is the one who most effectively imposes his will onto the world, by way of a linguistic and taxonomical mastery: "But that man who sets himself the task of singling out the thread of order from the tapestry will by the decision alone have taken charge of the world and it is only by such taking charge that he will effect a way to dictate the terms of his own fate" (208).

Such a man becomes a "suzerain of the earth," whose "authority countermands local judgments" (207), imposing order onto the chaos and can thus execute outrageous acts in the spirit of the frivolous strife of the cosmic dance. The acts of falsely accusing a minister of pederasty and turning the passions of his congregation against him, purchasing puppies for the sole purpose of drowning them, scalping an Apache child with whom he has just been playing, or cataloging cultural artifacts only to annihilate them from the Earth forever, all are simply part of the jubilant cosmic war dance, and "only that man who has offered up himself entire to the blood of war, who has been to the floor of the pit and seen horror in the round and learned at last that it speaks to his inmost heart, only that man can dance" (345).

Holden's title of "judge" suggests something operating with the force of law on its side, and indeed, Holden operates both within and beyond the sanction of state violence. Like the frontier town where we first meet him, his nature is one of both established order and untamed violence. He thus personifies the ambiguities inherent to founding violence itself, the founding violence that lies beneath the origins and perpetuation of every state, establishing itself only by way of displacement, expropriation, and destruction, and maintaining itself always through force; acting always beyond the limits of the law but in a mysterious fashion always with the protection and consent of the law.

The reflection of the judge is the face of the kid himself, the novel's nameless protagonist. The kid's introduction abounds in messianic signposts—

born in "thirty-three" (the alleged age of Christ at the time of his crucifixion), beneath the herald of a heavenly sign (the Leonids—a meteor shower), and the face of the kid holds, we are told, the whole of history (just as believers understand Christ to carry within him the whole of human sin) (4). The significance of the Leonids is also tied, as argued by John Sepich, to the "raining of fire," thus connecting the kid to that mystical dynamism discussed above (Sepich 51). The kid is, admittedly, not without moral complexity: "He can neither read nor write and in him broods already a taste for mindless violence" (McCarthy, *Blood Meridian* 4). But he nevertheless acts as something of a messianic foil against the order/chaos duality embodied in the figure of Judge Holden. The novel's narrative, amidst its magnificent caress of the English language, can be thought of as a backdrop against which takes place the ongoing dance between the judge and the kid.

In the novel's concluding chapters, after the Glanton Gang is gone, there remain the figures of the judge and the kid. And we are given to understand that their strange relationship is grounded on a moral innocence on the part of the kid, an inherent incorruptibility of sorts that is apparently impervious to the hideous brutality of the world in which he operates. This innocence (if it may be so called) holds a strange allure for the judge. Perhaps the most salient example of this incorruptibility is the kid's refusal to kill the judge when he, camouflaged with Tobin within the skeletons of dead mules, has Holden in his sights, and Holden, eventually, knows this: "I've passed before your gunsights twice this hour and will pass a third time. Why not show yourself?" (311). But it is precisely on account of the kid's persistence in his innocence that he becomes, for the judge, a disappointment: "There's a flawed place in the fabric of your heart. Do you think I could not know? You alone were mutinous. You alone reserved in your soul some corner of clemency for the heathen" (311–12). This mutiny, the character of forgiveness, is a betrayal not only of the judge, but more importantly, of the brutal, survival-of-the-fittest philosophy that he espouses. And it culminates, decades later, in the final confrontation of the two—Holden's expressed philosophy of cosmic order through violence, echoing the very origins of Western thought, against the kid's minimalist responses: "You aint nothin" (345). The kid hangs onto his mutinous innocence to the bitter end, refusing to dance the judge's dance, and paying for this refusal, apparently, with his life. And yet the judge dances on: "His feet are light and nimble. He never sleeps. He says that he will never die. He dances in light and in shadow and he is a great favorite. He never sleeps, the judge. He is dancing, dancing. He says that he will never die" (349).

But we would be remiss were we to overlook the novel's epilogue. Appearing in a single paragraph, following the words, "THE END," and providing a brief narrative apparently not connected in any way with the narrative of the novel, the epilogue speaks of a *"man progressing over the plain by means of holes which he is making in the ground. He uses an implement with two handles and he chucks it into the hole and he enkindles the stone in the hole with his steel hole by hole striking the fire out of the rock which God has put there"* (351). Beyond the brutality of the novel's world, after *the end* of that world, we have McCarthy's gesture, however modest, in the direction of the fire as an image of hope. That fire that Heraclitus identified as the cosmic principle, that heralded the birth of the kid, and that the judge sought, like a sagely sorcerer, to command; that fire becomes a freely given kernel of hope: *"He strikes fire in the hole and draws out his steel"* (351).

My Word Is Not Dead

In *No Country for Old Men*, the judge's ambiguous amalgamation of chaos and order is separated out, in almost Manichean fashion, into principles embodied by the characters of Sheriff Ed Tom Bell, who encapsulates the qualities of order, tradition, honesty, decency, and justice, and on the other side his counterpart, the psychopath Anton Chigurh, emissary of chaos and *"true and living prophet of destruction"* (McCarthy, *No Country for Old Men* 4). Like *Blood Meridian*, *No Country for Old Men* constructs a narrative, unfolding the consequences of the humanly weak miscalculations of Vietnam veteran Llewelyn Moss in his succumbing to the temptation to snatch the satchel of money from the bullet and corpse-riddled crime scene, but Moss's story is also the battlefield for the strife of the cosmic principles. Though they never meet, Chigurh and Bell are engaged in a battle, both material and philosophical, for the soul of Moss, and Bell finds himself outmatched. As Petra Mundik writes, "The burden of the metaphysical speculation is borne by the monologues of the aging sheriff Ed Tom Bell" (259). Everyone else—Carla Jean, Carson

Wells, the Mexican drug dealers, the young hitchhiker—are but pieces in this cosmic conflict playing itself out in Llewelyn's drama.

Chigurh is the very embodiment of chaos, "an evil, parodic version of the Second Coming" (Mundik 263). According to Linda Woodson, "he exists outside of society and is of indeterminate origin and purpose" (8). Devoid of both passion and compassion, he operates, like things in the material world, subject to the laws of chance and beyond the laws of men. The principles of chaos theory suggest that, even in a deterministic system, nature proceeds by way of negotiations of forces, and that subtle variations in any one of these negotiations can result in drastically different outcomes (and hence, a new and radically different and unforeseeable set of negotiations) (Gleick). Moss's decision to abscond with the briefcase, coupled with his later pangs of conscience and decision to return to the scene to provide water to the dying man, launched a chain of events that resulted in immeasurable violence and death. Though this violence is unnecessary and even pointless, once the decision is made, the series of subsequent encounters is inevitable, as Chigurh understands the world.

We see this clearly in Chigurh's exchanges with the gas station owner and Carla Jean. In both cases, Chigurh cites that each decision in our lives, each event, brings us to each subsequent event, that each negotiation inaugurates a path that produces subsequent negotiations. The gas station manager married a woman whose parents owned this small gas station, setting off a chain of events that brought him face-to-face with Chigurh and his quarter, dated "nineteen fifty-eight. It's been traveling twenty-two years to get here. And now it's here. And I'm here. And I've got my hand over it. And it's either heads or tails. And you have to say. Call it" (McCarthy, *No Country for Old Men* 56). For twenty-two years, the quarter had been in circulation—stamped by the U.S. Mint, paid by a bank for a worker's salary, dropped into vending machines, tumbling through laundry cycles—arriving, finally, into Chigurh's pocket, whence it will be pulled for this particular negotiation of forces. Carla Jean married Llewelyn, setting her on a path of working-class life and the simple desperation that tipped Llewelyn over the line into forces beyond his ken, and bringing Carla Jean face-to-face with Anton as well: "the shape of your path was visible from the beginning" (259). Anton acknowledges repeatedly, almost sympathetically, Carla Jean's innocence: "None of this was your fault:" but claims, nevertheless, that he has no choice: "I had no say in the matter" (257 & 259). He is subject, like all things, to the laws of chance, and they don't allow for exceptions, almost as though Anton believes that his acquiescence to the vicissitudes of chance is his greatest strength. The gas station owner won his coin toss, while Carla Jean lost hers, but either could have just as easily gone the other way. But they didn't. To Carla Jean, Chigurh says, "You can say that things could have turned out differently. That they could have been some other way. But what does that mean? They are not some other way. They are this way" (260).

On the other side, Sheriff Ed Tom Bell appears as the very instantiation of the Platonic ideal of order. His monological reflections, in particular about the institution of law and the various county sheriffs he's known in his life, revolve constantly around the importance of manners, traditions, propriety, decency, and justice. He laments the degradation of American life, and the loss of manners among America's youth. He expresses sheer exasperation at the darkness of the human heart, as evidenced by the countenance of modern crime: "*I think if you were Satan and you were settin around tryin to think up somethin that would just bring the human race to its knees what you would probably come up with is narcotics. Maybe he did*" (218). Bell is practically Kantian in his emphasis on honesty. Leaving his office, he asks his receptionist to call his wife and tell her that he has left, insisting, however, that she wait until he is gone, refusing to be a party to even the most seemingly insignificant of white lies (168). Through almost the entirety of the novel, the image painted of Bell is one of simple decency and humanity.

This understanding is severely complicated, however, by Bell's revelation to Uncle Ellis near the book's end. The revelation concerns his military service in World War II and the commendation he was awarded as a result. His unit, camped in a stone German farmhouse, comes under heavy artillery fire, leveling one of the home's outer walls and leaving a pile of rubble peppered with the mangled bodies of his fellow soldiers, many of whom lay severely wounded amidst the devastation. Bell manages to drive back the approaching Germans, and, as soon as night falls, he flees, abandoning his comrades on the battlefield. Bell is fully aware that, had he remained at his post, he would not have been able to singlehandedly hold it. He knows that, while he may have killed a few more Germans, they would have certainly succeeded in eventually killing him, and his death would have accomplished nothing more than a few more German deaths. Nonetheless, his Kantian ethics prod him with the conviction that standing his ground is precisely what he should have done: "you go into battle it's a blood oath to look after the men with you and I don't know why I didnt. I wanted to. When you're called on like that you have to make up your mind that you'll live with the consequences. But you dont know what the consequences will be" (278). Despite his protestations that he does not deserve it, the military awards him with the Bronze Star, only compounding the profound guilt that Bell carries: "Then I thought that maybe I could make up for it and I reckon that's what I have tried to do" (278). Bell thus indicates that this act of cowardice (as he understands it) and the accompanying military commendation he received have charted for him the life that he would ultimately lead, a life of bravery, honesty, decency, and selfless public service.

In the case of Moss, a momentary (and completely understandable) episode of human weakness set off a chain of events that terminated not only in his own death but in the death of his wife, who was undeniably innocent of everything having to do with Moss's acts. In Sheriff Bell's case, however, a momentary and no less relatable moment of human weakness had brought him a military commendation, an honorable discharge from the military, and the lifelong reputation of a war hero, and it charted the overall ethos of decency and public service that would eventually bring him into the path of Chigurh. Two momentary decisions in the face of negotiations of forces, two relatable moments of self-serving human weakness, a pivotal fork in the road, and an ensuing chain of events that maps out the remainder of a life.

But Chigurh is not without a vaguely Kantian deontological motivation of his own. Chigurh does what he does without passion or compassion, coldly, but not without a sense of cosmic duty or rationality. As Carson Wells says to Moss when he finds him in the Mexican hospital, "You could even say that he has principles. Principles that transcend money or drugs or anything like that" (153). To Carla Jean, he says, "I have only one way to live. It doesnt allow for special cases" (259). For Chigurh, each of us operates according to a rule, a guiding principle that helps us navigate the various coin tosses of the cosmic game, whether we know it or not, whether we acknowledge it or not. Just before killing Wells, Chigurh asks him, "If the rule you followed led you to this of what use was the rule?" (175). He tracks down and kills Carla Jean because, according to him, he had made a promise to her husband, and, even though her husband may be dead, Chigurh says, "my word is not dead" (255). Chigurh's word is his rule. It best enables him to speak order into the chaos of the universe. On the other hand, Bell's moral shortcoming lies in his failure to keep his word: "If I was supposed to die over there doin what I'd give my word to do then that's what I should of done" (278).

Most interesting in this transposition is the fact that there is an obvious symmetry that obtains between the law of Sheriff Bell and the chaos of Chigurh. Each is guided by a conviction of principle, however different these principles may appear. Each begins to resemble the other and reflect the other, even if these two antagonists never encounter one another face to face. Both are, moreover, ultimately insufficient ways of speaking into the darkness. In Bell's case, this is clear because his adherence to his principle is reactionary. It is motivated by an internal weight of unbearable guilt, one that, he claims, he wishes every day of his life he could go back and undo. His principled life of honorable integrity is really (or so he believes) an effort to quell the pangs of guilt and prevent such intense feelings of guilt from ever invading his heart again: "*I thought if I lived my life in the strictest way I knew how then I would not ever again have a thing that would eat on me thataway*" (282). His reactionary comportment is further witnessed in the existential exhaustion that he expresses in his every encounter with the world. For Chigurh, the shortcoming in his principle is evident in the fact that, at the novel's end, his "rule," his domineering faith in his own ability to impose his will onto the chaosmos, leads him into harm's way when, immediately upon leaving the home of Carla Jean, he is blindsided by a reckless driver running a stop sign. However principled he may be, Chigurh is no less at the mercy of fate than anyone else. The word imposes order and upholds law; but the word is insufficient.

Like *Blood Meridian*, *No Country for Old Men* ends with a coda, this time not an epilogue, after the novel's conclusion, but also not quite intrinsic to the narrative itself. Bell reflects on his father and, in the final pages, tells of dreams he had about his father shortly after he died. The first is a dream of squandered opportunity and perhaps of the prodigality and carelessness of youth. He and his father meet in town, where his father gives him some money, which Bell loses. The *second* dream, however, concerns an opening to the future, an ember of hope. In the dream, Bell is riding horseback through a snowy mountain pass, the cold beating against him. His father rides past him, "*carryin fire in a horn the way people used to do*" (309). Bell goes on, "*And in the dream I knew that he was goin on ahead and that he was fixin to make a fire somewhere out there in all that dark and all that cold and I knew that whenever I got there he would be there. And then I woke up*" (309). The light is but a glimmer, a whisper. As Bell says, the dream must always come to an end, when his eyes open once more onto the violent indifference of the world that has driven him to retirement. Nonetheless, the ember of hope flickers at the horizon beyond the waking reason of men.

You Didn't Give Me the Words

We return now to *The Sunset Limited*. This dramatic work deals in thorough detail with the questions of life, love, hope, and affirmation, wrestling with the challenge of whether or not life can ultimately be affirmed, and whether or not it is, after all, worth living. White's despair is not one born of circumstantial disadvantages or events—by all appearances, he lives a life of comfort and affluence, a white, male college professor, steeped in all the history, literature, philosophy, and culture that the Western tradition has to offer.

Like Camus's Sisyphean reflections, White's despair stems from reason itself, from the frank assessment that "Western Civilization finally went up in smoke in the chimneys at Dachau but I was too infatuated to see it. I see it now" (McCarthy, *The Sunset Limited* 27). He seeks to kill himself because he has arrived, at last, at the conclusion that the rationality of the Western tradition—the same rationality that gave the world Plato, Aristotle, Augustine, Descartes, Leibniz, Kant, etc.—also imposed bloody empire, colonialism, racism, slavery, policies of extractionism, forced religious conversions, Manifest Destiny, and ultimately culminated in the death camps of World War II and the dropping of the atomic bombs on Hiroshima and Nagasaki. The world, he says, "is basically a forced labor camp from which the workers—perfectly innocent—are led forth by lottery, a few each day, to be executed. I dont think that this is just the way I see it. I think it's the way it is" (122). Already in the nineteenth century, Friedrich Nietzsche characterized the history of Western thought as one with the history of nihilism, the progressive disinvestiture of all senses of value from the material world and into the beyond accumulating until finally, the beyond slips from our grasp entirely and, with it, the whole edifice of value itself. "For some time now, our whole European culture has been moving as toward a catastrophe, with a tortured tension that is growing from decade to decade: restlessly, violently, headlong, like a river that wants to reach the end, that no longer reflects, that is afraid to reflect" (Nietzsche et al., *Will to Power* 3). Nietzsche had seen the storm clouds forming, but it took the horrors of the first half of the twentieth century for the rest of the West, among whom we may count White, to catch up. The difference is that, where Nietzsche's entire project is geared toward confronting this nihilism head-on so as to think through and overcome it, White embraces it as the inevitable reality. None of the alternative views hold up to careful scrutiny, White argues: "The darker picture is always the correct one" (McCarthy, *The Sunset Limited* 112).

Black attempts to lure White back to the affirmation of life by way of a simplified teaching of the Christian gospel. "Simplified" in this context is not to be understood pejoratively, but rather, as a practice grounded in a basic affirmation of agapic, kenotic love. Black's Christian ethos is rooted in no specific theology, nor in any specific aspect of Christian doctrine. It has nothing to do with credal formulations or confessions; and less to do with "repentance," in the sense of self-directed chastisement, than it does with a properly understood love of the self. Black is perfectly comfortable in saying that the Bible is "true" without asserting that its truth is based in any literal understanding of its specific words. In fact, contrary to the fetishized way that many American Christians cherish the physical object of their Bibles, Black says of the book itself, "This book is a guide for the ignorant and the sick at heart. A whole man wouldnt need it at all" (68). He has no qualms about being labeled a heretic for denying the doctrine of original sin, choosing instead to seek the light in people: "I think for the most part people are good to start with. I think evil is somethin you bring on your own self" (67). Likewise, his acceptance of Christ is rooted not in an external faith in an historical event or in the singularly unique nature of Christ, but rather, in an internal faith in the possibility of redemptive and transformative love. Jesus, he says, "couldn't come down here and take the form of a man if that form was not done shaped to accommodate him" (95).

The point of the gospel, for Black, is not the one-and-done sacrifice reported to have taken place two thousand years ago, but rather, the power which that life and that death opened up within the human heart. And the redemption this offers is, he notes, eternal life, but not in the sense of the endless perpetuation of one's own personal consciousness and all its memories, but rather, in the very transfiguration of time itself, the saturation of the present moment with the sense and power of eternity, the kiss of God in the face of the stranger, the orphan, and the widow:

> He said you could have life everlasting. Life. Have it today. Hold it in your hand. That you could see it. It gives off a light. It's got a little weight to it. Not much. Warm to the touch. Just a little. And it's forever. And you can have it. Now. Today. But you dont want it. You dont want it cause to get it you got to let your brother off the hook. You got to actually take him and hold him in your arms and it dont make no difference what color he is or what he smells like or even if he dont want to *be* held. And the *reason* you wont do it is because he dont deserve it. And about that there aint no argument. He *dont* deserve it. (78–79)

That the brother (or the neighbor) does not deserve love indicates merely that there is nothing transactional about it. The love of Black's gospel is one that defies all modes of economic or calculative rationality. When the putative "expert in the law" asks of Christ, "And who is my neighbor?" he is asking. "To whom do I owe love?" Christ responds with the famous parable of the Good Samaritan, indicating that the question is badly formulated; one ought not ask, "Who is neighbor *to me?*" but rather, "*To whom* can I be the neighbor?" (Luke 10:25–37). In the famous parable of Lazarus and the rich man, we note that the rich man is not named; precisely because this parable belongs to Lazarus, the suffering other whom the rich man ignores (Luke 16:19–31). To love is to be redeemed.

This is Black's simple offer of salvation, echoing the ones made by Christ himself. The kingdom of God is within, as the rabbi said (Luke 17:20–21). To attain it requires nothing more than the total sacrifice of oneself in that offering of absolute risk mentioned earlier. And it is precisely because it defies all logic and rationality, that it is both simpler and infinitely more demanding than any philosophy, that Black can't ultimately find the *logos* to convince White. There, in Black's own personal Gethsemane, God remains silent because the words are not there to give. In his final, Mersaultian diatribe, White says to Black, "You tell me that my brother is my salvation? My salvation?

Well then damn him. Damn him in every shape and form and guise. Do I see myself in him? Yes. I do. And what I see sickens me" (McCarthy, *The Sunset Limited* 138). This is a reveling in nihilism itself, the nihilism that Nietzsche, in the *Genealogy of Morals*, characterizes as the great sympathy with man coupled with the great disgust with man (F. W. Nietzsche et al. 87). It is the nihilism sometimes casually ascribed to McCarthy himself, due to the unflinching brutality of his work. But the point seems to be not that we should embrace this nihilism, but rather that philosophy and the *logos* will not save us from it. Once White exits the apartment, Black collapses, grappling with why he was unable to save White from his despair. As he weeps, rocking back and forth, he prays, "That's all right. That's all right. If you never speak again you know I'll keep your word. You know I will. You know I'm good for it" (McCarthy, *The Sunset Limited* 142). This "word" is, again, not a doctrinal formulation or credal confession but the upsurge of love that wrests us from our atomized fragmentation and connects us to one another.

Not Yet . . .

Finally, we return once more to McCarthy's 2017 treatment of the Kekulé Problem. Referring to the German chemist, August Kekulé, this problem concerns "the configuration of the benzene molecule" (McCarthy, "The Kekulé Problem"). The solution to his problem appears to him in a dream, in the mythical image of the ouroboros, the circular symbol of the snake eating its own tail, causing Kekulé to awake and exclaim, "'It's a ring. The molecule is in the form of a ring'" (McCarthy, "The Kekulé Problem"). To address the question of why the resolution eludes Kekulé's conscious thought in spite of his ceaseless efforts, McCarthy looks to the unconscious (the "agent" of our dreams), thinking about this unconscious as, primarily, a biological mechanism, our naturally constituted "machine for operating an animal." In the multimillion-year history of the evolution of the unconscious, the faculty of language, by which we humans casually imagine ourselves to carry out our most sophisticated thinking, is little more than the blink of an eye, a thin and fragile veneer translucently covering a veritable sea of drives, impulses, desires, aversions, and instincts; an anarchic machine. McCarthy's "machinic" description of the unconscious hearkens to the work of 1960s

French thinkers Gilles Deleuze and Félix Guattari, who also characterize the unconscious as machinic, a factory rather than a theater: "It is at work everywhere, functioning smoothly at times, at other times in fits and starts. It breathes, it heats, it eats. It shits and fucks. What a mistake to have ever said *the* id. Everywhere *it* is machines—real ones, not figurative ones: machines driving other machines, machines being driven by other machines, with all the necessary couplings and connections" (Deleuze and Guattari, *Anti-Oedipus* 1). Drives, impulses, instincts, machines—the unconscious is already a collective, already "social," a "gathering of talents rather than just one" (McCarthy, "The Kekulé Problem"), operating always polyvocally, as happens any time we think. "That can't be right. Wait, did I . . . ? *Oh!*"

McCarthy speculates that our thinking is almost entirely unconscious, and this is supported by the fact that we may establish propositional formulations to express signposts on our path, to mark the trees through the forest, but it is much more difficult to recreate or justify the processes by which we arrived at our realizations. Very likely this is because, McCarthy claims, the "central idea of language" rests on the economic principle of exchange, "that one thing can be another thing" (McCarthy, "The Kekulé Problem"). A collection of phonetic letters pieced together in just such a way can be water. The problems of language, therefore, the problems of logic, are also predicated upon this principle of exchange, which requires substitutability. When taking our first baby steps in logic or critical thinking, one of the first things we learn is to substitute, in place of concrete designators, universalizable terms such as P, Q, R, etc., from which we articulate more formal representations of the propositions under consideration. Everything in this generic mode of thinking functions on the level of the general.

But genuine problems of thought and of life are so called precisely because they are irreducible, not easily solved by the substitution of universal terms. This is even more so when it comes to phenomena such as love. The problem of love, as Black formulates it, the problem of forgiveness, is one that cannot be addressed through universalizable terms of exchange. This is because love, as Black's gospel articulates it, is not the abstract, Enlightenment form of the love of humanity, but rather, the love of the neighbor. It is taking this person in your arms, regardless of who they are, where they come from, how they look, or how they smell. It is easy to love humanity in the abstract, infinitely more difficult to love the neighbor in their concreteness.

And the second reason that this love cannot be addressed through universalizable terms is that there is no step in the process whereby forgiveness can be justified, whereby the cosmic scales can be considered balanced, or that love can be earned. As Black says, "About that, there ain't no argument. He don't deserve it." It defies transactional reason in every guise.

Language, therefore, at least in its dominant propositional, philosophical modes, is insufficient for such considerations. But in at least one particular moment in the article, McCarthy suggests whispers of the possibility that language might evolve, or even that the human might evolve, so as to incorporate language into the material, biological functioning of the human body itself: "To repeat. The unconscious is a biological operative and language is not. Or not yet" (McCarthy, "The Kekulé Problem"). This not yet is a most curious formulation. McCarthy goes on to express the worry that to consider language in biological terms would be to risk "inviting Descartes to the table," that is, to reify consciousness as an independent component, bordering on substantiality, of the human. But, rightly taking that concern into consideration, one might nevertheless wonder if there are (or could be) uses of language that would operate more closely and immediately with the realm of the body, rather than the realm of sense.

Here again, Deleuze and Guattari are instructive. Writing of Kafka, they argue, "each language always implies a deterritorialization of the mouth, tongue, and the teeth. The mouth, tongue, and teeth find their primitive territoriality in food. In giving themselves over to the articulation of sounds, the mouth, tongue, and teeth deterritorialize" (Deleuze and Guattari, *Kafka* 19). The moment in human evolution when language first emerges constitutes a complex network of bodies (human, animal, object), sounds, and gestural indications, all in the service of organizing human activities with respect to the nonhuman world. Breath is emitted from the lungs; folds in the laryngeal flesh vibrate; the tongue, lips, and teeth form infinitely varied configurations of the stomatic aperture, all so as to emit sounds of varying intensity, arrangement, and timbre. Long before intellectuals had framed linguistics on the stratum of sense, language is, first and foremost, a bodily activity. Long before the philosophers were the poets, and maybe it is there that we may hope to find the hope of a new language: "thought as such begins to exhibit snarls, squeaks, stammers; it talks in tongues and screams, which leads it to create, or try to" (Deleuze and Guattari 55). McCarthy's not yet suggests that perhaps the artists, manipulators of language that they are, offer us glimpses of a language more attuned to the needs of the body, a language more in line with the power of the unconscious. One cannot help but wonder if this has not been McCarthy's project all along; if perhaps, beneath the patina of the "man of culture" lies the playful and immediate language of the poet-child; if the creation of a new language is not, for McCarthy, precisely the secret to "a philosophy in which craftsmanship is a sacred orientation toward human and nonhuman others" (Cooper 22).

In all likelihood, this is precisely why McCarthy more than once casts the image of God in the figure of a child: "See the child." The child knows no shame and does not naturally or instinctively project it onto others. Unencumbered by the binding shackles of exchange-oriented thinking, the child has no reservations about affirming nonsense, about longing for and believing in the impossible, and this includes the immediacy with which they love and forgive, the exuberance with which they welcome the new, the hope with which they greet each day. The kingdom, the rabbi said, is indeed within, but to enter, one must become the child (Matthew 18:3). The eloquent opening words of St. John's Gospel are, "In the beginning was the Word," the *logos* (John 1:1). But indeed, if this is true, this *logos* precedes the formalized language of the philosopher. The Word is not reducible to its formulaic expressions in accordance with the principles of logic; the Word speaks light into the darkness. In one of the most beautiful lines ever put to paper, McCarthy speaks through the mouth of an unnamed father the following: "He knew only that the child was his warrant. He said: If he is not the word of God God never spoke" (McCarthy, *The Road* 5).

WORKS CITED

Cooper, Lydia R. *Cormac McCarthy: A Complexity Theory of Literature*. Manchester University Press, 2023.

Deleuze, Gilles, and Félix Guattari. *Anti-Oedipus: Capitalism and Schizophrenia*. University of Minnesota Press, 1983.

———. *Kafka: Toward a Minor Literature*. University of Minnesota Press, 1986.

———. *What Is Philosophy?* Translated by Hugh Tomlinson and Graham Burchell, Columbia University Press, 1994.

Frye, Steven. *Understanding Cormac McCarthy*. University of South Carolina Press, 2009.

Gleick, James. *Chaos: Making a New Science*. Penguin, 2008.

Heraclitus et al. *Fragments: a text and translation.* Paperback edition, University of Toronto Press 1991.

Lincoln, Kenneth. *Cormac McCarthy: American Canticles.* 1. Palgrave Macmillan, 2009.

McCarthy, Cormac. *Blood Meridian or The Evening Redness in the West: 25th Anniversary Edition.* Vintage International, 1992.

———. "The Kekulé Problem." *Nautilus*, 17 Apr. 2017, https://nautil.us/the-kekul-problem-236574/.

———. *No Country for Old Men.* Knopf Doubleday Publishing Group, 2007.

———. *The Road.* Vintage Books, 2006.

———. *The Sunset Limited: A Novel in Dramatic Form.* Knopf Doubleday Publishing Group, 2006.

Monk, Nicholas. *True and Living Prophet of Destruction: Cormac McCarthy and Modernity.* University of New Mexico Press, 2016.

Mundik, Petra. *A Bloody and Barbarous God: The Metaphysics of Cormac McCarthy.* University of New Mexico Press, 2016.

Nietzsche, Friedrich, et al. *The Will to Power.* Vintage Books ed. Vintage Books, 1968.

Nietzsche, Friedrich Wilhelm, et al. *On the Genealogy of Morality: A Polemic.* Hackett Pub. Co., 1998.

Sepich, John. *Notes on Blood Meridian.* Revised and Expanded Edition. University of Texas Press, 2008.

Woodson, Linda. "'. . . You Are the Battleground': Materiality, Moral Responsibility, and Determinism in 'No Country for Old Men.'" *Cormac McCarthy Journal*, Volume 5, number 1, Spring 2005: 4–13.

McCarthy's Foundational Critique of Individualism and the Western Mythos in the Epilogue of *Cities of the Plain*

JONATHAN ELMORE AND RICK ELMORE

With the publication of *Cities of the Plain*, there was a widespread sense that scholars could see the critical arc of McCarthy's project as a whole. As Edwin Arnold and Dianne Luce proclaim in their 2001 *Companion to the Trilogy*, these novels "taken as a whole, represent McCarthy's working in the full maturity of his talent and in a scope surpassing anything he has done before" (xi). This maturation of McCarthy's project heralds, they argue, a new and equally mature era in McCarthy scholarship, "the lengthy and complex essays in [their] collection point[ing] the way for the kind of work [. . .] McCarthy's novels deserve" (xi). In the nearly twenty-five years since this programmatic call, the field of McCarthy studies has vigorously responded, arriving at rich and varied readings of McCarthy's turn west and his project as a whole. Yet, while the Border Trilogy has generated perhaps more critical attention than any other element of McCarthy's oeuvre, the epilogue to *Cities of the Plain* has remained curiously undertheorized, scholars in widespread agreement concerning its importance for understanding McCarthy's philosophical worldview and yet oddly reluctant to give a thorough and systematic analysis of the text. Hence this essay offers a close reading of the epilogue with an eye to how its philosophical claims concerning the nature of reality frame McCarthy's critical engagement with the genre of the Western.

In the epilogue to *Cities of the Plain*, McCarthy reiterates many of the philosophical themes found in *The Crossing*, insisting, for example, on the essentially dynamic and ever-changing nature of reality. Yet while in *The Crossing*, it is the dynamic nature of existence—epitomized in the oft-cited claim "all the world's a tale"—around which the narrative circles, in *Cities*, it is the ontological unity of existence and the way in which this unity troubles the distinction between self and other that takes center stage. More specifically, we argue that the epilogue reveals the ontology of McCarthy's philosophy, which holds that reality is fundamentally dynamic and holistically unified. Moreover, this ontological unity necessitates a complete rejection of Western individualism, this rejection revealing McCarthy's radical critique of the genre and mythos of the Western. It is, thus, McCarthy's thoroughgoing critique of individualism that, we argue, reveals the ultimate moral of the novel, McCarthy's rejection of individualism posing an essential challenge to the genre of the Western in a way yet to be fully appreciated by the scholarship.

While scholars have noted McCarthy's careful and thoughtful treatment of setting,[1] his attention to late twentieth-century American geopolitical and social issues,[2] as well as the narratological, formal, and aesthetic features of the Border Trilogy,[3] nearly all the scholarship takes up, in one way or another, the question of to what degree McCarthy's western turn develops, transforms, and/or challenges the genre of the Western. As Susan Kollin states, "with the publication of *Cities of the Plain* [. . .] McCarthy continues to be credited with transforming the genre [of the Western], taking on its cherished myths while subjecting them to new critical scrutiny" (558). Scholars have, as Kollin notes, tended to see McCarthy as revising the central thematics of the Western, critically updating the genre for a bleaker, modern world.[4] These studies have, unsurprisingly, tended to focus on the figure of the cowboy hero, as Dianne Luce proclaims "from the title *All the Pretty Horses* to the dedication of *Cities of the Plain*, the trilogy is a lullaby singing to sleep the vanishing cowboy" ("Vanishing World" 163).[5] Taking the decline of the American cowboy as their primary nexus of study, scholars have read John Grady Cole and, to a lesser extent Billy Parham, as icons of the fading American frontier spirit;[6] white males embittered by the loss of their artificial cowboy fantasies;[7] sites of homoerotic tension and desire;[8] or figures of masculine violence and sexual conquest run amok.[9] While the scholarship remains divided on how to understand McCarthy's fraught cowboys and his engagement with the Western generally, scholars overwhelmingly agree that this engagement and its consequences are brought to their full realization in the epilogue of *Cities of the Plain*.[10]

For example, Erik Hage contends that the "full philosophical burden [of the epilogue] must be weighed against the entire trilogy" (62), and Petra Mundik proclaims that the epilogue "can be seen as the culmination of the philosophical, metaphysical, and spiritual concerns raised throughout the Border Trilogy" (235). Similarly, Edwin Arnold concludes that "the almost thirty-page Epilogue to *Cities of the Plain* is the most elaborately conceived of [McCarthy's] endings, for it concludes not only the novel but the trilogy itself and, moreover, comments on the totality of McCarthy's work" ("Last of the Trilogy" 239), and Richard Wallach contends that the "epilogue reconfigures and summarizes the series of novels that lead up to it" (59). Thus scholars unanimously agree that the epilogue is critically important for understanding *Cities of the Plain*, the Border Trilogy, and what Scott Yarbrough calls "McCarthy's cosmology" (52). And yet, despite this widespread consensus regarding the importance of the epilogue, there has been surprisingly little textual analysis of the epilogue itself, scholars tending to treat its content in a speculative or gestural manner.

For example, Arnold surmises, in one of the first engagements with the epilogue, that it is "about many things, but chief among them, I think, is the role of the artist, or the dreamer, or the creator, and his responsibilities to the subjects of this dreams" ("Last of the Trilogy" 242). Similarly, Richard Wallach offers what he calls "an initial sketch of some of the ways" the epilogue concludes the trilogy, ultimately finding that the epilogue "correlates the trilogy's multiple notions of will and destiny with the narrative properties of diegesis and dream logic. It thereby consummates the series' currents of self-referentiality and its ongoing interrogation of narrative itself" (59). While provocative, neither of these initial ruminations include a thorough textual analysis of the epilogue itself. A few year later, Arnold returns to the epilogue saying that it "provides McCarthy's primary disquisition on the nature of dreams and dreaming, a summation of all that has gone before in his work" and yet he offers a mere three paragraphs of textual analysis ("Dreams and Visions" 66).[11] Over a decade after the novel's publication, Yarbrough briefly returns to the epilogue along very similar lines finding it to contain an alternative "answer" to the profound violence and "winner-take-all will to power" so characteristic of McCarthy's villains and novels in general. Yet he too chooses not to substantiate this reading via a detailed textual analysis. Hence, while scholars unanimously viewed the epilogue as the key to understanding the Border Trilogy and character of McCarthy's project as a whole, it took eighteen years for the first truly sustained close reading of the text to be published by Petra Mundik.

Appearing as a stand-alone chapter in her book *A Bloody and Barbarous God: The Metaphysics of Cormac McCarthy*, Mundik's analysis traces the Gnostic and Buddhist themes of McCarthy's work as part of the Perennial Philosophy she argues guides his fiction. Mundik finds in the epilogue's ruminations on death, dreams, narrative, and the Creator resonances with various metaphysical thinkers such as Grossman, Rudolph, Jung, James, Underhill, and Girard, all of which corroborate what she sees as the essentially Gnostic worldview underlying McCarthy's work. Yet while certainly the most thorough textual engagement with the epilogue to date, Mundik's reading positions the epilogue as merely another example of the sacred traditions and philosophical themes that she identifies across McCarthy's fiction. But such an approach attenuates the actual philosophical argument of the epilogue itself, obscuring the way in which the epilogue offers a sustained philosophical argument about the nature of reality and humanity's place within it. Hence, we offer a systematic analysis of the philosophical argument of the epilogue to *Cities of the Plain* in order to show how this text develops a unique and foundational account of the dynamic and ontologically unified nature of reality. It is on the basis of this unified ontology, moreover, that McCarthy offers, we contend, a fundamental critique of the genre of the Western, a critique that has yet to be fully appreciated by the existing scholarship.

In the epilogue to *Cities of the Plain*, a seventy-eight-year-old Billy, having been evicted from his hotel and with little in the way of material possessions, heads out on the road south. Early in his travels, he encounters another traveler headed north. The two share a meal of restaurant cracker packets under a highway overpass and have a long, complex discussion about the nature of life and existence. The man tells Billy of a dream he had that caused him to reevaluate his understanding of life. In this dream, a traveler comes to a mountain pass "where certain pilgrims used to gather in the long ago" (270). There is in the pass a "table of rock" on which "there were yet to be seen the stains of blood from those who'd been slaughtered upon it to appease the gods" (270). Pressed by Billy as to whether his companion is the traveler in the dream, the man replies "I dont think so. But then if we do not know ourselves in the waking world what chance in dreams?" (271). Pressed again a few lines later, the man remains uncertain: "I think the self of you in dreams or out is only that which you elect to see. I'm guessing every man is more than he supposes" (271). Against Billy's seemingly simple desire to establish the identity of the dream traveler, his companion complicates not only this possibility but the relationship between dreams and reality more generally.

Returning to the dream, the man tells Billy that having come to the mountain pass near dark, the traveler camps upon the stone table in order to "raise himself above the feasible paths of serpents in the night" (271). Upon this makeshift bed, the traveler falls asleep and, the stranger insists, dreams. Yet his insistence on this man's dream within a dream raises, for Billy, serious metaphysical questions, as it seems to violate our basic understanding of the relationship not only between dreams and reality but reality and its representation. As Billy puts the issue succinctly: "It's like the picture of your life in the map. [...] "Es un dibujo nada más [It's nothing more than a drawing]. It aint your life. A picture aint a thing. It's just a picture" (273).[12] The possibility of a dream within a dream smacks of metaphysical contradiction, insofar as it appears to ground a dream upon a dream or an unreality upon an unreality. Just as it would be nonsensical, ontologically speaking, to claim that a painting within a painting is distinct from the painting in which it appears, so too, Billy reasons, it must be nonsensical to insist on the independence of the dream man's dream. As Billy tells the stranger bluntly, this idea of a dream within a dream "just sounds like superstition," like something "that dont exist" (273). Yet while the stranger acknowledges the metaphysical complications of such a claim, he nonetheless insists on the independence of the dream man's dream from his own, this claim to independence revealing the difference between his and Billy's conceptions of life.

Responding to Billy's claim of an obvious difference between life and its representation, the stranger asserts, "You say that the life of a man cannot be pictured. But perhaps we mean different things. The picture seeks to seize and immobilize within its own configurations what it never owned. Our map knows nothing of time. It has no power to speak even of the hours implicit in its own existence. Not of those that have passed, not of those to come" (273–74). For the stranger, there is most certainly a difference between life and its representation, a picture of life different than life itself. Yet this difference is not, he insists, a result of the fact that "a picture aint a thing," life ontologically substantive in a way that its representation is not. Rather this difference emerges from the inability of representations to capture the dynamism of life, the fact that life "vanishes" the moment one tries to define it or represent, revealing life to be something dynamic rather than static, an action rather than a thing. For the stranger, life cannot be captured in a representation because the representation of life is only a static snapshot, a picture made immediately inaccurate insofar as life is always changing "moment to moment" (273).[13] Hence, while Billy and the stranger agree that there are limits to the possibility of representing life, they understand the cause of these limits in very different ways, the static nature of representations troubling our ability to represent not only life but any dynamic process.

Following out the implications of the static nature of representations, the stranger queries Billy, "But what is your life? Can you see it? It vanishes at its own appearance. Moment by moment. [. . .] When you look at the world is there a point in time when the seen becomes the remembered? How are they separate? It is that which we have no way to show. It is that which is missing from our map and from the picture that it makes. And yet it is all we have" (273). It follows from the static nature of representations that not only life's dynamism but any process, movement, or transition falls outside the image's ability to represent fully. How, the stranger insists, can something static ever capture something dynamic, the movement or moment of transition between, for example, the seen and the remembered, outside the ability of representations to completely encapsulate. Moreover, representations lack, the stranger stresses, even the capacity to represent the very processes of representation themselves, "our maps [. . .] hav[ing] no power to speak even the hours implicit in [their] own existence" (273). Hence, the recognition of the inability of representations to capture the dynamic nature of life forces on us a more general recognition of just how limited and uncertain our powers of representation actually are, representations unable to represent any process, even that of representation itself. For the stranger, the static character of representations complicates fundamentally our ability to represent, with any certainty, the nature of life or reality, the inability to reliably separate seen from remembered, dynamic from static, and life from its representation entailing that we can never be certain that any of our representations of life or the world are entirely true or accurate. Moreover, it is this essential uncertainty that explains the stranger's insistence on the independent existence of the dream man and his dream.

Returning to the question of the existence of the dream man, the stranger states,

> This traveler also has a life and there is a direction to that life and if he himself did not appear in this dream the dream would be quite otherwise and there could be no talk of him at all. You may say that he has no substance and therefore no history but my view is that whatever he may be or of whatever made he cannot exist without a history. And the ground of that history is not different from yours or mine for it is the predicate life of men that assures us of our own reality and that of all about us. (274)

While the substance of the dream man's existence remains uncertain, one cannot deny his appearance in the dream nor that it is this appearance that allows us to register his existence as such. Moreover, given the inability of representations to grant us reliable access to what is outside of representation, it follows that it is only by appearing in a representation that one can register the existence of anything, appearance in a representation the common "predicate" that "assures us of our own reality and that of all about us." Hence for the stranger, the justifications we have for asserting the dream man's existence turns out to be the same as the justifications we have for asserting the existence of anything, the grounds we have for believing in the existence of Billy or the stranger, the same as the grounds we have for believing in the existence of the dream man or his dream. It is, thus, "wiser," the stranger contends, to assert the independent existence of the dream man and his dream, since to deny this independence risks undermining our ability to assert the existence of anything at all. There is, for the stranger, thus, a common ground between our existence and that of the dream man, this common ground offering, he goes on to argue, fundamental insights into the nature of existence.

Having revealed the common ground between the dream man's claim to existence and that of all things, the stranger concludes, "Our privileged view into this one night of this man's history presses upon us the realization that all knowledge is a borrowing and every fact a debt. For each event is revealed to us only at the surrender of every alternate course. For us, the whole of the traveler's life converges at this place and this hour, whatever we may know of that life or out of whatever stuff it is made" (274–75). For the stranger, the recognition of the common ground between the dream man's claim to existence and that of our own reveals the dependence of all claims to knowledge and facticity on reality's essential ontological dynamism, "each event" or instance of life only a snapshot of the processes that are existence. While "for us" the representation of a thing at this moment, its apparent characteristics, attributes, relations, abilities, and modes of being, appears as the entirety of its existence, this appearance is, in reality, only one possible "course" or characterization of the entity, the dynamic nature of existence entailing that existence always exceeds, by definition, the capacity to represent it. Hence, while only ever appearing to us through its representation, existence is not reducible to representation. We are not, as one might first surmise, caught in an infinite regress of representation, reality, like the "sceptre" of the dream troupe's leader, a likeness inside a likeness inside a likeness, *ad infinitum* (275). Rather, what is revealed in the dream man's dream is the essential unity of existence, the dream man having in his encounter with the troupe an experience of reality as it truly is.

Having fallen asleep on the stone slab, the dream man dreams an encounter with a troupe of eight figures carrying a hostage woman on a litter. After some deliberation amongst themselves, three members of the troupe ceremonially present him "a cup of horn heated in a fire and shaped so it would stand" (279). Upon drinking its contents, the man "forgets" everything he had previously known, including even the very drinking of the concoction itself: "He drank it down [. . .] and almost at once all was taken from him so that he was like a child again and a great peace settled upon him and his fear abated to the point that he would become accomplice in a blood ceremony that was then and is now an affront to God" (280). In this child-like, *tabula rasa* state of having "abandoned all of his former views," a state in which, the stranger stresses, "there can be no lie or no dissemblance of the truth," the dream man is invited to "contemplate his surroundings," to see the world as it truly is:

> They seemed to be waiting for him to come to some decision. To tell them something perhaps. He studied everything about him that could be studied. [. . .] What he saw was the strangeness of the world and how little was

known and how poorly one could prepare for aught that was to come. He saw that a man's life was little more than an instant and that as time was eternal therefore every man was always and eternally in the middle of his journey, whatever be his years or whatever distance he had come. He thought he saw in the world's silence a great conspiracy and he knew that he himself must then be a part of that conspiracy and that he had already moved beyond his captors and their plans. If he had any revelation it was this: that he was repository to this knowing which he came to solely by his abandonment of every former view. And with this he turned to his captors and he said: I will tell you nothing. (282)

Having abandoned all his preconceived views about the world, and having observed everything about him from "the stars and mountains" to the delicate "panes of isinglass set into the caming" of his captors' torches, the dream man sees the true nature of reality. He sees the strangeness and contingency of reality, and how little humans can know and prepare for this contingency. He sees reality's essential dynamism, the way in which each life is but an instant in an ever-unfolding journey, every journey part of the eternally unfolding, never fully disclosed "conspiracy" of the whole. He sees that he, like all things, was always already a part of this conspiratorial unfolding, every seemingly discrete element of reality an inseparable instance of the same all-encompassing, ontological process. In this moment, the dream man sees reality as it truly is, the way in which all elements of reality are "borrowed" instances of the same ontologically unified and contingently unfolding process. Moreover, it is this knowledge of unity that, the text stresses, moves the dream man "beyond his captures and their plans," the recognition of reality's ontological unity leading to his execution.

Having come to see the true nature of reality and having refused to tell his captors the truth that he has seen, the dream man is promptly and ceremonially put to death: "the archatron came forward with his sword and raised it in his two hands above him and clove the traveler's head from his body" (282). In opposition to the dream man's recognition of the essential unity of reality, his beheading by the troupe appears as a kind of desperate attempt to reassert the primacy of ontological dualism, their literal separating of mind from body resonant with the most iconic element of Cartesian dualism. And yet, just as Billy's earlier assertion of the ontological difference between life and its representation was shown to be problematic, so too, the troupe's reassertion of ontological dualism also falters, the stranger's beheading, much to Billy's surprise, not the end of the story:

> I guess you're fixin to tell me that he survived havin his head lopped off.
> Yes.
> He woke from his dream. [. . .] In the selfsame desolate pass. The selfsame barren range of mountains. The selfsame world. (283)

Against Billy's repeated assumption of an ontological dualism between life and death, mind and body, reality and representation, the stranger insists on the unity of all things, the failure of the dream man's beheading and the repetition of "selfsame" emphasizing this unity from the local to the cosmic. Reality is simply not, this scene suggests, defined by ontological dualism, reality's ontological unity so complete that it complicates even the supposed limits between life and death, mind and body, reality and representation.

Articulating the significance of dreaming, the stranger tells Billy, "These dreams reveal the world also. [. . .] We wake remembering the events of which they are composed while often the narrative is fugitive and difficult to recall. Yet it is the narrative that is the life of the dream while the events themselves are often interchangeable" (283). Dreams reveal the essential ontological unity of reality, the narrative unity of the dream, like the conspiratorial unity of the world, the "life of the dream," while the events of the dream are the more or less interchangeable expressions of this essential unity. For the stranger, the power of dreams is that they offer us the possibility of a pure or child-like glimpse of reality, allowing us to see, even if obscurely, the narrative unity of existence, each of us in dreams like "pilgrims" in the "great democracy of the possible," going "forth to meet what we shall meet," open to the dynamic and contingent unfolding or narrative flow that is reality as such (284). Yet while in dreams humans can experience the dynamic unity of existence, "the events of the waking world" are another matter entirely, these events "forced upon us," while "the narrative is the unguessed axis along which they must be strung" (283).

In the waking world, humans are bombarded by events with no clear narrative, the dynamic unity of the world so obscured that all we see are singular, unconnected instances. Blind to reality's narrative, ontological unity, humans experience themselves as the creators of that very unity: "Each man [...] the bard of his own existence," "assembl[ing]" the events of the world "into the story which is us," each of us crafting our existence out of the seemingly unconnected events we encounter, this act of creation giving reality its character and meaning (283). Unable to see the unity of existence, humans, in the waking world, misunderstand both the nature of reality and their place in it, seeing themselves as creators rather than creations, independent authors of existence rather than unfolding elements of it. This misunderstanding leads humans into constant contradiction: "Our waking life's desire to shape the world to our conveniences invit[ing] all manner of paradox and difficulty," as "all in our custody seethes with an inner restlessness" (283–84). At odds with the restless ontological dynamism of all things, the human desire to dictate and determine human existence *ex nihilo* necessarily falters. As the man tells Billy, humans simply do not have the power to "call forth the world as they will. [...] Nor is this life of yours by which you set such store your doing, however you may choose to tell it. Its shape was forced in the void at the onset and all talk of what might otherwise have been is senseless for there is no otherwise" (285). For the stranger, humans cannot be the creators of their existence, since their lives are, like all things, elements of reality's dynamic unfolding. Given the unity of existence, there is, the stranger insists, no ontological distinction between the human world and the world in general, the fact that humans can imagine the world differently doing nothing to change this basic ontological truth. Yet while the notion of existence as "forced in the void at the outset" leads the dream man into a kind of crisis over how to understand human existence, the stranger sees in this unity a new understanding of existence and humanity's place in it.

Holding his hand "palm out," he asks Billy to "hold up" his own hand:

> You see the likeness? Yes. Yes. It is senseless to claim that things exist in their instancing only. The template for the world and all in it was drawn long ago. Yet the story of the world, which is all the world we know, does not exist outside of the instruments of its execution. Nor can those instruments exist outside of their own history. And so on. This life of yours is not a picture of the world. It is the world itself and it is composed not of bone or dream or time but of worship. Nothing else can contain it. Nothing else be by it contained. (286–87)

Reflecting on the likeness between their outstretched hands, the stranger insists again on the fundamental unity of existence, "the story of the world" both more than its "instancing" and yet inseparable from those very instancings. Reality is, the stranger reiterates, neither reducible to appearance nor independent of it, existence a story within a story and a process within a process *ad infinitum*. Yet what this shows is not, as the dream man fears, the loss of any meaning for human life, but its essential nature, our lives not a representation or "picture of the world" but the world itself, everything an instance of the same dynamic and unfolding process that is reality. Given the dynamic, ontological unity of existence, human life cannot be, the stranger concludes, something substantive, a "bone" or object whose reality is defined in opposition to the nonsubstantive, since this dualism of substantive and nonsubstantive is at odds with reality's ontological unity. Nor can life be a mere illusion or dream constructed by the powers of human discourse, since humans are not the bards of their own existence but elements of unfolding forces of which they cannot be the authors. Nor can human life be simply the expression of temporal or causal necessity, the contingency and spontaneity of reality's unfolding clearly at odds with any thinking of teleological or mechanistic determinism. Hence, given that life cannot be at root a substance, an illusion, or a mechanistic unfolding, the stranger argues that it is best understood as a form of "worship," a kind of reverence and veneration contained by itself and yet uncontainable in itself.

To think life as worship, as simultaneously both contained and uncontainable, is to understand life as a kind of difference within ontological unity. As the etymology of worship suggests, worship derives from the same root as "worth," which itself derives from the Proto-Germanic "wertha," meaning "toward" both in the sense of "opposition" and "equivalence" (Etymology). To understand existence as worship, thus, is to recognize that the different, opposed manifestations of life are, at the same moment, an element of the same ontological whole: life is difference within unity. Taking the example of the desert in front of them, the stranger tells Billy, "This desert about us was once a vast sea [. . .] can such a thing vanish? Of what are seas made? Or I? Or you?" (286). The present is necessarily "composed" of the past, insofar as there is "no other material [. . .] at hand," and yet the present remains irreducible to the past, the past both with us and yet not determinative of us. As the stranger puts it to Billy, "the log of the world is composed of its entities, but it cannot be divided back into them. And at some point this log must outdistance any possible description of it" (286). To think of existence as worship is to recognize the present as both entirely composed of the past and yet not identical to it. It is, the stranger admits, difficult to think reality in this way, since "however it may be construed within men's dreams or by their acts it will never make a fit," the dynamic nature of existence making it something that one can never totally represent (287). And yet, as the stranger stresses, this inability of humans to represent, acknowledge, or accept the nature of reality does nothing to change that nature. Nor does it leave our understanding of existence and our place in it undisturbed, the recognition of existence as a dynamic and contingently unfolding, unified process leading the stranger to a thinking of human existence in terms of love.

Having concluded the retelling of his dream, Billy's conversation with the stranger ends with a redefinition of human existence:

> Every man's death is a standing in for every other. And since death comes to all there is no way to abate the fear of it except to love that man who stands for us. We are not waiting for his history to be written. He passed here long ago. That man who is all men and who stands in the dock for us until our own time come and we must stand for him. Do you love him, that man? Will you honor the path he has taken? Will you listen to his tale? (288–89)

Given the ontologically unified nature of existence, the fact that every human life is a moment in the same unfolding process, a process whose only material is the past and yet one that unfolds in ways irreducible to that past, it follows that human life must be, in the deepest sense, unified. We are, the stranger stresses, radically connected, every human death standing in for every other in a spaced or differential repetition, the recognition of this radical collectivity framed through the ability to love another as oneself. To love in this way radically reconfigures our sense of being an autonomous and discreet individual, as it forces us to admit that what we are, in the most fundamental, ontological sense, is defined and created by our connections to others. We are nothing but these connections, even if, like "the log of the world," we are not simply reducible to these connections. Hence for the stranger, the recognition of the dynamic unity of existence forces on us both an understanding of existence as worship and a rethinking of human existence in terms of love, the recognition of the ontological collectivity that is human existence best expressed in the notion of loving another as oneself. It is, the epilogue suggests, this redefinition of existence and thinking of love that expresses the central philosophical insight of *Cities of the Plain* and the Border Trilogy as a whole. Yet, while there is certainly much to say about how this understanding of love and reality is taken up in the various love stories of the novels and how it dovetails with the philosophy laid out, for example, in *The Crossing*, it is also in light of these philosophical commitments that one must assess McCarthy's engagement and critique of the Western as a genre, his insistence on the ontological unity of reality entailing not simply a fundamental critique of ontological dualism but that of individualism as well.

Given McCarthy's insistence on the ontological unity of existence and his redefinition of human life in terms of love and radical collectivity, one finds in the epilogue to *Cities of the Plain* a thoroughgoing rejection of ontological dualism, the notion of reality as an ontologically unified process at odds with any notion of ontologically discrete individuals. For McCarthy, nothing is truly discrete and self-contained at an ontological level, neither the sea nor the desert neither you nor I. For McCarthy, a careful account of the ontology of the world shows us that each of us are moments of the same process, moments whose apparent differences are but differences of a moment and whose sameness is forever. As McCarthy puts it in the dedication that ends the epilogue, "*I will be your child to hold / And you be me when I am old*" (293). Hence, one finds in *Cities* a thoroughgoing critique of the most essential metaphysical convictions of the Western genre, the mythos of the rugged, purely self-determined individual with all it entails in terms of morality, ethics, and politics at odds with the very ontological nature of reality itself. To follow the philosophical argument of the epilogue is to not only see McCarthy's essential account of ontology and metaphysics, but to recognize the way in which McCarthy's so-called "Western Turn" is nothing less than a confrontation with, and refutation of, the Western mythos in American cultural identity all the way down, a mythos on which, for McCarthy, it is far past time to "*turn the page*" (293).

NOTES

1. Specifically, Chris Dacus's "The West as Symbol of the Eschaton in Cormac McCarthy," Ashley Bourne's "'Plenty of signs and wonders to make a landscape': Space, Place, and Identity in Cormac McCarthy's Border Trilogy," John Blair's "Mexico and the Borderlands in Cormac McCarthy's *All the Pretty Horses*."

2. For example, Josh Crain's "'Mojado-reverso': Illegal Immigration and Cormac McCarthy's Border Trilogy," Meg King's "'Where is your country': Locating White Masculinity in *All the Pretty Horses*," and Tom Pilkington's "Fate and Free Will on the American Frontier: Cormac McCarthy's Western Fiction."

3. For example, George Guillemin's "'As of some site where life had not succeeded': Sorrow, Allegory, and Pastoralism in Cormac McCarthy's Border Trilogy" and Christopher White's "Dreaming the Border Trilogy: Cormac McCarthy and Narrative Creativity."

4. See for example Vince Brewton's "The Changing Landscape of Violence in Cormac McCarthy's Early Novels and the Border Trilogy"; Brian Edwards' "Refiguring the West(ern): Cormac McCarthy's Border Trilogy and Old Markers in American Culture"; Trenton Hickman's "Against Nostalgia: Turning the Page of Cormac McCarthy's *Cities of the Plain*"; and Susan Kollin's "Genre and Geographies of Violence: Cormac McCarthy and the Contemporary Western."

5. Evidencing the thoroughness of scholarly interest in McCarthy's treatment of the Western, there are two full-length articles devoted to the role of horse and horsemanship in his Western fiction: See Wallis R. Sanborn's "Reconsidering Horses and Horseman in *Blood Meridian* and the Border Trilogy" and Stacey Peebles' "Hang and Rattle: Horsebreaking from Novel to Film in *All the Pretty Horses*."

6. See Phillip Snyder's "Cowboy Codes in Cormac McCarthy's Border Trilogy"; Russell Hillier's "'Like some supplicant to the darkness over them all': The Good of John Grady Cole in Cormac McCarthy's *Cities of the Plain*"; and Vahit Yasayan's "*Cities of the Plain*: The End of the All-American Cowboy."

7. See Dianne Luce's "'When You Wake': John Grady Cole's Heroism in *All the Pretty Horses*."

8. Notably, in the earliest full-length treatment of *Cities of the Plain*, Edwin Arnold points out that "Billy's feelings for John Grady run deeper than Billy might admit, and McCarthy, I think, does address the sexual ambivalence that is a part of their relationship" ("Last of the Trilogy" 238). More recently Joey Isaac Jenkins, drawing on Sullivan, offers a compelling, and to date most thorough, queer reading of the trilogy's central characters in "'The carnage in the woods': Queerness and Interspecies Violence in Cormac McCarthy's Border Trilogy."

9. See Jennifer Reimer's "All the Pretty Mexican Girls: Whiteness and Racial Desire in Cormac McCarthy's *All the Pretty Horses*"; Nell Sullivan's "Boys Will Be Boys and Girls Will Be Gone: The Circuit of Male Desire in Cormac McCarthy's Border Trilogy"; Josef Benson's *Hypermasculinities in the Contemporary Novel: Cormac McCarthy, Toni Morrison, and James Baldwin*; and Vahit Yasayan's "*Cities of the Plain*: The End of the All-American Cowboy."

10. In fact, early treatments of the epilogue found such a sense of closure in it that there was speculation that it might close McCarthy's career entirely: "The twenty-nine pages that end the book, the Border Trilogy, perhaps the western novels, and—though let's hope against it—could even be McCarthy's last work of fiction entirely" (Peebles 105).

11. Also in *A Cormac McCarthy Companion: The Border Trilogy* and thus shortly after *Cities* was published, Phillip Snyder, Jacqueline Scoones, and Douglas Canfield all briefly touch upon the epilogue.

12. We're grateful to Lt. Jim Campbell for his translation of the Spanish passages within the novel. All translations to follow are his. http://cormacmccarthy.cookingwithmarty.com/wp-content/uploads/COTPTrans.pdf

13. For more on McCarthy's dynamic conception of reality in the Border Trilogy, see Elmore and Elmore's "The World as Tale: Ontological Dynamism and Metaphysical Unity in Cormac McCarthy's *The Crossing*."

WORKS CITED

Arnold, Edwin T. "The Last of the Trilogy: First Thoughts on *Cities of the Plain*." In *Perspectives on Cormac McCarthy*. By Edwin T. Arnold and Dianne C. Luce. University of Mississippi Press, 1999: 221–248.

———. "'Go to Sleep': Dreams and Visions in the Border Trilogy." In *A Cormac McCarthy Companion: The Border Trilogy*. Edited by Edwin T. Arnold and Dianne C. Luce. University of Mississippi Press, 2001: 37–72.

Arnold, Edwin T., amd Dianne C. Luce. "Introduction." In *A Cormac McCarthy Companion: The Border Trilogy*. Edited by Edwin T. Arnold and Dianne C. Luce. University of Mississippi Press, 2001: vii–xi.

Benson, Josef. *Hypermasculinities in the Contemporary Novel: Cormac McCarthy, Toni Morrison, and James Baldwin*. Rowman and Littlefield: 2014.

Blair, John. "Mexico and the Borderlands in Cormac McCarthy's *All the Pretty Horses*. *Critique: Studies in Contemporary Fiction*. Volume 42, number 3, 2010: 301–7.

Bourne, Ashley. "'Plenty of signs and wonders to make a landscape': Space, Place, and Identity in Cormac McCarthy's Border Trilogy." *Western American Literature*, Volume 44, number, 2, 2009: 108–25.

Brewton, Vince. "The Changing Landscape of Violence in Cormac McCarthy's Early Novels and the Border Trilogy." *Southern Literary Journal*. Volume 37, number 1, 2004: 121–43.

Canfield, J. Douglas. "Crossing from the Wasteland into the Exotic in McCarthy's Border Trilogy." In *A Cormac McCarthy Companion: The Border Trilogy*. Edited by Edwin T. Arnold and Dianne C. Luce. University of Mississippi Press, 2001: 256–70.

Crain, Josh. "'Mojado-reverso': Illegal Immigration and Cormac McCarthy's Border Trilogy." *Cormac McCarthy Journal*, Volume 11, number 1, 2103: 59–79.

Dacus, Chris. "The West as Symbol of the Eschaton in Cormac McCarthy." *Cormac McCarthy Journal*, Volume 7, number, 1, 2009: 7–15.

Edwards Brian. "Refiguring the West(ern): Cormac McCarthy's Border Trilogy and Old Markers in American Culture." *Australian Journal of American Studies*. Volume 22, number 2, 2003: 1–9.

Elmore, Jonathan and Rick Elmore. "The World as Tale: Ontological Dynamism and Metaphysical Unity in Cormac McCarthy's *The Crossing*." *Mississippi Quarterly*. Volume 75, number 1, 2022: 61-78

Etymology Dictionary Online. Etymonline.com. October 28, 2022.

Guillemin, George. "'As of some site where life had not succeeded': Sorrow, Allegory, and Pastoralism in Cormac McCarthy's Border Trilogy," In *A Cormac McCarthy Companion: The Border Trilogy*. Edited by Edwin T. Arnold and Dianne C. Luce. University of Mississippi Press, 2001: 92–130.

Hage, Erik. *Cormac McCarthy: A Literary Companion*. McFarland, 2010.

Hickman, Trenton. "Against Nostalgia: Turning the Page of Cormac McCarthy's *Cities of the Plain*." *Western American Literature*, Volume 42, number 2, 2007: 142–64.

Hillier, Russell M. "'Like some supplicant to the darkness over them all': The Good of John Grady Cole in Cormac McCarthy's *Cities of the Plain*." *Cormac McCarthy Journal*, Volume 14, number 1, 2016: 3–36.

Jenkins, Joey Isaac. "'The carnage in the woods': Queerness and Interspecies Violence in Cormac McCarthy's Border Trilogy." *Cormac McCarthy Journal*. Volume 19, number 1, 2021: 21–45.

King, Meg. "'Where is your country': Locating White Masculinity in *All the Pretty Horses*," *Cormac McCarthy Journal*. Volume 12, number, 1, 2014: 69–88.

Kollin, Susan. "Genre and Geographies of Violence: Cormac McCarthy and the Contemporary Western." *Contemporary Literature*, Volume 42, number 3, 2001: 557–88.

Luce, Dianne C. "The Vanishing World of Cormac McCarthy's Border Trilogy." In *A Cormac McCarthy Companion: The Border Trilogy*. Edited by Edwin T. Arnold and Dianne C. Luce. University of Mississippi Press, 2001: 161–97.

———. "'When You Wake': John Grady Cole's Heroism in *All the Pretty Horses*." *Sacred Violence: A Reader's Companion to Cormac McCarthy*. Edited by Wade Hall and Richard Wallach. Texas Western Press, 1995: 155–67.

McCarthy, Cormac. *Cities of the Plain*. Vintage Books, 1998.

Mundik, Petra. *A Bloody and Barbarous God: The Metaphysics of Cormac McCarthy*. University of New Mexico Press, 2016.

Peebles, Stacey. "Lo fantástico: The Influence of Borges and Cortázar on the Epilogue of *Cities of the Plain*." *Southwestern American Literature*. Volume 25, number 1, 1999: 105–9.

———. "Hang and Rattle: Horsebreaking from Novel to Film in *All the Pretty Horses*." In *Cormac McCarthy: All the Pretty Horses, No Country for Old Men, The Road*. Edited by Sara Spurgeon. London: Continuum, 2011: 43–57.

Pilkington, Tom. "Fate and Free Will on the American Frontier: Cormac McCarthy's Western Fiction." *Western American Literature*. Volume 27, number 4, 1993: 311–22.

Reimer, Jennifer. "All the Pretty Mexican Girls: Whiteness and Racial Desire in Cormac McCarthy's *All the Pretty Horses*." *Western American Literature*, Volume 48, number 2, 2014: 422–42.

Sanborn, Wallis R. "Reconsidering Horses and Horsemanship in *Blood Meridian* and the Border Trilogy." *Cormac McCarthy Journal*. Volume 19, number 2, 2021: 178–202.

Scoones Jacqueline. "The World on Fire: Ethics and Evolution in Cormac McCarthy's Border Trilogy." In *A Cormac McCarthy Companion: The Border Trilogy*. Edited by Edwin T. Arnold and Dianne C. Luce. University of Mississippi Press, 2001: 131–60.

Snyder, Phillip A. "Cowboy Codes in Cormac McCarthy's Border Trilogy." In *A Cormac McCarthy Companion: The Border Trilogy*. Edited by Edwin T. Anold and Dianne C. Luce. University of Mississippi Press, 2001: 198–227.

Sullivan, Nell. "Boys Will Be Boys and Girls Will Be Gone: The Circuit of Male Desire in Cormac McCarthy's Border Trilogy." In *A Cormac McCarthy Companion: The Border Trilogy*. Edited by Edwin T. Arnold and Dianne C. Luce. University of Mississippi Press, 2001: 228–55.

Wallach, Richard. "Three Dreams: The Bizarre Epilogue of *Cities of the Plain*. Proceedings of the First European Conference on Cormac McCarthy. Edited by David Halloway. Cormac McCarthy Society, 1999.

White, Christopher T. "Dreaming the Border Trilogy: Cormac McCarthy and Narrative Creativity." *Cormac McCarthy Journal*. Volume 13, number 1, 2015: 121–42.

Yarbrough, Scott. "Tricksters and Lightbringers in McCarthy's Post-Appalachian Novels." *Cormac McCarthy Journal*. Volume 10, number 1, 2012: 46–55.

Yasayan, Vahit. "*Cities of the Plain*: The End of the All-American Cowboy." *Journal of American Studies of Turkey*, Volume 55, number 1, 2021: 207–42.

Contributors

Vernon W. Cisney is chair and associate professor of interdisciplinary studies at Gettysburg College in Pennsylvania. He is the author of *Deleuze and Derrida: Difference and the Power of the Negative* and *Derrida's Voice and Phenomenon: An Edinburgh Philosophical Guide*, as well as the translator or coeditor of a number of works in continental philosophy. He researches and teaches at the intersections of continental philosophy, film, literature, religion, and politics.

David Deacon is a senior lecturer at BIMM University, London. He completed his PhD at University College Dublin with a thesis exploring atheism in post-9/11 U.S. fiction. He has published on Cormac McCarthy and neoliberalism, popular music studies, and postwar-U.S. fiction.

Jordan J. Dominy is assistant professor of English in southern literature at Auburn University at Montgomery, where he teaches courses in composition and literature. His book *Southern Literature, Cold War Culture, and the Making of Modern America* was published in 2020. His current research interests include Cormac McCarthy and contemporary U.S. southern and American fiction and popular culture.

Jonathan Elmore is associate professor of English at Louisiana Tech University and the managing editor of *Watchung Review*. He is the editor of *Fiction *and the Sixth Mass Extinction: Narrative in an Era of Loss* and coauthor of *An Introduction to African and Afro-Diasporic Peoples and Influences in British Literature and Culture before the Industrial Revolution*. His scholarship has been published in the *Cormac McCarthy Journal, Mississippi Quarterly*, the *British Fantasy Society Journal, Orbit*, the *Journal of Liberal Arts and Humanities*, and *Criterion*, among others.

Rick Elmore is associate professor of philosophy at Appalachian State University and senior managing editor of book reviews at *Symposium*. He is the coeditor of *The Biopolitics of Punishment: Derrida and Foucault*. His articles and essays have appeared in *Politics and Policy, Symplokē, Symposium, Mississippi Quarterly*, and the *Cormac McCarthy Journal*, among others.

Rachel B. Griffis is associate professor of English at Spring Arbor University, where she teaches literature and writing courses. She has published articles in the *Cormac McCarthy Journal, Nathaniel Hawthorne Review, Christianity and Literature, Studies in American Indian Literatures, Literature and Theology*, and elsewhere. Her book on reading practices is forthcoming with Baker Academic.

Alex Harmon is assistant professor of English at Montana State University. She researches and teaches in twentieth- and twenty-first-century Native American literature, film, and material culture, federal Indian law, private property and public lands in the United States, and the Western.

Ahmed Honeini is an honorary research associate in American literature at Royal Holloway, University of London. He is the author of *William Faulkner and Mortality: A Fine Dead Sound* (2021) and *Tennessee Williams's America: Homes, Families, Exiles* (forthcoming 2025). He is also the founder of the Faulkner Studies in the U.K. Research Network and an associate editor of the *Journal of American Studies*.

Trevor Jackson received his PhD in interdisciplinary humanities in 2018 from the University of California at Merced. His research is on contemporary American culture and the intersection of philosophy and literature. His work has appeared in *Modern Language Studies, Studies in the Novel, The Cormac*

McCarthy Journal, and elsewhere. He lives and works in the Central Valley of California, lecturing for the University of the Pacific in Stockton.

Kateřina Kovářová is a lecturer at the University of South Bohemia in České Budějovice. Her research focuses on the interdependence of American nature and culture in Cormac McCarthy's fiction. She has published her work in the collections *Speculative Ecologies: Plotting through the Mesh* (2019), *Transnational Interconnections of Nature Studies and the Environmental Humanities* (2020), and *Mediating Vulnerability: Comparative Approaches and Questions of genre* (2021).

Peter Lurie is associate professor of English and film studies at the University of Richmond. He is the author of *Vision's Immanence: Faulkner, Film, and the Popular Imagination* (2004) and *American Obscurantism: History and the Visual in US Literature and Film* (2018) and the editor, with Ann J. Abadie, of *Faulkner and Film: Faulkner and Yoknapatawpha 2010* (2014). His current project, *Black Evanescence: Seeing Racial Difference from the Slave Narrative to Visual Media*, is forthcoming.

John Vanderheide is associate professor of English and cultural studies at Huron College, Western University, in London Ontario Canada. He is the coeditor of *Cormac McCarthy's Violent Destinies: The Poetics of Determinism and Fatalism* (2018).

Index

9/11, 14, 186, 199, 202, 203, 267; era of, 185, 188–89, 202

Absalom, Absalom! (Faulkner), 144, 147, 148, 150, 152
Africanist lens/caricatures, 110, 111, 118, 121, 123, 129
Agamben, Giorgio, 219, 220
Alejandra, 6, 69, 71, 78, 110, 123
All the Pretty Horses (CM), 1, 2, 16, 65, 67, 68, 69, 76, 78, 89, 90, 95, 110, 123, 126, 250
American Dream, 76, 77, 78, 156
American exceptionalism, 5, 11, 65, 66, 67, 68, 69, 70, 71, 77, 81; critique of, 79; ideology of, 67; myth of, 11, 65, 66, 70, 77, 78
Anasazis, 172, 173, 174
Animals, 23, 35, 73, 74, 75, 77, 90, 91, 92, 93, 94, 95, 96, 97, 98, 99, 100, 102, 104, 157, 167, 206, 224, 225, 231, 244, 246
Animalization, 123
Anglo-Saxon elements, 12, 109, 110, 111, 113, 114, 115, 117, 120, 125, 127, 129
Anthropocentric perspective, 12, 98, 103
Alienation, 3, 22, 46, 116, 219
Allegory, 109, 112, 114, 115, 118, 119, 126, 129, 208, 227, 262; allegorical method, 118; religion and, 46, 200

Apaches, 167, 168, 234
Appalachia, 45, 52; elements of, 5, 6, 23, 52, 60, 109, 110, 112, 113, 113, 114, 115, 125, 140
Aristotle, 241
Army, 77, 78, 158; armed forces, 77
Atheism, 184, 185, 186, 190, 191, 192, 193, 200, 202; new, 185, 189, 201, 202; radical, 13, 14, 184, 185, 190, 191, 192, 193, 194, 203. *See also* Atheists
Atheists, 14, 184, 186, 187, 188, 189, 190, 193, 198, 200, 201, 202, 203, 222
Atomic bomb, 65, 241

Barbarism, 221, 222, 225
"Barn Burning" (Faulkner), 141
Beckett, Samuel, 186, 209, 210, 212, 227
Bell, Ed Tom, 17, 236, 238, 239, 240, 241
Bell, Vereen, 2, 9, 16, 16, 25, 45, 62, 83, 187, 202, 206
Benjamin, Walter, 143, 144, 145, 146, 219, 221, 228
Beowulf, 42
Berlant, Lauren, 78, 167, 169, 170
Bible, 113, 119, 120, 139, 167, 168, 209, 211, 221, 227, 242; Old Testament, 119, 168
Billy the Kid, 232
Biopolitics, 16, 62, 220

Blackness, 109, 111, 112, 114, 115, 116, 117, 118, 122, 124, 130, 153
Blood Meridian (CM), 13, 42, 63, 66, 88, 93, 96, 123, 129, 130, 132, 133, 134, 135, 136, 140, 141, 142, 144, 147, 148, 149, 151, 152, 155, 156, 157, 158, 159, 160, 161, 166, 167, 169, 170, 174, 178, 179, 200, 201, 206, 231, 232, 233, 234, 236, 240, 263
Border Trilogy, the, 6, 9, 11, 15, 16, 64, 66, 67, 68, 72, 74, 76, 79, 80, 82, 83, 84, 88, 89, 91, 93, 94, 101, 106, 110, 122, 187, 206, 249, 250, 251, 252, 262, 263, 264
Buddhism, 252

Camus, Albert, 241
Cannibalism, 5, 11, 17, 45, 49, 59, 60, 81, 157, 196
Capitalism, 5, 7, 47, 49, 51, 62, 63, 117, 159; critique of, 46, 61, 63
Catholicism, 113, 184, 185, 201, 205; Irish, 120; Roman, 3
Celtic elements, 113, 114, 115, 117, 124, 125, 129
Chamberlain, Samuel, 232
Chaos, 34, 168, 231, 234, 235, 236, 237, 240; as theory, 237
Cherokees, 124
Child of God (CM), 5, 6, 10, 11, 16, 20, 21, 22, 28, 33, 40, 41, 42, 45, 46, 47, 48, 49, 50, 53, 57, 58, 59, 61, 62, 109, 112, 113, 116, 117, 118, 122
Christians, 3, 49, 80, 145, 159, 167, 202, 208, 209, 212, 242. *See also* Christianity
Christianity, 120, 159, 165, 210, 211
Christ, Jesus, 211, 225, 242
Cinema, 90, 96, 111, 145, 146, 150, 153
Cities of the Plain (CM), 15, 68, 71, 75, 76, 77, 78, 89, 91, 93, 96, 98, 110, 123, 249, 250, 251, 252, 262, 263
Civilization, 56, 68, 80, 124, 160, 165, 168, 189, 211, 212, 218, 221, 223, 225; Western, 187, 218, 219, 225, 227, 241

Colonialism, 164, 166, 173, 177, 178, 241
Coloniality, 6, 169, 174
Colonization, 123, 160, 161, 168, 169, 179; settler, 123, 157, 158, 159, 161, 165, 179
Comanches, 71, 167, 168, 180
Concentration camps, 219. *See also* Labor camps
Contingency, 14, 15, 146, 193, 198, 199, 200, 201, 225, 226, 257, 260; radical, 14, 186, 192, 200
Conservative (political), 6, 17; anticonservative, 199; neoconservative, 189
Cowboys, 66, 68, 69, 71, 77, 78, 250, 263
Counselor, The (CM), 63, 91, 104
Crossing, The (CM), 11, 12, 15, 65, 72, 77, 84, 89, 90, 91, 92, 93, 95, 97, 98, 99, 101, 102, 104, 105, 106, 110, 122, 123, 124, 125, 126, 127, 128, 129, 130, 249, 250, 262, 264

Deconstruction, 16, 124, 133, 186, 191, 193
Delaware Scouts, 136, 177, 179
Deleuze, Gilles, 245, 246
Derrida, Jacques, 147, 148, 152, 184, 186, 191, 192, 193, 194, 195, 196, 197, 198, 203. *See also* Derridean philosophy
Derridean s philosophy, 142, 193
Descartes, René, 241, 246; Cartesian elements, 8, 228, 257
Despair, 11, 65, 66, 67, 68, 71, 72, 74, 78, 79, 80, 82, 194, 208, 212, 230, 241, 244
Determinism, 186, 188, 189, 260
Deities, 186, 187, 192, 195, 198
Doctrine of Discovery, the, 164, 165
Dostoevsky, Fyodor, 208
Divine, 71, 72, 73, 74, 79, 99, 122, 187, 194, 195, 20, 209, 210, 211, 227
Dogs, 41, 73, 93, 100, 101, 105
Dreams, 67, 71, 72, 75, 76, 77, 78, 102, 222, 223, 226, 240, 244, 251, 252, 256, 258, 261
Drugs, 63, 121, 216, 217, 237, 239
Dualism, 8, 15, 228, 257, 258, 260, 262

Ecocritical readings, 5, 198
Eco-Marxism, 5, 17
Eduardo, 75, 76, 81
Elegiac elements, 2, 6, 17, 83, 142, 164, 166
Ely, 80, 191, 197, 198, 199
Enlightenment, the, 8, 187, 212, 245
Entropy, 186, 187, 202
Ethics, 4, 7, 8, 9, 14, 16, 28, 36, 37, 80, 84, 93, 104, 118, 194, 197, 202, 213, 214, 226, 227, 239, 262; communal, 11, 66, 79, 81
Environmental concerns, 11, 89, 91, 102, 104
Erskine, Albert, 98
Europe, 124, 160, 161, 164, 165
European colonialism, 123, 161, 165
Evil, 3, 4, 5, 10, 20, 27, 51, 54, 67, 90, 101, 112, 157, 193, 196, 197, 203, 233, 237, 242; as radical, 194, 197, 203, 226
Exceptionalism, 11, 66, 70, 76, 78, 80, 82, 83, 208; American, 5, 11, 65, 66, 67, 68, 69, 70, 71, 77, 78, 79, 80; critique of, 67, 74, 75, 77, 81; ideology of, 66, 67, 68, 74
Existentialism, 187, 202
Extinction, 90, 93, 102

Faith, 14, 15, 69, 79, 80, 120, 186, 195, 202, 207, 209, 211, 222, 224, 240, 242
Fatalism, 126
Faulkner, William, 12, 13, 105, 132, 134, 135, 136, 137, 138, 140, 141, 142, 143, 144, 146, 147, 149, 148, 150, 151, 152
Federal government (U.S.), 13, 155, 156, 158, 162, 163, 165, 166, 169, 172, 174, 175; and regulation, 158
Feminine, the, 6, 7
Fetishization, 56, 110, 123, 145, 242
Formalism, 133
Freedom, 14, 37, 81, 116, 122, 180, 195, 226
Free will, 20, 27, 263
Frontier, the, 32, 52, 67, 155, 160, 162, 169, 231, 250, 263; setting, 6; towns, 231, 234; Western, 7

Genesis, book of, 221
Genocide, 7, 15, 111, 123, 126, 129, 130, 164, 219, 231
Girard, Rene, 252
Glanton, John Joel, 123, 134, 135, 136, 137, 232
Gangs, 13, 133, 134, 136, 140, 142, 153, 156, 157, 158, 162, 167, 168, 169, 172, 174, 175, 176, 180, 232, 235
Gnosticism, 185
Gnostics, 3, 201, 208, 252
Go Down, Moses (Faulkner), 142, 146
God, 58, 62, 67, 76, 79, 80, 81, 84, 100, 113, 120, 121, 130, 137, 151, 157, 159, 160, 175, 185, 186, 187, 188, 191, 192, 195, 196, 197, 198, 199, 201, 202, 208, 211, 213, 215, 216, 217, 222, 223, 224, 225, 228, 230, 233, 236, 243, 247, 256
Gold rush, 158, 167
Gospel, the, 242, 243, 245, 247
Gothic, 41; southern, 6, 201
Grace, 3, 4, 83

Hemingway, Ernest, 91, 228
Heraclitus, 232, 233, 234, 236
Heroism, 67, 68
Herzog, Werner, 202
Hiroshima, 241
Holocaust, the, 187, 211
Homo economicus, 15, 231
hooks, bell, 109, 111
Horses, 68, 69, 93, 96, 126, 127

Ideology, 66, 67, 68, 69, 74, 75, 77, 78, 80, 156, 159, 161, 162, 175, 176
Imperialism, 6, 7, 66, 83, 126, 163
Indian law, 13, 156, 163, 164, 169, 171, 174, 178
Indian Removal Act, the, 158, 167, 219
Indians, 123, 124, 125, 157, 158, 163, 164, 166, 168, 169, 170, 172, 175, 176, 178, 179, 180
Indigenous people, 110, 111, 123, 124, 125, 126, 129, 165, 169, 174; critique of, 15, 250; individualism of, 8, 16, 46, 262; as

Indigenous people (continued)
  rugged, 52; tribes, 262. *See also*
  Genocide
Industrialization, 5, 46
Interviews, 1, 2, 16, 82, 104, 105, 185, 195, 202
Isolationism, 161

Jail, 25, 27, 37, 53, 54, 55, 115, 176, 210, 223
Jim Crow, 150
Jingoism, 178
Job, book of, 227
Johnson v. M'Intosh, 163, 164, 169, 170, 171, 172, 173, 174, 175, 178, 180

Kafka, Franz, 209, 218, 219, 246
Kant, Immanuel, 241
Kantian philosophy, 203, 238, 239
"Kekulé Problem, The" (CM), 127, 224, 231, 244, 245, 246
Kierkegaard, Søren, 211, 212
Knoxville, 112
Krauss, Laurence, 185, 202
Ku Klux Klan (The Klan), 57, 116, 143, 144

Labor camps, 187, 207, 219, 220, 241
Language, 4, 5, 14, 15, 16, 101, 116, 127, 128, 132, 133, 136, 148, 152, 160, 165, 173, 174, 175, 180, 207, 210, 224, 225, 226, 227, 230, 231, 232, 233, 235, 244, 245, 246, 247; and body, 99; critique of, 15, 127, 245; constructive power of, 225; nature of, 90; religious, 67, 82, 159, 200, 201
Law, 7, 13, 36, 57, 156, 158, 159, 162, 164, 165, 168, 170, 171, 175, 176, 178, 219, 231, 234, 238, 240. *See also* Indian law
Lawlessness, 156, 157; and morality, 7, 157; and settlers, 13, 159
Lazarus, 159, 243
Light in August (Faulkner), 13, 140, 141, 143, 144, 145, 150, 152
London, Jack, 91, 104, 135
Love, 3, 15, 99, 102, 113, 134, 197, 201, 211, 218, 219, 231, 241, 242, 243, 244, 245, 246, 247, 261, 262
Lukács, Georg, 133

Magdalena, 6, 69, 76, 77, 81, 110, 123
Manifest Destiny, 5, 83, 157, 159, 160, 161, 162, 178, 211, 241
Marshall, Chief Justice, 163, 164, 165, 171, 172, 174, 175, 176, 179, 180
Masculinity, 5, 228
Materialism, 49, 99
Melancholia, 187
Melville, Herman, 90, 227
Messianism, 193
Messianic foil/signpost, 234, 235
Metaphysics, 4, 5, 8, 9, 10, 12, 15, 16, 83, 110, 123, 147, 185, 195, 252, 253, 262; antimetaphysics, 191, 202
Mexican Revolution, 75
Mexico, 7, 68, 69, 70, 72, 73, 98, 105, 126, 127, 128, 158, 159, 160, 180; and U.S. border, 5, 6, 110, 123, 155, 158
Military, 158, 159, 161, 180, 232, 239; and paramilitary, 58; and service, 77, 238
Modernism, 147, 190; and postmodernism, 191
Modernity, 188, 190, 191, 207, 214, 215, 218, 220, 221, 225, 227
Monroe Doctrine, The, 158, 159, 160, 161, 162, 163, 164, 165, 166, 169, 170
Monster (term), 20, 21, 24, 27, 28, 33, 39, 42, 54, 99
Monstrosity, 10, 20, 23, 24, 25, 27, 28, 29, 31, 32, 33, 35, 37, 38, 39, 40
Morality, 4, 10, 15, 16, 79, 133, 231, 262
Morrison, Toni, 110, 123, 263
Misanthropy, 213
Misogyny, 6, 29, 41, 53, 54. *See also* Patriarchy; Sexism
Murder, 15, 20, 26, 28, 31, 32, 33, 35, 36, 37, 41, 48, 51, 53, 54, 59, 133, 134, 135, 144, 146, 169, 175, 231

Myth, 15, 94, 99, 156, 157, 168, 177, 189, 226, 244; and mythmaking, 167, 178
Mythology, 106, 160, 200
Mythologizing, 13, 156, 174

Nabokov, Valdimir, 190
National borders, 155, 162
Nationalism, 7, 18, 49, 170, 189
Native people, 13, 138, 155, 158, 163, 164, 166, 167, 170, 176, 178, 179, 180
Nature, 11, 12, 70, 83, 88, 89, 91, 93, 94, 96, 102, 103, 232, 237
Naturalism, 83, 185
Neoliberalism, 5, 11, 45
New Orleans, 139, 230
Nietzsche, Fredrich, 187, 209, 241, 242, 244
Nietzschean philosophy, 16, 202, 232
Nihilism, 3, 11, 14, 65, 66, 70, 71, 74, 79, 80, 81, 82, 83, 184, 185, 187, 200, 206, 210, 219, 241, 242, 244
No Country for Old Men (CM), 5, 8, 17, 231, 236, 237, 240
Nostalgia, 66, 83, 263

Objectification, 6, 53
O'Connor, Flannery, 201
Old Man and the Sea, The (Hemingway), 89, 105
Ontology, 16, 106, 111, 117, 191, 192, 196, 199, 200, 201, 250, 252, 262
Ontological dynamism, 15, 256, 259, 264
Ontological unity, 15, 250, 257, 258, 260, 262; and social/political, 12, 109, 111, 114, 117, 118, 122, 129
Orchard Keeper, The (CM), 8, 91
Oprah, Winfrey, 185, 195
Optical democracy, 151, 156, 157, 179, 232
Optimism, 7, 32, 62, 69, 70, 71, 78, 81, 187, 215; cosmic, 212; cruel, 78
Other, the, 123, 136, 167
Otherness, 24, 32, 99, 104, 117, 118, 129; and racial, 110, 118, 123, 129, 157

Pastoralism, 5, 6, 139
Patriarchy, 7, 8, 12, 45, 46, 109, 111, 117, 122, 124, 125. *See also* Misogyny; Sexism
Patriotism, 77
Personification, 34
Pessimism/pessimistic, 2, 3, 8, 14, 16, 74, 75, 77, 79, 80, 117, 122, 212, 227; Afropessimism, 12, 111, 112, 115, 116, 117, 122, 123
Philosophy, 7, 184, 190, 191, 196, 203, 212, 213, 221, 235, 241, 243, 244, 247, 250, 252, 262
Physics, 202
Piankashaw, 166, 180
Plato, 3, 212, 238
Poetry, 190, 224
Politics, 6, 7, 16, 133, 262; racial, 13, 134
Positivism, 185, 189
Postmodern philosophy, 66, 83, 210
Poststructuralism, 16, 195
Patriotism, 77
Postapocalyptic world, 5, 47, 79
Poverty, 46, 128, 129
Protestantism, 113, 119, 120, 151; and work ethic, 121
Proust, Marcel, 190
Psychology, 133, 149, 169
Puritanism, 67, 69, 72, 211

Queer, 263
Quijada, 12, 101, 126, 127, 128, 129

Race, 6, 12, 13, 109, 110, 111, 112, 113, 117, 118, 119, 120, 121, 123, 129, 130, 138, 160, 211, 228, 231
Racial differences, 12, 13, 109, 110, 111, 118, 119, 120, 122, 129, 148
Racism, 7, 8, 12, 13, 120, 121, 138, 139, 171, 241. *See also* White supremacy
Radio, 55, 143, 150
Rape, 25, 26, 27, 30, 36, 41, 53, 54, 114, 197
Rawlins, Lacey, 69, 70

Realism, 99
Reconstruction, 121
Redemption, 3, 4, 34, 83, 114, 178, 189, 193, 196, 199, 222, 243
Religion, 93, 94, 105, 120, 159, 165, 186, 190, 191, 193, 196, 202, 207
Road, The (CM), 2, 5, 8, 10, 11, 14, 16, 17, 24, 45, 46, 47, 48, 49, 50, 52, 58, 59, 60, 61, 62, 63, 65, 66, 79, 80, 81, 82, 103, 104, 184, 185, 186, 187, 188, 189, 190, 191, 192, 193, 194, 195, 196, 197, 198, 199, 200, 202, 206, 207, 214, 247

Sacred, the, 184, 186, 194, 196, 210, 224, 225, 252
Schopenhauer, Arthur, 212, 213
Science, 10, 14, 185
Screenplays, 90
Second Coming, the, 237
Self-interest, 5, 8, 11, 15, 231
Serial killers, 39, 49
Settler colonialism, 123, 157, 158, 159, 160, 162, 165, 179
Settler violence, 158, 162
Sevierville, 10
Sevier County, 20, 21, 22, 23, 25, 26, 27, 28, 34, 35, 36, 37, 40, 45, 46, 47, 48, 49, 50, 52, 54, 55, 56, 58, 61, 62, 115
Sexism, 6, 7, 157. *See also* Misogyny; Patriarchy
Sisyphean reflections, 241
Slave state, 134
Slavery, 7, 15, 116, 120, 130, 139, 141, 157, 231, 241
Slow death, 167, 169, 170, 172. *See also* Berlant, Lauren
Social death, 115, 116, 117, 121, 125
Southwest, American, 83, 92, 105, 110, 123, 126
Spanish language/descent, 72, 127, 135, 175, 264
Spengler, Oswald, 189

Stonemason, The (CM), 12, 109, 118, 119, 121, 122, 128, 129, 186, 211
Subjectivity, 7, 133, 149, 220, 234
Suicide, 14, 37, 121, 186, 208, 210, 211, 212, 213, 214, 217, 222, 223, 225, 228, 230
Sunset Limited, The (CM), 14, 184, 185, 186, 189, 190, 199, 200, 206, 207, 208, 210, 211, 212, 214, 215, 218, 223, 227, 230, 231, 241, 242, 244
Suttree (CM), 3, 6, 8, 42, 110, 111, 112, 118, 201

Taylor, Charles, 206, 224, 225, 226
Tennessee, 57, 104, 139; period in, 63
Theology, 14, 113, 117, 118, 120, 122, 190, 191, 201, 202, 222, 223, 242
Toadvine, 135, 139, 140, 141, 148
Tobin, 143, 235
Tolstoy, Leo, 209
Trauma, 26, 27, 39, 48, 95, 170, 175, 189, 218
Treaty of Guadalupe-Hidalgo, 155, 158, 160

Unbelievers, The, 185, 189
Unconscious, the, 15, 231, 244, 245, 246, 247
Utilitarian, 102, 106
Utopia/utopian, 15, 63, 128, 129, 195

Virgin Mary, 72, 73
Vietnam War, the, 83, 236

West, the, 7, 13, 156, 207, 220, 232; myth of, 83, 156, 262
Western (genre), 6, 16, 66, 67, 250, 262
"Whales and Men" (CM), 11, 89, 90, 91, 92, 93, 94, 95, 96, 97, 98, 99, 100, 101, 102, 103, 104, 105, 106
White Caps, 57, 58n16
White supremacy, 7, 12, 13, 117, 119, 129. *See also* Racism
Whiteness, 110, 111, 113, 118, 263
Whiskey, 77
Wilderson, Frank, III, 12, 111, 112, 115, 116
Witnessing, 157, 167, 171, 174, 179

Wittliff Collections, the, 88
Woodward, Richard, 82, 195
Woolf, Virginia, 190, 228
World War II, 77, 238, 241
Wolf/wolves, 11, 72, 73, 74, 75, 76, 78, 81, 82, 89, 91, 92, 93, 94, 95, 96, 97, 98, 99, 101, 102, 103, 104, 105, 106, 123, 126

Xenophobia, 157

Yoknapatawpha, 132, 136, 137, 142, 147, 151, 152
Yuma, 129, 167

Milton Keynes UK
Ingram Content Group UK Ltd.
UKHW031028011224
451733UK00006B/92